D1562430

The Place of Christ in Liturgical Prayer

Bryan D. Spinks, editor

Foreword by Martin Jean

The Place of Christ in Liturgical Prayer

Trinity, Christology, and Liturgical Theology

A PUEBLO BOOK

Liturgical Press   Collegeville, Minnesota

www.litpress.org

BV
185
.P53
2008

The cover image is a painting by Dragan Mojović and is reproduced with kind permission of Irinej, Bishop of Novi Sad and Dekan of the Faculty of Orthodox Theology of the University of Belgrade. The painting was completed in Belgrade in 1990 and was introduced into the main hall of the Orthodox Theological Faculty of Belgrade University by Bishop Danilo Krstić in 1996. From the English translation of Bishop Danilo Krstić's text explaining Mojović's painting: "The mystery of Divinity is indescribable. However, we use this intellectual 'icon' to indicate three aspects in one God . . . *The aspect of Essence*: let us envisage that the white sun is the unknowable essence of Divinity . . . *The aspect of Personhood*: let us imagine that three circles of light surrounding the sun are three Divine Persons (the Holy Trinity). The first is the Father. From Him the Son shines through, and the Spirit proceeds forth as the Third . . . *The aspect of Energy*: let us regard these silvery rays as different uncreated energies which eternally irradiate from the essence of God through three rings of light, as a gift by the Holy Trinity. One ray represents the energy of love (*agape*) . . . The other beams of radiance represent the other energies of Divinity: beauty, wisdom, truth, justice, compassion, humbleness." (The complete text of this essay is published in Episkop Danilo Krstić, *U početku beše Smisao*, Beograd 1996, 204–5 [The English translation of this collection of essays is *In the Beginning was Meaning*].)

A Pueblo Book published by Liturgical Press

Excerpt from the English translation of *The Roman Missal* © 1973, International Committee on English in the Liturgy, Inc. (ICEL). All rights reserved.

Unless otherwise noted, Scripture is translated by the authors. Where noted, Scripture is from the New Revised Standard Version Bible © 1989, Division of Christian Education of the National Council of the Churches of Christ in the United States of America. Used by permission. All rights reserved.

Cover design by David Manahan, OSB

© 2008 by Order of Saint Benedict, Collegeville, Minnesota. All rights reserved. No part of this book may be reproduced in any form, by print, microfilm, microfiche, mechanical recording, photocopying, translation, or by any other means, known or yet unknown, for any purpose except brief quotations in reviews, without the previous written permission of Liturgical Press, Saint John's Abbey, P.O. Box 7500, Collegeville, Minnesota 56321-7500. Printed in the United States of America.

Library of Congress Cataloging-in-Publication Data

The place of Christ in liturgical prayer : Trinity, christology, and liturgical theology / Bryan D. Spinks, editor ; foreword by Martin Jean.
     p. cm.
    "A Pueblo book."
    ISBN-13: 978-0-8146-6018-8
    1. Liturgies, Early Christian.   2. Jesus Christ—History of doctrines.
 3. Prayer—History.   I. Spinks, Bryan D.

BV185.P53 2008
264—dc22   2007034200

Contents

Foreword

The Yale Institute of Sacred Music (ISM) is an interdisciplinary graduate center dedicated to the study and practice of sacred music, worship, and the arts. Since 1973, one of our chief goals has been to assemble practitioners, scholars, and artists from these fields for common learning and conversation. The meeting of sixteen presenters and several dozen other participants in 2005 around the topic of christology and trinitarian theology in liturgical prayer is one of the most successful such events, for it gathered scholars and clergy from nearly a dozen religious traditions and from over five countries.

David Tracy speaks of three great "fractures" in the modern academy: the gaps between form and content, thinking and feeling, and theory and practice. The ISM strives boldly to jump over these chasms by holding in tension the daily experience of congregant and clergy-person with the knowledge of the scholar. Oftentimes, the training of religious leaders does not embrace critical scholarship or find ways to make this knowledge useful. Likewise, scholars of religion are too often trained to be so dispassionate as to exclude the experience of religious communities on the ground.

The ISM was constituted to hold these circles in harmony so that daily life can be shaped and bettered by the learned academy and so that this academy can itself be held accountable by the forces of the culture and of human experience itself. In the liturgy, like no other place, do these worlds converge. Finally, we are all characters in a grand narrative of meaning making that spans time and space.

May the reader be enlivened by the pages within this volume as were we who experienced the conversation firsthand.

Martin Jean

Acknowledgments

The 2005 Conference and subsequent publications of these papers would not have been possible without the untiring work of a number of people at the Yale Institute of Sacred Music and Liturgical Press. Special thanks due to Melissa Maier, ISM manager of external relations and publications, and the special projects assistant and conference coordinator John Hartmann and his assistant Burke Gerstenschlager, for the success of the initial conference. Meticulous editing and proofreading of the papers was undertaken at ISM by John Leinenweber, and he has worked closely with Mary Stommes, Colleen Stiller and Susan Sink of Liturgical Press. A deep dept of gratitude is owed to them in making this such a successful volume.

* * * * * * * * * * * * * * * *

Excerpts from *The Office of Vespers in the Byzantine Rite* (London: Darton, Longman and Todd, 1965). By permission of Darton, Longman and Todd.

Excerpts from *Prayerbook* (Cambridge, N.Y: New Skete, 1976). By permission of the Monks of New Skete.

Excerpts from "Odes of Solomon" by Charlesworth, JH (1973). By permission of Oxford University Press.

Excerpts from *Service Book of the Holy Orthodox-Catholic Apostolic Church: Compiled, Translated, and Arranged from the Old Church-Slavonic Service Books of the Russian Church and Collated with the Service Books of the Greek Church*, ed. I. F. Hapgood. 4th ed. (Brooklyn: Syrian Antiochian Orthodox Archdiocese, 1965); excerpts from *Divine Prayers and Services of the Catholic Orthodox Church of Christ*, ed. and trans. S. Nassar (Brooklyn: Syrian Antiochian Orthodox Archdiocese of New York and All North America, 1961). By permission of The Self-Ruled Antiochian Orthodox Christian Archdiocese of North America.

Excerpt from *Ephrem the Syrian—Hymns*, translated and introduced by Kathleen E. McVey. Copyright © 1989 by Kathleen E. McVey. Paulist Press, Inc., New York/Mahwah, NJ. Reprinted by permission of Paulist Press, Inc. www.paulistpress.com.

Excerpts from S. Brock, "Mary in Syriac Tradition," in *Mary's Place in Christian Dialogue*, ed. A. Stacpoole. By permission of St. Paul's (formerly St. Paul Publications), UK.

Excerpts from N. Constas, "Weaving the Body of God: Proclus of Constantinople, the Theotokos, and the Loom of the Flesh," *Journal of Early Christian Studies* (1995) in *Vigiliae Christianae*, Volume 24 (1970). By permission of Koninklijke Brill NV.

Excerpts from *Praising God: The Trinity in Christian Worship.* © 1999 Ruth Carolyn Duck and G. Ronald Kastner. By permission of Westminster John Knox Press.

Excerpts from "Christus Paradox" in *Common Praise* (Toronto, ON: Anglican Book Centre, 1998). © 1991 GIA Publications, Inc. Used by permission.

* * * * * * * * * * * * * * * *

We have made every attempt to obtain permission to reprint the following and will gratefully acknowledge in future editions or reprints should the copyright holders inform us:

Excerpts from Jungmann's *The Place of Christ in Liturgical Prayer.* 2d rev. ed., trans. A. Peeler (Staten Island, NY: Alba House, 1965).

Excerpts from Jungmann's "The Defeat of Teutonic Arianism and the Revolution in Religious Culture in the Early Middle Ages" in *Pastoral Liturgy* (New York: Herder and Herder, 1962).

Abbreviations

ACO   *Acta Conciliorum Oecumenicorum*

BELS   Bibliotheca *Ephemerides Liturgicae,* Subsidia

CCSL   Corpus Christianorum: Series Latina

CSCO   Corpus Scriptorum Christianorum Orientalium

DOP   Dumbarton Oaks Papers

HBS   Henry Bradshaw Society

NPNF   Nicene and Post-Nicene Fathers

OCA   Orientalia Christiana Analecta

OCP   *Orientalia Christiana Periodica*

ODB   *The Oxford Dictionary of Byzantium*

PG   Patrologia Graeca

PL   Patrologia Latina

SC   Sources chrétiennes

TLG   *Thesaurus Linguae Graecae*

Introduction

In 1925 the Austrian Roman Catholic liturgical scholar Josef A. Jungmann (1889–1975) published a seminal work, *The Place of Christ in Liturgical Prayer*. Basic to his thesis was that in the early church public prayer was addressed to the Father, through the Son, and in the Spirit, and that because of the Arian and miahysite/diaphysite controversies, prayer came to be addressed directly to the Son, and then to the Spirit. Jungmann's work is often cited by scholars as an authoritative work. The title of his book formed the catalyst to revisit trinitarian doctrine and christology in worship from the New Testament to the present at a conference held at Yale Institute of Sacred Music in February 2005. Scholarship since Jungmann has done much to undermine his views. In this introduction the editor revisits Jungmann's work and shows where some of its core arguments are no longer tenable.

Chapter 1

The Place of Christ in Liturgical Prayer: What Jungmann Omitted to Say

Bryan D. Spinks
Yale Institute of Sacred Music and Yale Divinity School

It was never a great mystery that the title of this conference is that of the English title of Josef Andreas Jungmann's groundbreaking book published in 1925 as *Die Stellung Christi im liturgischen Gebet*. The thesis of that book was one to which he returned in an essay in 1947, "The Defeat of Teutonic Arianism and the Revolution in Religious Culture in the Early Middle Ages." This conference was never intended to be about Jungmann, but rather to center on the important subjects raised by his title, namely christology and the Trinity in liturgical prayer. Yet, since Jungmann's arguments and assessment of the liturgical evidence are still from time to time quoted with authority, by those whose fields are dogmatics and systematic theology as well as liturgics, it seems fitting and right at the outset of our deliberations to reflect on what Jungmann said, and to draw attention to some factors that confirm Balthasar Fischer's comment in his Foreword to the 1989 edition of *The Place of Christ in Liturgical Prayer*, namely, that "sound liturgical piety depends on both the *ad Christum* and the *per Christum*."[1]

In his 1925 book Jungmann divided his study into two parts. The first was a general survey of liturgical texts from the *Didache* and the so-called *Apostolic Tradition*, then believed to be ca. 215, through the Egyptian and Syrian Church Orders, to the great classical rites of St. Mark, and the Byzantine Rite, the Syrian Orthodox and East Syrian Rites, to the Gallican, Visigothic, and Roman Rites. He paid particular attention to the doxologies, and was generally concerned to stress that the earliest

---

[1] Joseph Jungmann, *The Place of Christ in Liturgical Prayer*, foreword by Balthasar Fischer (Collegeville, MN: Liturgical Press, 1989) x. In English translations Jungmann is variously called Josef A. Jungmann, Joseph A. Jungmann, and Joseph Jungmann.

traditions addressed prayer to God the Father through Christ as, in the words of 1 Timothy 2:5, the "one mediator between God and human-kind, Christ Jesus, himself human."[2] He noted that some diaconal prayers were addressed to Christ, but generally sacerdotal prayers were addressed to God the Father. Some doxologies were addressed to the Father and the Son, and later also to the Holy Spirit as equal. In the East Syrian tradition the eucharistic prayers were addressed to the Trinity, but in the Syrian Orthodox some parts of some anaphoras were addressed to the Son as God.

In the second part of the work Jungmann turned to consider this development. The New Testament passages were discussed to show that generally Christ's humanity is the focus of prayer through him as mediator. The invocations to Christ and the Spirit in the *Acts of Thomas* and *John* were isolated as Gnostic aberrations, but the Cappadocian defeat of semi-Arianism, and the Constantinopolitan consolidation of trinitarian theology with the *homoousios* of the Spirit, resulted in new forms of doxologies. Public or liturgical prayer to Christ came about in a twofold manner. First, in the Syrian Orthodox and Coptic traditions Monophysite christology absorbed the humanity into the divinity. Secondly, as an overreaction against Arianism the divinity of Christ and *homoousios* were stressed by orthodoxy, and devotional prayers directed to Christ came into the liturgy. In the West this took place through the Visigothic Rite; it then came into the Gallican, and finally into the Roman Rite. Jungmann devoted a chapter to tracing how the term "high priest" for Christ in Hebrews was later transformed from meaning "mediator" to indicating the divine presence that brought about consecration at the Eucharist. The main conclusion of the work was that the primitive tradition, preserved in much of the Roman rite, and particularly the *canon missae,* was to address public liturgical prayer to God through Christ as mediator. To address Christ directly carried the danger of obliterating his humanity.

The essay of 1947 took up the same theme, though in terms of the Western Rites and in a wider cultural context.[3] The struggle over

[2] Scripture for this chapter taken from the *The New Revised Standard Version.*

[3] Joseph Jungmann, "The Defeat of Teutonic Arianism and the Revolution in Religious Culture in the Early Middle Ages," in *Pastoral Liturgy* (New York: Herder and Herder, 1962) 1–101, a revised translation of "Die Abwehr des germanischen Arianismus und der Umbruch der religiösen Kultur im frühen Mittelalter." *Zeitschrift für katholische Theologie* 69 (1947) 36–99.

Arianism in Spain led to a zealous anti-Arianism that spread to France and elsewhere. Jungmann cited the Council of Toledo (583 C.E.) where the aim was "to ensure that equal honour and adoration is given to all three Persons of the Trinity."[4] In the *Missale mixtum* he discovered examples of trinitarian statements being transferred to christology. A pronounced trinitarian emphasis is found in the Frankish liturgy. Jungmann argued that the focus on the Trinity and the anti-Arian emphasis led to a stress on the divine nature of Christ and a modalist intermingling of Christ and God. In turn this led to the cult of Mary, with her taking on the mediating role once attributed to the humanity of Christ, and to over-concern with the passion of Christ. These currents shaped not only the language of liturgy but also visual representation— of the Trinity, for example: the Father seated with a crucified Son in his lap, and the Spirit as a dove hovering above. Wide ranging effects, according to Jungmann, included the widening gulf between clergy and laity, and a quest for moral goodness replacing the concept of partaking of Christ's holiness.

It is reasonably clear that in this essay of 1947 Jungmann attempted to paint an evolutionary grand narrative using very broad brush strokes. The accusations he made—that late medieval Western liturgy and spirituality were the direct outcome of overreaction to Arianism—are too general and simplistic to be convincing. However, he built this new essay on the foundations of the earlier work, *The Place of Christ in Liturgical Prayer*, where he had implied that Origen's dictum that prayer be directed to "the Father of all through Jesus Christ and in the Holy Spirit"[5] exemplified the true pattern of liturgical prayer.

It is somewhat odd that Jungmann—who professed the Catholic faith and therefore the *homoousios* of Son and Spirit—should have seen Origen as an authority on this particular matter; odd because many patristic scholars have seen the type of subordinationism found in Origen as an underlying symptom of the deep suspicion, and even open hostility, toward Nicene terminology by figures such as Eusebius of Caesarea. Why did Jungmann feel uncomfortable with public prayer addressed to the Son or Spirit? Did this unease account for his less-than-full treatment of the New Testament evidence, and his rush to explain the development as either overreaction to Arianism or the

[4] Jungmann, *Pastoral Liturgy*, 27.
[5] Jungmann, *The Place of Christ*, 157.

development of monophysite christology? By his own admission all traditions still addressed prayer through Christ as well as to Christ, yet he seemed unhappy with the dual tradition.

The need to redress the balance is seen in James B. Torrance's Didsbury Lectures, *Worship, Community, and the Triune God of Grace* of 1996. Like his brother, T. F. Torrance, James Torrance was concerned with the dogmatic implications of Chalcedonian christology, arguing for a God-humanward movement in Christ's divinity, and a human-Godward movement in his humanity: a double movement of grace. We are taken up in the vicarious obedient life of Christ, and we come to God in, with, and through Christ. Under the title "The Sole Priesthood of Christ," Torrance outlined Jungmann's thesis to reinforce the dogmatic point that "we come to God our Father both in Christ and through Christ, and only through Jesus Christ."[6]

Torrance here rightly underlined the patristic teaching that what was not assumed cannot be redeemed; the full humanity of Christ means that we are saved in, with, and through Christ. We also worship in, with, and through Christ. However, in his chapter entitled "Worship— Unitarian or Trinitarian," Torrance clearly qualified Jungmann. Trinitarian worship, argued Torrance, takes place in three ways. One is indeed that we pray to the Father, through the Son, in the Spirit. But second,

> We pray to each of the three persons. We pray to the Father and to the Son ("even so come, Lord Jesus") and to the Holy Spirit (*Veni Creator Spiritus*) "who with the Father and the Son together is worshipped and glorified" (Nicene Creed). Here we see the significance of the Nicene "one in being" (*homoousios*). We only pray to one God, but we have a warrant in the New Testament and in the Church's life to pray to each of the three persons.[7]

The third manner, according to Torrance, is to glorify the One God, Father, Son, and Holy Spirit, as when we sing the doxology at the end of psalmody.

The implication is not that what Jungmann said about the mediatorship of Christ is wrong, but rather that he omitted to discuss the posi-

---

[6] James B. Torrance, *Worship, Community, and the Triune God of Grace* (Carlisle: Paternoster, 1996) 54–55.

[7] Ibid., 25.

tive liturgical implications of christology and trinitarian faith. This trinitarian link with christology is muted in Jungmann, and he did not explore the implications of not addressing public prayer to Christ, and of a less-than-orthodox doctrine of the Trinity. It is to some of the evidence and implications Jungmann passed over, missed, or would not have had the slightest interest in, that I now wish to turn.

NEW TESTAMENT IMPLICATIONS

In chapter 9 of *The Place of Christ in Liturgical Prayer*, Jungmann examined the instructions and beginnings of prayer in the New Testament. He noted that Jesus directed his followers to make prayer to the Father, and to make their requests to God in his name. Jungmann put great emphasis on 1 Timothy 2:5, Ephesians 5:10, Colossians 3:17, Hebrews 13:13, Romans 1:8, and 2 Corinthians 1:20. The implications of Philippians 2:10 were only briefly conceded with the comment, "Nevertheless, the actual use of the prayer addressed solely to Christ was rather an exception."[8] It is not what Jungmann said here but what he omitted to say that makes his case unbalanced.

The recent book by Jerome H. Neyrey, *Render to God: New Testament Understandings of the Divine*, seems to contain much that supports Jungmann. Neyrey considers the term Father as used in the Synoptics, and concludes that it is frequently used with the idea of God as patron and Jesus as client, though also with the idea of Jesus as mediator and Israel as client. However, Neyrey concludes with two chapters, the titles of which both begin with the question, "Who Else is Called 'God'?" One chapter looks at John, and the other at Hebrews. Neyrey concludes that the Johannine community called Jesus God. On Hebrews he argues that when Hebrews 1:8 called Jesus God, and compared him with Melchizadek, the writer was making ontological not just functional statements about the divinity of Christ.[9] Although Neyrey does not specifically consider the address of prayer, it would seem that the implications of his discussion are that the Johannine community and the author of Hebrews would have regarded prayer to Christ as God as quite legitimate.

Neyrey's work is in the historical-critical and socio-cultural genre, and this approach is followed by Adela Collins in a paper on the wor-

---

[8] Jungmann, *The Place of Christ*, 131.
[9] Jerome H. Neyrey, *Render to God* (Minneapolis: Fortress, 2004) 241–42.

ship of Jesus.[10] Agreeing that early Christians worshiped Jesus, she found the catalyst for this in the Greek and Hellenistic practice of offering veneration to heroes, benefactors, and rulers, and particularly in the cult of the Roman emperors.

Those working from a more canonical and narrative approach seem to find more to say, for example, Margaret Barker in her book, *The Great High Priest: The Temple Roots of Christian Liturgy*. It must be admitted that at times in this work Barker's imagination fills in gaps where we have no evidence. That, however, does not in itself invalidate all of her observations and suggestions. For example, Barker argues that the high priest functioned as Yahweh in making atonement; in fact, his role was to remove the damaging effects of sin from the community and the creation, and she sees the figure of the high priest behind the Son of Man in 1 Enoch, and behind this the high priest as representing prelapsarian Adam.[11] She suggests that Isaiah 53 could have been inspired by the Day of Atonement ritual, and argues that all these ideas explain the designation of Jesus in Hebrews as high priest. Elsewhere she considers the evidence that the Massoretic text has been changed to rule out early Christian interpretations, and she makes much of the tradition that Elyon and Yahweh had been Father and Son. Barker says:

> If we read the Hebrew Scriptures in the way that the first Christians read them, we should understand that Yahweh was the son of God Most High (El Elyon), and the Second Person (to use an anachronism), and that Yahweh was incarnate in Jesus. Thus Gabriel announced to Mary, "He shall be called Son of God Most High" (Luke 1.32). We should know why Paul could proclaim one God, the Father, and one LORD, Jesus the Messiah (1 Cor 8.6). We should know why two early texts of the New Testament came to describe Jesus as the one who brought Israel out of Egypt (Jude 5). We should know why the Fourth evangelist believed that Isaiah's vision of the LORD had been a vision of Jesus (John 12.41). . . . We should also understand why ikons of Christ have in the halo *ho on*, the Greek form of Yahweh.[12]

---

[10] Adela Collins, "The Worship of Jesus and the Imperial Cult," in *The Jewish Roots of Christological Monotheism*, ed. C. C. Newman et al. (Leiden: Brill, 1999) 234–57.

[11] Margaret Barker, *The Great High Priest* (London: T&T Clark, 2003) 42–55.

[12] Ibid., 309–10.

As I have already indicated, although I find Barker's allusions and connections highly suggestive, there are times when a fertile imagination replaces solid evidence. Her conclusions, however, find endorsement from Crispin Fletcher-Louis who, after considering Old Testament and intertestamental texts, argued that "the worship offered to Jesus by early Christians must now be seen in continuity with this older tradition. Jesus functions as had the high priest, the post-lapsarian Adam and the eschatological Son of Man for some pre-Christian Jews. Jesus is slotted into a preconceived pattern, theology and even practice of worship."[13]

C. Kevin Rowe's essay, "Luke and the Trinity: An Essay in Ecclesial Biblical Theology," has none of Barker's speculations. His thesis is that the identity of God in the narrative of Luke-Acts compels us to speak in trinitarian terms. He focuses on the titles of Lord and Savior, which, so he argues, in the Old Testament are both crucial terms in the identity of the God of Israel. In Luke 1:5-38, it is clear that *kurios* refers only to Yahweh. He notes:

> Between 1:38 and 1:39, however, there is a narrative gap during which time the conception of Jesus occurs. In light of 1:43 this narrative gap can be seen as the moment of the incarnation of YHWH, passed over in silence, but captured in the overlapping identity of the κύριος. For in 1:43 Elizabeth, filled with the Holy Sprit, addresses Mary as ἡ μήτηρ του κυρίου μου (the mother of my Lord!). This is the first time that Jesus himself appears in the narrative, and it is at this point that Jesus takes on the title/name κύριος. This dramatic moment in the narrative identifies YHWH with the human Jesus within Mary's womb by means of the overlapping resonance of κύριος. There is a fundamental correspondence between the one God of the OT and the person of Jesus such that they share the same name. The doubleness that this overlap creates in the referent of the κύριος finds its theological interpretation in an incarnational unity between YHWH and Jesus.[14]

Rowe goes on to note that it is impossible to speak of this incarnation without reference to the Holy Spirit, described as the power of the

---

[13] Crispin Fletcher-Louis, "The Worship of Divine Humanity as God's Image," in *The Jewish Roots of Christological Monotheism*, ed. C. C. Newman et al. (Leiden: Brill, 1999) 112–28.

[14] C. Kevin Rowe, "Luke and the Trinity: An Essay in Ecclesial Biblical Theology," *Scottish Journal of Theology* 56 (2003) 14.

Most High. The synonym of the Holy Spirit and the power of the Most High is, says Rowe, fully consonant with the OT as an expression of the dynamism of the one Lord of Israel. God's Spirit is indeed God himself but in repetition or doubleness in the conception of Jesus. Rowe notes: "Thus in the Lukan birth narrative there is a triplicity in the life of God that is made known in the conception of Jesus. . . . This God incarnates himself in the person of Jesus with an intensity that justifies the overlapping identification and doublenesss in referentiality of the single divine name κύριος,"[15] Rowe observes that in the *Magnificat* Mary adores God as *kurios* and as "God my Savior." The only other time *soter* is used in the gospel is 2:11, where the angel of the Lord announces the baby as their *soter*. "Regarding the two texts together in the narrative produces a unified soteriological identity between YHWH and Jesus (κύριος) in their role as savior (σωτήρ)."[16]

Richard Bauckham draws attention to Matthew's use of *proskunein*, which from Matthew 2:2 onward is reserved for expressing worship to Jesus.[17] The climax and theological rationale, according to Bauckham, is in Matthew 28:18, "All authority in heaven and on earth has been given to me." Joel B. Green observes that Stephen and Ananias offer prayer to Jesus, and adds, "so routine, in fact, is christocentric prayer to the identity of the early Christians that they can be known as 'those who call upon the name' of Jesus."[18] And Larry Hurtado has much more to say on the binitarian worship of the New Testament.[19]

I am not suggesting or implying that there is a consensus among New Testament scholars on these issues and exegesis. My point is that Jungmann was highly selective in the New Testament texts he discussed and in the authorities he quoted, both in 1925 and in the revised edition of his work. Certainly there are texts that clearly witness to offering

[15] Ibid., 15.

[16] Ibid., 16.

[17] Richard Bauckham, "The Throne of God and the Worship of Jesus," in *The Jewish Roots of Christological Monotheism*, ed. C. C. Newman et al. (Leiden: Brill, 1999) 67.

[18] Joel B. Green, "Persevering Together in Prayer: The Significance of Prayer in the Acts of the Apostles," in *Into God's Presence: Prayer in the New Testament*, ed. R. N. Longenecker (Grand Rapids: Eerdsmans, 2001) 188, citing Acts 2:21; 7:59; 9:14, 21; 22:16.

[19] Larry Hurtado, *Lord Jesus Christ: Devotion to Jesus in Earliest Christianity* (Grand Rapids: Eerdmans, 2003).

prayer to the Father through the Son, but also texts and passages that suggest, support, and invite the practice of prayer to Christ as God.

JUNGMANN'S LITURGICAL EVIDENCE

Although Jungmann provided a wide selection of liturgical texts, his concern was to show that public prayer addressed to Christ or the Spirit was generally located in heterodox liturgical texts, Gnostic, Nestorian, and Monophysite. Thus the liturgical evidence of the apocryphal *Acts*, together with the anaphoras of Addai and Mari, Gregory of Nazianzus, and Syriac James, for example, were cited as exceptions that proved his rule. In hindsight, his treatment of those texts was too simplistic.

The apocryphal *Acts* have preserved a number of prayers in the context of baptism, and bread only, or bread and water, eucharistic celebrations, and, as Andrew McGowan has shown, it is anachronistic to dismiss the latter as not real Eucharists.[20] Likewise, the term gnostic is now regarded as a blanket term covering a wide range of faith communities, many of whom regarded themselves as enlightened Christians, and it may well be the case that in many parts of Syria, Asia Minor, and Egypt, those groups later deemed gnostic represented a majority of those who considered themselves Christian.[21] The *Acts of John*, according to Knut Schaferdiek, comes from the second or third century; it springs from a bilingual milieu, and is possibly even of an original Syriac form and a tradition close to the *Acts of Thomas*.[22] The latter exists in Greek and Syriac; both of these are regarded as dependent upon a Syriac Ur-text, and are third-century works, perhaps from Edessa, but certainly representative of early Syrian Christianity. In the *Acts of John* one eucharistic prayer offered by the apostle begins, "We glorify your Name which converts us from error and pitiless deceit,"[23] and proceeds to give thanks to "you, Lord Jesus Christ." In a second

[20] Andrew McGowan, *Ascetic Eucharists: Food and Drink in Early Ritual Meals* (Oxford: Clarendon Press, 1999).

[21] See B. A. Pearson, *Gnosticism and Christianity in Roman and Coptic Egypt* (New York: T&T Clark International, 2004).

[22] In *New Testament Apocrypha*, ed. W. Schneemelcher; English translation ed. R. McL.Wilson, rev. ed. (Louisville: Westminster John Knox, 1991–92) 2:152ff. The texts of the *Acts* and introductory essays have been consulted for the discussion here. [Text modernized.]

[23] Ibid., 2:200–201.

prayer the apostle John prays, "We glorify your name that was spoken by the Father; we glorify your name that was spoken through the Son,"[24] and the prayer seems to be addressed to the Lord, or *Adonai/kurios*. In the *Acts of Thomas* an invocation, or epiklesis, is addressed to the Holy Spirit, where the Son is seen as being begotten by the Father and Mother, or Holy Spirit.[25] Another prayer is addressed to the bread of life, and another directly to the crucified holy body.[26] In the *Acts of Peter*, which is probably late second-century, and from either Rome or Asia Minor, a short eucharistic prayer is addressed to "You God Jesus Christ."[27]

It is not that these documents do not know of prayer addressed to the Father—in the *Acts of John* the "Hymn of Christ" begins "Glory be to thee, Father."[28] It is true that these works seem to presuppose ideas of redemption, and of a trinity of persons, that were by later standards less than orthodox. However, these authors, and we may assume their communities too, were not on the Marcionite wing of gnosticism—which rejected the God of the Old Testament in preference for Jesus—which might otherwise account for the christomonism. They did acknowledge the Father, but clearly bear witness to public prayer addressed directly to Christ and the Holy Spirit.

The fact that two of these documents are probably representative of Syrian Christianity is significant. When turning to the East Syrian tradition Jungmann made much of the fact that all three eucharistic prayers of this tradition are addressed to the Trinity, Father, Son, and Holy Spirit. In fact, however, Addai and Mari is addressed to the Name, as is, *pace* Jungmann, the anaphora of Theodore the Interpreter—just as we found in the Syrian eucharistic prayers in the *Acts of John*. Most of those endeavoring to find the "original text" of Addai and Mari have regarded the reference to Father, Son, and Holy Spirit as a later addition, and that the prayer was originally simply addressed to the Name. In fact, unless one is to maintain that any reference to Father, Son, and Spirit outside a baptismal context is "late,"

---

[24] Ibid., 2:202. This can also be rendered "We glorify your name of the Father which was spoken by you; we glorify your name of Son which was spoken by you." See M. R. James, *The Apocryphal New Testament* (Oxford: Clarendon Press, 1924) 268.

[25] Ibid., 2:359–60.

[26] Ibid., 2:391 and 401.

[27] Ibid., 2:291.

[28] Ibid., 2:182.

there is no reason why the Matthean triune names should not be regarded as original to this anaphora, which is almost certainly one of our earliest eucharistic prayers, and the oldest still in use.[29]

However, regardless of this fact, Addai and Mari is notorious for its apparent oscillation between addressing the Father and the Son. Bernard Botte suggested that the theology of the author was monarchianism, and that his modalism was probably unconscious and not at all aggressive.[30] Anthony Gelston also appealed to modalism to explain this switch of address.[31] More recently Sarhad Jammo has suggested that the first and third sections are addressed to the Father, and the second part to the Son, though this suggestion is made on the dubious assumption that the prayer is derived from the *birkat ha-mazon*.[32] On the other hand, Edward Ratcliff had suggested that it was originally addressed to the Son throughout, and this is supported by its Maronite twin, Sharar.[33] Jungmann's argument was that eucharistic prayers addressed either in part, or entirely, to the Son are the result of monophysitism, and post-date 451 C.E. This suggestion loses its credibility when an ancient prayer is found, on the one hand, in an East Syrian community which later espoused a diophysite position, and on the other, in the Maronite Church which was Chalcedonian.

It was the Egyptian anaphora attributed to Gregory of Nazianzus, addressed throughout to the Son, that Jungmann regarded as typifying his monophysite theory. A. Baumstark had suggested that this prayer was the ancient anaphora of Nazianzus which Gregory had himself expanded, and which had been taken to Egypt by Syrian monks.[34] José

---

[29] The reference to "arcane knowledge of the anaphora of Addai and Mari" in R. Giles (*Creating Uncommon Worship* [Collegeville, MN: Liturgical Press, 2004]) seems an insensitive and unecumenical dismissal of an ancient Eastern Church's living liturgy. Knowledge of the 1549 *Book of Common Prayer* is far more arcane!

[30] Bernard Botte, "L'Anaphore Chaldéenne des Apôtres," OCP 15 (1949) 266.

[31] Anthony Gelston, *The Eucharistic Prayer of Addai and Mari* (Oxford: Clarendon Press, 1992) 68.

[32] Sarhad Jammo, "The Anaphora of the Apostles Addai and Mari: A Study of Structure and Historical Background," OCP 68 (2002) 5–35.

[33] Edward Ratcliff, "The Original Form of the Anaphora of Addai and Mari: A Suggestion," *Journal of Theological Studies* 30 (1929) 23–32.

[34] A. Baumstark, "Die Chrysostomosliturgie und die syrische Liturgie des Nestorios," *Chrysostomika* (1908) 846–48.

Manuel Sánchez Caro made a close examination of the "I-thou" style of the Post-sanctus, comparing it with the homilies and poems of Gregory, and argued that this section could well have been written by Gregory to express an anti-Arian theology.[35] This was taken even further in the extended examination by Albert Gerhards, who effectively showed that this prayer had nothing specifically monophysite about it but contained much material that could be paralleled in Gregory of Nazianzus, and suggested that in some churches the eucharistic prayer had been addressed to Christ as God.[36]

Jungmann's blanket assumption that being monophysite in doctrine produced eucharistic prayers addressed to the Son needs careful reconsideration. At least with regard to examples such as Syriac James, where the anamnesis is addressed to the Son, this may be due less to monophysitism and more with reflecting a tradition found in the *Acts of John* and *Acts of Thomas*, in Addai and Mari, and in Sharar—that is, a Syrian rather than a monophysite symptom.

In a study of the anaphora attributed to Severus of Antioch I have suggested that although it is impossible to demonstrate that Severus wrote all or any of the prayer, it is equally impossible to rule out the possibility. There are traces of his theological position in the prayer, be they from him or from a redactor. I have argued that the three levels of *theoria* that Roberta Chesnut identified in the theology of Severus are present.[37] The first of these is the *theoria* of the visible, natural universe, and the creation itself declares the wonder of God. This leads to the *theoria* of the intelligences, where the mind is led to cross the realm of angels and archangels. This in turn leads to the *theoria* of the Trinity, and divinization. These are given expression both prior to the Sanctus, and in the Post-sanctus. Nothing in the anaphora, however, conflicts with a Chalcedonian christology—the address of the anamnesis to

[35] José Manuel Sánchez Caro, *Eucaristia e historia de la salvación* (Madrid: Ed. Católica, 1983) 310ff.

[36] Albert Gerhards, *Die griechische Gregoriosanaphora: Ein Beitrag zur Geschichte des eucharistischen Hochgebets*. Liturgiewissenschaftlichen Quellen und Forschungen 65 (Münster-Westfalen: Aschendorff, 1984).

[37] See R. Chesnut, *Three Monophysite Christologies* (London: Oxford University Press, 1976); B. Spinks, "The Anaphora Attributed to Severus of Antioch: A Note on Its Character and Theology," in Θυσία αἰνέσεως: *Mélanges liturgiques offerts à la mémoire de l'archevêque Georges Wagner (1930–1993)*, ed. J. Getcha and A. Lossky (Paris: Presses Saint-Serge, 2005) 345–51.

Christ as God is hardly un-Chalcedonian. Although Severus was a zealous supporter of the teaching of Cyril of Alexandria, we find no trace of heavy Cyrilline technical terms in the anaphora. The theology that seems to be reflected is not mia-physite per se, but Severus's interpretation of sanctification. A full study of the Syriac anaphoras is still to be undertaken, but few are openly monophysite in terminology, and the address of the anamnesis to the Son is perhaps simply a continuation of a Syrian convention of having part of the anaphora address the Son, which is at least as old as Addai and Mari.

The cumulative evidence is sufficient to indicate that public prayer addressed to Christ, at least in the Syrian tradition, but perhaps also in Asia Minor, was not uncommon, and cannot be dismissed by appeals to overzealous anti-Arianism or to a non-Chalcedonian christology.

THE WESTERN WEAKNESS: TWO CASE STUDIES

Jungmann was at pains to argue that the Roman tradition had loyally conserved what he insisted was the older and more primitive form of public prayer, namely prayer addressed to the Father. Such a practice was reinforced in liturgical legislation from African councils; for example, Canon 21 of the Council of Hippo Regius (393 C.E.), stated: "No one shall name the Father for the Son or the Son for the Father in prayers; and when one assists at the altar the oration shall be directed always to the Father."[38] Two versions of this canon are found in later collections of African councils. The *Liber canonum temporibus sancti Aurelii* read at the Council of Carthage (525 C.E.) stated: "No one shall name the Father for the Son or the Son for the Father in prayers, but the intention shall be directed always to the Father; and the prayers themselves shall be discussed with the more prudent." Then, in a collection composed between 526 and 546 by a deacon at Carthage, we find the statement: "No one shall direct the oration in prayers except to the Father and he shall discuss them previously with the better instructed."

Edward Kilmartin noted that this seems to outlaw, on the one hand, prayer that presupposes the Son but names the Father, and on the other, naming the Son in prayers traditionally addressed to the Father. Following Jungmann, he suggests that both modalism and an over-reaction to Arianism are envisaged, and notes the emphatic teaching

[38] Citations are from E. Kilmartin, "The Liturgical Prayer in Early African Legislation," *Ephemerides liturgicae* 99 (1985) 105–27.

that *oratio*—speech in prayer—shall be directed toward the Father.[39] How far this African legislation had an impact on Roman usage is difficult to know. However, Jungmann was quite correct to observe that, in distinction from the Christian East, and from Gaul and Spain, the Roman tradition was reticent to address public prayer directly to Christ. Examples such as the *Agnus Dei* have their origins elsewhere, and are imported into Roman usage. But what Jungmann presented as a strength of the Roman Rite can in other contexts be seen to be a potential theological weakness.

The Reformation tradition inherited the broadly Roman medieval prayer tradition, and thus in the *Book of Common Prayer* of the Church of England, prayer was mainly addressed to the Father, or to a generic God, and only in propers for Trinity Sunday, in doxologies, and the inclusion of the Athanasian Creed, do we find full liturgical expression of a trinitarian faith. The fragility of this inherited Western tradition may be demonstrated by two leading Newtonian theologians of the eighteenth century, William Whiston and Dr. Samuel Clarke.

Whiston was Newton's successor in the Lucasian Chair of Mathematics at the University of Cambridge, and was a brilliant polymath. However, using Newtonian philosophy, or state-of-the-art methodology, he concluded that Athanasius had deceived the whole church and led it astray; as a consequence Arius was right, and the doctrine of the Trinity was a corruption of biblical teaching. Whiston was convinced that the *Apostolic Constitutions* was a genuine apostolic document. James Force observed: "With his arian hypothesis confirmed by historical research in the earliest Christian documents, Whiston, in July of 1708, wrote to inform the archbishops of York and Canterbury that as a result of a fourteen-hundred-year conspiracy, the church had been teaching false doctrine and that he, William Whiston, could prove its falsity and also show how to reform Christian teaching by bringing it into conformity with the original."[40] For his pains Whiston was deprived of his Cambridge chair, but, undeterred, in 1711 he published a full defense of the *Apostolic Constitutions*, and in 1713 he published *The Liturgy of the Church of England reduc'd nearer to the primitive Standard,*

[39] Ibid., 108–9.
[40] James Force, *William Whiston: Honest Newtonian* (Cambridge: Cambridge University Press, 1985) 16.

Humbly propos'd to Publick Consideration.[41] Whiston emended the Prayer Book rites and added material from the *Apostolic Constitutions* to bring it in line with what he regarded as primitive Christianity. One of the casualties of his liturgical reforms was the doxology in psalms and canticles at Morning and Evening Prayer, replaced by "Glory be to the Father through the Son, and in the Holy Ghost"—the very formula that Jungmann championed.

The other Newtonian, a friend of Whiston, Dr. Samuel Clarke, was even more brilliant, and was tipped as a future bishop until he published his *Scripture-Doctrine of the Trinity* in 1712. Though Eusebian rather than Arian, it was evident to most readers that this was a heterodox doctrine of the Trinity in which the term God was reserved for the Father, and the Son and Holy Spirit were subordinated to the first person of the Trinity. In this work of 1712 Clarke suggested how the *Book of Common Prayer* might be brought into line with his corrected doctrine of the Trinity. In later years, in a 1724 edition of the *Book of Common Prayer* now in the British Library, Clarke made his own manuscript alterations to the Anglican liturgy, in which the *Gloria Patri* was replaced by either "Glory be to God, by Jesus Christ, through the heavenly assistance by the Holy Ghost," or "Unto God be glory in the Church, by Christ Jesus, Throughout all Ages, world without end. Amen." Alterations were made to the *Te Deum*, the Litany, and Creed; the Athanasian Creed was completely struck out. God and Lord were terms interchangeable only with Father, and reserved for the first person of the Trinity.[42]

What is significant here is not Whiston's and Clarke's heterodoxy but rather just how few alterations were needed to make the *Book of Common Prayer* Arian or semi-Arian. It is no accident that Clarke's suggestions were taken up enthusiastically in a whole number of liturgies published for Unitarian use.[43] Whiston and Clarke alert us to the

[41] See B. Spinks, "Johannes Grabe's Response to William Whiston: Some Reflections on a Lutheran Convert's Contribution to 18th-Century Anglican Orthodoxy and Liturgy," in *Lord Jesus Christ, Will You Not Stay: Essays in Honor of Ronald Feuerhahn on the Occasion of His Sixty-Fifth Birthday*, ed. J. Barth Day et al. (St. Louis: Concordia, 2002) 91–104.

[42] B. Spinks, "Trinitarian Belief and Worship: A Historical Case," in *God's Life in Trinity*, ed. M. Volf and M. Welker (Minneapolis: Fortress, 2006) 211–22.

[43] See A. E. Peaston, *The Prayer Book Reform Movement in the XVIIIth Century* (Oxford: B. Blackwell, 1940).

inherent problems in an inherited liturgical tradition that mainly addresses either a generic God, or God the Father, in prayer, and only exceptionally has prayers direct to God the Son and God the Spirit. It is not sufficient to claim Nicene and trinitarian orthodoxy in doctrine, and then to avoid expressing this in prayers and hymns in public worship. This is to invite a theoretical doctrinal orthodoxy alongside an actual public doxological heterodoxy.

LEX CREDENDI, LEX ORANDI:
THE CASE OF VINEYARD THEOLOGY AND WORSHIP

Though the lessons of Whiston and Clarke were available to Jungmann, it is most unlikely that he would have had the slightest interest in eighteenth-century Anglican heterodox liturgical revision. Vineyard worship of course post-dates Jungmann, but one suspects that even if it had been in existence in his lifetime it would have been of even less interest than Anglican liturgy. The Vineyard movement comes out of the charismatic revival ministry associated with the American evangelist John Wimber. Central to Vineyard worship are choruses that praise God in a gathering conscious of the majesty of Christ and the power of the Spirit. As James Steven has shown, in much charismatic worship is to be found praise addressed specifically to each of the persons of the Trinity.[44] However, Martyn Percy's discussion of Wimber and the Vineyard songs suggests that all is not well. Percy notes:

> Wimber and his song-writing colleagues are perhaps peculiar in addressing all three persons of the Trinity; in fact, no one person appears to be substantially more preferred to another. But what does emerge from even the most casual analysis of *Songs of the Vineyard* is that individuality and corporate nature of Trinitarian personhood (which might include distinctiveness in identity, functionality, space and time, yet mutuality and relationship), is dissolved. God as Father, Son and Holy Spirit assumes the same dissolved character throughout: intimate, loving, precious, refreshing, fulfilling, mighty and omnipotent, all without qualification. The data suggests that it is not so much God who is being addressed, but rather favourable concepts of God—an ideology—

[44] James Steven, *Worship in the Spirit: Charismatic Worship in the Church of England* (Carlisle: Paternoster, 2002).

16

that has rooted itself in the individual and corporate identity of the worshippers.[45]

Elsewhere Percy observes that despite the intimacy of the songs, with their preference for addressing God as "You" and "Lord," Jesus becomes the model for the Christian, and the power of his works is the Spirit. Emphasis is on the Spirit as unstoppable force rather than a person who gives gifts or whose presence yields fruits. Percy notes that "the power of Jesus is actually the power of the Spirit, given by the Father, working through the most effective agent possible: the person of Christ. In other words, there is a latent doctrine of subordination present in Wimber's thinking, which is explicitly exposed when the theme of power is used as an interpretive key to his theology."[46]

Indeed, Percy suggests that Wimber's subordinationist trinitarian theology most closely resembles that of Origen.[47] Although "Lord" is a key word in Vineyard worship, it functions as a code word for power and authority and not as a literal description of Jesus in relation to the Father and the Spirit. In Wimber's books and the Vineyard songs, Percy suggests, the manner in which Lordship is used tends, on the one hand, to deny the real humanity of Jesus in the life of the Trinity, and on the other, fails to give Jesus himself the same level of power that the Father or the Spirit possess. Jesus is subordinate both to the will of the Father and the power of the Spirit.[48] James Steven, Martyn Percy, and most recently, Pete Ward in *Selling Worship*,[49] all observe the tendency in Vineyard's choruses and other similar songs to concentrate on the majesty of Jesus, and the kingship and lordship of God, and to ignore any extended narrative of salvation history, especially the concept of self-emptying and the scandal of the cross. In the context of the Vineyard songs and Wimber's writings, the *lex orandi* can

[45] Martyn Percy, *Words, Wonders and Power: Understanding Contemporary Christian Fundamentalism and Revivalism* (London: S.P.C.K., 1996) 61.

[46] Ibid., 87.

[47] Ibid., 181 n. 9.

[48] Ibid., 88.

[49] Pete Ward, *Selling Worship* (Blatchley: Paternoster, 2005). R. Parry (*Worshipping Trinity* [Milton Keynes: Paternoster, 2005]) examined twenty-eight albums produced by Vineyard Music between 1999 and 2004, containing 362 songs. Only five fall into what Parry termed "Three–person songs."

disguise a distortion of orthodox doctrine that has a domino effect on how a Christian community envisions itself and its task in the world.

So, what does this have to do with Jungmann? The point is that Jungmann was certainly correct in stressing that the humanity of Christ must be a crucial part of liturgical prayer. Simply to address prayer to God the Son and God the Holy Spirit, be it in prose or song, does not in itself guarantee an orthodox doctrine of the Trinity or an orthodox christology. Consubstantiality of Son and Spirit with the Father cannot be separated from the consubstantiality of the Son with us. As T. F. Torrance puts it:

> The saving reality with which we are concerned here is the twofold but indivisible activity of God, of God as God upon man and of God as man towards himself, the movement of saving love which is at once *from* the Father, through the Son and in the Spirit, and *to* the Father, through the Son and in the Spirit. This has already taken place once and for all in the self-giving of God to us through the incarnation of his Son and the self-offering of Jesus Christ through his ascension to the Father.[50]

Worship must be grounded in the *katabasis* and *anabasis* of God. However, this needs far greater articulation than simply appending "through Christ" to a prayer addressed to God. The kenosis of God in Christ and the death on the cross cannot be avoided. In a post-Moltmann context, the so-called non-Chalcedonian versions of the *Trisagion* must surely be regarded as a totally orthodox liturgical unit in which christology and trinitarian theology are fittingly juxtaposed.

In this introduction I have attempted to show that Jungmann's concern for the human nature of Christ, as crucial as it is for soteriology, was argued at the expense of much New Testament evidence that at the very least invited the practice of addressing Christ as God. Likewise, his discussion of the early Eastern material seems to have been predetermined by his preference for what he regarded as a more primitive and still predominantly Roman form of liturgical prayer. The reluctance of the West—that is Rome and the Reformation Churches—to give fuller liturgical expression to the consubstantiality of the Son and Spirit, far from being an asset, has in fact always been a potential breeding ground for Arianism *redivivus*. But addressing Father, Son, and Spirit

---

[50] T. F. Torrance, *Theology in Reconciliation* (London: G. Chapman, 1975) 118.

without regard for the incarnation and atonement can be equally perilous. A full and sufficient *lex orandi* will give expression to both Nicene christology as well as the Nicene-Constantinopolitan trinitarian faith. It must also give full expression to the consubstantiality of the Son with us and for us, "who for us and our salvation came down from heaven." Of course, there is much more to be said on the topics of Trinity, christology, and liturgical theology, far beyond Jungmann's concerns, as subsequent papers I am sure will show. But by way of introduction I want to urge, with Balthasar Fischer, that sound liturgical piety absolutely depends on both the *per Christum* and the *ad Christum*.

Part 1

The New Testament and
Some Classical Worship Traditions

What picture does the New Testament yield on Christology and Trinitarian belief? When did Christians begin to address Christ as God in prayer? New Testament scholar Larry Hurtado examines the "binitarian" shape of devotion in the New Testament in which Jesus is linked with God the Father in a notable manner. This involves a whole constellation of practices in which Jesus figures prominently, including hymns, prayers, prophetic words, and the use of Jesus' name in healing, baptism, and other actions. Far from its being an appropriation of pagan notions of multiple deities and apotheosis of humans, Hurtado suggests that it arose from the use of categories from biblical tradition to express Jesus' status as sharing in, and being an expression of, God's name.

The New Testament trajectories are taken further by Paul Bradshaw, who traces some of the complexities of the forms and addressees of Christian praying in the first few centuries as it evolved from its Jewish matrix and was gradually shaped by the growing need to adhere to emerging doctrinal orthodoxy. How was this emerging orthodoxy appropriated and developed in later worship forms and formulae? Robert Taft examines the Byzantine Divine Office, which is a synthesis of the liturgical traditions of Constantinople and Palestine. A "neo-Chalcedonianism" is strongly developed in the liturgy, a liturgy which the Byzantines believed was not only a representation but also a re-presentation of the earthly saving work of Christ. What of non-Chalcedonian communities? Baby Varghese examines the early Syriac tradition and the Syriac prayers of the Eucharist in the Maronite and Syrian Orthodox traditions and shows that addressing prayer to Christ is not simply an expression of miaphysite Christology, but is an ancient strand in the Syriac-speaking tradition. Gabriele Winkler looks more closely at the "Oratio Christologica" or Post-sanctus in the eucharistic prayers of Basil, in the Egyptian redactions and the Armenian, Syriac, and Byzantine redactions, showing how a tradition evolved theologically. Peter Jeffery challenges Jungmann's conclusion about the *Kyrie* of the Roman Mass. Jungmann believed it was addressed to Christ, and this is so in the newly created "tropes" of the 1970 missal. Jeffery demonstrates how both a trinitarian and christological understandings of the *Kyrie* circulated from early times.

Chapter 2

The Binitarian Pattern of Earliest Christian Devotion and Early Doctrinal Development

L. W. Hurtado
University of Edinburgh

I begin this discussion with an explicit statement of my thesis and a connected critical observation. The observation is that (at least in my own New Testament/Christian Origins field) little has been made of the importance of earliest Christian devotional practice for historical understanding of developments in beliefs. My thesis is that the pattern of devotional practice that we see reflected already in our earliest Christian sources is both a notable phenomenon in its own right and was also a significant influence upon doctrinal development, particularly with reference to beliefs about God and Jesus.

Lest my complaint be misunderstood, I want to acknowledge that, to be sure, there is a large and generally helpful body of scholarship on first-century Christian worship. For the most part, however, these studies tend to be either general surveys, or more focused analyses of the sort that fit more readily within history-of-worship/liturgy concerns.[1] In particular, there is, of course, a body of substantial studies

---

[1] Surveys of earliest Christian worship include, e.g., O. Cullmann, *Early Christian Worship* (London: SCM, 1953); G. Delling, *Worship in the New Testament* (Philadelphia: Westminster, 1962); R. P. Martin, *Worship in the Early Church* (Grand Rapids: Eerdmans, 1974); A. Cabaniss, *Patterns in Early Christian Worship* (Macon: Mercer University Press, 1989); J. F. Nielen, *Gebet und Gottesdienst im Neuen Testament: Eine Studie zur biblischen Liturgie und Ethik* (Freiburg: Herder, 1937); J. Marty, "Étude des textes culturels de prière contenus dans le Nouveau Testament," *Revue d'histoire et de philosophie religieuses* 9 (1929) 234–68, 366–76; F. Hahn, *The Worship of the Early Church* (Philadelphia: Fortress, 1973); C. D. F. Moule, *Worship in the New Testament* (Bramcote: Grove Books, 1978). Among history-of-liturgy studies are J. Jungmann, *The Early Liturgy to the Time*

focused on the origins and development of Christian eucharistic practice, such as Lietzmann's classic.[2] Moreover, in the discussion of earliest (first-century) worship, the major tendency among historians of liturgy has been to explore whether and how it anticipates worship practices (e.g., Eucharist, baptism, fixed times, and forms of prayer) more formally/fully developed and more fully attested/described in somewhat later times.[3] As well, the traditional history-of-religions question has repeatedly been posed, especially as to whether/how earliest Christian eucharistic and baptismal practice may have been shaped by, or at least been reflective of, religious meals and initiation rites in the wider Roman-era environment.[4] These are fully appropriate lines of investigation, to be sure, but my own heuristic concerns are somewhat different, and are less frequently addressed.

To clarify these concerns further, if much of the available scholarship has tended to look "upstream" at first-century Christian phenomena of worship from a later standpoint, assessing how earlier practices anticipate and prefigure later practices, my own approach has been to

---

of Gregory the Great, trans. Francis A. Brunner. Liturgical Studies 6 (Notre Dame: University of Notre Dame Press, 1959) esp. 10–49, and the more recent incisive analysis and critique of previous studies by P. F. Bradshaw, The Search for the Origins of Christian Worship. 2nd ed. (London/New York: S.P.C.K., 2002) 47–72. Bradshaw stated, "The number of studies in the last 50 years relating to various aspects of worship in the New Testament has been so great that a comprehensive and detailed account is quite impossible within the limits of this chapter" (47).

[2] H. Lietzmann, Mass and Lord's Supper: A Study in the History of the Liturgy, trans. by D. H. G. Reeve (Leiden: E. J. Brill, 1979). Another well-known classic that gives some attention to earliest Christian practice is G. Dix, The Shape of the Liturgy (London: Dacre Press, 1975). Other, more recent, studies include I. H. Marshall, Last Supper and Lord's Supper (Exeter, UK: Paternoster, 1980); J. Kodell, The Eucharist in the New Testament (Wilmington: Michael Glazier, 1988); B. D. Chilton, A Feast of Meanings: Eucharistic Theologies from Jesus through Johannine Circles. Novum Testamentum Supplements 72 (Leiden: E. J. Brill, 1994); J. Koenig, The Feast of the World's Redemption: Eucharistic Origins and Christian Mission (Harrisburg: Trinity Press International, 2000).

[3] E.g., P. F. Bradshaw, Daily Prayer in the Early Church (New York: S.P.C.K., 1982).

[4] E.g., H.-J. Klauck, Herrenmahl und hellenistischer Kult (Münster: Aschendorff, 1982); and more recently D. E. Smith, From Symposium to Eucharist: The Banquet in the Early Christian World (Minneapolis: Fortress, 2003).

consider earliest Christian devotional practice in its own right, examining Christian phenomena in light of precedents and the synchronous context. In particular, I have tended to focus more on analysis of Christian worship in the context of the immediate and earliest religious matrix of the Christian movement, second-temple Jewish tradition.[5] I am especially interested in how earliest Christian devotional practice may represent a significant religious development in that context, and also how it both reflected and perhaps helped to stimulate and shape the religious convictions and beliefs that came to characterize Christian tradition.

Patristics scholars will perhaps immediately think of an important earlier discussion of this matter by Maurice Wiles in *The Making of Christian Doctrine*.[6] Certainly, Wiles makes the basic point that doctrine can be prompted and shaped by worship, and I am happy to point to this eminent scholar for precedent and support of what I wish to propose. He focused mainly on illustrations of how, in christological debates of the early centuries, worship practices were invoked and seen as relevant, and he cogently showed that in order to succeed ultimately in these debates, "any interpretation of the person of the Son had to be one which came to terms with the place given to him in the Christian practice of devotion" (74).

I broadly agree with his discussion, and readily defer particularly to his far greater acquaintance with the evidence of the third century c.e. and later. I am not persuaded, however, by his attribution of so much to an early "popular" piety that can be readily distinguished from a more officially-sanctioned liturgical practice. To be sure, a distinction between a "popular" piety and the piety and doctrinal understanding preferred in more official and learned circles of the early church is both plausible and demonstrable, perhaps more readily so in

---

[5] Esp. L. W. Hurtado, *One God, One Lord: Early Christian Devotion and Ancient Jewish Monotheism* (Philadelphia: Fortress, 1988; 2nd ed., Edinburgh: T&T Clark, 1998); idem, *At the Origins of Christian Worship: The Context and Character of Earliest Christian Devotion* (Grand Rapids: Eerdmans, 2000); idem, *Lord Jesus Christ: Devotion to Jesus in Earliest Christianity* (Grand Rapids: Eerdmans, 2003).

[6] Maurice Wiles, *The Making of Christian Doctrine: A Study in the Principles of Early Doctrinal Development* (Cambridge: Cambridge University Press, 1967) esp. ch. 4, "Lex Orandi," 62–93.

the third century and later.[7] But the worship practices and expressions
that Wiles cites from the New Testament as indicative of "popular" piety
are also all affirmed by the writers of these texts, and these writers
clearly intended their writings to be instructive, even authoritative
(certainly the case for Paul!), for approved Christian beliefs and practice.[8] For example, the heavenly scene of worship given to "the
Lamb" in Revelation 5 is hardly to be treated as indicative of a "popular" and "informal" piety, if that means a piety that can be distinguished from what was promoted and practiced by Christian leaders
such as the author of Revelation.[9] Likewise, it is misleading to characterize the singing of hymns about and to Christ (reflected in Pliny's famous letter about Christians in Bithynia, and represented in the *Phos
Hilaron* and the hymn with which Clement of Alexandria concludes the
Paidagogos) as evidence of "popular piety," if this connotes something
that exceeded a supposedly more cautious approach toward reverencing Jesus.[10] There is simply no evidence of such a more cautious approach advocated in Christian circles of the period of these texts. To
cite the last example, Clement gives no hint that he sees the hymn as
particularly reflective of a piety that he regards as less admirable or
learned than his own.

In short, Wiles rightly judged that early worship practice was important for understanding the development of beliefs in the period reflected
in the New Testament, particularly beliefs to do with Jesus.[11] But the remarkable reverence for Jesus reflected in the New Testament appears to
represent a piety/devotion that was both popularly embraced and also
affirmed and promoted by those who taught and led first-century circles
of Christians. In that sense this influential reverence/piety is to be seen
as, at the same time, both "popular" and "official."

---

[7] See e.g., J. Lebreton, "Le désaccord de foi populaire et de théologie sa-
vante dans l'Église chrétienne du IIIe siècle." *Revue d'histoire ecclésiastique* 19
(1923) 481–506, and 20 (1924) 5–27.

[8] Wiles, *The Making of Chirstian Doctrine*, 62–67.

[9] Revelation 4–5 is a two-scene dramatic unit that reflects a notable expression of first-century Christian faith. See, e.g., L. W. Hurtado, "Revelation 4–5
in the Light of Jewish Apocalyptic Analogies." *Journal for the Study of the New
Testament* 25 (1985) 105–24; L. Mowry, "Revelation 4–5 and Early Christian
Liturgical Usage." *Journal of Biblical Literature* 71 (1952) 75–84.

[10] Cf. Wiles, *The Making of Christian Doctrine*, 66–67.

[11] Ibid., 63.

There is another way in which my observations here can be distinguished from Wiles's discussion, while also being intended to complement it. Wiles focused on the influences of early Christian worship upon doctrines about Jesus. I will have some things to say about that as well, but I want to broaden the focus here somewhat to explore how the early Christian understanding of God and of Jesus' relationship to God (the "Father") were driven and shaped by the pattern of earliest Christian devotional practice. I will reserve a fuller explication for later in this paper.

In addition to Wiles's stimulating discussion, I gratefully acknowledge a few other valuable contributions. An insightful and very fruitful article by Richard Bauckham is especially worth noting, and was in fact influential in helping to shape my own research program at a very early point.[12] Bauckham focused on several passages in Jewish apocalyptic texts in which a human seer is confronted by an angel whom the seer at first mistakes for God, and so attempts to worship. In each case the angel forbids this, emphasizing that God alone is to be worshiped. Among these scenes are two instances in the book of Revelation (19:9-10; 22:6-9), which reflect an ancient author well aware of this Jewish tradition and fully sympathetic to the rather exclusivist worship scruple that it represents.[13] Bauckham then notes the rather striking evidence that Revelation also reflects with full approval the inclusion

---

[12] Richard Baukham, "The Worship of Jesus in Apocalyptic Christianity." *New Testament Studies* 27 (1981) 322–41. There is a revised and expanded version of this essay in idem, *The Climax of Prophecy: Studies on the Book of Revelation* (Edinburgh: T&T Clark, 1993) 118–49. See also R. T. France, "The Worship of Jesus: A Neglected Factor in Christological Debate?" in *Christ the Lord: Studies in Christology Presented to Donald Guthrie*, ed. H. H. Rowdon, 17–36 (Downers Grove: Inter-Varsity Press, 1982).

[13] It is commonly thought that the author of Revelation was a Jewish Christian (e.g., "John" at this early point was almost certainly used solely among Jews). It should also be noted that he had a strong concern about worship practice. His condemnation of the teachings and practices of "Nicolaitans" (Rev 2:6, 15), "Balaam" (2:14), and the "Jezebel" who claimed to be a prophet seems to have been particularly directed against what he regarded as questionable cultic practices. These he labelled "fornication" and eating "food sacrificed to idols," drawing upon the condemnatory labels used in the Old Testament against what the writers regarded as illegitimate cultic practices that brought the wrath of God upon Israel and Judah.

of the glorified Jesus with God as rightful recipients of heavenly (and so idealized) worship (most fully in Revelation 5:6-14), and he rightly judges that this is a clear indication of a notable development that must comprise a remarkably exalted view of Jesus.[14] Baukham's key contribution in this article was to draw attention to early Christian worship practice as a particularly important expression of such beliefs. His emphasis is especially appropriate and correct in analysis of Roman-era religion, for in that environment cultic practice was *the* key expression and test of one's religion.

Martin Hengel has also contributed to the discussion, especially in emphasizing the importance of the earliest Christian hymns/odes about Christ as evidence of—and as influential upon—christological beliefs.[15] As he noted, it is significant that the key New Testament passages in which we have the most extended and explicit presentations of Jesus' high importance are widely thought to be (or to draw upon) hymns/odes chanted in first-century Christian worship settings (e.g., Phil 2:6-11; Col 1:15-20; John 1:1-18).[16] Indeed, Hengel has contended

---

[14] Bauckham's observations were developed further by L. T. Stuckenbruck, *Angel Veneration and Christology*. Wissenschaftliche Untersuchungen zum Neuen Testament 2/70 (Tübingen: J.C.B. Mohr, 1995).

[15] Martin Hengel, "Hymns and Christology," in *Between Jesus and Paul*, 78–96 (London: SCM, 1983); idem, "The Song about Christ in Earliest Worship," in *Studies in Early Christology*, 227–91 (Edinburgh: T&T Clark, 1995). See also R. P. Martin, "Some Reflections on New Testament Hymns," in *Christ the Lord: Studies Presented to Donald Guthrie*, ed. H. H. Rowdon, 37–49 (Downers Grove: Inter-Varsity Press, 1982). Also still important is J. Kroll, *Die christliche Hymnodik bis zu Klemens von Alexandreia* (Königsberg: Hartungsche Buchdruckerei, 1921).

[16] See L. L. Thompson, "Hymns in Early Christian Worship." *Anglican Theological Review* 55 (1973) 458–72; R. J. Karris, *A Symphony of New Testament Hymns: Commentary on Philippians 2:5-11, Colossians 1:15-20, Ephesians 2:14-16, 1 Timothy 3:16, Titus 3:4-7, 1 Peter 3:18-22, and 2 Timothy 2:11-13* (Collegeville, MN: Liturgical Press, 1996); J. T. Sanders, *The New Testament Christological Hymns: Their Historical Religious Background* (Cambridge: Cambridge University Press, 1971); R. Deichgräber, *Gotteshymnus und Christushymnus in der frühen Christenheit: Untersuchungen zu Form, Sprache und Stil der frühchristlichen Hymnen*. Studien zur Umwelt des Neuen Testaments 5 (Göttingen: Vandenhoeck & Ruprecht, 1967); K. Wengst, *Christologische Formeln und Lieder des Urchristentums* (Gütersloh: Gütersloher Verlagshaus Gerd Mohn, 1972); G. Kennel, *Frühchristliche Hymnen? Gattungskritische Studien zur Frage nach den Liedern der frühen Christenheit*. Wissenschafliche Monographien zum Alten und

(persuasively in my view) that among the earliest expressions of Jesus' high significance in Christian circles were christologically interpreted biblical psalms (involving insights likely received as revelations prompted by the Holy Spirit) and also newly composed odes about Jesus that believers saw as inspired by the Holy Spirit, and that these psalms and odes "had a quite essential significance for earliest Christian worship as for the formation of Christology."[17] Indisputably, "psalms and hymns and spiritual songs" that flowed from the religious exaltation attributed to the Holy Spirit (Eph 5:18-20; Col 3:16-17), sung/chanted expressions of Jesus' redemptive work and exalted significance, predate considerably the developed doctrinal elaborations of the second to fourth centuries, and, as I aim to underscore in this essay, helped to generate and shape them.[18] In what follows, I wish to build further upon these studies and my own previous observations about early Christian devotion to consider further how worship practice of the first century or so both reflects religious convictions and also shaped further doctrinal developments.

Neuen Testament 71 (Neukirchen-Vluyn: Neukirchener Verlag, 1995). On the all-important Philippians passage, see now the essays in R. Martin and B. Dodd, eds., *Where Christology Began: Essays on Philippians 2* (Louisville: Westminster John Knox, 1998), and on the Colossians passage, C. Stettler, *Der Kolosserhymnus: Untersuchungen zu Form, traditionsgeschichtlichem Hintergrund und Aussage von Kol 1,15–20*. Wissenschaftliche Untersuchungen zum Neuen Testament 2/131 (Tübingen: Mohr Siebeck, 2000).

[17] Hengel, "Hymns and Christology," 88.

[18] We cannot linger here over the question, but I take the phrase "psalms and hymns and spiritual songs" to reflect the use of somewhat distinguishable types of sung/chanted expressions in early Christian worship (e.g., biblical Psalms and also fresh Christian compositions inspired by the Spirit). Commentators also debate whether the ψαλμός in 1 Cor 14:26 refers to the use of biblical Psalms or to Spirit-prompted odes. Cf., e.g., A. C. Thiselton, *The First Epistle to the Corinthians* (Grand Rapids: Eerdmans, 2000) 1131–37; G. D. Fee, *The First Epistle to the Corinthians* (Grand Rapids: Eerdmans, 1987) 690–91. Also disputed is whether praying and singing τῷ πνεύματι (1 Cor 14:15) connotes "charismatic" hymnody and prayer under the inspiration of the Holy Spirit (so, e.g., Fee, 670–71) or prayer/singing in the "innermost spiritual being" of the believer (so Thiselton, 1110–13). I find Fee's analysis more adequate, but the matter is not crucial for the present discussion.

THE "BINITARIAN SHAPE" OF EARLIEST CHRISTIAN DEVOTION[19]

In several publications over the last couple of decades or so I have drawn attention to what I term the "binitarian" character of earliest Christian devotion. Here I again focus on this. Before going further, therefore, it will be helpful to summarize briefly what I mean.

Inclusion of Jesus

First, I use the term "binitarian" to underscore the inclusion of Jesus with God as recipient of devotion. In earliest Christian devotional practice these two distinguishable and yet closely related figures are referred to and treated as the rightful and sole recipients of the sorts of devotional actions that early Christians characteristically refused to offer to other figures, whether humans (e.g., the Roman emperor), heavenly beings such as angels, or, most emphatically, other putative deities. That is, on the one hand, their devotional practice exhibits a stout exclusivity, a characteristic refusal to extend full cultic reverence to the many other recipients of devotion available in the religious environment of the early Roman period. In taking this stance, of course, early Christian circles exhibited their derivation from, and continuing faithfulness to, the strong Jewish religious scruple against undue reverence of anything or anyone other than the one God, a scruple that the Christian movement inherited from its Jewish religious matrix.[20]

---

[19] I lift here the title of a previous essay, and I draw upon the more extended analysis of earliest devotional practice offered there: Hurtado, "The Binitarian Shape of Early Christian Worship," in *The Jewish Roots of Christological Monotheism: Papers from the St. Andrews Conference on the Historical Origins of the Worship of Jesus*, ed. Cary C. Newman, James R. Davila, Gladys S. Lewis. Supplements to the Journal for the Study of Judaism 63 (Leiden: Brill, 1999) 187–213. This essay also forms chapter 3 of Hurtado, *At the Origins of Christian Worship*.

[20] Hurtado, "First Century Jewish Monotheism." *Journal for the Study of the New Testament* 71 (1998) 3–26. Of course, devout Roman-era Jews combined this scruple with a readiness to venerate martyrs (e.g., with tombs built in their honor), and to ascribe great status to principal angels and/or great biblical figures such as Enoch and Moses. The "monotheism" of ancient Jews and Christians was exhibited primarily in an avoidance of the *cultic worship* (as they practiced and understood it) of any figure other than the biblical deity, i.e., sacrifice, prayer, ritual praise/adoration, etc.

On the other hand, and all the more notably, the early Christians whose devotion is reflected in the New Testament seem entirely ready to extend to Jesus the sort of reverence that they otherwise reserved for the one God of biblical tradition, reverence that they refused to extend to other figures. Indeed, they appear to have considered this reverence of Jesus not only fully permissible and appropriate, but even as requisite. John 5:23 is perhaps the most explicit expression of this attitude, declaring that it is God's will that "all should reverence [τιμῶσι] the Son just as they reverence the Father," and that "whoever does not reverence the Son does not reverence the Father."[21] Other passages more implicitly, but in my view just as clearly, reflect this view that God now wills that Jesus be given the sort of reverence that links him with God in remarkable ways.

Of these, Philippians 2:6-11 is among the earliest. This much-studied text proclaims that God has exalted Jesus and given him "the name above every name" with the intention that Jesus should be given universal acclamation (vv. 9-11). Moreover, it is important to note that this acclamation, [Κύριος Ἰησοῦς Χριστός], reflects precisely the acclamation and invocation of Jesus that appears to have characterized earliest Christian worship. That is, the divine intention asserted in Philippians 2:9-11 is not simply a submission to Jesus after the fashion of submission to an enthroned or conquering king. The early Christians whose piety is reflected in the passage saw their own *corporate, cultic* acclamation of Jesus in their worship-gatherings as the full acknowledgement of God's exaltation of Jesus, and the anticipation of the universal acclamation of Jesus that the passage heralds.

In fact, the other instances of the very earliest confessional formulae that we know also indicate a provenance in gathered worship. In addition to Philippians 2:9-11, there is also the confession Κύριος Ἰησοῦς attested in 1 Corinthians 12:3 and Romans 10:9. In each instance we have a cultic acclamation of Jesus' exalted status, that is, a formula used in, and forming a crucial feature of, their corporate worship.[22]

---

[21] Translations are the author's.

[22] Cf. V. H. Neufeld, *The Earliest Christian Confessions* (Grand Rapids: Eerdmans, 1963), who focused on the "confession" of Jesus primarily in the context of arraignment and evangelism, in my view neglecting the true provenance of the action in worship.

This is easily demonstrable in the case of 1 Corinthians 12:3, for the larger context of 1 Corinthians 11-14 is explicitly concerned with various questions to do with behavior in corporate worship.[23] 1 Corinthians 12 opens with a contrast between the former idolatrous cultic activities of his addressees and what Paul sets forth as the proper devotional stance (12:1-3), which is enabled by the Holy Spirit, and expressed in the acclamation "Lord Jesus" (or "Jesus is Lord," 12:3). Then the various charismatic phenomena itemized in the verses that follow immediately (12:4-11) are apparently all exhibited in the worship gathering. Yet the context also indicates that this cultic acclamation of Jesus as Κύριος is set within worship that is prompted by God (the one "who activates them all [these spiritual gifts] in everyone," 12:6), and is also ultimately directed to God (as reflected in the frequent reference to God as recipient of prayer, tongue-speaking, and praise in these chapters).

Likewise in Romans 10:8-13, confessing (ὁμολογέω, v. 9) Jesus as "Lord" appears to be a devotional act that is linked in redemptive efficacy with faith in his resurrection (vv. 9-10) and with the obviously cultic action "[to call] upon the name of the Lord" (v. 13). Indeed, it appears that to "confess" Jesus as Lord here may be simply another way of referring to the same corporate invocation of Jesus that is also designated by the verb "call upon" (ἐπικαλέω), with its rich Old Testament association with cultic worship.[24]

I emphasize, however, that this inclusion of Jesus as a second, distinguishable recipient of devotion is characteristically presented with a clear concern to avoid a simple di-theism, and to maintain a monotheistic stance, howbeit in an innovative form. The reverence of Jesus is linked to God's exaltation of him, and Jesus' status and significance

[23] Women's attire in public worship (11:2-16); behavior at the Lord's Supper (11:17-34); "spiritual gifts" in worship (chapters 12-14). In addition, we may note 1 Cor 8-10, which is mainly concerned with questions about Christians' participation in various activities and settings where devotion to other deities may be involved.

[24] Romans 10:13 is a direct quotation of Joel 3:5 (LXX; 2:32 in the Hebrew text). On this use of the verb see, e.g., W. Kirchschläger, "ἐπικαλέω," in *Exegetical Dictionary of the New Testament*, ed. Horst Balz, Gerhard Schneider (Grand Rapids: Eerdmans, 1990-93) 2:28-29. On the christological significance of the expression, see C. J. Davis, *The Name and Way of the Lord: Old Testament Themes, New Testament Christology*. Journal for the Study of the Journal for the New Testament Supplement Series 129 (Sheffield: Sheffield Academic Press, 1996).

is expressed with reference to God ("the Father"). This is what I mean by "binitarian": not simply two figures, but a linkage and, indeed, a clear functional subordination of Jesus to God, a "shaped two-ishness" exhibited in the characteristic expressions of belief and in cultic practices.

Specific Devotional Actions

My second point is that this "binitarian" worship is exhibited in quite specific phenomena. In work on this topic over the last couple of decades or so, one of my concerns has been to avoid abstractions and to focus on matters that can be tested critically, building up conclusions inductively on the basis of specifics. To be sure, as Paul Bradshaw showed in his influential analysis of the study of early liturgy, we do not have sufficient evidence to construct a putative form of worship for first-century Christianity. Moreover, in any case we should probably posit diversity in this earliest period rather than supposing that there was any one form of worship to be sought in the extant evidence.[25] But although the New Testament writings do not furnish us with the sort of evidence needed to say what kind of first-century "liturgies" or orders of worship there might have been (if any), I contend that a number of relevant devotional actions set within the context of gathered worship are reflected in these texts, and that these form a constellation of considerable historic significance. In their historical context the devotional acts in question are simply remarkable. What evidence that we have of Jewish religious practice of the time gives us no real analogies for them, either individually or as a constellation of devotional practices. The reason appears to be that these sorts of practices were regarded by devout Jews as inappropriately directed to anyone other than the one God.[26] This makes the appearance of these practices in early Christian circles all the more notable. I refer readers to previous

[25] Bradshaw, *The Search*, esp. 47–72.

[26] It is important to emphasize that we are looking for analogies to *public, corporate* worship/devotional practices that functioned as characteristic and identifying features of a religious group. This means that "magical" practices, usually involving private/secret invocation of powerful spirits and/or other beings, are not directly relevant. A good many Roman-era Jews may have engaged in such practices, but this would have been the actions of individuals. "Magical" practices did not function openly as identifying, characteristic devotional actions expressive of devout Jewish religion.

publications for a more extended discussion,[27] and content myself here with a summary presentation of the basic data.

Where we have references to prayer in the New Testament, it is typically offered to God, but often prayer is offered "through" Jesus (e.g., Rom 1:8) or in Jesus' name (e.g., John 16:23-24).[28] Moreover, particularly in Pauline texts, prayer is offered to "the God and Father of our Lord Jesus Christ" (e.g., 2 Cor 1:3; Eph 1:3; Col 1:3). That is another way of distinguishing Christian prayer, the God to whom one prays being (re)defined with reference to Jesus. Though fewer, there are indications of prayer to Jesus, both jointly with God (e.g., 1 Thess 3:11-13) and also to Jesus alone (e.g., 2 Cor 12:8-9; Acts 7:59-60).[29] In further support, we may note the "Grace and peace" salutations (which invoke God and Jesus), and the "Grace" benedictions (which typically invoke Jesus) in Paul's letters, formulae commonly thought to have been appropriated by him from contemporary use in worship gatherings.

I have already referred to ritual invocation/confession of Jesus in early Christian worship. In 1 Corinthians 1:2, Paul characterizes Christians simply as "all those who everywhere call upon [ἐπικαλέω] the name of our Lord Jesus Christ," which suggests that this practice (described in biblical language for worship of God) is ubiquitous in first-century Christian circles. Indeed, the little fragment of Aramaic worship cited in 1 Corinthians 16:22, *Marana tha* (which probably means "Come, O/our Lord!"), is commonly taken as addressed to Jesus, and is rather clear evidence that the ritual invocation of him was operative in Aramaic-speaking Christian circles as well as among Pauline congregations.

---

[27] Hurtado, *At the Origins*, esp. 70–94.

[28] Still worth consulting is the discussion in J. Jungmann, *The Place of Christ in Liturgical Prayer*. 2nd rev. ed., trans. A. Peeler (Staten Island: Alba House, 1965) 127–43. The initial publication of this work (German first ed., 1925) we justly celebrate in this conference.

[29] See R. J. Bauckham, "Jesus, Worship of," in *Anchor Bible Dictionary*, ed. D. N. Freedman, 3:812–19 (Garden City: Doubleday, 1992) esp. 813; A. Klawek, *Das Gebet zu Jesus. Seine Berechtigung und Übung nach den Schriften des Neuen Testaments: Eine biblisch-theologische Studie* (Münster: Aschendorff, 1921). On the Pauline evidence, see esp. A. Hamman, *La prière: Le Nouveau Testament* (Tournai: Desclée, 1959) 245–337.

As a related matter, we may also point to Jesus' prominence in early baptismal practice. As is well known, extant evidence indicates that the initiation rite observed in first-century Christian circles typically included the invocation of Jesus' name (e.g., Acts 2:38; 8:16; 10:48). This was certainly intended to mark ritually the persons baptized, linking them with Jesus.[30] But it is also another devotional action in which Jesus had an unparalleled prominence, and his name was thought to have special power. The New Testament also reflects somewhat similar ritual uses of Jesus' name in healing (e.g., Acts 3:6; 4:30), exorcism (e.g., Acts 16:18), and perhaps also in the sort of ritual of judgment that Paul directs the Corinthian church to carry out against the incestuous man in 1 Corinthians 5:3-5.[31]

To cite another well-known practice, some sort of common meal of religious/sacred significance also appears to have been a characteristic feature of Christian circles from the earliest period onward. Moreover, in spite of apparent variations in wording, prayers used, and specific interpretations of the religious meaning/nature of the meals, it seems clear that in all known instances Jesus figured prominently.[32] The earliest and comparatively extended evidence is in 1 Corinthians, where Paul calls the event "the Lord's Supper" (κυριακὸν δεῖπνον, 11:20), that is connected with "the Lord Jesus" (11:23), reflecting a new covenant made "in [his] blood" (v. 25).[33] The meal is to be celebrated "for my

[30] See now L. Hartman, *"Into the Name of the Lord Jesus": Baptism in the Early Church* (Edinburgh: T&T Clark, 1997).

[31] In this passage it is not entirely clear whether "in the name of [the/our] Lord Jesus" (v. 4) goes with Paul's act of judging the situation (v. 3) or with the direction to the church to assemble that follows in verse 4. The Nestle-Aland 27th ed. text punctuates the wording in support of the latter option, and I tend to favor it as well. But either way, the centrality of Jesus as powerful "Lord" and the ritual use of his name are clearly reflected.

[32] I submit that whether one takes the Pauline evidence (1 Cor 11:17-34), or the gospels' Last Supper accounts (Matt 26:26-30; Mark 14:22-25; Luke 22:14-23, with their own variations), or the relevant material in *Didache* (9–10), there is a clear focus on Jesus in all cases.

[33] In addition to commentaries on 1 Corinthians, see also A. Eriksson, *Traditions as Rhetorical Proof: Pauline Argumentation in 1 Corinthians* (Stockholm: Almquist & Wiksell International, 1998) 174–96, for analysis of the church situation and the rhetorical aims and devices in Paul's handling of it. It is worth noting (but cannot be explored here) that the term κυριακός was also used in the Roman period to designate something as "imperial" (e.g., imperial

[Jesus'] remembrance" (εἰς τὴν ἐμὴν ἀνάμνησιν, vv. 24-25), and Paul's statement that the celebration is a proclamation of "the death of the Lord . . . until he comes" (v. 26) may represent a specific interpretation of this ἀνάμνησις.[34] In short, Jesus has a prominence in this meal that rather closely resembles the roles of deities in other religious meals of the Roman period. Indeed, Paul makes such a direct comparison, declaring that participation in the Christian sacred meal is completely incompatible with participation in the meals in honor of other deities (1 Cor 10:19-22). Just as importantly, Jesus' centrality in this core worship action is completely unprecedented and unparalleled in all extant evidence of observant Jewish groups of the time.

We have already noted the place of hymns *about* Jesus, and even hymns sung *to* Jesus, in early Christian worship, and we cannot linger further over the several putative examples widely thought to have been identified in the New Testament writings.[35] My point here is simply to underscore the significance of Jesus-hymns having such a characteristic and core function. That is, in addition to *what* the hymns say about Jesus, it is at least as significant *that* such hymns had such a prominent place in early Christian worship. It is without parallel in the Jewish context of the time, except for the way in which God is praised (e.g., in the chanting of Psalms).

Still another feature of early Christian worship has not received adequate attention, that is, prophetic oracles uttered in Jesus' name. In

---

treasure). So did the use of the term by Christians (as also ἡ κυριακὴ ἡμέρα, Rev 1:10) represent an implicit appropriation to Jesus of imperial-like status? In defense of this suggestion, see A. Deissmann, *Light from the Ancient East*, trans. by L. R. M. Strachan (Grand Rapids: Baker Book House, 1965) 357–58.

[34] For a recent discussion of the interpretative options and issues, see Thiselton, *The First Epistle*, esp. 878–82, who emphasizes that ἀνάμνησις here involves both a mental recollection of, and "self-involvement" with, Jesus' death, and also a "living out of this Christian identity" in relations with other members of the church at the table.

[35] The reference to "singing and making melody to the Lord in your hearts" (Eph 5:18) likely means praise directed to the exalted Jesus. "Worshiping the Lord and fasting" (Acts 13:2) is probably also to be taken as worship directed to Jesus. The simple absolute "the Lord" (ὁ κύριος) usually designates Jesus in the New Testament. E.g., when the author of Luke-Acts wishes to make it clear that he makes reference to God, he prefers the word "δεσπότης" (e.g., Luke 2:29; Acts 4:24).

his major analysis of early Christian prophecy, David Aune identified nineteen instances in the New Testament where the risen Jesus is either the speaker or is identified as the source or authority of the prophetic speech, and he pointed to nine further instances in the early Christian collection known as the *Odes of Solomon*.[36] In light of the traditional concern against prophecy in the name of any god other than YHWH (e.g., Deut 13:1-5), the early Christian evidence is extraordinary in its implications about Jesus' place in the devotional life of the circles whose practice is reflected in the relevant texts.

Early and Widely Represented

The final point I want to underscore is that these devotional phenomena focused on Jesus appear to have emerged amazingly early and were widely characteristic in first-century Christian circles. I have already noted briefly 1 Corinthians 1:2, where Paul refers to "all those who in every place call on the name of our Lord Jesus Christ." Early in his epistolary effort to correct problems of divisiveness and the misguided notions of spiritual superiority of some in the Corinthian church, Paul strikes this note of ecumenical relationship in the common devotional practice of invoking Jesus, here using a biblical phrase that connotes worship offered to Jesus.[37] Indeed, here and elsewhere (e.g., Acts 9:14) "call[ing] upon the name" of Jesus is simply another way of designating believers, so widespread and uncontroversial among them is this ritual action!

Lest we suspect that the ecumenical circle referred to might extend solely to other Pauline churches of Gentile converts, there is the fragment of Aramaic-speaking devotional practice preserved in 1 Corinthians 16:22, *Marana tha*, already noted. Moreover, as I have argued previously,[38] there is no indication that the devotion to Jesus reflected

---

[36] D. E. Aune, *Prophecy in Early Christianity and the Ancient Mediterranean World* (Grand Rapids: Eerdmans, 1983) 328–29. NT texts = the seven oracles to churches in Rev 2–3; Rev 16:15; 22:12-15, 16, 20; plus 2 Cor 12:9; Acts 18:19; 23:11; 1 Thess 4:15-17; 1 Cor 14:37-38; 1 Thess 4:2; 2 Thess 3:6, 12. We might also note Acts 9:10-17.

[37] See the discussion in Fee, *The First Epistle*, 33–34, and further literature cited in n. 16; and also Hurtado, *Lord Jesus Christ*, 108–13. Biblical (OT) instances where the crucial verb-form appears include Gen 4:26; 12:8; Ps 50:15; and esp. Joel 3:5.

[38] Hurtado, *Lord Jesus Christ*, e.g., 135–36, 165–67, 172–76.

in Paul's letters represents any significant innovation in the sort of devotional practices that characterized other sectors of first-century Christianity, such as the Jerusalem church. In short, Paul's reference to this devotion to Jesus as characterizing believers "everywhere" (ἐν παντὶ τόπῳ, 1 Cor 1:2) seems not to be an exaggeration, but rather a justifiably confident claim.

In addition to this *Marana tha* fragment, Paul's letters refer to another Aramaic prayer/worship expression, this one referring to God, *Abba* (Rom 8:15; Gal 4:6). As I have noted elsewhere, this is another instance of Paul apparently passing on to his Greek-speaking converts prayer-expressions used by their Aramaic coreligionists (and older siblings in the faith); this reflects a concern to promote some sense of being united in a common devotional stance. Indeed, I have suggested that, taken together, these two Aramaic expressions, the one an invocation of Jesus, the other reflecting prayer to God (the "Father"), can be seen as representing what we may call a "binitarian" pattern of devotion, both Jesus and God featured as recipients, with its origin among Aramaic-speaking Jewish believers in Roman Judea and then promoted among Greek-speaking Pauline churches.[39]

In sum, the data quickly reviewed here indicate that there was a constellation of first-century Christian devotional practices in which Jesus featured prominently along with God in what we may call a "binitarian" devotional pattern exhibiting a concern both to include Jesus and also to assert a monotheistic stance; that these appeared surprisingly early in the Christian movement and that the devotional pattern is not a late development; and that the devotional practices involved were widely characteristic in first-century Christianity. In view of these findings, it is all the more plausible to ask whether this devotional pattern may also have had a powerful effect in stimulating and shaping developments in belief, or at least in the articulation and elaboration of belief.

CASE STUDIES

In the remaining part of this study I will examine a selection of texts that I believe exhibit an impact of early Christian devotional practice upon belief, in particular early Christian efforts to articulate belief about God.

---

[39] Ibid., 110–11.

A New Testament Example?

Although it is easier to identify what seem to us more readily recognizable instances of doctrinal reflection shaped by devotional practice in extra-canonical Christian sources of the second century and later, we may find some evidence of this already within the New Testament as well. In the New Testament texts, which include our earliest extant Christian sources, taking us back to scarcely more than twenty years after Jesus' execution, one of the principal modes of efforts to reflect upon and articulate beliefs involved the (re)interpretation of biblical (Old Testament) texts. In its earliest stages this interpretative effort seems to have been very much accompanied and stimulated by religious experiences that were received by believers as divine revelations. These experiences helped to generate reconfigured beliefs, and to reorient the recipients of these experiences (and other believers influenced by them) to perceive things in biblical texts that they had not been able to notice before. It seems to me that this sort of experience of new "revelatory" insight into Scripture is reflected in Paul's (autobiographically informed?) image of a "hardened" Israel, who read Moses with a veil over their minds. But, Paul continues, "when one turns to the Lord, the veil is removed" and one is enabled to see "the glory of the Lord (Jesus)" (2 Cor 3:14-18; NRSV). This sort of experientially-prompted "discovery" of the exalted significance of Jesus in the Old Testament texts has been referred to as "charismatic exegesis."[40]

Granted, it is difficult to be sure precisely what the reciprocal relationships and dynamics may have been between these new insights into biblical texts, other religious experiences such as visions and prophetic oracles, and the devotional practice of treating Jesus as a rightful recipient of cultic reverence. Indeed, it may be a bit artificial to assume a one-way relationship, as if, for instance, "charismatic exegesis" simply gave rise to devotional practice or vice versa. Were early circles of believers moved by the Spirit to feel obliged to extend cultic reverence to the exalted Jesus, and thereafter found a basis for this practice in their Scriptures? Or did new insights from "charismatic exegesis" of their Scriptures help to generate their reshaped devotional practice?

---

[40] D. E. Aune, "Charismatic Exegesis in Early Judaism and Early Christianity," in *The Pseudepigrapha and Early Biblical Interpretation*, ed. James H. Charlesworth and Craig A. Evans (Sheffield: JSOT, 1993) 126–50; Hurtado, *Lord Jesus Christ*, 73–74, 184–85.

Or should we allow for a more complex and dynamic interaction especially lively in the first few years and decades? I have suggested that in the earliest moments of the young Christian movement religious experiences of "revelational" impact, together with (indeed, perhaps happening in the process of) prayerful pondering of scriptural texts, were crucial in generating the new conviction that "God required them to assent to his exaltation of Jesus in cultic action."[41] But it also seems reasonable to think that, as the earliest Christians reflected on how to affirm both this cultic reverence of Jesus and the exclusivist monotheism inherited from the Jewish matrix of their faith, they were driven again and again back to their Scriptures to find resources for themselves, and justification for outsiders (perhaps especially other devout Jews) who objected.

To turn to a specific text that may preserve an instance of this, in Philippians 2:9-11 we have a rather clear reflection of an unprecedented and remarkable reading of Isaiah 45:22-25 as referring to an eschatological acclamation and triumph of *two* distinct but linked figures, the "Lord" (Jesus) and also "God" (the "Father").[42] I submit that it is unlikely that this way of reading the Isaiah passage would ever have arisen except in the light of powerful prior convictions that God had exalted Jesus to a glorious status, and, perhaps, that obedience to God now required an unprecedented reverence for Jesus. The basic effects of this "binitarian" reading of Isaiah 45:22-25 are to base and justify reverence for Jesus in God's exaltation of him, and also firmly to portray reverence for Jesus as actually serving "the glory of God the Father." In short, behind Philippians 2:9-11 is an exegesis of Isaiah 45:22-25 that reflects a concern to show how the cultic reverence of these two figures, Jesus and God, is really compatible with the exclusivist monotheistic stance of the biblical/Jewish tradition. Might this creative exegesis of the Isaiah passage represent an early instance of "exegetical theology," "faith seeking understanding" in the earliest years, that was prompted at least in part by powerful religious experiences and the answering devotional practices that we have surveyed? (So, should we characterize this early effort better as religious experi-

[41] Hurtado, *Lord Jesus Christ*, 185.

[42] One of the best analyses remains unpublished: T. Nagata, "Philippians 2:5-11. A Case Study in the Contextual Shaping of Early Christology." Ph.D. diss., Princeton Theological Seminary, 1981.

ence seeking understanding?) And might this kind of early exegetical effort also have helped to justify and reinforce Christian devotional practices?

Justin's Theological Exegesis

We see further examples of the kind of exegetical work that seems to have been prompted by early Christian devotional practice in Justin Martyr's *Dialogue with Trypho*. It is worth noting that, although a great amount of the argument concerns demonstrating that the biblical (Old Testament) writings foretell the coming of Jesus, his virginal conception, his messianic status, and his redemptive death and resurrection/ exaltation, Trypho is presented as making his most strenuous objections against worshiping Jesus (esp. in *Dial.* 38.1; 64.1; 65).[43] In response to these repeated objections, and in defense of Christian devotional practice, Justin offers creative exegesis of key biblical texts.[44] We do not have the space here for more than limited analysis of key elements of Justin's handling of the scriptural texts.

In *Dialogue* 63.4-5, after presenting several biblical passages in support of claims about Jesus' preexistence and redemptive significance, Justin then also cites Psalm 45:6-11 (LXX 44:6-11) as specific scriptural justification for worshiping Jesus. Justin claims that the import of this Psalm is that all who believe in God truly are to worship Jesus "as God

---

[43] For the purposes of my argument here it is unnecessary to judge whether Trypho was a real figure or a literary creation by Justin. All that is needed is the considerably more widely accepted view that Trypho gives expression to the sorts of objections to Christian faith and practice that were lodged by many devout Jews of that time. In the following discussion, I work from the text of Justin in E. J. Goodspeed, *Die ältesten Apologeten: Texte mit kurzen Einleitungen* (Göttingen: Vandenhoeck & Ruprecht, 1914; reprint, 1984). For ease of reference, I use the English translation in *Ante-Nicene Fathers*, 1, ed. A. Roberts and J. Donaldson (Peabody: Hendrickson, 1994 [1885]), but with amendments to modern English.

[44] See O. Skarsaune (*The Proof from Prophecy. A Study in Justin Martyr's Proof-Text Tradition: Text-Type, Provenance, Theological Profile*. Novum Testamentum Supplements 56 [Leiden: E. J. Brill, 1987] 199–203), who structures the argument in *Dialogue* 48–107 as almost entirely to do with proving Jesus as Messiah, and (curiously, to my mind) portrays *Dial.* 64–65 as "a digression caused by Trypho" from what Skarsaune sees as Justin's main concern which is to demonstrate Jesus' virginal conception (201). I respectfully submit that this is a misjudgment on Skarsaune's part.

and as Christ" (cf. 64.1, "as Lord and Christ and God"). Justin takes the psalm as admonishing believers to "forget old ancestral customs" (i.e., their previous idolatrous practices) in the call to "forget your people and the house of your father" (Ps 45:10/LXX 44:11); and Justin presents the exhortation in Psalm 45:10-11 (LXX 44:11-13), "because he [Christ] is your Lord, and you shall worship him," as a direct justification for the cultic reverence offered to Jesus in Christian worship.[45]

Thereafter, in response to Trypho's reiterated objection to worshiping Jesus (*Dial.* 64.1), Justin cites Psalm 99:1-7 (LXX 98:1-7) as further scriptural basis (*Dial.* 64.4), implicitly positing Jesus as the exalted Lord who reigns and before whom worship is now to be offered ("worship at the footstool of his feet," Ps 99:5/LXX 98:5). Justin then (64.6) goes on to present references in Psalm 72:17-19 (LXX 71:17-19), directing praise both for "the Lord God of Israel who alone does wonders," and also for "his glorious Name," as a scriptural basis for what I have termed the "binitarian" worship of God and Jesus. For Justin, Jesus is the one referred to in the scriptural mention of God's "Name" here; so, he is to be worshiped along with "the Lord God" (*Dial.* 64.6).[46]

This intriguing christological interpretation of scriptural references to God's "Name" is even more explicit in *Dialogue* 65. In this passage Trypho, portrayed as shaken by Justin's exegetical moves, again strenuously objects to such reverence for Jesus by invoking the ringing declaration from Isaiah 42:8, "I am the Lord; this is my name; my

---

[45] The standard LXX text (Ps 44:13) has προσκυνήσουσιν αὐτῷ ("they [the daughters of Tyre] shall bow to/worship him"), but Justin's citation more closely reflects the Masoretic text (Ps 45:12), which exhorts the princess-bride to reverence (השתחוי) her king-groom. Here we see one of a number of instances where Justin reflects knowledge/use of "non-LXX" biblical manuscripts, and also Christian "testimony sources" that seem to have contained renderings reflecting Hebrew and Targumic texts. See esp. the conclusions on the matter in Skarsaune, *The Proof*, 90–91.

[46] On early Christian understanding of Jesus as God's "Name," see, e.g., J. Daniélou, *The Theology of Jewish Christianity*, trans. and ed. J. A. Baker (London: Darton, Longman and Todd, 1964) 147–63. This conception is reflected in the eucharistic prayer in *Didache* 10:2, where God is thanked for "your holy name, which you made dwell in our hearts." As K. Niederwimmer observed (*The Didache: A Commentary* [Minneapolis: Fortress, 1998]), God's "name" here must connote "God's epiphany, God in person" (156), and "here stands for what the Greeks would call οὐσία" (156 n. 13).

glory I will not give to another."[47] Trypho's obvious point is that this scriptural text clearly forbids inclusion of any second figure in cultic devotion. But, after declaring his faith that Scripture does not contradict itself, Justin proceeds to claim that Isaiah 42 actually teaches that God *does* share his glory with "his Christ *alone*" (*Dial*. 65.3). To make this point, Justin first quotes the entirety of Isaiah 42:5-13, and then focuses on the references in the passage to a figure whom God calls, strengthens, and makes "a covenant of the people" and "a light of the Gentiles"; and Justin takes these all as references to Jesus, the Christ. Still more remarkably, however, Justin then interprets Isaiah 42:8 (the very statement that Trypho cites, and one of the most emphatic declarations of God's exclusivity in the Old Testament) as in fact declaring that God does share his glory exclusively *with Jesus*. As Justin reads the statement, "this is my Name" directly refers to the figure addressed in the preceding verses in Isaiah 42, and Justin understands this figure as Jesus, the Christ. For Justin, thus, Isaiah 42:8 is an explicit declaration of a closed circle of *two* (God and his "Name") who exclusively *share* the same divine glory (*Dial*. 65.7)! "Have you not perceived, my friends, that God says He *will* give Him whom He has established as a light of the Gentiles, glory, and *to no other*; and not, as Trypho said, that God was retaining the glory to Himself?"[48]

Actually, it seems to me that behind Justin's treatment of these particular texts lies a rather thoroughly worked out and very early Christian interpretation of whole passages of Isaiah (perhaps even the entirety of Isaiah?), in which God and another allied figure, variously referred to as God's "arm," "servant," "light," and "name," are understood as forming an exclusive pairing.[49] For Justin, and the prior Christian exegetical tradition that he reflects, Jesus is the second figure, with whom exclusively God shares his glory; and for Justin this gives scriptural justification to include Jesus as recipient of worship

[47] The same statement appears also in Isaiah 48:11.

[48] I quote the translation from Ante-Nicene Fathers 1.231, emphasis mine. The LXX reads "τὴν δόξαν μου ἑτέρῳ οὐ δώσω" and Justin appears to have taken the word ἑτέρῳ as meaning that the divine glory was exclusively shared by the Lord God and his Name, *and no other* beyond this closed circle of two.

[49] The early Christian exegesis of Isaiah that I refer to is reflected prior to Justin in, e.g., John 12:27-41, as elaborated below. See also R. Bauckham, *God Crucified: Monotheism and Christology in the New Testament* (Carlisle: Paternoster, 1998) 47–69.

with God in the "binitarian" pattern that we have noted as characteristic of Christian circles in our earliest evidence.

To make sure that my argument is clearly perceived, I reiterate for emphasis that the crucial issue in several passages in the *Dialogue* is the worship of Jesus with God. It is that to which Trypho makes his most strenuous objection, and it is this that Justin explicitly seeks to justify in his exegesis of the biblical passages that we have noted here.[50] That is, Justin here endeavors to give a biblical basis for the Christian "binitarian" devotional practice, already long characteristic in Christian circles. In these passages in the *Dialogue* we see how Christian worship practice demanded and shaped the intensive exegetical attention to biblical passages that Justin reflects.

Although I do not have the space here to develop the evidence fully, I also want to contend that Justin's exegetical efforts probably reflect a prior Christian tradition of such exegetical theology in defense of Christian worship. It seems to me most unlikely that Christians were first confronted with the objections to Christian worship that are mouthed by Trypho in this second-century text. Surely, from earlier years as well, a good many devout Jews would have hurled Isaiah 42:8 against what they perceived as the compromising of God's uniqueness through unwarranted reverence for any second figure. I have attempted to show elsewhere that in fact we have evidence of first-century Christian efforts to justify reverence for Jesus through asserting that he does share the divine glory.[51]

What else are we to make of the emphasis in the Gospel of John that Jesus is the manifestation of divine glory (1:14), that his miracles reveal his glory (e.g., 2:11; 11:40), that Jesus does not seek human glory or his own but only the glory of God (e.g., 5:41; 8:50, 54), and that Jesus is given divine glory and that he bore it even before his earthly appearance (17:5)? I propose that this well-known Johannine emphasis on Jesus' glory/glorification reflects in part the sort of antagonistic engagement with Jewish opposition to devotion to Jesus that is well recognized by scholars in the Gospel of John. The intensity of this

[50] Note that Justin returns to the issue in *Dialogue* 68.3, reasserting an exclusivist "binitarian" stance. "Do you think that any other one is said to be worthy of worship and to be called 'Lord and God' in the scriptures except the maker of everything and Christ, he who by so many scriptures was proved to you to have become a man?"

[51] Hurtado, *Lord Jesus Christ*, esp. 374–81.

glory-emphasis was prompted by Jewish objections such as that also ascribed to Trypho, that Christians compromised God's unique glory in their reverence for Jesus.[52]

Indeed, an intriguing passage in John may give direct evidence that in these first-century controversies texts from Isaiah were crucial (just as texts from Isaiah are central in *Dialogue* 64-65). John 12:37-43 laments Jewish unbelief in Jesus in spite of his signs, and then declares this a fulfilment of Isaiah 53:1, a text that decries unbelief among those "to whom the arm of the Lord has been revealed" (John 12:38). It seems to me that this reflects the specific identification of Jesus as "the arm of the Lord." Then, after citing Isaiah 6:9-10, which refers to the (divinely) blinded eyes and hardened hearts of Israel, the author goes on to declare that "Isaiah said this because he saw his glory and spoke about him" (John 12:41). This must indicate that the author of John understood the vision-scene in Isaiah 6:1-5 as a vision of the glorious/glorified Jesus![53] The divine "glory" referred to in Isaiah 6:3 as filling all the earth is interpreted/appropriated christologically.

Had we space to do so here, we might even consider whether Pauline references to Jesus as manifestation and reflection of God's glory represent still earlier textual evidence of this ancient Christian articulation and defense of Jesus' right to a status uniquely associated with God.[54] For my part, this seems most likely the case. In addition to trying to satisfy themselves about how properly to accommodate reverence for Jesus with their inherited concern for the uniqueness of God, the earliest circles of the embryonic Christian movement must have needed to answer objections from outsiders. In particular, I find it hard to avoid the judgment that the sort of devotional practices that we have surveyed briefly must have generated sharp antagonism from devout Jews, and I have argued that in fact we have good evidence that this was the case at a very early point.[55]

---

[52] See esp. J. L. Martyn, *History and Theology in the Fourth Gospel* (Nashville: Abingdon, 1979).

[53] Sirach 48:24-25 reflects a tradition that the prophet Isaiah foresaw eschatological events, and John 12:41, thus, indicates an early Christian conviction that Isaiah foresaw the appearance of Christ.

[54] The key work is C. C. Newman, *Paul's Glory-Christology: Tradition and Rhetoric*. Novum Testamentum Supplements 69 (Leiden: E. J. Brill, 1992).

[55] See Hurtado, "Pre-70 C.E. Jewish Opposition to Christ-Devotion." *Journal of Theological Studies* 50 (1999) 35–58.

In short, I contend that Justin's *Dialogue*, and these New Testament texts as well, exhibit an early form of exegetical theology that was intended to articulate Jesus' unique significance and justify an unprecedented devotion to him, and that involved appropriation of key biblical categories, particularly divine "name" and "glory."

Justin's Further Theological Efforts

In addition to the exegetical theology that we have noted, Justin also exhibits an early effort to articulate and justify Christian belief and devotional practice by drawing upon a wider store of vocabulary, imagery, and conceptual categories drawn from beyond his Scriptures. I restrict myself to a couple of examples where the focus is the same: to explain and justify joining Jesus with God in faith and worship.

In *Dialogue* 61.1, after claiming for Jesus a whole string of biblical titles and categories (e.g., "Beginning," "Wisdom," "Angel," "Logos," and "Captain"), Justin explains that this second figure was "begotten of the Father by an act of will" (ἐκ τοῦ ἀπὸ τοῦ πατρὸς θελήσει γεγεννῆσθαι, 61.1). Then, invoking as analogy how kindling a fire from another fire does not lessen the latter, Justin emphasizes that this second figure does not involve any diminution of the Father. Later, in *Dialogue* 126-129, Justin returns to this emphasis that it is fully right to recognize a second divine figure uniquely linked with "the Father." Again, he claims a string of biblical titles for Jesus (126.1), and then goes on to identify him as the divine figure who appeared to Abraham and in other theophanic scenes (126.2-6).

In *Dialogue* 128 we see more efforts to articulate both a distinction and also a close linkage between "the Father" and Christ. In particular, note the use of another analogy, likening Christ's indivisible and inseparable relationship with the Father to the relationship of the light of the sun to the sun itself (128.3). Yet Justin then notes the limitation of this analogy (128.4); for, unlike the light of the sun, Christ is not merely notionally distinct from the Father (οὐχ ὡς . . . ὀνόματι μόνον ἀριθμεῖται), but "indeed is something numerically distinct" (καὶ ἀριθμῷ ἕτερόν τί ἐστι).[56] But, repeating his earlier statement, Justin insists that this distinction does not involve a diminution (ἀποτομήν) of/in God "as if the essence [οὐσία] of the Father were divided"

[56] This interesting phrase, "numerically distinct" (ἀριθμῷ ἕτερόν ἐστι) appears also in *Dialogue* 129.4.

(128.4), and once again Justin resorts to the analogy of fire kindled from fire to make this point.

In *1 Apology*, which is directed more toward a non-Jewish readership (and was officially addressed to Antoninus Pius, the emperor), it is also clear that Christian worship is a controversial matter that requires theological explanation and justification. Early on, in *1 Apology* 5–6, Justin rebuts the charge that Christians are "atheists," which has to do entirely with matters of worship. Acknowledging freely that Christians refuse to worship the many pagan deities, Justin insists, however, that the charge is not really fair, for Christians do worship "the most true God," along with the Son, and also "the prophetic Spirit."[57] A bit later (*1 Apol.* 13), Justin returns to the matter, emphasizing that Christian worship does not involve animal sacrifice or incense, but invocation, hearty praise and thanksgiving, and petition, directed to "the Maker of this universe" (13.1-2), and to Jesus Christ "the Son of the true God," whom Christians hold "in the second place [ἐν δευτέρᾳ χώρᾳ ἔχοντες]," and also "the prophetic Spirit in third place [ἐν τρίτῃ τάξει]" (13.3). The following statement, however, makes it clear that in addition to their refusal to worship the many gods, the really controversial feature of Christian worship in the eyes of pagan critics was the inclusion of Jesus as recipient of reverence with God, which Justin refers to as giving the crucified man, Jesus, "a place second after [μετὰ] the unchangeable and eternal God, the creator [γεννήτορα] of all things" (13.4). In *1 Apology* 14.1, Justin quickly characterizes Christians as rejecting as demons the pagan deities, and following "the only unbegotten God through his Son."

In short, what I have termed the "binitarian" shape of Christian worship was a key feature of early Christianity objected to by pagan and Jewish critics, and so for Justin was an important matter to explain and justify. Justin refers to the "mystery" that lies behind the inclusion

---

[57] Justin also appears to include "the host of other good angels who follow and are like him" among those whom Christians reverence. From other passages in Justin's writings (e.g., *1 Apol.* 13, 16, 61), however, it is fairly clear that he did not advocate or practice the worship of angels. Instead, it looks as though the mention of angels here is to emphasize that, though Christians reject the pagan pantheon, they do acknowledge and show due respect for a whole host of heavenly beings. On this, see W. R. Schoedel, "A Neglected Motive for Second Century Trinitarianism." *Journal of Theological Studies* 31 (1980) 356–67.

of Jesus as recipient of worship with God (1 Apol. 13.4), and indicates that his aim in 1 Apology is to try to set forth this mystery (ἐξηγουμένων ἡμῶν προτρεπόμεθα) so that readers may give it heed. To be sure, Justin can also characterize Christian worship in what looks more like what we might call "proto-trinitarian" language, as in 1 Apology 67.2, where he says that "we bless the Maker of all things through his Son, Jesus Christ, and through the Holy Spirit."[58] But the really central issue that required his attention was the Christian profession and practice of an exclusivist monotheism that nevertheless involved reverencing Jesus as well as the creator God.

In the course of justifying Christian devotional practice, Justin gives us our earliest extant uses of some theological terms and categories. He emphasizes that the genuine distinction between Christ and God the Father does not mean any diminution or partition in God's οὐσία ("being," "substance"). In defense of his claim that the relationship of Christ and the Father is pre-temporal he asserts that the pre-incarnate Son is already witnessed to in Old Testament theophanies. He also refers to the utterances of biblical prophets under inspiration from "the divine Word," who sometimes spoke "as from the person of God the Father the Lord of all [ἀπὸ προσώπου τοῦ δεσπότου πάντων καὶ πατρός θεοῦ], and sometimes as from the person of Christ [ὡς ἀπὸ προσώπου τοῦ Χριστοῦ]" (1 Apol. 36.2).[59] Justin here gives us the earliest (extant) uses of this term πρόσωπον as a way of trying to represent the unity of and distinction between the Father and the Son. Obviously, the subsequently more familiar *substantia* and *persona* represent the deployment of Latin equivalents to the pioneering Greek-language theological efforts that Justin's writings attest.

CONCLUSION

I conclude with a summary statement of my argument. The "binitar-ian" devotional pattern exhibited in the specific devotional actions surveyed here was characteristic in Christian circles from the earliest

[58] Note also Justin's description of Christian baptism in 1 Apol. 61, where he mentions the invocation of the name of the Father, Jesus, and the Holy Spirit (61.3, 12–13).

[59] Justin also refers here to the Word speaking through the prophets "some-times as from the person of the people answering the Lord or his Father." His other uses of the term πρόσωπον refer to the Father and/or to Christ: e.g., 1 Apol. 37–38.

days about which we know anything. This remarkable inclusion of Jesus with God as recipient of cultic reverence was unprecedented in Jewish tradition, and required both a powerful impetus, and also innovative efforts to understand God and God's purposes in such a way that this intense devotion to Jesus could be accommodated within the strong concern for God's uniqueness that marked Jewish tradition in its Roman religious environment. This concern inherited from Jewish tradition also remained central in the young religious movement that identified itself with reference to Jesus and that came to be what we call "Christianity."

There were, to be sure, other things that prompted Christian exegetical activity and theological reflection. Initially, of course, believers needed to try to understand things for themselves, perhaps especially Jesus' crucifixion and the powerful experiences that generated the unexpected conviction that God had raised him from death and exalted him to a place of unprecedented honor and glory, and that God now required them to respond accordingly in obedience, including cultic obedience. But these radical and momentous convictions expressed in christological claims and in cultic actions required Christians to invest in still further theological effort beyond satisfying themselves that scriptural texts could be read as supportive of their stance. They had to give justification also to those outside their circles, especially critics, both Jewish and pagan. They also had to find ways to explain how it was not a violation of their professed exclusivist monotheism for Jesus to have a place as recipient in their cultic practice. That is, one of the major driving forces in early exegetical and theological efforts was the pattern of earliest Christian worship.

Moreover, the binitarian pattern of worship also helped to shape the content and directions of these efforts. Simple appropriation of the apotheosis concept would not do; in the eyes of at least the most influential believers it was not reconcilable with their professed monotheistic commitment and their disdain for pagan religion. Nor was it finally adequate to think of Jesus as either a uniquely inspired prophet or even as a high angelic being. It proved difficult to square either notion with what had been the Christian worship pattern from the earliest memories of the movement, in which Jesus was given a place that linked him with the one God in unparalleled ways.

Quite simply, this required some creative theological efforts. With all due recognition that early Christians drew upon resources in Jewish tradition and in the wider cultural environment of the first few centuries, I contend that these early believers also produced ideas about God that involved some genuinely novel features.[60] In particular, their efforts to affirm God's unity and uniqueness, while also according such a high status to Christ, produced a novel form of exclusivist monotheism. This remarkable theological development was, at least in part, also an attempt to construct an understanding of God that explained, justified, and measured up to the remarkable pattern of Christian binitarian worship/devotion.

---

[60] I emphasized connections with, and crucial distinctions from, Jewish "principal agent" traditions in *One God, One Lord*. For an emphasis on second-century Christians' engagement with philosophical traditions in developing their views of God, see, e.g., E. Osborn, *The Emergence of Christian Theology* (Cambridge: Cambridge University Press, 1993).

Chapter 3

God, Christ, and the Holy Spirit in
Early Christian Praying

Paul Bradshaw
University of Notre Dame

It is commonly asserted that liturgical prayer in the early church was made *to* the Father, *through* the Son, and *in* the Holy Spirit. Indeed, this is the very pattern that Origen in the third century said should always begin and end prayer (*De oratione* 33.1), and evidence can certainly be marshaled from early Christian sources to support the argument that it was so. Because the conviction that Jesus was the sole mediator through whom God's salvation had been brought to humankind is fundamental to the writings of the New Testament, it is not surprising to find that he was also regarded there as the mediator through whom worship and praise were now to be offered to God. Thus, Hebrews 13:15 exhorts its readers: "Through him, then, let us continually offer a sacrifice of praise to God, that is, the fruit of lips that confess his name";[1] Colossians 3:17 similarly urges: "do everything in the name of the Lord Jesus, giving thanks to God the Father through him" (see also Eph 5:20; 1 Pet 4:11); and Paul begins his letter to the Romans by thanking "God through Jesus Christ for all of you" (1:8), includes the acclamation "Thanks be to God through Jesus Christ" in the body of the text (7:25), and ends it with the doxology, "to the only wise God, through Jesus Christ, to whom be the glory forever" (16:27). Similar doxologies become widespread in post-New Testament sources, beginning possibly with the *Didache* ("yours is the glory and the power through Jesus Christ for evermore," 9.4), though it may be a later

---

[1] Scripture for this chapter taken from the *New Revised Standard Version*.

addition here,[2] but certainly with the *First Letter of Clement* ("We give thanks to you through Jesus Christ, the high-priest and guardian of our souls . . . ," 61.3), and continuing constantly thereafter. Interestingly and somewhat surprisingly, however, in spite of the fact that Jesus is commonly described in such early writings as being our high-priest, that the letter to the Hebrews portrays him as ever living to make intercession (7:25), and that in John 14:14 he says "If in my name you ask me for anything, I will do it," nevertheless it is praise that is almost invariably addressed to God through him in the prayers of the early centuries, and it is not until considerably later that we have extant examples of liturgical texts in which he is explicitly represented as also the mediator of the Church's petitions and intercession. But is praying through Christ the whole story of early Christian practice? As is so often the case, the truth is by no means as simple as many earlier scholars have asserted it to be.

First, we need to recognize that there has in recent years been a marked paradigm shift in the way in which the evidence for early Christian liturgy is interpreted, and this affects our understanding of its prayer patterns. Earlier generations of scholars tended to presume a high degree of uniformity of practice across the ancient Christian world, and a strong current of continuity from the apostolic age itself down to the alleged golden age of the fourth century. Nowadays, however, many of us would be more inclined to acknowledge the existence of a much greater pluriformity of liturgical practice from one place to another, and to be alert to the presence of as many discontinuities as continuities between one age and the next. Thus, earlier scholars were generally quite content to assemble a selection of examples of what they wanted to regard as mainstream Christian practice from a variety of sources and regard that as settling the argument. Any evidence that did not fit their theory was then explained away, usually either by ascribing it to deviant groups, whose practices could not therefore be taken seriously as evidence for what orthodox Christians were doing, or more commonly in the case of prayer patterns by claiming the existence of a sharp distinction between private and public prayer. Thus, for instance, Joseph Jungmann himself could say, "up to the fourth century, the prayer directed to Christ was widely used,

---

[2] See Kurt Niedewimmer, *The Didache: A Commentary* (Minneapolis: Fortress, 1998) 150–51.

both privately and in the form of hymns and acclamations. It is not among the official prayers said by the leader of the liturgical assembly. For the latter, the rule was prayer offered to God 'through Christ'"; or as he puts it more succinctly, "although the prayer to Christ was in use by the faithful from the earliest times, it was denied a home for a long time in the solemn public worship of the community."[3]

Not only is the existence of such a clear division between "mainstream" and "deviant" Christian groups highly questionable for the early centuries of Christianity, but the alleged distinction between "public worship" and "private prayer" also has an anachronistic ring about it. At least until the end of the second century, and in many places in the third century as well, all Christian worship and prayer could in a sense be described as domestic. Whether people were praying on their own, or with a spouse or friend, or with their whole household, or with a number of households gathered together for the eucharistic meal, their prayer is likely to have shared some common characteristics. This is not to say that there were not conventions that shaped the way in which particular communities prayed—indeed they are mentioned in several early sources[4]—but there is no evidence that there were universally agreed norms or enforced rules for praying that tried to extend such conventions more widely across provinces until the late fourth century. Thus, what may have lain outside the conventions for one group of Christians may have been perfectly acceptable in another. Nor can we confidently assert that what Christians said when they were, for example, praying on their own each day cannot possibly have influenced what they said when they were gathered with others around the eucharistic table. There may well have been some differences, but equally one would expect that the one might have some effect on the other. If not, it would be the equivalent of asserting—as some scholars indeed would do—that the references to prayer in Saint Paul's letters were entirely governed by the epistolary conventions of the time and so cannot possibly tell us anything about how he actually prayed, whether alone or with others.

[3] Joseph Jungmann, *The Place of Christ in Liturgical Prayer* (London: Geoffrey Chapman, 1965) 170–71, 213. See also ibid., 160: "even in the earliest Fathers there is evidence of private prayers to Jesus and of hymns of praise to him."

[4] For these conventions, see Allen Bouley, *From Freedom to Formula: The Evolution of the Eucharistic Prayer from Oral Improvisation to Written Texts* (Washington: Catholic University of America Press, 1981).

In any case, there is a circularity of argument in declaring that any examples of direct prayer to Christ that are found must belong to the category of "private" prayer, and then saying that the evidence proves that direct prayer to Christ did not take place in "public" worship until the fourth century. There are so very few examples of liturgical texts as such that can be dated with any confidence prior to the middle of the fourth century that it is hard to know to what sort of context references to forms of Christian praying might have belonged. A hymn to Christ, for instance—was that sung in a communal gathering or by an individual in the privacy of his or her own room?

On the other hand, it is important to draw a distinction between Jesus being honored alongside the Father and prayer actually being addressed directly to him. The two are not the same. It would have been perfectly natural for Christians to have wanted to ascribe praise and honor to Jesus for what he had done for them, without their necessarily viewing him as equal to the Father or as one to whom prayer could legitimately be addressed. Some, though certainly not all, of the examples cited by Larry Hurtado in his important studies on devotion to Jesus fall into the category of honor rather than the object of prayer as such.[5] So, for example, when in the Book of Revelation both God and Christ are conjoined in a hymn of praise such as "To the one seated on the throne and to the Lamb be blessing and honor and glory and might forever and ever" (Rev 5:13-14), that is not the same as offering prayer directly to Jesus. Similarly, when praise is ascribed to Jesus independently of God, as in 2 Peter 3:18 ("grow in the grace and knowledge of our Lord and Savior Jesus Christ. To him be the glory both now and to the day of eternity"; see also 2 Tim 4:18), once again it does not mean that prayer as such was being made to him.

---

[5] See Larry Hurtado, *One God, One Lord: Early Christian Devotion and Ancient Jewish Monotheism* (Philadelphia: Fortress, 1988; 2nd ed. Edinburgh: T&T Clark, 1998); "The Binitarian Shape of Early Christian Worship," in *The Jewish Roots of Christological Monotheism: Papers from the St. Andrews Conference on the Historical Origins of the Worship of Jesus*, ed. C. C. Newman et al., 187–213. Supplements to the Journal for the Study of Judaism 63 (Leiden: Brill, 1999); "The Origin and Development of Christ-Devotion: Forces and Factors," in *Christian Origins: Worship, Belief and Society*, ed. K. J. O'Mahony, 52–82. Journal for the Study of the New Testament Supplement Series 241 (Sheffield: Sheffield Academic Press, 2003); *Lord Jesus Christ: Devotion to Jesus in Earliest Christianity* (Grand Rapids: Eerdmans, 2003).

If I may insert here another small footnote to Hurtado's valuable work, nor can references to "confessing Jesus as Lord" or "calling upon" him in the New Testament be cited as unquestionably clear indications that prayer was addressed directly to Jesus in the apostolic era. Although they may appear to do so, what is meant may be no more than the practice either of praying through him, or simply of naming him in connection with God. For early Christians did not merely bless God, but they blessed "the God and Father of our Lord Jesus Christ" (see Eph 1:3; 2 Cor 1:3; 1 Pet 1:3); and they did not just give thanks to God, they thanked "God, the Father of our Lord Jesus Christ" (Col 1:3). Thus confessing Jesus as Lord might well be referring to some such formula as we find there, or of course to the baptismal confession of faith, and not to prayer as such at all. Equally, calling upon him might imply no more than referring to him in prayer in a similar way rather than invoking him directly, whatever the verb itself might seem to be saying.[6] Hence, on its own, the New Testament evidence can be regarded as no more than inconclusive in this respect, and so leaves us with very few explicit examples of Jesus being directly addressed in prayer.

But to return to my main theme, it is therefore necessary to be especially careful when citing doxological material from early Christian sources not to extrapolate from that evidence conclusions about the wider question of the offering of prayer. It is in any case important to be cautious when quoting what appear to be the texts of very early Christian doxologies, as they are particularly susceptible to emendation by later hands, as appears to have been the case with a number of those that are found in the so-called *Apostolic Tradition* of Hippolytus.[7] Sometimes such emendations may have been done quite unconsciously as the copyist wrote down the doxological form with which he was personally familiar from liturgical use in his own generation rather than reproducing exactly the particular prepositions that lay in the manuscript before him. Nor should we expect early Christian writers themselves to have been completely consistent in the form that they used. So far as we can tell, there were no standardized prayer

[6] For a study of this expression, see Carl J. Davis, *The Name and Way of the Lord: Old Testament Themes, New Testament Christology.* Journal for the Study of the New Testament Supplement Series 129 (Sheffield: Sheffield Academic Press, 1996) 118–39.

[7] See Paul F. Bradshaw, Maxwell E. Johnson, and L. Edward Phillips, *Apostolic Tradition: A Commentary* (Minneapolis: Fortress, 2002) 52–54.

conclusions among the conventions of the first few centuries, and it was only in the christological and pneumatological debates of the fourth century that the choice of prepositions assumed major doctrinal significance. Thus we should expect that earlier authors might adopt a number of different forms for such doxological endings, as indeed they do.

The writer of the *First Letter of Clement*, for instance, can use a doxology addressed to God through Jesus Christ: "The grace of our Lord Jesus Christ be with you and with all everywhere who have been called by God through him, through whom be to him glory, honor, power," etc. (65.2; see also 58.2); or in a more elaborate form: "to the well-pleasing of his name through our high-priest and guardian Jesus Christ, through whom be to him glory and majesty, power and honor," etc. (64).[8] At the same time he is also able apparently to offer praise to Jesus alone: "This blessing came upon those chosen by God through Jesus Christ our Lord, to whom be glory for ever and ever" (50.7). The *Martyrdom of Polycarp* reveals somewhat parallel constructions. Polycarp ends his prayer before death with the following complex doxology: "for this reason and for all things I praise you, I bless you, I glorify you through the eternal and heavenly high-priest Jesus Christ, your beloved child, through whom to you and with him and holy spirit be glory both now and for the ages to come" (14.3; see also 22.2); elsewhere in the account glory is offered to God alone (20.2) and also to Jesus alone: ". . . but with Jesus Christ reigning for ever, to whom be glory, honor," etc. (21).

I have said that such acclamations of praise should not be treated as being the same as prayer. Yet, at the same time I have to admit that it is highly likely that they were instrumental in encouraging the idea that prayer might be offered not just to God but also to Christ. It is quite a small step from expressing praise to Christ to making prayer to him. While to our modern eyes acclamations, hymns, and prayers would be thought of as belonging to quite distinct literary and liturgical genres, the ancients did not apparently categorize things in such a rigid manner. As Albert Gerhards has pointed out in a critique of Jungmann's book, it is interesting to observe that when in the fourth century Basil is arguing for the legitimacy of a particular form of doxological conclusion that he has employed when "praying with the people," it is an example drawn from a traditional hymn, the *Phos*

---

[8] Translations, unless otherwise noted, are by Paul Bradshaw.

hilaron, and not a prayer that he uses in order to justify his practice.[9] Thus, the crossover from one type of liturgical unit to another seems to have been seen as a perfectly natural step.

Nevertheless, were earlier scholars right in saying that all such prayer to Christ belonged only to the category of private devotion and never to what they described as the official prayer of the church? Let us prescind from the question of whether it is possible to distinguish a category of "official prayer" at this period, and simply examine the clues that exist. Origen is both the most forceful advocate for prayer being offered only to the Father ("if we give heed to what prayer properly is, surely prayer is to be addressed to no man born of woman, not even to Christ himself, but to the God and Father of all alone . . ." (*De oratione* 15.1)[10] and also our principal witness to the practice by others of praying to Christ. He asks: "Are we not divided if some of us pray to the Father and some to the Son, inasmuch as they who pray to the Son, whether with or without the Father, commit a foolish sin in great simplicity because of their lack of discernment and criticism?" (*De oratione* 16.1) This certainly seems to suggest that there were some who were praying to Christ, or perhaps to Christ together with the Father. In his *Conversation with Heraclides*, Origen is more explicit as to where this praying takes place. He insists that "the offering" should be made to God through Christ, and that it should "not be made twice," that is, that the eucharistic prayer should not be addressed both to the Father *and* to the Son.[11] Such an admonition only makes sense if there were actually people who were doing just that. Some scholars would try to minimize the significance of these remarks, claiming that they were directed to the activities of some small heretical group and so not testimony for more widespread deviancy from an alleged norm. But there is no evidence that it should be restricted in this way. And indeed, the fact that North African ecclesiastical legislation at the end of the fourth century finds it

---

[9] Basil, *De spiritu sancto* 29; see Albert Gerhards, "Prière adressée à Dieu ou au Christ? Relecture d'une thèse importante de J. A. Jungmann à la lumière de la recherche actuelle." In *Liturgie, spiritualité, cultures: Conférences Saint-Serge XXIXe semaine d'études liturgiques*, ed. A. M. Triacca & A. Pistoia (Rome: C.L.V.-Edizioni liturgiche, 1983) 112–13.

[10] All quotations from this treatise are taken from *Origen's Treatise on Prayer*, trans. E. G. Jay (London: S.P.C.K., 1954).

[11] *Conversation with Heraclides* 4. For this interpretation of the phrase, see Bouley, *From Freedom to Formula*, 140–41.

necessary to stipulate, "let no one in prayers name either the Father instead of the Son, or the Son instead of the Father; and when one stands at the altar, let prayer always be directed to the Father,"[12] demonstrates just how widespread and persistent the practice was.

What is more, even Origen himself was not above addressing his own prayers to Christ. Having said that supplication may be made to those who are saints, he continues: "Now if these prayers are rightly offered to men who are saints, how much more ought we to give thanks to Christ who has shown us such great kindness by the will of the Father! But we must also make intercession to him . . ." (*De oratione* 14.6). Now, this statement might perhaps be understood to mean that intercession should be addressed to God through Christ, but in his *Contra Celsum* he is more specific: "We have to send up every petition, prayer, intercession, and thanksgiving to the supreme God through the high-priest of all angels, the living and divine Logos. We will even make our petitions to the very Logos himself and offer intercession to him and give thanks and also pray to him, if we are capable of a clear understanding of the absolute and the relative sense of prayer" (5.4).[13] What he seems to be saying here is that it is wrong for others to pray directly to Christ because they do not have a proper understanding of what they are doing and of the relationship of Christ to God, but that it is acceptable for him to do so because he knows that such an address is only relative and not absolute. As he explains later in the same work, "we ought to pray to the supreme God alone, and to pray besides to the only-begotten Logos of God, the firstborn of all creation; and we ought to beseech him, as a high-priest, to bear our prayer, when it has reached him, up to his God and our God and to his Father and the Father of people who live according to the word of God" (*Contra Celsum* 8.26). To this evidence may be added a whole catalogue of brief prayers to Christ scattered throughout Origen's writings.[14]

Further evidence for prayers addressed to Christ occurs in the Apocryphal Acts. There has been a common reluctance to admit these texts as

[12] Canon 21 of the Council of Hippo Regius (393), repeated as Canon 34 of the Third Council of Carthage (397); Latin text in Charles Munier, ed., *Concilia Africae a. 345-a. 525.* CCSL 149 (Turnholt: Brepols, 1974) 39, 183.

[13] English translations from *Contra Celsum*, trans. Henry Chadwick (Cambridge: Cambridge University Press, 1953).

[14] For examples, see C. W. Bigg, *The Christian Platonists of Alexandria* (Oxford: Clarendon Press, 1913) 228–29 n. 1.

evidence for what so-called mainstream Christianity might have been doing in its praying. Jungmann, for instance, rejected them as deriving "for the most part, not from Catholic but from heretical, especially Gnostic and Docetic, circles," and argued against them either as perhaps embodying the remains of forms of popular devotion once current in early Christianity or instead as elements taken over from primitive Christianity into Gnostic circles and preserved there when they disappeared from more orthodox settings.[15] Such a judgment, however, contrasts with the widespread use by modern scholars of the very same sources as good evidence for early Syrian baptismal practice. Almost all of what is asserted about the latter is based on this material. Why then should we be so unwilling to draw upon it when it comes to saying anything about prayer patterns? There seems to be an illogical inconsistency here, fueled no doubt by a disinclination to admit into court any testimony that might point to a conclusion that the scholars a priori had decided was simply not true of what they thought of as mainstream Christianity.

The *Acts of John*, usually dated in the late second or early third century and commonly thought to have originated in Syria, contains two different prayers supposedly spoken by the apostle John, each at a Eucharist involving bread alone. They clearly address praise to Christ, even though they do not actually make petition as such to him, as the following extracts indicate: "we praise thy gracious name, O Lord, <which> has convicted those that are convicted by thee; we thank thee, Lord Jesus Christ . . . who hadst need <. . .> of (our) nature that is being saved. . . . What praise or what offering or what thanksgiving shall we name as we break this bread, but thee alone, Jesu . . ." (*Acts of John* 85, 109).[16]

Yet while these particular formularies may not petition Christ directly, there are others that do. We may begin with the Aramaic invocation *marana tha*. Although this expression has been the object of considerable discussion by New Testament scholars,[17] it is commonly ignored by liturgical scholars. Jungmann himself passed over its appearance in the *Didache* with the brief comment: "'Hosanna to the God of David,' 'Maranatha,' not being formal prayers, do not concern us

---

[15] Jungmann, *The Place of Christ*, 165–68.
[16] English translation from *New Testament Apocalypse*, ed. W. Schneemelcher, 2. 2nd ed. (Cambridge: James Clark & Co., 1992).
[17] See for example Davis, *The Name and Way*, 136–39.

here."[18] Such dismissals by liturgical scholars arise because the invocation does not fit within the traditionally dominant paradigm for the evolution of Christian liturgical prayer, and especially eucharistic prayer, which was of a single seamless whole, derived from the Jewish grace after meals, the *Birkat ha-mazon*, and addressed throughout to God the Father. I have tried elsewhere to expose some of the flaws in that particular theory, and to support those who instead would see eucharistic praying as originating in a series of shorter individual prayer units of diverse kinds that were gradually expanded in length, increased in number, and blended into composite oration.[19] Even though *marana tha* is found in a meal context in *Didache* 10.6, I am not suggesting that its root is specifically eucharistic, but only that it appears to have been a fairly common feature of primitive Christian worship, as an eschatological entreaty for the return of the Risen Lord. It is true that besides its occurrence in the *Didache*, there are only two other extant instances of the expression, in 1 Corinthians 16:22 and in Greek in Revelation 22:20. Yet, all three are of sufficiently diverse provenance as to suggest a quite wide dispersion of its use.

Nevertheless, granted that such may once have been the case, did not its use then die out as the expected *parousia* did not materialize, and hence leave no mark upon later patristic prayer? I do not think so. Although it does not recur in later texts in precisely this form, there are indications of a possible line of development. Justin Martyr in the middle of the second century speaks of eucharistic consecration taking place either "through a word of prayer which is from him" or "through a prayer of the word which is from him" (*I Apology* 66.2)—the Greek may be translated either way. The correct meaning of this phrase has been much disputed,[20] but one possible interpretation is that the reference to "the word" is to the Logos—a key element in Justin's theology—and the phrase should therefore be understood as saying that the principal agent of eucharistic consecration is Christ. 1 Timothy 4:4 had already stated

[18] Jungmann, *The Place of Christ*, 4.

[19] See Paul F. Bradshaw, *Eucharistic Origins* (London: Oxford University Press, 2004), chapter 7.

[20] See G. J. Cuming, "ΔΙ᾽ ΕΥΧΗΣ ΛΟΓΟΥ (Justin, *Apology*, i.66.2)." *Journal of Theological Studies* 31 (1980) 80–82; Anthony Gelston, "ΔΙ᾽ ΕΥΧΗΣ ΛΟΓΟΥ (Justin, *Apology* i.66.2)." *Journal of Theological Studies* 33 (1982) 172–75; Michael Heintz, "δι᾽ εὐχῆς λόγου τοῦ παρ᾽ αὐτοῦ (Justin, *Apology* 1.66.2): Cuming and Gelston Revisited." *Studia Liturgica* 33 (2003) 33–36.

that "everything created by God is good, and nothing is to be rejected, provided it is received with thanksgiving; for it is sanctified by God's word and by prayer"; and so what we have here may well be a development of that idea. It does not follow of course that Justin's eucharistic prayer itself included an explicit invocation addressed to Christ: to believe that Christ is the agent of consecration and to invoke him liturgically are two quite different things. But when we add to Justin's testimony the witness of other early sources, the case is strengthened.

First there is Irenaeus, writing some years later than Justin. He introduces the Greek word *epiklesis* in eucharistic discourse, using it in his description of the heretical activities of the Valentinian Gnostic Marcus, who "pretending to eucharistize cups mixed with wine, and protracting to great length the word of invocation, makes them appear purple and reddish" (*Adv. haer.* 1.13.2). But he also applies it to the orthodox process of consecration: "as bread from the earth, receiving the invocation of God, is no longer common bread but eucharist, consisting of two realities, earthly and heavenly, so also our bodies, receiving the eucharist, are no longer corruptible, having the hope of the resurrection to eternity" (4.18.5). In another place he adopts a variant of this idea: "the cup that has been mixed and the bread that has been made receive the word of God and become the eucharist of Christ's body and blood" (5.2.3). Once again, these passages by themselves do not necessarily mean that Irenaeus was familiar with an explicit liturgical formula invoking the Logos within the prayer itself,[21] but they may be said to add strength to the case when taken in conjunction with certain passages of a similar kind in both Clement of Alexandria and Origen to which Maxwell Johnson has drawn attention, and above all the explicit invocation of the Logos in the eucharistic prayer of Sarapion in the fourth century: "let your holy Word come upon this bread . . . and upon this cup. . . ."[22]

At this point it may rightly be objected that all that I have shown is the emergence of a prayer to God to let the Logos come, and not the existence of such a prayer addressed directly to Christ, and hence lacking any clear connection with the primitive *marana tha* invocation. But in order to make that link, we need now to consider the role of the Holy Spirit in early Christian prayer. So far I have said scarcely anything about

---

[21] See S. Agrelo, "Epiclesis y eucharistía en S. Ireneo." *Ecclesia orans* 3 (1986) 7–27.

[22] Maxwell E. Johnson, *The Prayers of Sarapion of Thmuis: A Literary, Liturgical, and Theological Analysis.* OCA 249 (Rome: Pontificio Istituto Orientale, 1995) 249ff.

this, and that is because the ancient sources themselves have much less to say about the place of the Spirit in Christian praying than they do about the place of Christ. However, from what they do say it is clear that the alleged standard formula "through Christ and in the Holy Spirit" was anything but universal. Although Ephesians 6:18 counsels Christians to "pray at all times in the Spirit," that formula does not seem to occur in prayer texts as such until several centuries later, and Origen is our sole witness in commending its use prior to that. On the other hand, prayer through Christ and through the Holy Spirit is attested to some extent in this earlier period. Thus Justin Martyr in his description of eucharistic practice speaks of the president sending up "praise and glory to the Father of all through the name of the Son and of the Holy Spirit" (*I Apology* 65.3) and Clement of Alexandria ascribes to God "glory and honor through the servant Jesus Christ, the Lord of the living and the dead, and through the Holy Spirit" (*Quis dives salvetur?* 42.20).

The main reason why the Holy Spirit is less frequently mentioned in early sources seems to be because there was not then as completely clear a differentiation between what later orthodoxy would regard as the Second and Third persons of the Holy Trinity. The Spirit could be thought of as the Spirit of God or of Christ, and hence to speak of Christ was the same as to speak of his spirit, and vice versa. Thus, when in some third-century Syrian texts we encounter references to the invocation of the Spirit, that may be seen as no more than a regional variation of the invocation of the Logos found in other sources. In parallel fashion to Justin and Irenaeus, therefore, the *Didascalia Apostolorum* affirms that "the eucharist is accepted and sanctified through the Holy Spirit" and is "sanctified by means of invocations" (6.21, 22), and this theological understanding of consecration is found embodied in actual liturgical formulae in other later Syrian sources. Once again, because these occur in apocryphal Scriptures, they tend to have been passed over by many liturgical historians on the grounds that they belong to fringe groups and so cannot tell us anything about liturgical practice in mainstream Christianity. But if we are able to set aside such prejudices, the texts may be able shed some considerable light on third-century praying. Our principal source here is the *Acts of Thomas*, in spite of the critical problems and difficulties of interpretation presented by this work.[23] Scat-

---

[23] For editions of the text and a brief discussion of some of the problems associated with it, see Paul F. Bradshaw, *The Search for the Origins of Christian Worship*. 2nd ed. (London: S.P.C.K., 2002) 107.

tered throughout its narrative are quite a number of prayers of very diverse kinds, including some that are made up of a series of short acclamations of praise and others that are entirely petitionary in character. Some are addressed directly to the heavenly counterparts of physical elements, such as to "waters from the living waters" (ch. 52), to "holy oil given to us for sanctification" (ch. 121), and to "bread of life" (ch. 133). But two of the many prayers in this work are addressed to the Holy Spirit (chs. 27, 50), and they both consist of a repeated series of short invocations. For example, the second begins as follows: "Come, gift of the Exalted; come, perfect mercy; come, Holy Spirit. . . ."

What is their source? Such direct invocations for the deity to be present are not characteristic of Jewish prayers from this period nor of Graeco-Roman prayers. Caroline Johnson has argued that their closest parallel is in the magic spells of the ancient Mediterranean world,[24] and she may well be right in seeing that tradition as having influenced the development of the repetitive character of the forms of invocation found here. But what of the origin of the invocation as such? Taken in conjunction with the other references that I have outlined, the most likely origin does seem to lie in the primitive Christian *marana tha* ejaculation. As the expectation of an imminent *parousia* began to decline, it would not have been unnatural for that invocation to have been interpreted by some no longer as an entreaty for the risen Lord to return, but as a call for him to be present at the act of worship, and used in some places either outside the eucharistic prayers, as we find in the *Didache,* or as part of the petitionary element of the prayer itself, as we find in the *Acts of Thomas.* The close association between Christ and Spirit in the *Acts of Thomas* appears to be emphasized in the prayers that I have cited by the Holy Spirit being addressed as "the name of the Messiah" in one of its invocations (or perhaps the prayer is to be understood as being addressed to both Christ and the Spirit).

Most of the credit for unraveling the evolution of the eucharistic epiclesis goes to Gabriele Winkler, who has shown that in the Syrian tradition the earliest forms all have this imperative form "Come," addressed to the Messiah and/or his Spirit, although she has more recently modified her conclusions somewhat to claim that the very

[24] "Ritual Epicleses in the Greek Acts of Thomas," in *The Apocryphal Acts of the Apostles: Harvard Divinity School Studies,* ed. F. Bovon et al., 171–204 (Cambridge, MA: Harvard University Center for the Study of World Religions, 1999).

oldest form was addressed to "the name of the Messiah," by which the Spirit was always meant. Other forms of epiclesis addressed either to Christ, such as "may the spirit of holiness come and dwell," or to the Father, such as "may the Spirit come and rest and abide," or imperatives addressed to the Father, as in "Send your Holy Spirit" or "Let your holy Word come upon this bread," or petitions to the Father to send the Spirit, all reflect later stages of development.[25]

So what may we conclude from these many and scattered pieces of evidence about the place of Father, Son, and Holy Spirit in Christian praying in the first three centuries? In many traditions prayer undoubtedly continued to be addressed consistently to the Father, as it had been in the Jewish traditions that preceded it, albeit with some reference to the relation of Christ to the Father and/or through the meditation of Christ, and less frequently with some reference to the Spirit. Nevertheless, there is enough evidence to suggest that in other traditions liturgical prayer addressed directly to Christ was known, either alongside the Father or in place of him. While in some instances this invocation of Christ may quite rapidly have been transformed into prayer to God to let his Word come—and this may well be what was already known to Justin, Irenaeus, and others—yet in Syrian circles, and more widely still if we take the witness of Origen seriously, direct address to Christ or to the Spirit continued to be a characteristic part of Christian praying in the third century. It was thus only in the harsher climate of the fourth century, when liturgical praying became part of the battleground on which matters of doctrine were fought out, that the language of prayer was subject to greater scrutiny, and largely—but, it must be noted, never entirely—brought into concord with the orthodoxy of the age.

[25] See Gabriel Winkler, "Nochmals zu den Anfängen der Epiklese und des Sanctus im Eucharistischen Hochgebet." *Theologische Quartalschrift* 74 (1994) 216–19; "Further Observations in Connection with the Early Form of the Epiklesis," in *Le sacrement de l'initiation*, 66–80 (Antelias, Lebanon, 1996); and "Weitere Beobachtungen zur frühen Epiklese (den Doxologien und dem Sanctus): Über die Bedeutung der Apokryphen für die Erforschung der Entwicklung der Riten." *Oriens Christianus* 80 (1996) 177–200.

Chapter 4

Christ in the Byzantine Divine Office

Robert F. Taft, S.J.
Pontifical Oriental Institute

THE BYZANTINE LITURGY OF THE HOURS: HISTORY
The Byzantine Divine Office and its largely unstudied theology[1] are
the product of an extremely complex process of cultural interaction
and cross-fertilization resulting in the synthesis of the two completely
distinct and independent liturgical cults and cultures of Constantinople and Palestine.[2] The first millennium saw the development of the

---

[1] See the ample bibliography in Robert F. Taft, *The Liturgy of the Hours in
East and West: The Origins of the Divine Office and its Meaning for Today*, 2nd rev.
ed. (Collegeville, MN: Liturgical Press, 1993) 375–77, 384–87; updated in the
2nd Italian edition: idem, *La Liturgia delle Ore in Oriente e in Occidente: Le orig-
ini dell'Ufficio divino e il suo significato oggi*, 2a edizione revisionata con nuova
traduzione di Sara Staffuzza (Rome: Lipa, 2001) 443–46, 453–58; idem, "Select
Bibliography on the Byzantine Liturgy of the Hours," OCP 48 (1982) 358–70.

[2] See Miguel Arranz, "Les grandes étapes de la liturgie byzantine: Palestine—Byzance—Russie Essai d'aperçu historique," in *Liturgie de l'église particu-
lière, liturgie de l'église universelle. Conférences Saint-Serge 1975*, BELS 7 (Rome:
Ed. liturgiche, 1975) 43–72; Aleksej M. Pentkovskij, "Konstantinopol'skij i ierusalimskij bogosluzhebnye ustavy," *Zhurnal Moskovskoj Patriarxii* 4 (2001) 70–
78; idem, "Studijskij ustav i ustavy studijskoj tradicii," ibid. 5 (2001) 69–80;
Robert F. Taft, *The Byzantine Rite. A Short History*, American Essays in Liturgy
(Collegeville, MN: Liturgical Press, 1992); idem, *Liturgy of the Hours*, passim in
chs. 3, 5, 9–11, 17; idem, "Mount Athos: A Late Chapter in the History of the
'Byzantine Rite,'" DOP 42 (1988) 179–94; idem, "In the Bridegroom's Absence:
The Paschal Triduum in the Byzantine Church," in *La celebrazione del Triduo
pasquale: anamnesis e mimesis. Atti del III Congresso Internazionale di Liturgia,
Roma, Pontificio Istituto Liturgico, 9–13 maggio 1988*, Analecta Liturgica 14 =
Studia Anselmiana 102 (Rome: Pontificio Ateneo Sant'Anselmo, 1990) 71–97;
idem, "A Tale of Two Cities: The Byzantine Holy Week Triduum as a

cathedral rite of Constantinople from the fourth to the tenth centuries. By the end of that period it had already been subjected to hagiopolite contamination during the monastic ascendancy provoked by the struggle against Iconoclasm (725–843), culminating in the reform of the Studite era, when these two disparate traditions, the imperial rites of the capital and the ruder monastic usages of the Palestinian wilderness, courted and eventually entered an unlikely morganatic marriage.

Here is how this came about. Toward the beginning of the ninth century, Saint Theodore Studites appealed for some monks of the Laura of Saint Sabas in the wilderness beyond Jerusalem to help in the struggle against Iconoclasm.[3] These monks brought with them the hagiopolite *Horologion* or *Book of Hours* they knew in Palestine, and when, in 799, Theodore and some of his monks left their Monastery of Sakkoudion in Bithynia to take over the Monastery of Stoudios in the capital, these usages entered Constantinople and mingled with the *akolouthia asmatike* or "sung" cathedral rite of Hagia Sophia still in use there.[4] The Studite monks grafted the Constantinopolitan *Euchologion* or *Prayer Book*, with its prayers, diaconal litanies, and exclamations for the Hours and other services, onto the quite different Office of the Sabaitic monastic *Horologion*. At the same time, the Constantinopolitan

Paradigm of Liturgical History," in *Time and Community: In Honor of Thomas Julian Talley*, ed. J. Neil Alexander, NPM Studies in Church Music and Liturgy (Washington: The Pastoral Press, 1990) 21–41—the last three studies are reprinted in idem, *Liturgy in Byzantium and Beyond*, Variorum Collected Studies Series CS494 (Aldershot/Brookfield: Ashgate-Variorum, 1995) chs. 4–6; idem, "Holy Week in the Byzantine Tradition," in *Hebdomandae sanctae celebratio: Conspectus historicus comparativus: The Celebration of Holy Week in Ancient Jerusalem and its Development in the Rites of East and West*, ed. Antony G. Kollamparampil, BELS 93 (Rome: CLV—Ed. liturgiche, 1997) 67–91; also the bibliographical material cited the previous note.

[3] On Saint Sabas and his laura, see Joseph Patrich, *Sabas, Leader of Palestinian Monasticism: A Comparative Study in Eastern Monasticism, Fourth to Seventh Centuries*, Dumbarton Oaks Studies 32 (Washington: Dumbarton Oaks, 1995); idem, ed., *The Sabaite Heritage in the Orthodox Church from the Fifth Century to the Present*, Orientalia Lovaniensia Analecta 98 (Louvain: Peeters, 2001).

[4] Thomas Pott, *La réforme liturgique Byzantine: Étude du phénomène de l'évolution non-spontanée de la liturgie Byzantine*, BELS 104 (Rome: CLV—Ed. liturgiche, 2000) ch. 4; Taft, *The Byzantine Rite*, ch. 5; Pentkovskij, "Konstantinopol'skij i ierusalimskij bogosluzhebnye ustavy"; idem, "Studijskij ustav."

cathedral psalter or *Antiphonarion* was abandoned in favor of the hagiopolite monastic *Psalterion.*[5]

The period from ca. 800–1204 was dominated liturgically by the progress of this Studite synthesis, a monastic rite that would ultimately supplant the quite different asmatike cathedral rite of the Constantinoplitan *Typikon of the Great Church*[6] in the restoration following the Latin conquest and occupation of 1204–1261. Though the final stage in the evolution of this Office, which I have christened "neo-Sabaitic,"[7] would gradually modify and ultimately supplant this Studite rite everywhere during the Athonite hesychast ascendancy,[8] this neo-Sabaitic usage represents, basically, no more than a second wave of influence of the monastic usages of the Laura of Saint Sabas in the wilderness between Jerusalem and the Dead Sea.[9]

THE NEW HYMNOGRAPHY[10]

But that is still only half the story. Characterizing the revival of monastic worship in Palestine in the restoration following the Persian depredations of 614 C.E. was a veritable explosion of hymnographic

---

[5] On the Byzantine liturgical books of the two traditions, the *asmatike* and hagiopolite, and their fusion, see Robert F. Taft, "Le ufficiature liturgiche: i libri liturgici della Chiesa bizantina," in Guglielmo Cavallo (ed.), *Lo spazio letterario del medioevo: Le culture circonstanti*, ed. G. Cavallo, et al. 3 vols. (Rome: Salerno editrice, 1992–2006) 229–56.

[6] Juan Mateos, ed., *Le Typicon de la Grande Église: Ms. Sainte-Croix n°. 40, Xe siècle*. Introduction, texte critique, traduction et notes. 2 vols. OCA 165–166 (Rome: Pontificio Istituto Orientale, 1962–63). The definitive work on this office is now the doctoral dissertation written under my direction: Gregor M. Hanke, *Vesper und Orthros des Kathedralritus der Hagia Sophia zu Konstantinopel. Eine strukturanalystische und entwicklungsgeschichtliche Untersuchung unter besonderer Berücksichtigung der Psalmodie und der Formulare in den Euchologien*, Inauguraldissertation zu Erlangung des akademischen Grades eines Doktors der Theologie, Philosophisch-Theologische Hochschule Sankt-Georgen, Frankfurt am Main, 29 Oktober 2003, being prepared for publication in OCA.

[7] Taft, *The Byzantine Rite*, ch. 7.

[8] What this means is well summarized by John Meyendorff, "Mount Athos in the Fourteenth Century: Spiritual and Intellectual Legacy," DOP 42 (1988) 157–65; on the liturgy see Taft, "Mt. Athos."

[9] Taft, *The Byzantine Rite*, ch. 7; idem, "Mt. Athos"; idem, "Select Bibliography," pars. 6, 27–28.

[10] Taft, "Select Bibliography," pars. 114–152.

composition.[11] Famous hymnographers like Saint Andrew of Crete (ca. 660–740), Saint John Damascene (ca. 675–753/4), and Theophanes Graptos (ca. 778–845) immortalized this tradition, and when Theophanes was sent to join Saint Theodore at Stoudios, this hymnographic tradition also set down roots in Constantinople and was carried on there by Theodore himself, his brother Joseph, and others.[12]

Just why Palestinian monasticism took this turn in the road remains something of a mystery.[13] At any rate it was in Jerusalem that Saint John Damascene, monk of the Anastasis and "last of the Greek Fathers," put the finishing touches on what has been called "the final synthesis" of Byzantine theology.[14] And that may be why it was also in Palestine that "the final synthesis" found theological expression in this avalanche of new liturgical poetry.[15]

This history still remains to be written, and many of its chapters are obscure. We have no idea, for instance, why this poetry caught on everywhere,[16] despite the fact that Palestinian solitaries remained obstinately opposed to the startling innovation it represented.[17] What we

[11] Aristarchos Peristeris, "Literary and Scribal Activities in the Monastery of St. Sabas," in Patrich, *The Sabaite Heritage*, 171–94; Christian Hannick, "Hymnographie et hymnographes sabaïtes," ibid., 217–28.

[12] Elena Velkovska, "Libri liturgici bizantini," in *Scientia Liturgica: Manuale di liturgia*, ed. Anscar J. Chupungco, 1: *Tempo e spazio liturgico* (Casale Monferrato: Piemme, 1998) 243–58, here 251.

[13] See Hannick, "Hymnographie et hymnographes sabaïtes."

[14] How the Laura of Saint Sabas acquired this influence also remains somewhat of a mystery: see Andrew Louth, "St. John of Damascus and the Making of the Byzantine Theological Synthesis," in Patrich, *The Sabaite Heritage*, 301–4.

[15] Patrich, *The Sabaite Heritage*; Albert Ehrhard, "Das griechische Kloster Mâr-Saba in Palästina: seine Geschichte und sein literarischen Denkmäler," *Römische Quartalschrift* 7 (1893) 32–79.

[16] W. Weyh, "Die Akrostichis in der byzantinischen Kanonesdichtung," *Byzantinische Zeitschrift* 17 (1908) 1–68, esp. ch. 1: Geschichte der Kanonesdichtung, 5–37, here 7, attributes "der große Erfolg" of the canons to the musical aspect, but that, while not improbable, remains to be demonstrated.

[17] See, for instance, the opposition expressed in such texts as Augusta Longo, "Il testo della «Narrazione degli abati Giovanni e Sofronio» attraverso le «Hermeneiai» di Nicone," *Rivista di studi bizantini e neoellenci* 12–13 (1965–66) 223–67, here 254–55, 261–63; *Vita* 2 of Saint Theodore Studites, attributed to Theodore Daphnopates, PG 99:216B–17A; further examples in Irénée Hausherr, *Penthos: The Doctrine of Compunction in the Christian East*, Cistercian Studies

do know is that this new liturgical poetry quickly conquered the terrain to become *the* characteristic of the Byzantine Divine Office, as described in the famous 1924 essay of Lev Gillet, "Le génie du rit byzantin."[18]

This corpus eventually grew to comprise a staggering amount of material. On each of the 366 days of the year (there is a proper for Saint Cassian on February 29 in leap years), the proper for the Divine Office occupies some thirty pages in a normal edition and includes about seventeen refrains for Vespers, 140 for Matins, and half a dozen for Compline. Multiply all that by 366, add the mountain of chants in the manuscripts that have never been incorporated into the printed books (it is enough to recall the 5,320 pages of material in twelve volumes, one per month, of Italo-Byzantine Greek liturgical poetry edited by the Istituto di studi bizantini e neoellenici di Roma under the direction of the late Professor Giuseppe Schirò[19]), and one will have

Series 53 (Kalamazoo: Cistercian Publications, 1982) 106–9; Robert F. Taft, "Christian Liturgical Psalmody: Origins, Development, Decomposition, Collapse," in *Psalms in Community. Jewish and Christian Textual, Liturgical, and Artistic Traditions*, ed. Harold W. Attridge and Margot E. Fassler, Society of Biblical Literature Symposium Series Number 25 (Atlanta: Society of Biblical Literature 2003) 7–32, here 11–15; idem, "Saints Lives and Liturgy: Hagiography and New Perspectives in Liturgiology," in *In God's Hands: Essays on the Church and Ecumenism in Honour of Michael A. Fahey, S.J.*, ed. J. Z. Skira and M. S. Attridge, 33–53 (Louvain: Leuven University Press, 2006). Compare this opposition with the encomia of such poetic refrains in the texts cited by Nancy Patterson Ševčenko, "Canon and Calendar: The Role of a Ninth-Century Hymnographer in Shaping the Celebration of the Saints," in *Byzantium in the Ninth Century: Dead or Alive. Papers from the Thirtieth Spring Symposium of Byzantine Studies, Birmingham, March 1996*, ed. Leslie Brubaker, Society for the Promotion of Byzantine Studies Publications 5 (Aldershot/Brookfield/Singapore/Sydney: Ashgate Variorum, 1998) 101–14, here 102–3.

[18] *Les Questions liturgiques et paroissiales* 9 (1924) 81–90, modeled, as Gillet himself confirms, on the magistral 1899 essay of Edmund Bishop (1846–1917), "The Genius of the Roman Rite," reprinted in revised form in idem, *Liturgica Historica: Papers on the Liturgy and Religious Life of the Western Church* (Oxford: Clarendon, 1918) 1–19. On this great autodidact English Catholic liturgical scholar, see the wonderful academic biography by Nigel Abercrombie, *The Life and Work of Edmund Bishop* (London: Longmans, 1959).

[19] *Analecta hymnica Graeca e codicibus eruta Italiae Inferioris*, 13 vols. (Rome 1966–1983). Vol. 13 has the indices with 334 pages of incipits alone.

some idea of the massive quantity of material in the Byzantine fixed liturgical cycle alone. If we add the propers of the temporal or movable cycle, the quantity of material increases by about a third. The five volumes of Enrica Follieri's indispensable indices comprise 2,551 pages of Byzantine Greek hymnographic poetry incipits, averaging up to thirty per page or almost 69,000 poetic pieces in all![20] And only those totally innocent of the hard grind of sifting through Greek and Slavonic liturgical manuscripts—the latter preserve many canons and chants no longer in use in the Greek books—would even dream of thinking this encompasses all there is.

The main unit of this poetry was the canon, which in the eighth century would supersede the older Constantinopolitan *kontakion* as the centerpiece of Matins (*orthros*).[21] Originally, the canon comprised the nine biblical canticles of the hagiopolite psalter with accompanying refrains or *troparia*, not the poetic odes later substituted for them.[22]

It is this enormous quantity of new ecclesiastical poetry, covering each day page after page in the hymn books, that forced the development of a new series of anthologies to unify this material originally scattered in disparate manuscript collections of *heirmologia, kanones, kathismata, kontakaria, sticheraria, tropologia* in manuscripts of the

[20] Henrica Follieri, *Initia hymnorum Ecclesiae Graecae*. 6 vols. Studi e Testi 211–215bis (Vatican: Bibliotheca Apostolica Vaticana, 1960–1966).

[21] Elizabeth M. Jeffreys, "Kanon," ODB 2:1102; idem, "Kontakion," ODB 2:1148. On the history of the canon see Enrica Follieri, "L'innografia bizantina dal contacio al canone," in *Da Bizanzio a San Marco. Musica e liturgia*, ed. Giulio Cattin, Quaderni di «Musica e storia» 2, Fondazione Ugo ed Olga Levi (Venezia: Società il Mulino, 1997) 10–32; Nancy Patterson Ševčenko, "Canon and Calendar"; idem, "The Five Hymnographers at Nerezi," *Palaeoslavica* 10/2 (2002) 55–68; Egon Wellesz, *A History of Byzantine Music and Hymnography*, 2nd ed. (Oxford: Clarendon Press, 1961) esp. 198–245; Weyh, "Die Akrostichis in der byzantinischen Kanonesdichtung," esp. Erstes Kapitel: Geschichte der Kanonesdichtung, 5–37. Weyh says the name "canon (κανών)" was first used for this liturgical unit in the mid-ninth century, and Saint Andrew of Crete (ca. 660–d. 740) was the first composer of canons (ibid., 7). We are still light years away from an adequate history of these developments.

[22] The earliest manuscripts with *troparia* for the biblical canticles are the seventh-century Egyptian papyrus *Rylands 466* and the fragment *Heidelberg 1632*, and by the eighth century the nine odes and their refrains have been systematized.

eighth–ninth centuries.[23] These new anthologies appear in the centuries indicated: the *oktoechos* with the hymnic propers of the mobile or temporal cycle of Sundays from Pentecost to Lent begins to be formed in the eighth century, though the name *oktoechos* first appears in the eleventh-century manuscripts, and the weekday cycle is added only later, to form the *"great (mega) oktoechos"* or *parakletike*; the *triodion-pentekostarion* with the Lenten and paschal propers by the tenth century; and the *menaion* or "monthly" for the twelve-month fixed cycle in the same era.

THE CHRISTOLOGY OF THE BYZANTINE DIVINE OFFICE

As one might imagine, this massive quantity of highly theologized liturgical poetry in the Byzantine Divine Office leaves no theme untouched. But some common elements that return time and again can be identified:

1. The notion that *everything* Christ did, he did for our salvation.

2. The belief that this saving work is still operative as salvific for us now.

3. The incessantly reiterated theme of the resurrection, the central mystery in Byzantine soteriology and liturgical theology.

4. The theme of light, Christ as the light of the world, our illuminator—i.e., savior, often in conjunction with the mystery of the Transfiguration as one of the saving mysteries whereby Christ effected our illumination—i.e., transfiguration.

The Agrypnia

This theology finds expression in the texts of both the "Ordinary," those unchangeable components that make up the permanent skeleton of a liturgical service regardless of the day or feast; and the "proper," those texts that pertain to the celebration of a particular festivity.[24]

---

[23] Paul Géhin and Stig S. Frøyshov, "Nouvelles découverts sinaïtiques: à propos de la parution de l'inventaire des manuscrits grecs," *Revue des études Byzantines* 58 (2000) 167–84, here 175–81; Robert F. Taft and Nancy Patterson Ševčenko, "Oktoechos," ODB 3:1520.

[24] The Byzantines themselves called the texts proper to a celebration its *akolouthia* ("order," or "office"), though the term *akolouthia* has a wider extension and is not limited to this sense: Robert F. Taft, "Akolouthia," ODB 1:46–47.

Since these two fonts exist intermingled in the actual liturgical celebrations, I shall exploit them together as their theological themes appear in the *agrypnia* or centerpiece of the neo-Sabaitic office. This "All-night Vigil," originally a monastic service that came to be used also as a festive cathedral vigil in parish worship, is a composite office uniting in one unbroken service solemn Vespers; the nocturns of Matins or Orthros, which in monastic usage are drawn out through the night with long monastic psalmody;[25] the Sunday Resurrection Vigil; and Lauds.[26] The several segments of this single composite service include all the substantial theological meat of the Byzantine Hours.[27]

Vespers and Matins

A service of unparalleled beauty, the *agrypnia* begins in a flood of light and incense, as the doors of the brilliantly illumined sanctuary are opened onto the darkened church, and the celebrant proclaims in solemn chant: "Glory to the holy, consubstantial, and undivided Trinity, always, now and ever, and unto the ages of ages!" Then the deacon

[25] On the monastic psalmody of the Byzantine Office, see Juan Mateos, "La psalmodie variable dans le rite byzantin," in *Acta philosophica et theologica* 2 (Rome: Societas Academica Dacoromana, 1964) 325–39.

[26] Taft, *The Liturgy of the Hours*, 277–90; Miguel Arranz, "L'office de la veillée nocturne dans l'Eglise grecque et dans l'Eglise russe," OCP 42 (1976) 117–55, 402–25; idem, "N. D. Uspenskij: The Office of the All-Night Vigil in the Greek Church and in the Russian Church," *St. Vladimir's Theological Quarterly* 24 (1980) 83–113, 169–95 (trans. of the previous article); Juan Mateos, "Quelques problèmes de l'orthros byzantin," *Proche-orient chrétien* 11 (1961) 17–35, 201–20. I resume here some material from Robert F. Taft, *Beyond East and West: Problems in Liturgical Understanding*, 2nd rev. and enlarged ed. (Rome: Edizioni Orientlia Christiana, 1997) ch. 3. Chant pieces cited below that are not attributed to a particular translation are from that source.

[27] I shall prescind for the most part from the twenty-two prayers, nine in Vespers and thirteen in Matins, originally distributed as collects at various points throughout the *agrypnia*. Most of them are addressed to God the Father, and even those addressed to Christ can hardly be said to contain any developed christology, though they do refer to some of the themes I develop below. On these prayers, the basic work is Miguel Arranz, "Les prières presbytérales des matines Byzantines," OCP 37 (1971) 406–36; 38 (1972) 64–115; idem, "Les prières sacerdotales des vêpres Byzantines," OCP 37 (1971) 85–124; idem, "Le sacerdoce ministériel dans les prières secrètes des vêpres et des matines byzantines," *Euntes docete* 24 (1971) 186–219.

and priest call the congregation to prayer with verses adapted from Psalm 94:6, after which the deacon, lighting the way with a huge candle, symbol of Christ who lights up our path, leads the celebrant through the whole church incensing.

Meanwhile, the choir is chanting the invitatory psalm of Vespers, Psalm 103/104,[28] a psalm of creation. In the East, liturgy is not just a service. It is also the place of theophany, and in the vigil, as in the Bible, the very first theophany is creation. In chanting the invitatory psalm, special emphasis is given to the christological theme of darkness and light, the base-symbolism of this office. The psalm verses expressing this theme (Ps 103/104:19b-20a, 24a) are repeated twice:

> The sun knows when to set; you bring darkness and it is night.
> How manifold are your works, O Lord! In wisdom, you wrought them all![29]

This light theme is resumed immediately in the central rite of Evensong, the *lucernarium*, which opens with Psalm 140/141, the heart of traditional Christian vesperal psalmody:

> O Lord I cry to you: hear me O Lord!
> Let my prayer rise like incense before you, the lifting up of my hands like the evening sacrifice.

While clouds of incense once again fill the church as a sign of the congregation's prayers rising to the throne of God (as the psalm says), every candle in the church is lit, and the choir chants the proper refrains with which the psalmody is farced, refrains showing how the mystery of light that transforms creation is fulfilled in the dying and rising of Christ. Here are some of the variable refrains from Sunday Vespers in the third tone:[30]

---

[28] Where the Hebrew and LXX psalm numberings differ, I give first the Greek Septuagint numbering, which is that of the Byzantine rite. For the respective numberings see the Psalter Table in Taft, *The Liturgy of the Hours*, x.

[29] Translations of biblical texts, with the exception of Phil 2:5-11 on pages 83–84 (RSV), are Robert Taft's. Psalms are translations from the Septuagint.

[30] English version adapted from *The Office of Vespers in the Byzantine Rite* (London: Darton, Longman and Todd, 1965) 42–43.

Everything has been enlightened by your resurrection, O Lord, and paradise has been opened again; all creation, extolling you, offers to you the perpetual hymn of praise.

We, who unworthily stay in your pure house, intone the evening hymn, crying from the depths: "O Christ our God, who have enlightened the world with your resurrection, free your people from your enemies, you who love humankind!"

O Christ, who through your Passion have darkened the sun, and with the light of your resurrection have illumined the universe: accept our evening hymn of praise, O you who love humankind!

You underwent death, O Christ, so that you might free our race from death; and having risen from the dead on the third day, you raised with you those that acknowledge you as God, and you have illumined the world. O Lord, glory to you!

During the chanting of the final refrain, the priest and deacon, bearing the smoking censor, make the Introit of solemn Vespers, processing through the church to the central "Holy Doors" of the sanctuary. There the age-old Hymn of Light is intoned, the *Phos hilaron*, which for over sixteen centuries, day after day, without variation or change, has proclaimed that the true Light of the World is not the sun of creation by day, nor the evening lamp by night, but the eternal Son of God, "the true light that enlightens everyone," in the words of John 1:9. Saint Basil the Great (d. 379), who quotes this hymn in far-off fourth-century Caesaria in Cappadocia, says it was already so old by then that no one remembers who composed it.[31] A literal version of the original Greek text reads:

O joyous light of the holy glory of the immortal Father,
    heavenly, holy, blessed Jesus Christ!
Having come to the setting of the sun, and beholding the
    evening light,
We praise God Father, Son and Holy Spirit!
It is fitting at all times that you be praised with auspicious voices,
    O Son of God, giver of life;
Wherefore the whole world glorifies you![32]

---

[31] *On the Holy Spirit* 29:73; Basile de Césarée, *Sur le Saint-Esprit*, ed. Benoît Pruche, SC 17bis (Paris: Cerf, 1968) 508–10 = PG 32:205.

[32] Trans. adapted from Antonia Tripolitis, "PHOS HILARON: Ancient Hymn and Modern Enigma," *Vigiliae christianae* 24 (1970) 189–96, here 189. See

The collect at the end of the vesperal intercessions resumes the themes of the service:

> O great and exalted God! You alone are immortal and dwell in unapproachable light! In your wisdom, you created all things: You separated light from darkness, establishing the sun to govern the day, and the moon and stars to rule the night. . . . Clothe us in the armor of light, rescue us from the fears of night. . . . Then, gladdened by your joy and enlightened by your precepts, may we rise to glorify your goodness . . . [33]

"God is light," says the First Letter of John (1:5), and this light shines in our world to transfigure us through the transfigured face of Christ, "The true light that enlightens everyone" (John 1:9). In Byzantine Sunday worship, this theme serves as symbolic matrix to express the unity of the Sunday mystery—the passover of Christ—and its sacramental symbols: baptism, called *photismos* or "illumination," and Eucharist.

This is a theme that pervades all of Byzantine spirituality and mysticism. In a moving passage of his Sermon on the Transfiguration, Anastasius of Sinai (ca. 700) has the transfigured Christ say:

> It is thus that the just shall shine at the resurrection. It is thus that they shall be glorified; into my condition they shall be transfigured, to this form, to this image, to this imprint, to this light and to this beatitude they shall be configured, and they shall reign with me, the Son of God.[34]

Similarly, on the August 6 feast of the Transfiguration, the liturgical refrains attribute our transfiguration to Christ's:[35]

---

also Peter Plank, *PHOS HILARON. Christushymnus und Lichtdanksangugng der frühen Christenheit*. Hereditas: Studien zur alten Kirchengeschichte 20 (Bonn: Borengässer, 2001).

[33] English version adapted from *The Office of Vespers in the Byzantine Rite*, 42–43.

[34] André Guillou, "Le Monastère de la Théotokos au Sinaï: Origines; épiclèse; mosaïque de la Transfiguration; Homélie inédite d'Anastase le Sinaïte sur la Transfiguration (étude et texte critique)," *Mélanges d'archéologie et d'histoire* 67 (1955) 253.

[35] Trans. adapted from *The Festal Menaion*, trans. Mother Mary and Kallistos Ware, *The Service Books of the Orthodox Church* (London: Faber and Faber, 1969) 468.

Come, let us rejoice . . . let us be transformed this day into a better state . . . For in his mercy, the Savior of our souls has transfigured disfigured man and made him shine with light upon Mount Tabor. (Small Vespers)
. . . On Mount Tabor he makes bright the weakness of man and bestows enlightenment upon our souls. (Small Vespers)
Today, Christ on Mount Tabor has changed the darkened nature of Adam, and filling it with brightness has made it godlike. (Small Vespers)

This light symbolism pervades the propers especially on Sunday. At Sunday Vespers on Saturday evening, refrains like this one in tone 5 farce the vesperal psalms (LXX Pss 140, 141, 129, 116):

We offer the evening worship to you, the light that never sets. In the fullness of time you shone on the world, and descended even into hell to dispel the darkness that was there, and showed the light of the resurrection to the nations. O Lord the giver of light, glory to you!

And in the First Ode of the canon of Sunday Matins, tone 2:

O pure one, through the inaccessible door of your closed womb the Sun of righteousness passed and appeared to the world.

The Resurrection Vigil

After the monastic psalmody of Matins, the *agrypnia* passes immediately to the three psalms of the third nocturn, which on Saturday night is transformed into the psalmody of the age-old Resurrection Vigil described as early as the 380s by Egeria's *Diary* 24:8-11,[36] and the *Apostolic Constitutions* 2, 59:3-4.[37] The three components of this service are three psalms in remembrance of Jesus' three days in the tomb; an incensation in remembrance of the aromatic spices brought by the women to anoint the body of the Lord, thus inaugurating the first watch before the tomb, model of all Christian resurrection vigils, including what we call a wake in English; and a solemn proclamation of

[36] Égérie, *Journal de voyage (Itinéraire)*, ed. Pierre Maraval, SC 296 (Paris: Cerf, 1982) 242–45; English trans. John Wilkinson, *Egeria's Travels* (London: S.P.C.K., 1971) 124–25. The seminal study on the topic is Juan Mateos, "La vigile cathédrale chez Égérie," OCP 27 (1961) 281–312.

[37] *Les Constitutions apostoliques*, ed. M. Metzger, vol. 1, books 1–2, SC 320 (Paris 1985) 324–27.

the Gospel of the Resurrection, in remembrance of the angel who stood at the rolled-back stone of the tomb announcing the Resurrection.

Egeria describes this service as she saw it over sixteen hundred years ago in the rotunda of the Anastasis or "resurrection" basilica in Jerusalem:

> But on the seventh day, the Lord's Day, there gather in the courtyard before cock-crow all the people, as many as can get in, as if it were Easter. Soon the first cock crows, and at that the bishop enters, and goes into the cave in the Anastasis. The doors are all opened, and all the people come into the Anastasis, which is already ablaze with lamps. When they are inside, a psalm is said by one of the presbyters, with everyone responding, and it is followed by a prayer; then a psalm is said by one of the deacons, and another prayer; then a third psalm is said by one of the clergy, a third prayer, and the Commemoration of All. After these three psalms and prayers they take censers into the cave of the Anastasis, so that the whole Anastasis basilica is filled with the smell. Then the bishop, standing inside the screen, takes the Gospel book and goes to the door where he himself reads the account of the Lord's resurrection . . . [38]

In the Byzantine *agrypnia* this Resurrection Vigil opens with the solemn chanting of select verses from Psalms 134, 135, and 118, accompanied by the refrains of the "myrrh-bearing women," the pious women who went to the tomb to anoint the body of the Lord and thus became the first witnesses to the resurrection. As soon as the cantors intone "Praise the name of the Lord" from Psalm 134, the doors of the sanctuary are opened, all the lights and candles in the church are again lit, and the celebrant, preceded once more by the deacon and his candle, incenses again the whole church. The refrains of the myrrh-bearers give the sense of this service as a Resurrection Vigil:

> By the tomb stood an angel radiant in light, and thus did he speak to the myrrh-bearing women: "Let not your sorrow mingle tears with precious ointment. You see the tomb before you; look for yourselves. He is not here; he has risen!"
> With the first rays of dawn they had set out for the tomb, sobbing and lamenting as they walked along. But when they reached the tomb,

[38] Wilkinson, *Egeria's Travels*, 124–25.

they were startled by an angel who said: "The time for tears and sorrow is now over. Go! Tell his friends that he has risen!"

Your women friends had come with ointment, Lord, hoping to anoint your bruised and battered body cold in death. But the angel stood before them, saying: "Why seek the living among the dead? He is God! He has risen from the grave."[39]

The responsory and the solemn chanting of the Gospel of the Resurrection follow, after which the Book of the Gospels, symbol of the risen Christ in our midst, is solemnly borne in procession to the center of the church and enthroned there, while the choir sings the Resurrection Hymn professing faith that, having heard the paschal Gospel, we too have seen and tasted the glory of God:

Having seen Christ's resurrection, let us adore the holy Lord Jesus Christ, who is alone without sin. We worship your cross, O Christ, we sing and tell the glory of your holy resurrection. For you are our God, we know of no other than you, we call on your name. Come all you faithful, let us worship Christ's holy resurrection. For behold, through the cross has joy come to all the world. As we continually bless the Lord, we sing of his resurrection, for he has endured the cross and destroyed death by death![40]

Lauds

The same themes of light and paschal triumph are found throughout the rich poetry of Lauds, especially in the Odes of the Canon, a series of refrains composed according to the themes of the biblical canticles. The same basic realities are proclaimed: darkness and light; the darkness of sin overcome by the illumination of the risen Christ.

In this poetry one notes especially the Pauline sense that whatever was accomplished was done for our salvation: the incarnation, the cross, the tomb, the resurrection on the third day—all are hymned as instruments of our salvation active now. Here are a few examples from the Sunday *Oktoechos* proper, tone 1:[41]

[39] *Prayerbook* (Cambridge, NY: New Skete, 1976) 110–11.
[40] *The Byzanatine Liturgy*, 2nd ed. (New York: The Russian Center, 1956) 58–59.
[41] English translations downloaded from http://www.anastasis.org.uk/oktoich.htm, copyright Archimandrite Ephrem (Lash), and slightly adapted.

Rejoice, you heavens! Sound the trumpet foundations of the earth! Shout aloud your joy, you mountains! For see, Emmanuel has nailed our sins to the Cross, and he who gives life, has slain death and raised up Adam, for he loves humankind.

Let us sing the praise of him who was willingly crucified in the flesh for our sakes, suffered and was buried and rose from the dead, as we say: establish your Church in right belief, O Christ, and give peace to our life, for you are good and love humankind.

As we, the unworthy, stand at your tomb that received life, we offer a hymn of glory to your ineffable compassion, Christ our God; because you accepted Cross and death, O sinless one, that you might give resurrection to the world, for you love humankind.

Let all creation rejoice, let the heavens be glad, let the nations clap their hands with gladness! For Christ our Savior has nailed our sins to the Cross, and by slaying death has granted us life, raising all Adam's fallen race, since he loves humankind.

Note the frequent use of paradox and simile to express these realities, as in the following refrains:

Christ incarnate makes me divine. Christ being humbled exalts me. Christ the Giver of life, by suffering the passion in the flesh, makes me dispassionate. Therefore I raise a song of thanksgiving, for he has been glorified![42]

Christ being crucified lifts me up. Christ put to death raises me with himself. Christ grants me life. Therefore as I clap my hands in gladness I sing to the Savior a song of victory, for he has been glorified.

A fearful, awesome mystery is performed today!
The releaser of Adam is arrested!
He who tries hearts is unjustly tried!
The God before whom angels stand in fear stands before Pilate!
The creator is struck by the hand of the creature!
The judge of the living and the dead is judged to death on a tree!
The destroyer of hell is sealed in a tomb!
Compassionate Lord and Redeemer, glory to you! (Good Friday Vespers)

Gracious Lord, you ride upon the Cherubim, and are praised by the Seraphim; now you ride like David on the foal of an ass.

The children sing hymns worthy of God, while the priests and scribes blaspheme against you.

---

[42] Ibid.

By riding an untamed colt, you have prefigured the salvation of the gentiles, those wild beasts, who will be brought from unbelief to faith! Glory to you, o merciful Christ, our King and the lover of humankind! (Palm Sunday Vespers)

He who clothes himself with light as with a garment stood naked for trial.

He was struck on the cheek by hands that he himself had formed.
A people that transgressed the law
nailed the Lord of Glory to the cross.

Then the curtain of the temple was torn in two; then the sun was darkened, unable to bear the sight of God outraged, before whom all things tremble. Let us worship him!

The disciple denied him but the thief cried out: "Remember me, Lord, in your kingdom!" (Good Friday Matins)

BYZANTINE CHRISTOLOGY

What conclusions can we draw from what we have seen of the theology expressed in the Byzantine Divine Offices? Gerhard Delling has said:

> Worship is the self-portrayal of religion. In worship the sources by which religion lives are made visible, its expectations and hopes are expressed, and the forces which sustain it are made known. In many respects the essence of a religion is more directly intelligible in its worship than in statements of its basic principles or even in descriptions of its sentiments.[43]

What Delling says here of the phenomenological/epistemological level is even more true on the existential: not only in worship is faith *known*; through worship faith *is fed and lives*.

I think this is eminently true of the christology expressed in the Byzantine Hours: it is an accurate reflection of the soul of Byzantine Orthodoxy. Byzantium saw itself as a conservative society, something quite different from how we view our twenty-first century pace-setting culture.[44] We view theology as creative, but in Byzantine times creativity in theology was about as welcome as creative bookkeeping

[43] Gerhard Delling, *Worship in the New Testament*, trans. P. Scott (Philadelphia: Westminster, 1962) xi.

[44] In this context, see the astute remarks of Paul Speck, "Byzantium: Cultural Suicide?" in L. Brubaker, ed., *Byzantium in the Ninth Century: Dead or Alive* (Aldershot/Brookfield: Ashgate, 1998) 73–84.

to the IRS. If one accused a Byzantine Orthodox theologian of being creative, he would have fled in horror.[45] Before modern times the rule of theology was what was believed *"quod semper et ubique et ab omnibus*—always and everywhere and by everyone." Whether or not this was verified in fact is beside the point: we are dealing with perceptions. But theology has always been an unstable compound because one of its elements, human beings, is always changing, and history shows the church dancing a minuet between ongoing change and explicitly proclaimed adherence to Pope Saint Stephen I's (254–257) famous dictum, *"Nihil innovetur nisi quod traditum est*—Let there be nothing new that has not been handed down."[46]

So, late antique and medieval Christians, especially the Byzantines, were interested in continuity, not change. Byzantium was a backward-looking civilization: traditional models, not innovations, were its ideal.[47] Byzantine theology was traditional and apophatic. It did not seek new ways to explain old things, but old ways to explain everything. Indeed, since they considered the mysteries unfathomable, they were reluctant to explain them at all.[48] So they talked around them, as

[45] See Eric D. Perl, ". . . 'That Man Might Become God': Central Themes in Byzantine Theology," in *Heaven On Earth: Art and the Church in Byzantium*, ed. Linda Safran (University Park: Pennsylvania State University Press, 1998) 39–57, here 39–40 and passim.

[46] See Peter Stockmeier, "'Alt' und 'Neu' als Prinzipien der frühchristlichen Theologie," in *Reformatio Ecclesiae: Beiträge zu kirchlichen Reformbemühungen von der Alten Kirche bis zur Neuzeit. Festgabe für Erwin Iserloh*, ed. Remigius Bäumer (Paderborn/Munich/Vienna/Zürich: F. Schöningh, 1980) 15–22. Gerhart B. Ladner, however, in his seminal study *The Idea of Reform: Its Impact on Christian Thought and Action in the Age of the Fathers* (Cambridge, MA: Harvard University Press, 1959), maintains that the very notion of reform is Christian. On the whole issue see most recently the excellent discussion in Pott, *La réforme liturgique byzantin*, esp. Part 1.

[47] Cyril Mango, *Byzantium: The Empire of New Rome* (London: Weidenfeld & Nicolson, 1980) 218; idem, *Byzantium and its Image, History and Culture of the Byzantine Empire and its Heritage*, Variorum Collected Studies Series CS191 (London: Variorum, 1984) ch. 1, esp. 32.

[48] I do not wish to imply that the Orthodox approach to theology—and, indeed, to the very history of their own theology—is not without grave problems. One reflection of this is the fact that, since the death of John Meyendorff (1926–1992), almost all serious, reputable historians of Orthodox theology are non-Orthodox scholars. On the whole issue, see the excellent, penetrating

in their liturgical poetry, and defined their parameters in their councils. *But they did not pretend to explain them.*

Modern theologians forging new christologies "from below" will find, then, no consolation in "Sailing to Byzantium," as the title of Yeats's famous poem puts it. Byzantine christology, the christology of the Nicene-Constantinopolitan Creed and of the first seven ecumenical councils, sometimes called neo-Chalcedonian,[49] is "high christol-

---

analysis of Dorothea Wendebourg, "'Pseudomorphosis': A Theological Judgement as an Axiom for Research in the History of Church and Theology," *The Greek Orthodox Theological Review* 47 (1997) 321–42, translated from idem, "'Pesudomorphosis'—ein theologisches Urteil als Axiom der kirchen—und theologiegeschichtlichen Forschung," in *The Christian East. Its Institutions & Its Thought. A Critical Reflection. Papers of the International Scholarly Congress for the 75th Anniversary of the Pontifical Oriental Institute, Rome, 30 May–5 June 1993,* ed. Robert F. Taft, OCA 251 (Rome: Pontificio Istituto Orientale, 1996) 565–89; also numerous works of Gerhard Podskalsky cited ibid., note 29 and passim, among which esp. *Griechische Theologie in der Zeit der Türkenherrschaft (1453–1821): Die Orthodoxie im Spannungsfeld der nachreformatorischen Konfessionen des Westerns* (Munich: A.C.H. Beck, 1988); idem, "Entwicklung des griechisch-byzantinischen theologischen Denkens (bis zum Ende der Türkokratie), *Ostkirchliche Studien* 47 (1998) 34–43; and most recently, idem, *Zur Hermeneutik des theologischen Ost-West-Gesprächs in historischer Perspektiv,* Erfurter Vorträge zur Kulturgeschichte des Orthodoxen Christentums 2 (Erfurt: Universität Erfurt—Religionswissenschaft [Orthodoxes Christentum], 2002); and idem, *Von Photios zu Bessarion. Der Vorrang humanistisch geprägter Theologie in Byzanz und deren bleibende Bedutung,* Schriften zur Geschichte des östlichen Europa 25 (Wiesbaden: Harrassowitz Verlag, 2003). To savor the extremes, at times surpassing the ridiculous, to which an Orthodox anti-Western vision of their own theological history can reach, the reader with a sense of humor should read John S. Romanides, *Franks, Romans, Feudalism and Doctrine: An Interplay between Theology and Society,* Patriarch Athenagoras Memorial Lectures (Brookline: Holy Cross Orthodox Press, 1982); apropos of whose work see André de Halleux, "Une vision orthodoxe grecque de la romanité," *Revue théologique de Louvain* 15 (1984) 54–66. See also the history of contemporary Greek Orthodox theology by Yannis Spiteris, *La teologia ortodossa neo-greca* (Bologna: Edizoni Dehoniane, 1992).

[49] See Charles Moeller, "Le chalcédonisme et le néo-chalcédonisme en Orient de 451 à la fin du VIe siècle," in *Das Konzil von Chalkedon, Geschichte und Gegenwart,* ed. Alois Grillmeier and Heinrich Bacht. 3 vols. (Würzburg: Echter-Verlag, 1951–54) 1: *Der Glaube von Chalkedon,* 637–720; Alois Grillmeier in collaboration with Theresia Hainthaler, *Christ in Christian Tradition,* 2: *From the*

ogy." Its Christ is the incarnate Logos of the Prologue of John 1:1-18 and Philippians 2:5-11, preexisting from all eternity.

So the Jesus of the Byzantine Office is not the historical Jesus of the past, but the heavenly High Priest interceding for us constantly before the throne of the Father, as in Romans 8:34, Hebrews 9:11-28, and actively directing the life of his church, as in Revelation 1:17–3:22 (and passim).[50] It is this consciousness of Jesus as the Lord not of the past but of contemporary history that is the aim of all Orthodox-Catholic spirituality and liturgical anamnesis. The liturgy is a *present encounter* with God. Salvation is now. The death and resurrection of Jesus are past events only in their historicity. But they are eternally present in God, and have brought the presence of God among us to fulfillment in Jesus.

This Byzantine worldview is based on the mystery of Christ announced in the New Testament, defined in the ecumenical councils, and developed in the texts of the liturgy itself. One of the earliest (61/2 C.E.) New Testament texts, Philippians 2:5-11 (RSV), captures the entire kerygma:

> . . . Christ Jesus,
> though he was in the form of God,
> did not count equality with God a thing to be grasped,
> but emptied himself,
> taking the form of a servant,
> being born in the likeness of men.
> And being found in human form,
> he humbled himself and became obedient unto death,
> even death on a cross.
> Therefore God has highly exalted him,
> and bestowed on him the name which is above every name,

Council of Chalcedon (451) to Gregory the Great (590–604), part 2: *The Church of Constantinople in the Sixth Century*, translated by John Cawte and Pauline Allen (London: Mowbray/Louisville: Westminster John Knox Press, 1995) 563: "neo-Chalcedonianism" in the index; Hans-Joachim Schulz, *Die byzantinische Liturgie: Glaubenszeugnis und Symbolgestalt*, Sophia Bd. 5, dritte, völlig überarbeitete und actualisierte Auflage (Trier: Paulinus Verlag, 2000) 86–87.

[50] That this contemporary, active, risen Christ present in the church through his Spirit was the chief focus of the New Testament church can be seen in the earliest New Testament writings, the authentic Pauline epistles, which say next to nothing about the historical details of Jesus' earthly life.

that at the name of Jesus every knee should bend,
in heaven and on earth and under the earth,
and every tongue confess that Jesus Christ is Lord,
to the glory of God the Father![51]

This lyrical creed summarizes the doctrinal basis for both Orthodox and Catholic liturgical theology in the paschal mystery of Christ, from his passover via the kenosis or self-emptying of his incarnation, passion, and crucifixion; then his exaltation via resurrection, ascension, and session at the right hand of the Father; to ultimate glorification in his celestial liturgy with the angels and saints before the throne of God.

These interdependent doctrines, seminal to the Byzantine worldview, are like successive links in a chain, each one an essential aspect of the Byzantine vision, each flowing directly from its predecessor, the whole grounded in the incarnation of the God-man Jesus. This incarnation not only bridged the gulf between divinity and humankind. It also made God's saving dispensation a permanently present reality one could represent in icon and actually re-present again in ritual, thus turning Christian ritual into a dynamic, living icon of the saving work of Jesus.[52]

---

[51] It is paraphrased in the Post-sanctus of the Byzantine Anaphora of St. Basil: *L'Eucologio Barberini gr. 336*, ed. Stefano Parenti and Elena Velkovska. Seconda edizione riveduta con traduzione in lingua italiana, BELS 80 (Rome: CLV—Ed. liturgiche, 2000) par. 15.2; Frank E. Brightman, *Liturgies Eastern and Western* (Oxford: Clarendon, 1896) 403–4.

[52] Except, of course, for the Inconoclasts: see Alexander P. Kazhdan and Giles Constable, *People and Power in Byzantium: An Introduction to Modern Byzantine Studies* (Washington: Dumbarton Oaks Center for Byzantine Studies, 1982) 86–90; Vladimir Lossky, "Tradition and Traditions," in idem and Léonide Ouspensky, *The Meaning of Icons*, trans. G. E. H. Palmer and E. Kadloubovsky (Crestwood: St. Vladimir Seminary Press, 1982) 9–22, here 14: ". . . the defenders of the holy images founded the possibility of Christian iconography on the fact of the Incarnation of the Word." As Saint John Damascene (ca. 675–d. 749) teaches: "In former times God, who is without form or body, could never be depicted, But now when God is seen in the flesh . . . I make an image of the God whom I see": *First Apology Against Those Who Attack the Divine Images* 16, *Die Schriften des Johannes von Damaskos*, ed. Bonifatius Kotter. 6 vols. Patristische Texte und Studien 7, 12, 17, 22, 29, 60 (Berlin/New York: W. de Gruyter, 1969–2006) 3:89 = PG 94:1245A; English trans. from John of

In other words, Byzantine Orthodox Christians based the realism of their liturgy on faith in the reality of the risen Christ.[53] Because the risen Jesus is humanity glorified, he is present through his Spirit to every place and age not only as Savior, but as saving; not only as Lord, but as priest and sacrifice and victim. This is because nothing in his being or action is ever past except the historical mode of its manifestation. Hence Jesus is not extraneous to the heavenly-earthly liturgy of the church, but its first protagonist. As the Byzantine Liturgy prays: "You are the one who offers and is offered, who receives the offering and is given back to us!"[54] The Episcopalian theologian Thomas J. Talley put it this way:

> By virtue of the resurrection, Christ is now trans-historical and is available to every moment. We may never speak of the Risen Christ in the historical past. The event of his passion is historical, but the Christ who is risen does not exist back there, but here, and as we live on this moving division line between memory and hope, between the memory of his passion and the hope of his coming again, we stand always in the presence of Christ, who is always present to everyone. *This is where the real substance of our anamnesis lies.*[55]

Of course there is a sense in which every historical event lives on in its effects and in its remembering. But in the Catholic and Orthodox traditions, the basis for liturgical anamnesis is not psychological recall but theophany, an active, faith encounter *now* with the *present* saving activity of Christ. For what Christ was and did, he still is and does: it

---

Damascus, *On the Divine Images: Three Apologies Against Those Who Attack the Divine Images*, trans. David Anderson (Crestwood: St. Vladimir Seminary Press, 1980) 23.

[53] For a fuller presentation of these theological concepts, see Taft, *Beyond East and West*, chs. 1 and esp. 13; idem, *The Liturgy of the Hours*, ch. 21.

[54] Brightman, *Liturgies*, 378. On this prayer and the phrase in question, see Robert F. Taft, *A History of the Liturgy of St. John Chrysostom*, 2: *The Great Entrance. A History of the Transfer of Gifts and Other Preanaphoral Rites*, 4th ed., OCA 200 (Rome: Pontificio Istituto Orientale, 2004) ch. 3, esp. 135–41.

[55] From his unpublished class notes on the liturgical year, which Father Talley, then Professor of Liturgy at the General Theological Seminary of the Episcopal Church in New York, kindly placed at my disposition several years ago (emphasis added).

is he who both preaches his Word and is the Word he preaches, he who calls us to himself, he who binds the wounds of our sin and washes us in the waters of salvation, he who feeds us with his own life, he who is the pillar of fire leading us across the horizon of our own salvation history, lighting our sin-darkened path. He does it in word and sacrament—not only there, but certainly there. That is why at Christmas the Byzantine liturgy speaks in the present tense: "Christ is born, glorify him! Christ comes from heaven, go forth to meet him! Christ is on earth, exult!"—not *was* born, *came* from heaven, *was* on earth, but *is* born, *comes* from heaven, *is* on earth.[56]

In this theology, church ritual constitutes not only a *representation* but also a *re-presentation*—a rendering present again—of the earthly saving work of Christ. This vision, common also to the patristic West, was canonized for all time in the pithy summary of Pope Saint Leo I, the Great (440–461): "*Quod . . . Redemptoris nostri conspicuum fuit, in sacramenta transivit*—What was visible in our Redeemer has passed over into sacraments"[57]—i.e., what Jesus did during his earthly ministry remains permanently, visibly, tangibly available in mystery, through the liturgical ministry of the church. Saint Symeon of Thessalonika (d. 1429) puts the same teaching in Byzantine theological dress:

> There is one and the same church, above and below, since God came and appeared among us, and was seen in our form and accomplished what he did for us. And the Lord's priestly activity and communion and contemplation constitute one single work, which is carried out at the same time both above and here below, but with this difference: above it is done without veils and symbols, but here it is accomplished through symbols . . .[58]

---

[56] Irmos of Ode 1 of the canon of Christmas Matins: trans. adapted from *The Festal Menaion*, 269. On this theology see Perl, "Central Themes in Byzantine Theology," 53. For the identical liturgical theology in the Latin patristic tradition, see Marie-Bernard de Soos, *Le mystère liturgique d'après s. Léon le grand*, Liturgiewissenschaftliche Quellen und Forschungen 34 (Münster: Aschendorff, 1958).

[57] Pope Leo I, *Sermon 24—On the Ascension 2, 2*, PL 54:398.

[58] *Dialogue Against All Heresies 131*, PG 155:340AB (trans. adapted from Nicholas Constas).

For the Byzantines, then, the church's earthly song of praise is but the icon, the reflection—in the Pauline sense of *mysterion*, a visible appearance that is bearer of the reality it represents—of the heavenly liturgy of the risen Lord before the throne of God. As such, it is an ever-present, vibrant participation in the heavenly worship of God's Son. That is why the Byzantine would have found nothing surprising about the teaching of *Sacrosanctum Concilium*, the December 4, 1961, Vatican Council II Constitution on the Sacred Liturgy (pars. 7-8, 83), that when the church proclaims the Scriptures, preaches the Word, celebrates the Supper of the Lord, and sings the Divine Praises in the Hours, it is Christ himself who does so in and through the voice of the assembly.[59]

---

[59] See *Vatican Council II: The Conciliar and Post Conciliar Documents*, ed. Austin Flannery (Collegeville, MN: Liturgical Press, 1975) 4–5, 24.

Chapter 5

Prayers Addressed to Christ in the West Syrian Tradition

Baby Varghese
Kottayam

Early Syriac theology is characterized by a high christology in which a maximalism of the divine element in Christ is regularly found.[1] The mediatorship of Christ was not so central in early Syriac thought, which rather highlighted the glorified Christ seated at the right hand of God the Father. This christology finds its earliest liturgical expression in the concluding doxology of the Syriac *Didascalia*:

> Now to him . . . [who] was taken up to heaven by the power of God his Father and of the Holy Spirit, and sat on the right hand of the throne of God Almighty upon the cherubim; to him who is coming with power and glory to judge the dead and the living: to him be dominion and glory and majesty and kingdom, and to his Father and to the Holy

---

[1] This would perhaps explain why almost all early Syriac writers (*Acts of Thomas, Acts of John*, Aphrahat, Ephrem, *Doctrine of Addai*, etc.) speak of the incarnation as "putting on a body." The clothing imagery was suitable to emphasize the priority of the divinity in the life and work of Jesus Christ. For a study of this theme see S. Brock, "Clothing Metaphors as a Means of Theological Expression in Syriac Tradition," in *Typus, Symbol, Allegorie bei den östlichen Vätern und ihren Parallelen im Mitteralter*, ed. M. Schmidt and C. F. Geyer, Eichstäter Beiträge 4 (Regensburg: Pustet, 1982) 15–16, and the illustrative texts. Saint Ephrem even says that Mary conceived through her ear (*Hymns on the Church* 49:7, in *Hymnes de Ecclesia*, ed. E. Beck. CSCO 198/199, Scriptores Syri 84/85 [Louvain: Secrétariat du CorpusSCO, 1960]). See the references in R. Murray, "Mary, the Second Eve in the Early Syrian Fathers," *Eastern Churches Review* 3 (1971) 374–75.

Spirit; who was, and is, and endures, both now and for all generations to the ages of ages, Amen.[2]

The exaltation of the divine nature of Christ finds its expression in the liturgical tradition by addressing prayers to Christ, a usual feature of early Syriac prayers, attested since *The Odes of Solomon*. The forty-second ode has placed the following words on the lips of Christ, who descended into Sheol, and claims that the souls of the departed prayed to him:

> And I made a congregation of living among his dead;
> And I spoke with them by living lips;
> In order that my word may not be unprofitable.
> And those who had died ran towards me;
> And they cried out and said, Son of God, have pity on us.
> And deal with us according to Thy kindness,
> And bring us out from the bonds of darkness.
> And open for us the door
> By which we may come to Thee;
> For we perceive that our death does not touch Thee.
> May we also be saved with Thee,
> Because Thou art our Saviour.
> Then I heard their voice,
> And placed their faith in my heart.
> And placed my name upon their head,
> Because they are free and they are mine.[3]

PRAYERS ADDRESSED TO CHRIST IN THE APOCRYPHAL LITERATURE

The apocryphal literature, both in Greek and Syriac, attests a liturgical tradition in which prayers were usually addressed to Christ.[4] Scholars have often exaggerated the heretical character of the liturgical

---

[2] *Didascalia* 6.23, in *The Didascalia Apostolorum in Syriac*, ed. A. Vööbus, CSCO 402, 408, Scriptores Syri 176, 180 (Louvain: Secrétariat du CorpusSCO, 1979).

[3] *Ode* 42:14–20 in *The Odes of Solomon*, ed. J. H. Charlesworth (Oxford: Clarendon Press, 1973) 145–46. By permission of Oxford University Press.

[4] See A. Gerhards, *Die griechische Gregoriosanaphora: Ein Beitrag zur Geschichte des eucharistischen Hochgebets*. Liturgiewissenschaftlichen Quellen und Forschungen 65 (Münster-Westfalen: Aschendorff, 1984) 180–210.

elements in this literature. A large part of it enjoyed popularity in the Orthodox tradition; several works were written to popularize the ideas of martyrdom, asceticism, and spirituality, and to claim apostolic authority for liturgical practices. In the apocryphal acts or histories the apostles are presented as perfect missionaries who preach, perform miracles, convert, baptize, and celebrate the Eucharist. Prayers, both sacramental and non-sacramental, are attributed to them. Striking differences exist between the Syriac and Greek versions of the New Testament apocryphal works; this suggests that early Christian churches or sects felt free to adapt or revise them to suit their interests. Recent studies have demonstrated that at least some of them had their origin in Orthodox circles, and were used by the heretical groups with interpolations.[5]

The baptismal tradition witnessed by the *Acts of Thomas* agrees with the early Syriac baptismal liturgy and theology attested by the *Didascalia Apostolorum*, Aphrahat, and Saint Ephrem. The *History of John, Son of Zebedee* (or *Acts of John*) witnesses a rather developed fourth- or early-fifth-century baptismal liturgy, but the eucharistic prayers in it seem to be more archaic. A few prayers will illustrate the liturgical tendencies of the early Syriac tradition. The most striking aspect of the early Syriac liturgical tradition, as witnessed by the *Acts of Thomas*, is the prayers addressed to Christ with or without trinitarian reference. For the early Syriac Christians this was a way to confess their christology, giving emphasis to the divinity of Christ and his equality with God the Father. The person and work of the Holy Spirit was not yet clearly defined. A detailed discussion of the orthodoxy of the liturgical portions, and a comparison with the Greek or related versions, is not intended here.

The exaltation of the divinity is evident in the Syriac *Acts of Thomas*, an apocryphal work originally written in Syriac in the middle of the third century.[6] The liturgical portions of the *Acts* represent the late-second- and early-third-century liturgical traditions of the Syriac

[5] See H. J. W. Drijvers, "Facts and Problems in Early Syriac-Speaking Christianity," in *The Second Century. A Journal of Early Christian Studies* 2 (Abilene: Second Century Journal, 1982) 157–75; repr. in idem, *East of Byzantium: Studies in Early Syriac Christianity* (London: Variorum Reprints, 1984).

[6] Syriac text and English translation as *Acts of Judas Thomas* in W. Wright, *Apocryphal Acts of the Apostles*. 2 vols. (London: Williams and Norgate, 1871; repr. Amsterdam, 1968) (=AAA). Wright's translation was reproduced with di-

speaking churches of Mesopotamia.[7] The most striking feature of this tradition, as we have already noted, is the prayers addressed to Christ. In addition to the accounts of the baptism and Eucharist, there are more than a dozen prayers of various lengths addressed to Christ.[8]

The *Acts of Thomas* contains five baptismal accounts. Four of these contain formulae of anointing or blessing of the oil addressed to Christ or to the "Name of the Messiah."[9] They represent various stages of the development of the early Syriac liturgy and will be discussed in the order of their development.

1. In the baptism of General Sifur and his family (chs. 131–32)— which probably represents the oldest baptismal tradition attested in the *Acts*—oil was poured over the head of the candidates with a glorification of the Name of the Messiah:

> Glory to thee, (thou) beloved fruit!
> Glory to thee, (thou) name of the Messiah!
> Glory to thee, (thou) hidden power that dwellest in the Messiah![10]

Then they were baptized in the name of the Father, and the Son, and the Holy Spirit.

---

vision into chapters by A. F. J. Klijn, *The Acts of Thomas: Introduction, Text, Commentary.* Supplement to NovumTestamentum 5 (Leiden: Brill, 1962).

[7] As Yves Tissot has pointed out ("Les Actes de Thomas, exemple de recueil composite," in *Les actes apocryphes des apôtres* [Paris: Labor et Fides, 1981] 221–32), the *Acts of Thomas* is a composite writing and must first of all be analyzed and understood in its different parts. Thus we can see both orthodox and heretical elements in it.

[8] Chs. 10, 25, 39, 47, 53, 67, 80, 81, 97, 122, 153, 167. The final prayer of the apostle Thomas (ch. 167) is reminiscent of Saint Stephen's prayer (Acts 7:59-60). See also the prayer of the bridegroom (ch. 15) and prayer by a young man (ch. 35). The prayer of Thomas in chapter 70 is addressed to the Holy Trinity. The Hymn of Praise by Thomas (absent in Klijn's edition) is indifferently addressed to the Father and the Son (AAA, 2:245–51). Two confessions (chs. 65, 72) give an excellent summary of early Syriac christology.

[9] See B. Varghese, *Les onctions baptismales dans la tradition syrienne.* CSCO 512, Subsidia 82 (Louvain: E. Peeters, 1989) 3–33, and G. Winkler, "Original Meaning of the Pre-baptismal Anointing and Its Implications," *Worship* 52 (1978) 24–45.

[10] AAA 2:267.

2. In the baptism of King Gundaphorus (chs. 26–28), the Name of the Messiah is invoked over the oil, which is apparently identified with the Holy Spirit. As in Sifur's case, oil was poured over the head of the candidate with a prayer:

> Come, holy name of the Messiah; come, power of grace, which art from on high; come, perfect mercy; come, exalted gift; come, sharer of the blessing; come, revealer of hidden mysteries; come, mother of seven houses, whose rest was in the eighth house; come, messenger of reconciliation, and communicate with the minds of these youths; come, Spirit of holiness, and purify their reins and their hearts.[11]

Then follows the baptism in the name of the Holy Trinity.

3. In the baptism of Mygdonia (chs. 120–21), which represents a further stage, an epiclesis is addressed to Jesus. The apostle Thomas took the oil and poured it on her head and said:

> Holy oil, which was given to us for unction, and hidden mystery of the Cross, which is seen through it—Thou, the straightener of crooked limbs, Thou, our Lord Jesus, life and health and remission of sins,—let Thy power come and abide upon this oil, and let Thy holiness dwell in it.[12]

The apostle anointed her head, her nurse was asked to anoint her body, and then she was baptized in the name of the Holy Trinity.

4. In the baptism of Vizan the prince, and certain women (ch. 157), the invocation over the oil is directly addressed to Christ.

> Fair Fruit, that art worthy to be glowing with the word of holiness, that men may put Thee on and conquer through Thee their enemies, when they have been cleansed from their former works,—yea, Lord, come, abide upon this oil, as Thou didst abide upon the tree, and they who crucified Thee were not able to bear Thy word. Let Thy gift come, which Thou didst breathe upon Thine enemies, and they went backward and fell upon their faces, and let it abide upon this oil, over which we name Thy name.

Then the apostle poured the oil over their heads and said: "In Thy name, Jesus the Messiah, let it be to these persons for the remission of

---

[11] Ibid., 2:166–67.
[12] Ibid., 2:189.

offences and sins, and for the destruction of the enemy, and for the healing of their souls and bodies." Judas Thomas himself anointed the body of Vizan, and asked Mygdonia to anoint the body of the women. As usual, they were baptized in the name of the Holy Trinity.

There is no reason to doubt the orthodoxy of the baptismal rite, which follows the early Syriac tradition in which anointing always preceded the immersion. The baptism of Vizan (ch. 157) agrees with the rite attested by the Syriac *Didascalia* (ch. 16).

This helps us to believe in the orthodoxy of the accounts of the eucharistic celebrations found in the *Acts of Judas Thomas*. These usually follow the baptisms, and further attest the tradition of addressing prayers to Christ.[13] Among the six accounts of the Eucharist (chs. 26–27, 29, 49–50, 121, 133, and 158), three give the prayers, probably representing three different stages in the evolution of the rites.

1. The Eucharist that follows the baptism of Sifur (ch. 133) seems to represent the oldest liturgical tradition attested in the *Acts of Judas Thomas*. Immediately after the baptism the apostle brought bread and wine, placed it on the table, and said the following blessing:

> "Living bread, the eaters of which die not! Bread, that fillest hungry souls with thy blessing! Thou that art worthy to receive the gift and to be for the remission of sins, that those who eat thee may not die! We name the name of the Father over thee; we name the name of the Son over thee; we name the name of the Spirit over thee, the exalted name that is hidden from all." And he said: "In Thy name, Jesus, may the power of the blessing and the thanksgiving come and abide upon this bread, that all the souls, which take of it, may be renewed, and their sins may be forgiven them" (ch. 133).[14]

2. After the baptism of a certain woman who had been possessed by a devil and was healed (no anointing is attested), the apostle asked his

---

[13] See G. Rouwhorst, "Bénédictions, action des grâces, supplications: Les oraisons de la table dans le Judaïsme et les célébrations eucharistiques des chrétiens syriaques." *Questions liturgiques* 61 (1980) 211–40, esp. 221–29, and "La célébration de l'eucharistie selons les Actes de Thomas," in *Omnes Circumadstantes: Contributions towards a History of the Role of the People in the Liturgy, Presented to Herman Wegman*, ed. C. Caspers and M. Schneiders, (Kampen: J. H. Kok, 1990) 51–77.

[14] AAA, 2:268.

deacon to make ready the Eucharist (chs. 49–50). The deacon brought a bench, spread over it a linen cloth, and placed on it "the bread of blessing." Judas Thomas stood beside it and said:

> Jesus, who hast deemed us worthy to draw nigh unto Thy holy Body and to partake of Thy life-giving Blood; and because of our reliance upon Thee we are bold and draw nigh, and invoke Thy holy Name, which has been proclaimed by the Prophets as Thy Godhead willed; and Thou art preached by Thy Apostles through the whole world according to Thy grace, and art revealed by Thy mercy to the just; we beg of Thee that Thou wouldest come and communicate with us for help and for life, and for the conversion of Thy servants unto Thee, that they may go under Thy pleasant yoke and under Thy victorious power, and that it may be unto them for the health of their souls and for the life of their bodies in Thy living world (ch. 49).[15]

Then the Holy Spirit was invoked:

> Come, gift of the Exalted; come perfect mercy; come, holy Spirit . . . come, power of the Father and wisdom of the Son, for Ye are one in all; come and communicate with us in this Eucharist which we celebrate, and in this offering which we offer, and in this commemoration which we make.[16]

He made the sign of the cross upon the bread and gave it to everyone saying: "Let this Eucharist be unto you for life and rest, and for judgment and vengeance." And they said, "Amen" (ch. 50).

3. In the Eucharist that follows the baptism of Vizan and certain women, the prayer over "bread and mingled cup" is an invocation/ anamnesis addressed to Christ:

> Thy holy Body, which was crucified for our sake, we eat, and Thy life-giving Blood, which was shed for our sake, we drink. Let Thy Body be to us for life, and Thy Blood for the remission of sins. For the gall which thou drankest for us, let the bitterness of our enemy be taken away from us. And for Thy drinking vinegar for our sake, let our weakness be strengthened. And (for) the spit which thou didst receive for us, let us

---

[15] AAA, 2:189.
[16] Ibid., 2:189–90.

94

receive Thy perfect life. And because Thou didst receive the crown of thorns for us, let us receive from Thee the crown that withereth not. And because Thou wast wrapped in a linen cloth for us, let us be girt with Thy mighty strength, which cannot be overcome. And because Thou wast buried in a new sepulchre for our mortality, let us too receive intercourse with Thee in Heaven. And as Thou didst arise, let us be raised, and let us stand before Thee at the Judgment of truth (ch. 158).[17]

He broke the Eucharist and gave to Vizan and the women and said: "Let this Eucharist be to you for life and rest and joy and health, and for healing of your souls and of your bodies." And they said, "Amen."

Though the second account (ch. 50) mentions bread only, it may refer to the entire eucharistic celebration (Acts 2:42, 46; 20:7; Luke 24:30). When we consider the eucharistic rites in the *Acts of Judas Thomas* along with the baptismal accounts, we have no reason to doubt their orthodoxy.[18]

The most striking characteristic of the eucharistic prayers in the *Acts of Judas Thomas* is the invocation of the Name, which corresponds to the third part of the Jewish meal prayer *Birkat-ha-Mazon*. In *Birkat-ha-Yerusalayim* the Name is related to the "dwelling of God's glory": "Have mercy, JHWH our God, upon Thy people Israel, upon Thy city Jerusalem, upon Zion the abiding place of Thy Glory, upon the Kingdom of the house of David Thine anointed, and upon the great and holy house that was called by Thy Name . . ." In the eucharistic prayers of the *Acts of Judas Thomas* the idea of dwelling may be implied in the demand "come!" In the baptismal invocation in chs. 120–21 and 157 "come" and "dwelling" are mutually related: "let Thy power come and abide upon this oil, and let Thy holiness dwell in it" (121); "Lord, come, abide upon this oil . . . over which we name Thy name" (157).[19]

The invocation of the Name is a tradition that the early church inherited from Judaism. In Judaism "Name" stands for the person, and the invocation of the Name means the invocation of the personal presence

---

[17] Ibid., 2:290.

[18] I am mindful that scholars have pointed out elements of Encratism in the *Acts of Judas Thomas*; see Y. Tissot, "L'entratisme des Actes de Thomas," *Aufstieg und Niedergang der römischen Welt* 25–26 (1988) 4415–30.

[19] AAA, 2:158, 289.

of God.[20] According to Jean Daniélou, in the Pauline letters and in Saint John's Gospel "Name" seems to denote the divine nature of Christ that he shares with the Father and the Holy Spirit.[21] The application of the theology of the Name to Jesus Christ was a testimonial of his divinity, for Name means Jesus in his character as God and Savior. Invocation of the Name implies the knowledge of the person invoked and a personal relationship with him. It is a request with love and confidence for his presence and action. Above all, it is an act of communion. Thus the prayers addressed to Christ are, most probably, the survival of the Judeo-Christian tradition of invoking the Name of Christ.

The liturgical traditions attested by the Syriac *Acts of John* represent a further stage of development.[22] A long prayer by John (that he prayed on his way to Ephesus) narrates the *mirabilia Christi*, and it gives the theological basis for the prayer *ad Christum*: "And Thou hast said, and we have heard with our ears of flesh, 'I and My Father are one' (John 10:30), and 'he that hath seen Me, hath seen the Father' (John 14:9); and in this confidence, Lord, my youth beseeches Thee to hear my prayer."[23] According to this prayer no contradiction exists between prayer *ad Patrem* and prayer *ad Christum*, for Christ is coeternal with his Father: "And whatsoever I ask of Thy Father in Thy name, He will give to me (John 16:16); and nothing shall be too difficult for one

---

[20] See J. Dupont, "Nom de Jésus," in *Dictionnaire de la Bible, Supplément* 6:514–41 (Paris: Letouzy et Ané, 1960).

[21] See J. Daniélou, *Théologie du Judéo-christianisme* (Paris: Desclée, 1958), 20; for the use of "Name" in the baptismal and eucharistic liturgies, ibid., 206–9.

[22] In their edition of the *Acts of John* (Acta Iohannis. 2 vols. Corpus Christianorum, Series Apocrypha 1–2 [Turnhout: Brepols, 1983]), Eric Junod and Jean-Daniel Kaestli conclude that the work was edited in the second half of the second century in Egypt, and that chapters 94–102 and 109 are of Syrian origin, probably in the Oriental Valentinian milieu, and were inserted in the work during the third century. The baptismal liturgy of the Syriac *Acts* represents a fourth- or early fifth-century tradition. See A. F. J. Klijn, "An Ancient Syriac Baptismal Liturgy in the Syriac Acts of John." *Novum Testamentum* 6 (1963) 216–28. According to R. H. Miller, "Liturgical Materials in the Acts of John," in *Studia Patristica* 13, 375–81, Texte und Untersuchungen 116 (Berlin: Akademie-Verlag, 1975) 375–81, the liturgical materials in the *Acts of John* are orthodox.

[23] AAA, 2:6.

of those who believe in Thee (Mark 9:23), but whatsoever they ask, they shall receive (Matt 7:7; 21:22)."[24] Whether we pray to the Father or to the Son, the prayer is addressed to the one true God. Thus one of John's prayers begins by addressing the Father and then turns to the Son, a feature found in several West Syrian prayers, especially in the *Sedre*:

> Lord God, strong and mighty, long suffering and abounding in grace, Thou art He who from the first didst show Thy long suffering for a hundred years, on those (who were) called to repentance . . . until the flood came and swept away that whole generation. And Thou art He who didst send Thy only-(begotten and) dear Son, that the world might have life through Him; and He came and did good deeds like Thee, because He proceeded from Thee. . . . This mercy, then, which is eternally in Thee, is also found in Thy Son, for Ye are one. Turn, Lord! The heart of these erring ones, who, lo, are shouting and crying out before devils. . . . Thou didst die once, and didst raise us to life with Thyself. . . . Hear the prayer of Thy servant John, and let me enter this city, bearing the sign of Thy Cross; and direct my path to the right hand. . . .[25]

The Syriac document called *The Decease of Saint John* contains three prayers addressed to Christ, the second being a eucharistic prayer.[26] The Eucharist that John offered before his death makes no reference to the wine. A rather simple benediction was pronounced over the bread:

> What praise, or what offering [*qurbono*], or what thanksgiving, when we break the bread, shall we render unto Thee? But Thyself alone, Thee Jesus the Messiah, we praise, the Name of the Father which was spoken. We glorify Thy entrance by the door; we glorify the resurrection, which through Thee has been announced unto us; we glorify Thy word, Thy

[24] Ibid.

[25] Ibid., 2:10–11.

[26] Syriac text and English translation in AAA (2:61–68); Greek version in W. Schneemelcher, ed. *New Testament Apocrypha*, 2 (Louisville: Westminster John Knox, 1992). There is a striking difference between the Greek *Acts of John*, the Syriac *History of John*, and the Syriac *Decease of Saint John*. For the three prayers in question, see in the Greek version chapters 108, 109, 112. The Greek version, chapters 85–86, contains another account of the Eucharist, which is absent in the Syriac.

glory, Thy ineffable pearl, Thy treasury, Thy net, Thy greatness, Him who for our sake was called the Son of Man, the truth, the freedom of speech, the liberty which (is) in Thee as in the truth. For Thou art the Lord, who wast called the root of immortality, and the fountain of incorruption, and the foundation of the universe. Because of this we acknowledge Thy majesty, which is now invisible.[27]

John's last prayer is an example of the early Syriac tendency to exalt the divinity:

God, who hast chosen us for the apostleship of the nations; who hast sent us to the world; who hast shown Thyself through Thy Apostles; who hast never been at rest from the foundations of the world, but who constantly hast saved those who were able (to be saved); who hast made Thyself known through all nature, and hast proclaimed Thyself even among the beasts; who hast made the desolate soul that had become savage, be peaceable and quiet; who, when it was thirsting for Thy word, hast given Thyself to it; who, when it was dead, hast quickly appeared unto it: who, when it was plunged in sin, hast alone shown Thyself unto it; who, when it was overcome by Satan, hast already manifested Thyself unto it: who hast not left it to be agitated like a body; who hast shown it its enemy; who hast made a clean union; God Jesus, Father of those that are above the heavens, and Lord of the celestials, and God of the celestials (. . .); receive the soul of Thy John. . . .[28]

Similar prayers are found in the later West Syriac tradition. Though the account speaks of the offering of the bread only ("And when he had asked for bread, he prayed thus. . . ."; "And when he had broken the bread,"[29]), the prayers are rather orthodox in content.

Similar prayers are attested in the other apocryphal works such as *The History of Philip the Apostle and Evangelist*,[30] *The History of Mar Mathew and Mar Andrew, the Blessed Apostles*,[31] *The Epistle to the*

---

[27] AAA, 2:63–64; cf. Greek chs. 109–110, *New Testament Apocrypha*, ed. Schneemelcher, 2:201–2. In the Greek version the prayer is much longer.

[28] AAA, 2:65–66; cf. Greek chs. 112–14.

[29] AAA, 2:63, 64.

[30] AAA, 1:74–79; Syr 2:69–92 (English translation).

[31] AAA, 1:102–26; 2:93–115.

Laodiceans,[32] etc. These prayers are directed to Christ with or without a trinitarian reference. In *The History of Philip* Christ, in a prayer addressed to him, is qualified as "Son of God, Jesus the Messiah, the Power and Wisdom of His Father."[33] Similar prayers are found in the *The History of Mar Mathew and Mar Andrew*.

The liturgical tradition attested is apparently Syrian. Thus Philip made (*rsm*) the sign (*rûsmô*) upon the gate of the prison in which Mathew was imprisoned. Though Satan sent seven demons to kill Andrew, they fled as they saw "the seal (*hatmo*) of the Messiah between his eyes." Andrew baptized the inhabitants of the "City of Dogs" "in the name of the Father and the Son and the Spirit of holiness."[34]

PRAYERS ADDRESSED TO CHRIST
IN EARLY SYRIAN ORTHODOX EPIPHANY SERVICES
The structure of West Syrian liturgical services such as the consecration of water in baptism and on the feast of the Epiphany, the consecration of Myron, and the ordination, has been inspired by that of the anaphora. To a certain extent these services have retained the structure and orientation of the early Syriac anaphoras. Even when the anaphoras underwent revisions or interpolations, these liturgies remained rather faithful to the original form and spirit. We have a few manuscripts of the Epiphany service, written in the tenth or eleventh centuries. Most probably they represent an earlier tradition that might go back to the seventh or eighth century. Thus in a tenth- or eleventh-century manuscript (*London, BL Add. 14495*), the *Sedra* is absent. (The *Sedra* form of prayer has been attributed to the Patriarch John I, d. 648.) In its place we find an earlier form, known as the "prayer of incense," in which the *promiun* or introductory part of the *Sedra* is still absent. In *BL Add. 14495* a long prayer of incense that follows the

---

[32] This Marcionite document (attributed to Saint Paul) has placed the following prayer on the lips of Saint Paul: "I thank Christ in all my prayer that you are steadfast in him and persevering in his works, in expectation of the promise for the day of judgment" (*New Testament Apocrypha*, ed. Schneemelcher, 2:44).

[33] AAA, 2:79. See the prayers *ad Christum*, pp. 71, 79. A prayer with a trinitarian reference is: "The True God is One, Our Lord Jesus the Messiah, and with Him His Father, and His holy Spirit, to whom be glory and honour and praise and worship in all generations, forever and ever" (2:92).

[34] AAA, 2:121, 2:110, 2:102, 2:114.

censing ("the priest shall burn incense and shall say the following prayer") has been addressed to the Son and illustrates very well the contents of Syriac prayers *ad Christum* during the first millennium:

> O Maker of the Worlds and Creator of things, both those which are visible and those which are invisible; Thou Light immaterial Who wast born in the beginning; Who didst prepare for the angelic hosts a habitation which was fair . . .; Who didst lay the foundations of the earth with radiance upon the waters, and didst adorn it with flowers of divers kinds . . .; in Whose image and likeness man was created, and Who hast shown Thyself [to be] the King of the Universe: by Thy coming in the flesh Thou hast restored to his former divine estate man who had fallen therefrom through his own negligence, inasmuch as he erred through the counsel of a woman, and Thou hast washed away from him by the washing of the second birth the filth which had come upon him; do Thou now, O Lord, Who hast brought us unto this hour, be among us, and in driving away from our souls the darkness of ignorance fill us with that light which is above the world, and guide us [so that we walk] without fault to the wholly perfect and threefold light of the incomprehensible Trinity, and lighten the eyes of our minds with rays of heavenly light, and show us the sons of light, and by the descent (*magnnuto*) of Thy Most Holy Spirit change the nature of this water [so that it may become] a fountain of healing, and fill it with the heavenly gift, that it may be for a help unto those who draw therefrom, and may become the water which springeth up unto everlasting life . . .; for Thou Thyself art the Dispenser of perfect gifts, and to Thee are fitting glory and honour from all created beings, both those which are in heaven, and those which are upon earth; together with Thy Father and Thy Holy Spirit, now and always. Amen.[35]

This prayer shows that the Syrian Orthodox tradition had faithfully followed the early Syriac tendency of "the maximalism of the divinity." Christ is addressed using the same images and titles as God the Father; the Holy Spirit is understood as the "Spirit of Christ" ("Thy Most Holy Spirit"). The service contains four long prayers, and three are addressed to Christ. The fourth prayer, addressed to the Father, ends with a trinitarian doxology with a christological emphasis: "through Jesus, our Lord, unto Whom are meet praise, and honour,

---

[35] E. A. Wallis Budge, ed. and trans., *The Blessing of the Waters on the Eve of the Epiphany* (London: Henry Frowde, 1901) 67–70.

and dominion, with Thee, and Thy Most Holy, and good, and ador-
able, and life-making Spirit, Who is equal unto Thee in being,
now. . . ."[36]

Another Epiphany service is found in *London BL. Add. 14499* (tenth/
eleventh century).[37] The rite is more developed and begins with a trinitarian doxology: "Glory be to God (*âlôhô*), and to the Son, and to the
Holy Spirit."[38] This service contains four prayers, the first—a short
prayer—is addressed to the Trinity. The fourth prayer (the same as the
fourth prayer in *Add. 14495*) is addressed to the Father. The second
and the third are rather long and both are addressed to Christ, emphasizing his divinity and enumerating his attributes. Both are similar to
the prayer quoted above. In the second prayer the Holy Trinity has
been qualified as "Thy holy, and coequal, and uncreated, and everlasting Trinity."[39] The third prayer contains an invocation of Christ:

> Thou didst bless the child of nature, and Thou didst by Thy birth sanc-
> tify the virgin womb, and all creation praised Thee when Thou wast re-
> vealed. For Thou, O our God, didst appear upon the earth, and with the
> children of men Thou didst live and move. Thou didst sanctify for us
> the floods of Jordan when Thy Holy Spirit from heaven smote upon
> them, and Thou didst break the head of the dragon, which writhed
> therein. Do Thou then, O Lord Who lovest man, come (*thô*) now by the
> descent of Thy Holy Spirit, and sanctify these waters. Give unto them
> the grace of Jordan, and make them to be fountains of blessings, and
> gifts of holiness, and a loosing of sins, and a binding up of sickness, . . .
> For Thou art He Who by water and spirit didst renew our nature, which
> had become old through sin. Thou art He Who by water didst do away
> with the sin, which was in the days of Noah. Thou art He Who by the
> sea didst free the race of the Hebrews from the oppression of Pharaoh.
> Thou art He Who by water and fire didst deliver Israel from the error of
> Baal by the hands of Elijah the Prophet. And now, O our Lord, whilst
> sanctifying these waters by Thy Holy Spirit, grant unto those who touch
> them, or who partake of them, or who make use of them in any way
> whatsoever in true faith, praise, and holiness, and blessing, and purifi-
> cation, and health, so that by the material elements of the world, and by

[36] Ibid., 78.

[37] Ibid., 79–101.

[38] At least until the time of Moses Bar Kepha (d. 903) the Anaphora of Saint
James as well as other Syrian Orthodox anaphoras began with this doxology.

[39] Ibid., 91.

the children of men, and by angels, and by things visible, and by things invisible, [Thy Name may be praised, together with Thy Father and Thy Holy Spirit now] and always, and for ever and ever.[40]

A similar invocation of Christ is found in an ancient Coptic Epiphany service:

Thou didst sanctify the floods of the Jordan having drawn down upon them from heaven Thy Holy Spirit, and Thou didst break in pieces the heads of the dragons that were hidden therein. O Our Lord, Thou man-loving God, Jesus Christ, come again by the descent of Thy Holy Spirit.[41]

Prayers *ad Christum* can be found in the Epiphany services of the Syrian Orthodox, Coptic, and Armenian churches. The exaltation of the divinity, a common feature attested in them, is in no way a post-Chalcedonian phenomenon. Rather it is the survival of a pre-Nicene tradition. This would perhaps explain why the Epiphany was popular in the East in the early centuries, and also why Christian baptism was interpreted in terms of Christ's baptism and his anointing by the Holy Spirit.

PRAYERS ADDRESSED TO CHRIST IN THE ANAPHORA OF SAINT JAMES AND OTHER ANAPHORAS

In the Syriac anaphora of Saint James, as well as in all other West Syrian anaphoras, two prayers are addressed to Christ: the second part of the anamnesis and the final prayer of the anaphora. All other prayers are invariably addressed to God the Father. In the fourth century Antiochene anaphora, as we find it in the *Apostolic Constitutions* (8.12.38)

---

[40] Ibid., 91–96, here 94–96. An abridged version of this prayer is included in the present Epiphany service of the Syrian Orthodox Church. See Mar Athanasius Yeshue Samuel, ed., *Ma'de'dono: The Book of the Church Festivals* (Hackensack, NJ: Metropolitan Mar A. Y. Samuel, 1984), 65–69, and another version in Abraham Konat, ed., *Ktobo d-ma'de'dono* (Pampakuda: Mar Julius Press, 1984) 190–98.

[41] Budge, *The Blessing*, 130–31. The Coptic Epiphany service published by Budge (102–37) contains several prayers addressed to Christ. In the Armenian Epiphany service Christ is asked to sanctify the water; see F. C. Conybeare, *Rituale Armenorum* (Oxford: Clarendon Press, 1905) 177.

and in the Greek Saint James, the anamnesis is addressed to the Father. The Armenian and Ethiopian versions of Saint James follow the Syriac model. Does that mean that the West Syrians have modified these two prayers for christological reasons? I do not think that it is a post-Chalcedonian development. Most probably this is the survival of an earlier tradition. Originally the anamnesis of Saint James must have been addressed to the Father as a prelude to the epiclesis, and the West Syrians might have modified it, probably to make it conform to the Syro-Mesopotamian tradition, in which several prayers were addressed to Christ. The East Syrian Addai and Mari, and the Maronite Peter Sharar, have retained this feature. In the *Testamentum Domini* the anamnesis is addressed to the Son.

We have evidence that at least until the end of the ninth century prayers *ad Christum* existed in the West Syrian anaphoras, which were later modified. One of the letters of Jacob of Serug (d. 521) gives the impression that during his time the Sanctus was usually addressed to Christ:

> Now He alone, the Only Begotten, was born in a twofold way; one from the Father without body and without beginning; another corporeally, from the Virgin Mary, as it is said: "God was seen in the flesh" (cf. 1 Tim 3:16), and God had sent His Son, who was born from the woman (Gal 4:4). The Virgin Church was betrothed to Him Who was, Who is, (that is) to Jesus Christ, to Him, Who was yesterday, who is today and Who will be always (Ps 2:7). It is to that true bridegroom that the daughter of Light has been betrothed and therefore during the celebration of the mysteries, she addresses Him with the words of the Seraphim, as to His Father, because in the same way that she proclaims the Holy Father, she proclaims also a holy Son.[42]

Moses Bar Kepha (d. 903) also knew the tradition of addressing the Sanctus to the Son. Thus in his commentary on the Eucharist, after having explained the Sanctus as a prayer addressed to the Father, he writes: "Again, another manner of interpretation. Isaiah aforetime saw

[42] Jacob of Serug, "Lettre de Jacques de Saroug aux moines du couvent de Mar Bassus, et à Paul d'Edesse," trans. M. l'abbé Martin. *Zeitschrift der Deutschen Morgenländischen Gesellschaft* 30 (1876) 225.

one of the Holy Trinity, to wit the Son, who was to become man, sitting upon a high throne, and the seraphim standing about Him, etc."[43]

In the anaphora of John of Bosra, the conclusion of the institution narrative contains a prayer addressed to Christ, which is not found in any other West Syrian anaphoras:

> Do this for my remembrance. For when I said that I will be among you and I will give holiness to him who celebrates (it), for he who eats my body and drinks my blood abides in me and I in him, and as I live because of the Father, so he who eats me will live because of me. Therefore, as we have received this instruction as the institution of your laws, O Word of God, we prepare the bread and we mix the cup and therefore we proclaim your whole economy, from the former glory and the coming down and the condescension to passion, death and the cross and the God befitting resurrection.[44]

In the Anaphora of the Twelve Apostles, one of the oldest Syrian Orthodox anaphoras, the prayer over the veil is addressed to Christ:

> Before you, King of kings and Lord of lords, we worship and beseech You, O Lord, extend the right hand of Your mercies upon (us), Your servants who have bowed down before Your terrible might of greatness, and bless, protect, absolve, sanctify Your sheepfold that You have saved by Your pure blood. Make to shine Your terrible sign (*rûshmô*) upon them, so that the enemy may know that they are the saved sheep of your sheepfold.[45]

The usual anamnesis addressed to the Son follows.

In the ninth century, however, the Syrian Orthodox Church introduced a major liturgical reform. Thus in his commentary on the

---

[43] R. H. Connolly, ed., *Two Commentaries on the Jacobite Liturgy* (London: Williams and Norgate, 1931) 49. In his comments on the word *Hosanna* Bar Kepha writes: "The people then answer and say thus: Glory to the Son, who became incarnate for us and redeemed us" (51).

[44] H. G. Codrington, ed., "The Anaphora of John of Bosra," in *Anaphorae Syriacae* 11/1 (Rome: Pontificium Institutum Orientalium Studiorum, 1981) 20. The usual anamnesis addressed to the Son follows.

[45] A. Raes, ed., *The Anaphora of the Twelve Apostles (Prima)*, in *Anaphorae Syriacae* 1/2 (Rome: Pontificium Institutum Orientalium Studiorum, 1940) 214.

Eucharist, Moses Bar Kepha directs that if any prayer is addressed to Christ, it should be changed *ad Patrem*. After having commented on the last prayer of the anaphora of Saint James, Bar Kepha writes:

> Wherefore it is evident from these things that all the prayers of the Qurrabha are addressed to the Father, except this prayer, the last of all the prayers, which is addressed to the Son, wherein the priest confesses to the Son, because that through Him we have gained access to the Father, and He is the way that leads us, and the door that brings us in to the Father, according to His own unimpeachable and all-holy words. If therefore there be found in the Qurrabha any prayer whatsoever that is not addressed to the Father—whether it came about through the error of a scribe, or of a priest uninstructed and untrained in the divine Scriptures—we ought to correct it and cause it to be addressed to the Father, like the rest of the prayers throughout the Qurrabha, which are addressed to the Father; for the priest who offers holds the person of Christ, and in His place he acts as a mediator and stands between God and men. But it is right that that prayers which is the last of all the prayers should be addressed to the Son, because He became to us a means by which we might draw near to the Father. Wherefore let us confess and give thanks to Him in this prayer for that He is become to us the cause of this great benefit, and that when we were far off and rejected by His Father, in Him and through Him He called us and brought us near to Himself.[46]

According to Bar Kepha, the prayers of the anaphora are addressed to the Father, because "the priest who offers typically represents Christ Himself—who became a mediator of God and men."[47] The prayers *ad Patrem* are the prayers of Christ, addressed to his Father. Bar Kepha is the first Syrian Orthodox writer to explain the theological basis of the prayers of the anaphora, but his instruction was not strictly followed in the prayers of the preparation rites, pre-anaphora, *ordo communis*, and the post-Communion rites, which were composed between the eleventh and fifteenth centuries. Thus we can find several prayers *ad Christum* in them. Though the anaphora remained trinitarian in its orientation, the "accessories" of the eucharistic service were rather christological in their expression.

[46] Ibid., 90.
[47] Ibid., 89.

In the case of the preparation rites, most of the prayers are addressed to the Father, or to the three divine persons. The most ancient prayer of the preparation rites (found also in the Maronite liturgy) is a typical example: "Account us worthy, O Lord God, that having our hearts sprinkled (*kâd rsîsîn*) and cleansed from all things evil, we may enter into Thy great and exalted Holy of Holies. May we be enabled to stand in purity and holiness before Thy sacred altar, and in true faith offer reasonable and spiritual sacrifices unto Thee, O Father, Son and Holy Spirit, Amen."[48]

The preparation rites consist of two parts, each with a *Promiun-Sedro*. The *Promiun-Sedro* of the first part is addressed to the three divine persons, whereas that of the second part is to the Son (Athan. 7, 15-16). The *Hutomo* (conclusion) of both parts is addressed to the Son. Some of the prayers of the preparation of the bread and wine (also found in the Byzantine and East Syrian liturgies) are addressed to Christ.

All the seven prayers of commemoration said by the priest as he holds the paten and the chalice are addressed to the Son. Six among them begin with the following formula: "O God, Thou art the Sacrificial offering and to Thee the sacrifice is offered. Receive this offering from my weak and sinful hands . . ." (Athan. 13-14). Christ is both the one who receives the offering and the offering itself. The idea of Christ as the mediator is not as central in Syrian Orthodox liturgical thought as in the Latin West. Christ is regularly presented as "the one who receives the offering."[49] Even when the prayers refer to the sacrifice of Christ his role as the one who receives the sacrifice is emphasized. Thus in the *Hutomo* of the first part of the preparation rites we find:

[48] Samuel Athanasius, ed., *Anaphora: The Divine Liturgy of Saint James* (1967; published for liturgical use in the Syrian Orthodox Church of Antioch) (=Athan.), 9. This prayer is attested in the most ancient manuscripts of the pre-anaphora, e.g., *London, BL. Add. 14495* and *17128* (both tenth/eleventh century). On this prayer, see B. Varghese, 1998. "Early History of the Preparation Rites in the Syrian Orthodox Anaphora," in *Symposium Syriacum VII*, ed. R. Lavenant, 127–38. OCA 256 (Rome: Pontificio Instituto Orientale, 1998), and P. E. Gemayel, *Avant-messe Maronite*, OCA 174 (Rome: Pontificio Instituto Orientale, 1965).

[49] See the *Eqbo* (Termination) of the first part of the Preparation rites: "O Christ, who didst accept the sacrifice of the high-priest Melchizedek, accept, O Lord, the prayers of Thy servant and forgive the sins of Thy flock" (Athan. 8).

O pure spotless Lamb, Who offered Himself to the Father an acceptable offering for the expiation and redemption of the whole world, make us worthy that we may offer ourselves to Thee a living sacrifice well-pleasing to Thee after the manner of Thy Sacrifice for us. May we be accounted worthy to offer unto Thee, O Lord, sacrifices of praise and thanksgiving for a savour of spiritual sweetness. Let all our thoughts and words and actions be whole burnt-offerings unto Thee. Grant us, O Father, Son and Holy Spirit, to appear before Thee without blemish all the days of our life, and ever be well-pleasing to Thy Godhead.[50]

In the prayers Christ is always addressed as the Son of God, the second person of the Holy Trinity, who receives the prayers along with the Father and the Holy Spirit.

The pre-anaphora opens with the christological hymn *Ihydoyo* (*ho monogenes*), one of the oldest liturgical hymns of the Syrian and Byzantine traditions, which emphasizes that "one of the Trinity was crucified." The hymn most probably had its origin during the sixth-century christological controversies in the East. The christological orientation of the pre-anaphora is emphasized by the entrance hymn, the *Trisagion*, with the addition "he who was crucified for us have mercy upon us." The reading of the gospel with the accompanying hymns, silent prayers, deacons' acclamation, priest's proclamation, and blessings are christological in form and content.

Then follows the *Promiun*, prayer of pardon (*husoyo*), and *Sedro*. The prayer of pardon, introduced after the sixteenth century, is addressed to Christ: "O Christ, our King, the Lord of glory, our Lord and Master, be Thou for them [the departed] and for us, the Absolution and the Absolver." The variable *Promiun-Sedro* are indifferently addressed to the Father or to the Son and are concluded with a trinitarian doxology. The solemn blessing of the censer has been done in the name of the Trinity.

Originally the anaphora began with the trinitarian glorification or the modified form of a Pauline formula (2 Cor 13:14), but in its present form the West Syrian anaphoras begin with three prayers (prayer before peace, prayer of the imposition of the hand, and prayer over the veil) addressed to the Father. Alternate prayers for peace for Maundy

---

[50] Athan. 9. See also one of the *Promiun* of the pre-anaphora: "Glory be to Thee, O well-pleasing Sacrifice, Who offered Thyself upon the Cross; Who didst absolve our sins by Thy Sacrifice for us . . ." (ibid., 27).

Thursday and Holy Saturday are addressed to Christ. The alternate
prayer for peace prescribed for Christmas is addressed to the Father,
but is christological in content, and ends with a doxology *per Christum*:
"We . . . beseech Thee Lord . . . [to] make us worthy to give sincere
peace to one another by a holy kiss and to partake of the heavenly and
incorruptible gifts of our Lord Jesus Christ, *through Whom and with
Whom* praise, glory and sovereignty are worthy of Thee, together with
Thy all-Holy Spirit" (Athan. 32, italics added).

A *per Christum* doxology is rather rare in the Syrian Orthodox liturgy. The prayers of the anaphora and other liturgical services end
with the usual doxology: "Praise and glory to You, to Your Only-
Begotten Son and to Your Holy Spirit" ("to You and to Your Father and
Your Holy Spirit" if the prayer is *ad Christum*). The Syrian Orthodox
prayers always emphasize the equality of the Son with the Father,
rather than his mediatorship.

SYMBOLS, GESTURES,
AND CHRISTOLOGICAL INTERPRETATION

Liturgical commentaries East and West usually interpret liturgical
symbols and gestures in christological terms. In the reading of the gospel, Christ himself announces the "Life-giving message," and before
and after the reading the priest greets the congregation with the same
greeting of the risen Lord: "Peace be to you."[51]

The preparation of the bread and wine are always related to the incarnation and passion of Christ.[52] In the mixing of the water and wine,
the Syrian Orthodox tradition sees the ineffable mystery of the union
of the two natures in Christ. Thus the priest says the following prayer,

---

[51] John 20:21. The Old Syriac Version (*Sinaiticus*) and Peshitta have *shlomo
'amkun* and the Harklean reading is *shaino 'amkun*. In the present Syrian orthodox practice the former is used for the greetings before the reading and the
latter for the greetings after.

[52] See the East Syrian rite in *Liturgies Eastern and Western, Being the Texts
Original or Translated of the Principal Liturgies of the Church* 1: *Eastern Liturgies*,
ed. F. E. Brightman "on the basis of the former work by C. E. Hammond" (Oxford: Clarendon Press, 1896; repr. 1965) 251–52. [No other volumes published.]
Repr. with the title *Eastern Liturgies* (Piscataway, NJ: Gorgias Press, 2002).

as he mixes water and wine: "O Lord God, as Thy divinity was united with Thy humanity so unite this water with this wine."[53]

In the Syro-Antiochene tradition, the fraction is always associated with the passion of Christ.[54] The prayer of fraction, attributed to Dionysius Bar Salibi (d. 1171), is a vivid presentation of the Syrian Orthodox christology, and illustrates very well how christology was expressed in liturgical texts:

> Thus truly did the Word of God suffer in the flesh and was sacrificed and broken on the cross; and His soul was departed from His body, while His Godhead was in no way departed either His soul or from His Body. And He was pierced in His side with a spear and there flowed out blood and water for the atonement of the whole world, and His Holy Body was stained therewith. For the sins of the whole world, the Son died on the Cross, and His soul came and was united with His body. And he turned us from the wrong practice to the right deeds. By His blood He reconciled and united the Heavenly hosts with the earthly beings, and the people with the gentiles, and the soul with the body. The third day He rose again from the sepulcher, and He is One Immanuel, and is indivisible into two natures after the unity indivisible. Thus we believe and thus we confess and thus we confirm that this Flesh is of this Blood and that this Blood is of this Flesh.[55]

[53] Athan. 6; Brightman, *Liturgies*, 251. Cf. the East Syrian prayer: "Water is mixed with wine and wine with water, and let them both be one: in the name of the Father, and of the Son and of the Holy Ghost, for ever" (ibid., 251). There is striking similarity between the East and West Syrian rites of preparation of the bread and wine (ibid., 251–52).

[54] E.g., Theodore of Mopsuestia, *Commentary on the Lord's Prayers and on the Sacraments of Baptism and the Eucharist*, trans. A. Mingana. Woodbrooke Studies 6 (Cambridge: W. Heffer and Sons, 1933) 105–6; Narsai, *The Liturgical Homilies*, trans. R. H. Connolly, Texts and Studies 8/1 (Cambridge: Cambridge University Press, 1909), 23–24 [Hom. 17–A] and 59 [Hom. 21–A]); and Moses Bar Kepha, *Commentary on the Eucharist*, in *Two Commentries*, ed. Connolly (as in note 43) 67–68.

[55] Athan. 49–50. The prayer was probably not the composition of Bar Salibi but was inspired by the commentaries of Moses Bar Kepha and Bar Salibi. See B. Varghese, *The Syriac Version of St. James: A Brief History for Students*. Grove Liturgical Studies 49 (Cambridge: Grove Books, 2001) 42–43.

The *ad Christum* principle seems to be permanently marked in Eastern worship in two important liturgical postures. The liturgical orientation toward the East is an *ad Christum* posture. On the basis of Matthew 24:27 a popular belief developed that in the Second Coming Christ would come from the East. Following Zechariah 6:12 ("Orient is His Name": LXX and Peshitta), the East has often been understood as a symbol of Christ himself. The eastward orientation symbolizes our hope in the second coming of Christ as well as our desire to return to Paradise.[56] Similarly, standing was interpreted as an *ad Christum* posture. Standing in worship is an eschatological posture, an attitude of vigilant waiting for the glorious second coming of Christ.[57]

CONCLUSION

The eucharistic prayer was always christocentric in its formulation. From the earliest times the Syro-Antiochene tradition used the eucharistic prayers as an effective means to express its christological concerns. Thus in the anaphora of book 8 of the *Apostolic Constitutions* we find a long description of the mystery of the incarnation. Some of the early Syrian Orthodox anaphoras (those of Timothy of Alexandria, Severus of Antioch, and John of Bosra) as well as the earliest known Syrian Orthodox Epiphany services have followed this model.

In the early Syriac tradition eucharistic prayers were usually addressed to Christ. The East Syrian anaphora of Addai and Mari, and the Maronite anaphora of Peter Sharar, still contain prayers addressed to Christ. At least until the time of Moses Bar Kepha (d. 903), the Syriac version of St. James as well as other Syrian Orthodox anaphoras contained such prayers, which were later modified *ad Patrem* most probably under influence of the commentary of Bar Kepha and the revised Syriac version of St. James (the so-called New and Correct Recension attributed to Jacob of Edessa). However, the anamnesis and

[56] See B. Varghese, *West Syrian Liturgical Theology* (Aldershot: Ashgate, 2004) 109–10.

[57] According to Saint Basil, from Easter to Pentecost we stand to pray "in order to show that we are on our way towards the heavenly kingdom which will be the final and perfect Pentecost. As we journey, we are carrying within us the Spirit of the risen Christ, being in effect risen ourselves" (*On the Holy Spirit*, 27.66, in *De Spiritu Sancto. Sur le Saint-Esprit*, ed. Benoît Pruche. 2nd ed. SC 17bis (Paris: Cerf, 1968) 485.

the final prayer are still addressed to Christ; these are in no way a "Monophysite innovation" as J. A. Jungmann believed.

In the Syrian Orthodox tradition, as elsewhere in the East, Christ is above all the incarnate Logos, the Second Person of the Trinity, who is seated at the right hand of God the Father. Christ is the co-receiver of the prayers along with the Father and the Holy Spirit.[58] Thus sometimes the Sanctus has been addressed directly to Christ or understood as a glorification of Christ.

Prayers addressed to Christ are a witness to and a confession of his divinity and his consubstantiality with God the Father and the Holy Spirit, and their significance is to be understood in a trinitarian framework. The place of Christ in the liturgy has been expressed, both East and West, using various metaphors. Thus Christ has been called Priest, Lamb of offering, Sacrifice, Mediator, and above all has been addressed as the one who receives prayers and offerings along with the Father and the Holy Spirit. Since the Middle Ages the Latin tradition has emphasized the mediatorship of Christ, while in the Syriac liturgical theology Christ as mediator occupies a less important place. Among the various manifestations of Christ in liturgical celebrations his divinity always comes to the fore. I will conclude with a quotation from Saint Ephrem, the greatest of all Syriac poet-theologians, who always emphasized the divinity of Christ:

> Whom have we, Lord, like You—the Great One who became small, the
>   Wakeful who slept,
> the Pure One who was baptized, the Living One who died,
> the King who abased himself to ensure honour for all!
> Blessed is Your honour![59]

---

[58] Thus in the *Sursum corda* of the Syriac anaphora of Saint James we find: "Let our minds and our understanding and our hearts be above where our Lord, Jesus Christ sits at the right hand of God the Father."

[59] *Hymn on the Resurrection*, no. 1:22 in *The Harp of the Spirit: Eighteen Poems of Saint Ephrem*, ed. Sebastian Brock. 2nd ed. Studies Supplementary to Sobornost 4 (Oxford: Fellowship of St. Alban and St. Sergius, 1983) 30.

Chapter 6

The Christology of the Anaphora of Basil in its Various Redactions, with Some Remarks Concerning the Authorship of Basil

Gabriele Winkler
University of Tübingen

The anaphora of Basil is an excellent model to demonstrate the evolution of christological positions. Moreover this anaphora has come down to us in virtually all the extant languages of the Christian East, offering thus an interesting multifaceted perspective.

Any study of the anaphora of Basil has to begin with the seminal doctoral dissertation of Hieronymus Engberding of 1931. In his pioneering study Engberding established for the first time the prominence of the four most important versions of this anaphora:

1. the short Egyptian anaphora of Basil (in Greek, Coptic, Ethiopic);

2. the longer redaction based on a lost archetype Ω from which the first Armenian version emerged;

3. also dependant on Ω, the lost archetype Ψ, from which the Syriac redaction derives;

4. the Byzantine version, also deriving from Ψ, one of the youngest redactions.[1]

---

[1] H. Engberding, *Das eucharistische Hochgebet der Basileiosliturgie: Textgeschichtliche Untersuchung und kritische Ausgabe*. Theologie des Christlichen Ostens. Texte und Untersuchungen (Münster: Aschendorff, 1931) LXXXVII; see G. Winkler, *Die Basilius-Anaphora: Edition der beiden armenischen Redaktionen*

It seems highly unlikely that this anaphora was composed or redacted by just one person, for this eucharistic prayer encapsulates several layers of different ages and provenance.

I want to begin with a succinct overview of new editions and scholarly studies (2000–2005) of the anaphora of Basil on the basis of Engberding's stemma of the various redactions of Basil:

1. The short Egyptian Basil (extant in Greek, Coptic, and Ethiopic) was the main focus of an extensive study by Achim Budde. His investigation, based on the extant Greek and Coptic manuscripts, appeared in 2004.[2]

2. The longer redaction of Ω has survived in two Armenian redactions. In 2001 Erich Renhart published a critical edition of the older Armenian version accompanied by a German translation, however without a commentary.[3]

3. With regard to the versions of Ψ in Syriac and Byzantine Greek, the critical edition of the oldest Greek manuscript (*Barb. gr. 336*, eighth century) by Stefano Parenti and Elena Velkovska, published in 2000, deserves special attention.[4] The Syriac version awaits further scrutiny; we are still dependent on the Syriac edition by I. Rahmani.[5] The Georgian redaction dependent on the

---

und der relevanten Fragmente, Übersetzung und Zusammenschau aller Versionen im Licht der orientalischen Überlieferungen. Anaphorae Orientales 2, Anaphorae Armeniacae 2 (Rome: Pontificio Istituto Orientale, 2005) (= BA) 13.

[2] A. Budde, *Die ägyptische Basilius-Anaphora: Text—Kommentar—Geschichte.* Jerusalemer Theologisches Forum 7 (Münster: Aschendorff, 2004); for a detailed review see *Oriens Christianus* 89 (2005) 264–75. For the Ethiopic version see S. Euringer, ed., "Die äthiopische Anaphora des hl. Basilius nach vier Handschriften herausgegeben, übersetzt und mit Anmerkungen versehen." *Orientalia Christiana* 36 [No. 98] (1934) 135–223.

[3] E. Renhart, ed. "Die älteste armenische Anaphora: Einleitung, kritische Edition des Textes und Übersetzung," in *Armenische Liturgien: Ein Blick auf eine ferne christliche Kultur,* ed. E. Renhart and J. Dum Tragut, 93–241. Heiliger Dienst. Ergänzungsband 2 (Graz/Salzburg, 2001). For an assessment of Renhart's publication see Winkler, BA 25–27.

[4] S. Parenti and E. Velkovska, eds., *L'Eucologio Barberini gr. 336.* BELS 80 (Rome: CLV, 2000).

[5] I. Rahmani, ed. *Missale iuxta ritum ecclesiae apostolicae Antiochenae Syrorum* (Sharfé: Typis patriarchalibus in Seminario Sciarfensi de Monte Libano, 1922).

Byzantine recension was studied by Nino K'aĵaia on the basis of the Georgian manuscripts.[6]

4. A critical edition of the known Armenian manuscripts of both Armenian versions, including the extant fragments, was undertaken these past years in Tübingen. The edition is accompanied by an extensive study comparing the Egyptian versions (in Greek, Coptic, Ethiopic) and the Armenian, Syriac, and Byzantine (Winkler, *Die Basilius-Anaphora* = BA).

This present paper will explore: (1) the christological statements of the various redactions of the anaphora of Basil and their dependence on the christological formulae of the Synod of Antioch in 341 (BA 566–77, 579–82, 741–50, 844–61, 866–70); (2) the affinity between Ω and the Syriac tradition;[7] (3) the problem of the authorship of Basil (BA 16–18, 877).

I. THE CHRISTOLOGY

The christological tenets of the anaphora of Basil cannot be properly understood without taking into account the evolution of credal statements in the context of baptism, and the creeds of the fourth century Antiochene synods.

Major progress has been made over the past decades concerning the formation of the Syriac, Armenian, and Georgian creeds, including the Ethiopic evidence, via studies involving scholars from Louvain,[8] Oxford,[9]

---

[6] N. K'aĵaia, *Basili Kesarielis t'xzulebat'a jveli k'art'uli t'argmanebi* [= The Old-Georgian translations of the works of Basil of Caesarea] (Tbilissi: Mec'niereba, 1992).

[7] BA 287–88, 303–4, 314, 388–92, 416–17, 431–51, 471–77, 548–59, 566–73, 596–601, 698–721, 788–89, 796–804, 809–15, 818–26, 844–50, 854, 871–76.

[8] See A. de Halleux, "Le symbole des évêques perses au synode de Séleucie-Ctésiphone (410)," in *Erkenntnisse und Meinungen* 2, ed. G. Wiessner, 161–90. Göttinger Orientforschungen 1/17 (Wiesbaden: Harrassowitz, 1978); "La Philoxénienne du symbole," in *Symposium Syriacum 1976*, 295–315. OCA 205 (Rome: Pontificio Istituto Orientale, 1978); "Le deuxième lettre de Philoxène aux monastères du Beit Gaugal." *Le Muséon* 96 (1983) 5–79.

[9] See S. Brock, "Clothing Metaphors as a Means of Theological Expression in Syriac Tradition," in *Typus, Symbol, Allegorie bei den östlichen Vätern und ihren Parallelen im Mittelalter*, ed. M. Schmidt and C. F. Geyer, 11–38. Eichstätter Beiträge 4 (Regensburg: Pustet, 1982); "The Christology of the Church of the East in the Synods of the Fifth to Early Seventh Centuries: Preliminary Con-

and Tübingen,[10] as well as the precious work of B. M. Weischer for the Ethiopic version of the Nicaenum.[11] These studies not only

---

siderations and Materials," in *Aksum—Thyateira: A Festschrift for Archbishop Methodios of Thyateira and Great Britain* (London: Thyateira House, 1985) 125–42; "The Church of the East in the Sasanian Empire up to the Sixth Century and Its Absence from the Councils in the Roman Empire," in *Pro Oriente. Syriac Dialogue* 1 (Vienna: Tyrolia Verlag, 1994) 69–86; "The Nestorian Church: A Lamentable Misnomer." *Bulletin of the John Rylands University Library of Manchester* 78 (1996): The Church of the East: Life and Thought, 23–35.

[10] See G. Winkler, "Ein Beitrag zum armenischen, syrischen und griechischen Sprachgebrauch bei den Aussagen über die Inkarnation in den frühen Symbolzitaten," in *Logos: Festschrift für Luise Abramowski*, ed. H. Ch. Brennecke, E. L. Grasmück, and Ch. Markschies, 499–510. Beihefte zur Zeitschrift für die neutestamentliche Wissenschaft und die Kunde der älteren Kirche 67 (Berlin/New York: W. de Gruyter, 1993); *Über die Entwicklungsgeschichte des armenischen Symbolums: Ein Vergleich mit dem syrischen und griechischen Formelgut unter Einbezug der relevanten georgischen und äthiopischen Quellen.* OCA 262 (Rome: Pontificio Istituto Orientale, 2000); "Anhang zur Untersuchung »Über die Entwicklungsgeschichte des armenischen Symbolums« und seine Bedeutung für die Wirkungsgeschichte der antiochenischen Synoden von 324/325 und 341–345," in *The Formation of a Millennial Tradition: 1700 Years of Armenian Christian Witness (301–2001): In Honor of the Visit to the Pontifical Oriental Institute, Rome, of His Holiness Karekin II, Supreme Patriarch and Catholicos of All Armenians, November 11, 2000*, ed. R. F. Taft, 107–59. OCA 271 (Rome: Pontificio Istituto Orientale, 2004); "Zur Erforschung orientalischer Anaphoren in liturgievergleichender Sicht II: Das Formelgut der Oratio post Sanctus und Anamnese sowie Interzessionen und die Taufbekenntnisse," in *Acts of the International Congress Comparative Liturgy Fifty Years after Anton Baumstark (1872–1948), Rome, 25–29 September 1998*, ed. R. F. Taft and G. Winkler, 403–97. OCA 265 (Rome: Pontificio Istituto Orientale, 2001; eadem, "Das theologische Formelgut über den Schöpfer, das ὁμοούσιος, die Inkarnation und Menschwerdung in den georgischen Troparien des *Iadgari* im Spiegel der christlich-orientalischen Quellen." *Oriens Christianus* 84 (2000) 117–77; "A Decade of Research on the Armenian Rite 1993–2003," in *The Formation of a Millennial Tradition: 1700 Years of Armenian Christian Witness (301–2001). In Honor of the Visit to the Pontifical Oriental Institute, Rome, of His Holiness Karekin II, Supreme Patriarch and Catholicos of All Armenians, November 11, 2000*, ed. R. F. Taft, 183–210. OCA 271 (Rome: Pontificio Istituto Orientale, 2004); "Zur Signifikanz eines kürzlich erschienenen Aufsatzes zur Basilius-Anaphora." *Studi sull'Oriente Cristiano* 8 (2004) 23–45.

[11] B. M. Weischer, "Die ursprüngliche nikänische Form des ersten Glaubenssymbols im Ankyrōtos des Epiphanios von Salamis. Ein Beitrag zur Diskussion

demonstrated the significance of these oriental creeds for our knowledge of the evolution of christology in the East during the formative period, revolutionizing hitherto held positions, but they also greatly enhanced our awareness and appreciation of the richness and complementary character of these Syriac, Armenian, and Ethiopic christological expressions. On a more technical level it was possible to show the process of adaptation of the Greek vocabulary, with its technical terms, by the coining of Syriac and Armenian neologisms during the fifth to sixth centuries, which can be traced in the Syriac and Armenian sources.[12] The enormous progress made in our knowledge of the evolution of the credal statements during the formative period of the third to sixth centuries greatly assists our understanding of the evolution of the various redactions of the anaphora of Basil (see BA 23–25).

With regard to the christological disputes and the emergence of the anaphora of Basil we have to realize several important facts:

1. The inclusion of the creed in Eastern anaphoras during the fifth to sixth centuries was preceded by another process, namely the reshaping of all major parts of the anaphora of Basil by inserting credal formulae.[13] These credal statements emerged (1) from a baptismal context and (2) from the christological disputes of the epoch.

2. The anaphora of Basil, surprisingly, reflects to a considerable extent discussions in the aftermath of the Nicene Council (BA 566–77, 579–82, 741–50, 844–61, 866–70). We have to realize that the Nicene Creed was by no means initially considered normative. For example, the Antiochene bishops resisted the intrusion of speculative philosophical language into the creed, in particular the οὐσία- and

---

um die Entstehung des konstantinopolitanischen Glaubenssymbols im Lichte neuester äthiopischer Forschungen." *Theologie und Philosophie* 53: 407–14; idem, *Qērellos IV/1: Homilien und Briefe zum Konzil von Ephesos*. Äthiopistische Forschungen 4 (Wiesbaden: Harrassowitz, 1979).

[12] Besides the works of Halleux and Brock, see Winkler, *Entwicklungsgeschichte*, 286–87, 332–74, 375–466; "Anhang," 109–19; "Das theologische Formelgut," 133–77; "Zur Erforschung," 446–50, 456–58; "Zur Signifikanz," 31–38.

[13] See Winkler, "Zur Erforschung," 407–93; BA 24–25, 562–65.

ὁμοούσιος formulae, suggesting instead that biblical language be retained to express the relationship of the Son with the Father.[14]

3. Hieronymus Engberding assumed that the main characteristic of the longer versions consists in the inclusion of biblical quotations. Undoubtedly this is true, yet we are now able to identify several of the most important quotations in the anaphora of Basil as part of the formulae of the Antiochene Synod of 341 (BA 566–77, 579–82, 741–50, 844–61, 866–70).

4. Up to now we have known little about the *Rezeptionsgeschichte* of the Antiochene Synods of 324/325, 341, and 345. To my great surprise I discovered that these synods formed the basis on which the earliest Armenian creeds were shaped.[15] The most important witness is a fifth-century Armenian history known today as the *Buzandaran Patmut'iwnk'*. This mirrors the earliest layers of Armenian church history, and is also the main witness for the Syrian influence on the early Armenian Church during its formative period in the fourth to fifth centuries.[16]

Not only do the earliest Armenian patristic sources allow us to describe the *Rezeptionsgeschichte* of these synods, but the main surprise for me was the extent of the borrowings from the christological statements of the Antiochene Synod of 341 in the Armenian redactions of the anaphora of Basil, but by no means restricted to them (BA 566–77, 579–82, 741–50, 844–61, 866–70). The Egyptian shape of this intriguing anaphora shows this too, although not to the same extent (BA 868–69, 877, 879–80).

---

[14] See the extensive studies of: H. Ch. Brennecke, *Hilarius von Poitiers und die Bischofsopposition gegen Konstantius II. Untersuchungen zur dritten Phase des arianischen Streites (337–361)*. Patristiche Texte und Studien 26 (Berlin/New York: W. de Gruyter, 1984); *Studien zur Geschichte der Homöer: Der Osten bis zum Ende der homöischen Reichskirche*. Beiträge zur historischen Theologie 73 (Tübingen: Mohr, 1988); and W. A. Löhr, *Die Entstehung der homöischen und homöusian-ischen Kirchenparteien—Studien zur Synodalgeschichte des 4. Jahrhunderts*. Inaugural-Diss. (University of Bonn, 1986).

[15] See Winkler, "Anhang," 109–59.

[16] See N. Garsoïan, *The Epic Histories Attributed to P'awstos Buzand (Buzandaran Patmut'iwnk'): Translation and Commentary*. Harvard Armenian Text and Studies 8 (Cambridge: dist. by Harvard University Press, 1989) 8–9, 16, 26–27, 46–47, 492–93; BA 69–71.

The most prominent borrowings from the Antiochene Creed of 341 include, for example:

1. In the Oratio ante Sanctus reference to
   — the Creator as "Lord of All" (τῶν ὅλων) in both Armenian versions;[17]
   — the preexistence of the Son "before (all) eternity" in the first Armenian redaction and the Byzantine version;[18]
   — the characterization of the Son as the "living Logos—Wisdom —Power—True Light" of the Father, again in the first Armenian redaction and in the Byzantine text;[19]

2. In the Oratio post Sanctus
   — the depiction of the Son as εἰκών (+ χαρακτήρ) of the Father, based on Col 1:15 and Heb 1:3;[20]
   — in all likelihood an original statement concerning the incarnation ἐπ᾽ ἐσχάτου (ἐσχάτων τῶν ἡμερῶν) combined with "he took a body from the virgin"; this, probably the original text on the incarnation in the anaphora of Basil (BA 631–33, 665– 69, 868–69), was manipulated to a considerable extent in all versions, for example by
   — the inclusion of the Holy Spirit in all Egyptian redactions (still absent in Ω + Ψ; missing in the Armenian and Byzantine texts; in the Syriac version, however, present);[21] and by
   — the presence of neologisms: "he became em-*bodied*" in the Armenian versions (which was not coined before the fifth cen-

---

[17] BA 142/143 (= arm Bas I), 214/215 (= arm Bas II), 566–75, 868.

[18] BA 144/145 (= arm Bas I), 582, 868 (= the other versions); Parenti and Velkovska, *L'Eucologio*, 64 (= byz Bas).

[19] BA 144/145 (= arm Bas I), 579–81, 868 (= the other versions); Parenti and Velkovska, *L'Eucologio*, 64 (= byz Bas).

[20] BA 74/75 (= Fragment), 156/157 (= arm Bas I) 616–25, 868 (including the other versions); Parenti and Velkovska, *L'Eucologio*, 64 (= byz Bas).

[21] BA 156/157 (= arm Bas I), 226/227 (= arm Bas II), 645–50, 665–67 (including the other versions); Winkler, "Zur Erforschung", 416–17 (= boh Bas), 419 (= Ethiopic version), 421 (= byz Bas), 424/428 (= arm Bas I), 433 (= arm Bas II); Rahmani, *Missale*, 178 (= syr Bas); Budde, *Die ägyptische Basilius-Anaphora*, 148–49 (= gr + copt Bas).

tury) and "he was en*fleshed*" in the Syriac witness (stemming from the sixth century);[22]

— the resurrection formula, he rose "*from the dead* the third day," in all Egyptian versions;[23]

— the formulation of the Son's *parousia* "to judge everybody according to his deeds," present in all versions of the anaphora of Basil.[24]

3. The formulae of the anamnesis in all versions of the anaphora of Basil is based on the Antiochene Creed of 341.[25]

Several of these statements of the Antiochene Creed were mediated through Syriac influence, as for example the expression "Lord of All," typical for Addai and Mari and the Syrian baptismal *ordines*, in both Armenian redactions.

II. TRACES OF SYRIAC INFLUENCE PARTICULARLY IN THE Ω-REDACTIONS

The most important witnesses of Ω include the two Armenian redactions. These show many intriguing features, some of which are absent in the Egyptian and/or Byzantine redactions. That the second Armenian translation derives from the Byzantine text is assumed, yet obviously the Greek text was superimposed on a much older model, which sometimes differs considerably from the Byzantine version.[26] This is

---

[22] For the various neologisms in the Armenian and Syriac languages see BA 650–56, 666–67; Winkler, "Zur Erforschung," 424/428, 433; Rahmani, *Missale*, 178 (= syr Bas).

[23] BA 686–87, 869; "Zur Erforschung," 417 (= boh Bas), 420 (= Ethiopic text); Euringer, "Die äthiopische Anaphora," 152/153 (= Ethiopic version); Budde, *Die ägyptische Basilius-Anaphora*, 150–51 (= gr + copt Bas).

[24] BA 160/161(= arm Bas I), 230/231 (= arm Bas II), 851–853, 869 (including the other versions); Budde, *Die ägyptische Basilius-Anaphora*, 150–51; Euringer, "Die äthiopische Anaphora," 152/153; Parenti and Velkovska, *L'Eucologio*, 66 (= byz Bas); Rahmani, *Missale*, 181–82 (= syr Bas).

[25] BA 170/171 (= arm Bas I), 238/239 (= arm Bas II), 741–50, 869 (including the other versions); Winkler "Zur Erforschung," 373/374 (= arm Bas I + II), 378 (= byz Bas), 379 (= syr Bas); Rahmani, *Missale*, 181–82 (= syr Bas); Budde, *Die ägyptische Basilius-Anaphora*, 158–59 (= gr + copt Bas).

[26] BA 11, 128, 491, 881 (see also *Indices*, 888: "arm Bas unabhängig von griech. Vorlage").

also true—albeit in different ways—of the first Armenian redaction (BA 287–88, 388–92, 416–17, 431–51, 871–74), which was undoubtedly translated from an unknown text via Syrian mediation.

Striking parallels between the Syriac tradition and the Ω-redactions mark major parts of the anaphora, namely: the verbs and their sequence in connection with the praise before the Sanctus (BA 419, 431–51, 871, 879); the verbs and their sequence at the institution narrative (here, however, it is not so much the Armenian but Egyptian and Byzantine versions that reflect Syrian parallels) (BA 698–721, 874); the combination of the verbs "bless" and "sanctify" present in the epiclesis, which is normative for East-Syrian anaphoras (BA 788–89, 796–804, 809–15, 874).

A closer look at these verbs and their context in various parts of the anaphora will demonstrate my point.

1. *The praise-verbs of the Oratio ante Sanctus* (BA 431–51, 871). First of all, the beginning of the Oratio ante Sanctus in both Armenian versions seems not to depend on the *vere dignum* (BA 419–24). This is quite peculiar. In addition, the older Armenian translation contains no direct address to God, but begins with just one single verb of praise in the infinitive: "to glorify Thee" (namely *p'aṙaworel* = δοξάζειν) (BA 140/141, 388–92, 416–17, 431–51, 442–45, 447, 871) whereas anyone familiar with the Byzantine anaphora of Basil knows that the praise of the people in the Oratio ante Sanctus includes a string of six praise-verbs in the indicative (cf. αἰνεῖν, ὑμνεῖν, εὐλογεῖν, προσκυνεῖν, εὐχαριστεῖν, δοξάζειν).[27]

In the summary of the praise of God by the people, the older Armenian recension has the verb *awrhnen* (cf. εὐλογεῖν), repeated in connection with the praise of the highest ranks of angels (the cherubim and seraphim) immediately before the Sanctus (here in both Armenian versions); this is absent in the other versions (BA 438, 442, 444–45). With the other ranks of angels just one verb, namely προσκυνεῖν, is used; this occurs in all versions of this anaphora with the exeption of the Byzantine text, which has αἰνοῦσιν.[28]

According to Macomber's reconstruction of the anaphora of Addai and Mari, this anaphora began the Oratio ante Sanctus with "Glory be

---

[27] See Parenti and Velkovska, *L'Eucologio*, 64.

[28] BA 438, 442–45; Parenti and Velkovska, *L'Eucologio*, 64.

to Thee";[29] very likely it was once not a substantive but the verb δοξάζειν, which in the Syriac tradition regularly replaces εὐλογεῖν (BA 413, 415–17, 431–34, 437–39, 450–51, 871). The ranks of the angels "adore" (προσκυνεῖν), whereas the highest ranks of angels, namely the cherubim and seraphim, "glorify" (δοξάζουσιν) God.[30]

Thus the Armenian redaction has considerable affinity with the East-Syrian tradition, as the comparison between the Armenian version of Basil and the anaphora of Addai and Mari seems to indicate (BA 437–39, 871):

Addai + Mari		Armenian Anaphora of Basil
1. The Praise by the people:		
"Glory"	(δοξάζειν)	"to glorify"
2. The Praise-Verbs associated with the Angels		
a. the upper beings		a. the angels, archangels, etc.
"adore"	(προσκυνεῖν) (all versions of Bas, exeption: **byz Bas**)	"adore"
b. the camps and servants + *Cherubim – Seraphim*		b. *Cherubim – Seraphim*
"glorify" (= δοξάζειν = εὐλογεῖν)	(εὐλογεῖν)	"praise" (arm Bas I: 3 verbs) (arm Bas II: 1 verb!)

No other redaction of Basil shows such close affinity with the East-Syrian tradition as Ω, that is, the Armenian redactions.

In addition, all Ω-versions (not, however, the Egyptian versions) clearly indicate that the Sanctus is brought forth by the movement of

[29] For the original Syriac text see W. F. Macomber, "The Ancient Form of the Anaphora of the Apostles," in *East of Byzantium: Syria and Armenia in the Formative Period*, ed. N. G. Garsoïan et al. (Washington: Dumbarton Oaks, 1982) 71–88.

[30] For the original Syriac text see BA 432–34, 871; Macomber, "The Ancient Form," 84/86.

the wings of the seraphim (BA 463–77, 872). This tradition has its roots in the Targumim of Isaiah 6:2 and Ezekiel 1:24, which again points toward Syrian mediation (BA 463–77, 872).

2. *The Institution Narrative and Epiclesis.*[31] The entire Egyptian tradition, not just the second Armenian translation, has the verb-pair "bless" and "sanctify" in connection with the introduction to the Lord's words over the bread.[32] This verb-pair is characteristic of the Syrian tradition.[33] The primary place of these verbs, however, is not the Institution Narrative but the Epiclesis (BA 701, 788, 799–801, 874), where these verbs are normative for the three East-Syrian anaphoras (BA 799–800, 803–4, 809–10, 812–15, 874). The Epiclesis of the Byzantine and second Armenian version of Basil combines ἐλθεῖν with the verb-pair εὐλογῆσαι – ἁγιάσαι, as for example in the East-Syrian anaphora of the Apostles Addai and Mari (BA 244/245, 783, 786, 788, 814–15, 874).

The Verbs of the Epiclesis

Addai + Mari	Šarrar	Basil
I. come	come	ἐλθεῖν (nearly all versions of Bas)
—	dwell	—
rest	rest	—
II. Verb-Pair:		
bless + sanctify	—	εὐλογῆσαι – ἁγιάσαι
		byz Bas (+ 1 additional verb
		arm Bas II (+ additional Verb-Pair)

III. No Consecratory Verb: "make" (ποιήσῃ) (BA 777–78, 786, 789, 798–99, 802, 805–06)

—	—	sah Bas
		byz Bas

---

[31] BA 693–721 (= Institution Narrative), 753–830 (= Epiclesis) 874–75, 880.

[32] BA 234/235, 698–700, 702–06, 719, 874; Budde, *Die ägyptische Basilius-Anaphora,* 152–53 (= gr + copt Bas).

[33] So already S. Brock, "Invocations to/for the Holy Spirit in Syriac Liturgical Texts: Some Comparative Approaches," in *Acts of the International Congress Comparative Liturgy Fifty Years after Anton Baumstark (1872–1948), Rome, 25–29 September 1998,* ed. R. Taft and G. Winkler, 377–406. OCA 265 (Rome: Pontificio Istituto Orientale, 2001); see in addition BA 698–700, 702–06, 719, 799–801, 803–04, 809–10, 812–15, 874.

Moreover, the older nucleus of the Epiclesis of the anaphora of Basil was addressed to the Son (as in the Maronite *Šarrar*) (BA 822–26, 875) which was altered only through the interpolation of the consecratory verb "make" (ποιήσῃ) in Basil seemingly through the influence of Jerusalem, i.e., the anaphora of James (BA 825–26, 875).

Overview on the Institution Narrative and Epiclesis (BA 880)

a. Introduction to the "bread-words":

verb-pair:

"bless + sanctify,"	typical of East-Syrian tradition
so in Egyptian Basil	
arm Bas II	
byz Bas	

b. The Epiclesis

ἐλθεῖν and

"bless + sanctify,"

so in byz Bas	in the East-Syrian tradition the norm
arm Bas II	("bless + sanctify" missing in *Sarrar*[34])

III. THE ANAPHORAL INTERCESSIONS[35]

Not only do these central parts show close affinity with the East-Syrian anaphoras, but the basic division between the anaphoral intercessions in the commemoration for the "dead and the living" (in that sequence) is also typical of the oldest East-Syrian reference to the dead and the living in the context of the last judgment. This is the case in the earliest Syriac creeds and credal statements in patristic sources, in contrast to all other traditions, which mention in the creed first the living, then the dead.[36]

---

[34] So already S. Brock, "Towards a Typology of the Epicleses in the West Syrian Traditions." In *Crossroad of Cultures: Studies in Liturgy and Patristics in Honor of Gabriele Winkler*, ed. H.-J. Feulner, E. Velkovska, and R. Taft, 173–92. OCA 260 (Rome: Pontificio Istituto Orientale, 2000); see also BA 814.

[35] See Winkler, *Entwicklungsgeschichte*, 551–54, 581–83; "Zur Erforschung," 476–85; "Zur Signifikanz," 38–43; BA 842, 844–50, 856–61, 875, 880.

[36] See previous note. So already, for example, R. H. Connolly, "The Early Syriac Creed." *Zeitschrift für Neutestamentliche Wissenschaft und die Kunde des Urchristentums* 7 (1906) 202–23; Halleux, "Le symbole" (as in note 8) 163; and several others.

In the original shape of the intercessions of the anaphora of Basil they still are not separated from the epiclesis but flow out of the invocation of the Spirit with the petition for the saints (= reference to the dead) in the context of the parousia and last judgment. We see this most distinctly in the first Armenian redaction:

> . . . but may we find mercy
> *on the day of the appearance of your right judgment*
> with all the saints . . .
> [= beginning of the intercessions *for the dead,*
> followed by those of the living]
> (BA 178/179–180/181, 842–50, 856–61, 875).

This sequence is also found in the other Ω-versions, corresponding to the following earliest Syriac credal statements:[37]

> – *Acts of Thomas:* ". . . for he is the judge of the *dead and the living* . . ."
> – Aphrahat: "he is the judge of *the dead and the living* . . ."
> – East-Syr. baptismal creed: ". . . to judge the dead and the living . . .," etc.

Thus the order of the intercessions in the Byzantine anaphora of Basil, followed by the Liturgy of Chrysostom, is not a Byzantine peculiarity but has its roots in the early Syriac tradition.

In this context we have to remember that the most important sections of the anaphora of Basil, such as the Oratio ante Sanctus and, in particular, the Oratio post Sanctus—but also the anamnesis—include the Antiochene formulae of the creeds of 341; these were sometimes passed on via Syrian mediation, as is the case with the sequence of the intercessions, which, like the preceding parts of the anaphora, were shaped on the basis of the creed.

IV. ANOTHER IMPORTANT TRAIT

Besides these peculiar features of several redactions of this intriguing anaphora, another important trait demonstrates the complexity of its evolution. Sometimes the Armenian versions represent a fusion of the Egyptian branch of Basil with the genuine Ω-tradition, as is the case, for example, in the context of the Epiclesis (BA 784 n 13, 797 n 40, 798

---

[37] See Winkler, *Entwicklungsgeschichte*, 551–54, 581–83; "Zur Erforschung," 476–77; BA 845.

n 41, 799) and the reference to the last judgment either at the end of the Oratio post Sanctus or at the beginning of the intercessions (BA 842–43, 849). The beginning of the intercessions of the first Armenian version of Basil refers to the "*day* of the *appearance*" of the "just *judgement*"; this has parallels with the Egyptian versions at the end of the Oratio post Sanctus: . . . ὁρίσας ἡμέραν ἀνταποδόσεως καθ᾽ ἣν ἐπιφα- νείς κρῖναι . . . (BA 842–43, 849). The epiclesis of the second Arme- nian version reflects the Syrian tradition, on the one hand, with the verb-pair "bless and sanctify," and on the other with the verb-pair "purify (= "sanctify") + ἀναδείκνυμι" of the Coptic (i.e. Sahidic [+ Bo- hairic]) tradition (BA 784 n 13, 797 n 40, 798 n 41, 799).

THE IMPLICATIONS
What are the implications of these traits in the anaphora of Basil?

1. The christology of Ω (often also of the Egyptian branch) is clearly an adaptation of the Antiochene christological statements in the context of the anti-Arian aftermath of the Council of Nicaea, and thus seemingly antedates the evolution of the trinitarian teach- ings of Basil. Moreover, the Cappadocian christological reflec- tions are not a mirror of the Antiochene anti-Arian disputes of 341, in contrast to the anaphora named after the great Cappado- cian father, where the formulae of the Synod of Antioch in 341 figure prominently, especially in Ω.

2. The closeness of the Ω-redaction, and in particular the Armenian redactions, to the early Syrian traditions can no longer be simply dismissed, as has been done in a recent publication.[38]

3. This anaphora in its oldest layers, namely some sections of the Oratio ante Sanctus, plus the presence and the shape of the Sanc- tus (with the Benedictus missing *after* the Sanctus, BA 535–49, 872), and parts of the epiclesis, seem to antedate Basil. Various parts of this anaphora are very old indeed, as they also show close connections with the baptismal traditions.[39]

[38] See A. Budde, "Typisch Syrisch? Anmerkungen zur Signifikanz liturgischer Parallelen. Der Ursprung der Basilius-Anaphora in der Diskussion." *Jahrbuch für Antike und Christentum* 45 (2002) 50–61, and my reply, "Zur Signifikanz," 23–45.

[39] Studied in great detail in my analysis of the *Basilius-Anaphora* (BA; see also *indices*, 892).

The christological discussions of the Antiochene Synod in 341 are clearly reflected in the so-called anaphora of Basil, most prominently in the first Armenian redaction, and less dominant, though still present, in the Egyptian versions (BA 867–70, 877, 879–80).

These new findings imply that we may have to abandon the assumption of Basil's involvement in shaping the Basil-anaphora; moreover, we may have to modify Engberding's claim that the *longer* form of this anaphora always reflects the *younger*, and also the original idea of Anton Baumstark who considered the longer version the older one.[40] This assumption has to be accompanied by the following caveat: Ω has *sometimes* preserved older layers than the Egyptian tradition did, but there are undoubtedly later additions with the frequent biblical quotations. These *secondary* quotations from the New Testament have to be distinguished from those that served to express the relationship of the Son with the Father, taken over from the Synod of Antioch in 341.

The importance of attributing this anaphora to Basil lies in the fact that this anaphora has indeed something to do with the christological disputes and the struggle for orthodoxy. It does not, however, concern the Nicene formulation of orthodoxy, or the Cappadocian, but the Antiochene. This christological position was not in favor of the Nicene philosophical language, preferring biblical language to describe the relationship of the Son to the Father over against the Nicene ὁμοούσιος + οὐσία formulae.

[40] See A. Baumstark, *Die Messe im Morgenland* (München: J. Kösel, 1906) 72; BA 20, 568, 645–50, 666–68, 695, 726, 741, 749, 856–61, 878, 880.

Chapter 7

The Meanings and Functions of *Kyrie eleison*

Peter Jeffery
Princeton University

JUNGMANN ON LITURGICAL PRAYER

Josef A. Jungmann's scholarly writing, and his role in the Roman
Catholic liturgical reform of the twentieth century, reveal a "lifelong
engagement with his favorite idea, . . . namely, the role of Christ's
mediatorship in Christian prayer." As early as 1914, that is, Jungmann
was asserting the principle that "Only prayer to the Father through
Christ is prayer in the strict, true, original sense."[1] His opinion provided a major theme for many of his publications, which argued that
this original understanding—prayer is directed to the Father through
Christ—had become obscured over the centuries owing to regrettable
historical developments. The restoration of this alleged principle was,
therefore, an important goal of the liturgical reform that Jungmann
did so much to lead.

One of the most influential statements of Jungmann's view is his
seminal article "The Defeat of Teutonic Arianism and the Revolution
in Religious Culture in the Early Middle Ages."[2] This aims to show
that "indeed, we may safely assert that in all the two thousand years
of the Church's history, no period has ever seen a greater revolution of
religious thought and institutions than that which took place in the

---

[1] Balthasar Fischer, "Foreword," in *Source and Summit: Commemorating Josef
A. Jungmann*, ed. J. M. Pierce and M. Downey (Collegeville, MN: Liturgical
Press, 1999) ix–x.

[2] In *Pastoral Liturgy* (New York: Herder and Herder, 1962) 1–101. Revised
translation of "Die Abwehr des germanischen Arianismus und der Umbruch
der religiösen Kultur im frühen Mittelalter." *Zeitschrift für katholische Theologie*
69 (1947) 36–99. The book *Source and Summit*, ed. Pierce and Downey, consists
of seventeen reflections on and responses to Jungmann's article.

five centuries between the close of the patristic age and the dawn of scholasticism." To be more specific, these five centuries would extend from the lifetime of St. Gregory the Great (d. 604) to that of St. Bernard of Clairvaux (d. 1153).[3]

Although much of Jungmann's evidence is actually somewhat earlier than Gregory, Jungmann theorized that, between Gregory and Bernard, the church's reaction to Arianism and other heresies would have led to a certain "zeal to emphasize the divinity of Christ," even at the expense of slighting his humanity. "[T]he explanation of the contrast between the religious culture of the rising Middle Ages and that of the Patristic age is to be found to some extent in the handing down and the spread of forms of devotion which were created in theatres of anti-Arian warfare." In both pictorial art and liturgical texts, therefore, one can observe that, as late antiquity gave way to the Middle Ages, "Christ as Mediator becomes less important, the Trinity more so."[4] "The ancient Roman tradition held fast, as its inviolable norm, the universal practice of the early Christian liturgy. According to this usage the official prayer of the Church offered at the altar was always addressed to the Father and presented 'through Christ'; and prayer was thus offered to God while the mind was directed to the glorified Redeemer, the transfigured Head of the Church."[5] But during that five-century transitional period "[t]he Gallic-Carolingian Church departs from this rule. The practice of addressing Christ is more and more set on a par with that of addressing God the Father, and the latter practice, where it appears in newly formulated prayers, favours the form of address to the Blessed Trinity: *suscipe sancta trinitas*."[6]

The Latin quotation is the incipit of one of the private offertory prayers which became part of the Roman Mass during the Middle Ages, and was still in use in Jungmann's time.[7] The message is unmistakable: prayers addressed to the Trinity in this way represent a departure from the original Roman tradition of addressing the Father through Christ. Therefore they ought to be removed from the liturgical

---

[3] Jungmann, "The Defeat of Teutonic Arianism," 1.

[4] Ibid., 13, 22, 16.

[5] Ibid., 4.

[6] Ibid., correcting a misspelling in the Latin word *trinitas*.

[7] Josef A. Jungmann, *The Mass of the Roman Rite: Its Origins and Development (Missarum Sollemnia)*, trans. F. A. Brunner. 2 vols. (New York: Benziger Brothers, 1951–55) 2:46–52, 59.

books—as indeed this one was removed in the reforms following the Second Vatican Council.

As Jungmann saw it, the "Tridentine" Roman liturgy of his time was rife with instances like this, in which "medieval developments continue, but people do not look back to their origins"—to such an extent that, by the nineteenth century, "Liturgy ran the risk of becoming a subject for rubrical antiquarianism, an aesthetic show-piece."[8] But Jungmann was sure that through his own research and that of his contemporaries

> a great change has taken place since last century. Thanks to the emergence of historical theology, and Christian archaeology, too, the world of the Fathers and that in which our liturgy found its origin has been brought near once more. The ancient Christian world has revived. Much knowledge has become available to us. The early patterns of various liturgies are coming to light with increasing definition, and we are astonished to see their shapes in the liturgical forms we know today. And so they invite us once more to enter more deeply into their meaning.[9]

Thus the time was ripe to restore the liturgy to what was now understood to be its original spirit, removing medieval distortions to "revive . . . the ancient Christian world," "the world of the Fathers."

Prayers like *Suscipe sancta Trinitas* were easily disposed of, since their demonstrably medieval origin made it easy to target them as late deformations of the tradition. More problematic was the *Kyrie eleison*, which in Jungmann's time was also understood as a trinitarian prayer. The *Kyrie* had originated much earlier than *Suscipe*, and was more deeply rooted in many parts of the liturgy, so that it threatened to undermine Jungmann's argument. Jungmann adduced evidence that the trinitarian interpretation of the *Kyrie* dated to the Carolingian period, and could therefore be dismissed as a product of that regrettable medieval tendency to address prayers to all three persons. But this argument did not restore Jungmann's ideal pattern—for the *Kyrie*, he believed, had originally been addressed to Christ, not to the Father. How could one explain that? Jungmann's solution was that the *Kyrie* was originally not a liturgical prayer, strictly speaking, but a popular

---

[8] Jungmann, "The Defeat of Teutonic Arianism," 88, 93.
[9] Ibid., 93.

element that had come into the liturgy from the surrounding cultural milieu.

Jungmann on the Origins of the Kyrie

According to Jungmann, "the *Kyrie eleison* of our present liturgy of the Mass originally conveyed the same sense as the *Christe eleison; Kyrios* means Christ."[10] It contradicts the usual practice of addressing prayer to the Father, but that can be explained by the fact that it did not originate as one of the priestly or presidential prayers of the official liturgy. Instead, it came from the devotional prayers of the Christian laity, where it had roots in "the pagan cult of the Sun."

> We possess another manner of prayer of a popular kind, and of similarly venerable antiquity, in the *Kyrie eleison*. . . . The cry ἐλέησον [*eleison*], with the address κύριε [*kyrie*], in the Old Testament psalms directed to God, meets us in the New Testament on the lips of those who implore the aid of the Saviour.[11] In the pagan cult of the sun, which was in its prime in the Church's youth, it was customary to greet the rising sun with this cry, ἐλέησον ἡμας [*eleison hēmas*]. As late as the fifth century, [Pseudo-]Eusebius of Alexandria had to deny that Christians still did the same. Then it was all the more natural that the *Kyrie eleison* should be adopted increasingly as a cry to him whom the Christians were wont to think of as a sun of justice, as "oriens ex alto."[12]

However, this historical trajectory from sun-cult to popular Christian worship is not easy to trace. The earliest evidence that Jungmann cited for the Christian use of *Kyrie eleison* does not, in fact, confirm that this invocation was originally addressed to Christ—nor is there any

[10] *The Early Liturgy to the Time of Gregory the Great*, trans. F. A. Brunner. Liturgical Studies 6 (Notre Dame: University of Notre Dame Press, 1959) 20.

[11] Jungmann cites Psalm 6:2(3), "Eleison me, Kyrie," and Matthew 9:27, 15:22, 17:15 as examples.

[12] *The Place of Christ in Liturgical Prayer*. 2nd rev. ed., trans. A. Peeler (Staten Island, NY: Alba House, 1965) 215–16. Translation of *Die Stellung Christi im liturgischen Gebet*. Liturgiewissenschaftliche Quellen und Forschungen 19/20. 2nd ed. (Münster: Aschendorff, 1962). His information on the sun cult and Pseudo-Eusebius is from F. J. Dölger, *Sol Salutis: Gebet und Gesang im christlichen Altertum, mit besonderer Rücksicht auf die Ostung in Gebet und Liturgie*. Liturgiegeschichtliche Forschungen 4–5. 2nd ed. (Münster: Aschendorff, 1925) 61–62 (incorrectly cited in ibid., 216 n 1).

suggestion of sun symbolism. The earliest sources actually exhibit a disconcerting variety: in some of them, the *Kyrie* was addressed to the Father, in others to the Son, in still others it was left "indeterminate." But Jungmann dismissed all these differences by asserting that they are ultimately "of small moment," given the popular origin of the *Kyrie*.

> In liturgical usage, we find the Kyrie eleison first attested in the Ap[ostolic] Const[itutions] VIII—i.e., for the end of the fourth century— as a repeated response of the people to the prayer-intentions and petitions announced by the deacon litany-fashion. The calls of the deacon are here adapted to the ordinary order of address of the liturgical prayer (to God). In like manner, the eleison cry occurs also later, e.g. in the St James liturgy after the anamnesis, in both the Greek and the Syrian forms of that liturgy: "Have mercy on us, Lord, God, almighty Father!" Used in the same way as in the Apostolic Constitutions, i.e. as the people's response, now in Greek, now translated, the Kyrie eleison still continues more or less in all Eastern liturgies. But the diaconal litany to which it answers shows almost throughout the prayer-address to Christ, as is the case already in the fifth century in the Testament of our Lord. Or on the other hand the term "Lord" simply leaves open the question—which seems of small moment for this unassuming prayer of petition—of the exact sense of the address. The Acts [of the Apostles] use the word "Lord" in an equally indeterminate manner. . . .[13]

On the other hand, evidence from the Roman Missal appeared to uphold Jungmann's theory. The litany of the saints, sung at the Paschal Vigil on Holy Saturday, begins with the words *Kyrie eleison* and ends by connecting to the *Kyrie* of the Mass. Therefore the litany could be interpreted as an expansion of the original popular pattern: the invocations of the saints would be later additions to an originally christological *Kyrie*. Moreover, now that the litany has found its way into the liturgy itself, it has been properly tamed by being finished off with a priestly collect that reaffirms the correct and original pattern of prayer to the Father through the Son.

> In the Roman liturgy the invocation of the saints on Holy Saturday has won a place as a preliminary to the Mass in the setting of the *Litany of*

---

[13] Jungmann, *The Place of Christ*, 216, including note 4, wherein Acts 1:24f is cited.

the Saints. This is a perfect example of how popular forms of prayer may be not merely received but fitted into the structure of the liturgy. The invocations of the saints, which were inserted into the original prayer to Christ, now form the main substance of this prayer. It is followed by more petitions to Christ, ending in the *Agnus Dei* and the *Kyrie eleison*, *Christe eleison*. The earliest pre-liturgical litany texts either break off here or add only a few versicles and psalm verses. On Holy Saturday, on the other hand, the litany is rounded off by the collects of the Mass: the invocation of the saints merges into the petition to Christ [i.e., the Kyrie of the Mass Ordinary], and after the *Gloria* ends in a solemn prayer which, as always, is addressed to the Lord God through Christ. The Litany of the Saints undergoes a similar extension when, as on Rogation Days, it is recited as a prayer by itself. On these occasions it culminates in the *orationes* of the Church with their solemn ending, *Per dominum nostrum* ["through our Lord Jesus Christ . . ."], with which our prayer takes the place allotted to it by God himself, as it were, in the plan of divine salvation. The manner of its recital enhances the harmonious impression of its composition. Whereas the litany itself is sung by the choir and congregation, the *orationes* are recited by the officiating priest, who for this purpose goes up to the altar.[14]

There are at least two problems with this. First, Jungmann gives no examples here of "pre-liturgical litany texts" which would confirm the theory that the invocations addressed to the saints (and those to the Father and the Spirit!) came in more recently. He did adduce some examples later on, however, in his magnum opus, *The Mass of the Roman Rite* (1:341-42 and n. 49). But these, too, do not necessarily support Jungmann's claims. For example, Jungmann cites the litany of saints preserved in an eighth-century English manuscript, which begins and ends with *Christe audi nos*. The other petitions are either indeterminate or clearly addressed to the Son, except for the presumably secondary invocations of saints. And since this manuscript is a personal prayer collection, not a liturgical book, one could argue that any text found in it is popular or perhaps "pre-liturgical."[15] Unfortunately, however, Jungmann did not read the litany all the way to the end. It does not stop at

---

[14] Ibid., 272–73.

[15] *London, British Library, MS Royal 2 A. XX*. M. Lapidge and R. Sharpe, *A Bibliography of Celtic-Latin Literature 400–1200*. Royal Irish Academy Dictionary of Medieval Latin from Celtic Sources, Ancillary Publications 1 (Dublin: Royal Irish Academy, 1985) 338 no. 1278.

the bottom of the page (26b), but continues on to the next (27a), where it closes off with *"Summa trinitas una Diuinitas, auxiliare et miserere nobis—* Most high Trinity, one divinity, help and have mercy on us."[16]

The second problem for Jungmann's theory is that the Holy Saturday litany cannot be "a perfect example of how popular forms of prayer may be not merely received but fitted into the structure of the liturgy." At best it is only an imperfect example, for it contains some significant anomalies: the litany of saints here was not exactly "rounded off by the collects of the Mass." It actually merged into the ninefold *Kyrie* chant of the Ordinary of the Mass, and was followed by the lengthy Gloria in excelsis. Only after the Gloria did the priest finally arrive at the collect of the Mass. The interruption of the Gloria between the *Kyrie* and the collect(s) was no random anomaly, for whenever the Gloria was said at Mass it came between the *Kyrie* and the collects. What appeared to save Jungmann's interpretation was the serendipitous fact that, on less important days when the Gloria was omitted, the collects did follow immediately after the *Kyrie* because there was no Gloria. "The same stylistic rule can be found at work on other occasions, and not only in the Roman liturgy. In the ordinary Mass the congregational prayer of the *Kyrie* is followed in like fashion by the solemn prayer of the Church, the collect; it is only on feast days that the Gloria intervenes . . ."[17]

Rather than speculate about why a "stylistic rule" would be violated routinely on all the major days of the liturgical year, Jungmann made it the basis of a theological principle. This he said was known to all of "the great theologians": before addressing the Father in the liturgical collect, we approach by means of the popular and Christ-directed *Kyrie eleison,* thus anticipating the phrase "through our Lord Jesus Christ your Son" with which the collect will end. Jungmann evidently regarded this principle as timeless, for the one great theologian he cited did not belong to the formative era of the liturgy, but to the Counter-Reformation, the formative era of Jungmann's own Jesuit order.

---

[16] A. B. Kuypers, ed. *The Prayer Book of Aedeluald the Bishop, Commonly Called the Book of Cerne, Ed. from the MS. in the University Library, Cambridge* (Cambridge: Cambridge University Press, 1902) 211–12. The ending is also omitted from the edition in M. Lapidge, *Anglo-Saxon Litanies of the Saints.* Henry Bradshaw Society 106 (London [Woodbridge: Boydell], 1991) 212–13.

[17] Jungmann, *The Place of Christ,* 273.

It may be asked here whether perhaps the Kyrie is a way of asking Christ the Lord for his intercession, and his mediatorship for the solemn prayer which has thus been introduced. In principle, there is no objection to such a way of praying. The great theologians find it entirely admissible to approach Christ in his humanity to obtain his intercession. The preliminary Kyrie would then be a counterpart to the end formula [of the collect] *per Dominum*. The idea is not excluded, but neither is it given prominence. Its underlying purpose is more likely to have been that of St. Ignatius's instruction in his *Spiritual Excercises*: in praying one should turn, at the end of the meditation, either first to Christ and then to our heavenly Father, or, if the occasion requires it, first to Mary, then to Christ, and then to God the Father. The suppliant should approach the throne of the divine majesty step by step, as it were, and thus close the prayer with so much the more reverence and care. It is only another side of Christ's position as Mediator which thus comes out.

This meeting—especially in the Roman liturgy—with Christ the Lord, the Mediator between God and man, at all cross-roads, so to speak, is plainly characteristic of liturgical prayer in contrast to the free-growing, less restricted forms of popular piety.[18]

Not surprisingly, however, the ancient "stylistic rule" was forgotten during the confrontation with Arianism. The originally popular litany hardened into the ninefold *Kyrie* of the Mass ordinary: three repetitions of *Kyrie eleison*, three of *Christe eleison*, then three more of *Kyrie eleison*. And this arbitrary arrangement of thrice three led to the erroneous idea that the *Kyrie* is addressed to the entire Trinity, not to Christ alone. "The *Kyrie* of the Mass, which in the Roman tradition as in the eastern was a simple appeal to Christ wherein *Kyrie* and *Christe* are interchangeable, is given a rigid Trinitarian meaning in the Carolingian 9th century commentary of The Liturgy [*sic*]. This interpretation, dictated by the triple triad of the *Kyrie*, has come down to the present day."[19] Here the reference is to the ninth-century liturgical commentator Amalar of Metz, who does interpret the *Kyrie* as addressing the three members of the Trinity in turn.

Kyrie eleison, Domine Pater, miserere;
Christe eleison, miserere, qui nos redemisti sanguine tuo;

---

[18] Ibid., 274–75. "Thomas Aquinas, Suarez, Petavius, and Scheeben" are also cited as "great theologians" in note 1 on p. 275.
[19] Jungmann, "The Defeat of Teutonic Arianism," 35–36.

Kyrie eleison, Spiritus Sancte, miserere.[20]

Kyrie eleison, Lord Father, have mercy.
Christe eleison, have mercy, who redeemed us with your blood.
Kyrie eleison, Holy Spirit, have mercy.

Amalar's text somewhat resembles the medieval *Kyrie* tropes, or rather prosulae, in which the trinitarian interpretation is common but not universal. These texts were composed to fit the long, florid Gregorian chant melodies of the *Kyrie*, one syllable for each musical note. Though christological prosulae also exist,[21] it might be said that in this repertory the process has reached its logical conclusion: in an overreaction to the heretics who would subordinate the Son to the Father, what was originally a popular appeal to Christ became universally misunderstood as invoking the entire Trinity—and the misunderstanding would persist into the twentieth century.

The Reform of the Kyrie

The problem, then, for the twentieth-century liturgical reform, of which Jungmann was one of the most respected leaders, was what to do with the misunderstood, rigidly ninefold *Kyrie*. Perhaps some reformers favored abolishing it altogether, for we read with relief in Jungmann's last book that "The Kyrie itself has not been dropped." Both the number nine and the trinitarian intepretation had to go, however.

> Even as a simple invocation in which all human needs and intentions could be covered, the Kyrie eleison contained a built-in temptation to accumulation or repetition in some "mystical" number. In fact, the Byzantine breviary has a twelvefold and even a fortyfold "Kyrie eleison." No specific number of invocations was prescribed in the older Roman

[20] Amalar, *Liber officialis* 3.6, ed. J. M. Hanssens (Vatican City: Biblioteca Apostolica Vaticana, 1948–50) 2:283. As Jungmann points out, this text is only in the third edition, written ca. 823. The earlier editions contain a different text in which the first *Kyrie* is addressed to the Father, the *Christe* to the Son, and the last *Kyrie* expresses the Son's return to the Father (Hanssens 2:548–49, 1:143). Thus Amalar does appear to be the innovator of the trinitarian interpretation.

[21] P. Jeffery, *Translating Tradition: A Chant Historian Reads*, Liturgiam Authenticam (Collegeville, MN: Liturgical Press, 2005) 30–31.

liturgy. According to the first Roman Ordo (end of the seventh century), the litanizing carried on until the Pope gave a signal to stop.[22] A century later the number was fixed at nine, in the sequence in which it was known until the most recent liturgical reform (*Kyrie eleison*, three times; *Christe eleison*, three times; *Kyrie eleison*, three times).

While the Kyrie eleison was not intended originally in a Trinitarian sense—nor does the context warrant it—after the ninth century this interpretation became predominant at the hands of liturgists and spiritual writers carried away on a wave of devotion that was cresting at the time. From the very beginning, however, *Kyrie* meant Christ, and from St. Paul's time it was a popular name for Christ. He was being invoked at the beginning of his celebration; he was, so to speak, called into the midst of the community that had assembled in his name.[23]

In keeping with this view, the *Missale Romanum* of 1970 offered two new ways of performing the *Kyrie*. In the simplest method, the nine repetitions were reduced to six: the priest would say "*Kyrie eleison, Christe eleison, Kyrie eleison*" once each, and the people would repeat each phrase after him. A larger number of repetitions was also permitted, however, for instance if the musical setting called for it.

The 1969 Order of Mass provides for the priest's threefold invocation and its repetition each time by the people; this is a simplification compared to the former ritual of three-times-three invocations. On the other hand, there is nothing in the General Instruction (par. 30) to prevent increasing the number of invocations or even expanding the texts. The possibility of expanding them into a confession ritual has already been mentioned above.[24]

What "expanding the texts" meant was that additional wording could be inserted alongside *Kyrie eleison* and *Christe eleison*. Precedent for this was identified with the "tropes," or rather prosulae, of the medi-

---

[22] Here Jungmann cites Ordo Romanus 1 (ed. M. Andrieu, *Les Ordines Romani du haut moyen age.* 5 vols. [Louvain: Spicilegium Sacrum Lovaniense Bureaux, 1931–61], 2:84). In my forthcoming translation and commentary I expect to propose a somewhat later date.

[23] Joseph Jungmann, *The Mass: An Historical, Theological, and Pastoral Survey,* trans. J. Fernandes, ed. M. E. Evans (Collegeville, MN: Liturgical Press, 1976) 168–69, summarizing *The Mass of the Roman Rite,* 1:333–46.

[24] Jungmann, *The Mass: . . . Survey,* 169.

eval *Kyrie* chants. "During the late Middle Ages it became common practice to augment the Kyrie invocation by way of 'troping.' Kyrie tropes comprise almost half the contents of volume 47 of the collection *Analecta Hymnica*."[25] The medieval *Kyrie* prosulae were more important in the early Middle Ages than later on.[26] The (Tridentine) Roman Missal of 1570 did not include them, and they survived merely as convenient labels for the different *Kyrie* melodies.

The option of "expanding the texts" after Vatican II, however, was not intended to restore the medieval prosulae, many of which (after all) express trinitarian interpretations. What was envisioned instead was "the possibility of expanding them into a confession ritual." This referred to the Vatican II innovation we now call "the Penitential Rite." Traditionally, the priest and ministers quietly had recited the prayer Confiteor Deo among the prayers at the foot of the altar, at the very beginning of the Mass, covered (if there was music) by the singing of the Introit and *Kyrie*. The people, on the other hand, did not recite the Confiteor themselves until just before receiving Communion, near the end of the Mass, or even afterward. But in the twentieth century, the growth of the "dialogue Mass" had the people reciting the server's part, so that the second Confiteor before Communion came to seem superfluous. It was therefore dropped in 1962 in the last preconciliar edition of the Roman Missal.[27] After Vatican II the now-communal Confiteor before the Mass was given even more prominence as one alternative for the new Penitential Rite. Another alternative would remodel the *Kyrie* as a penitential prayer. "The Order of Mass does not restrict the penitential act to this Confiteor formula, but provides alternatives for invoking God's mercy. One of these utilizes the 'Kyrie eleison' because of the plea for mercy it contains, and expands it each time as an address to Christ, with an appeal to his coming as Redeemer; the actual wording is left to the celebrating priest."[28] By way of example, the new Missal gives:

[25] Ibid., 169.

[26] D. A. Bjork, *The Aquitainian Kyrie Repertory of the Tenth and Eleventh Centuries*, ed. R. L. Crocker (Aldershot: Ashgate, 2003).

[27] The procedure is described in "Ritus servandus in celebratione Missae" X.6; compare the 1962 edition (wherein the *Confiteor* has been dropped) with earlier editions.

[28] Jungmann, *The Mass: . . . Survey*, 168.

Priest: You were sent to heal the contrite: Lord have mercy.

People: Lord have mercy.

Priest: You came to call sinners: Christ have mercy.

People: Christ have mercy.

Priest: You plead for us at the right hand of the Father: Lord have mercy.

People: Lord have mercy.[29]

Strictly speaking, there is no precedent in the history of the Roman Mass for a penitential rite incorporating the *Kyrie* like this. There is something like it in the Holy Communion service in the *Book of Common Prayer*: the minister recites the Ten Commandments and the people respond to each commandment with "Lord have mercy upon us, and incline our hearts to keep this Law."[30] A pre-Reformation precedent for such a communal recitation of the Decalogue has been alleged in the "prieres du Prône" which were said after the sermon in many medieval French dioceses; they can be seen as comparable to what we now call the Prayer of the Faithful.[31]

What Went Wrong?

Only toward the end of his career, after the main work of liturgical reform had been done, did Jungmann begin to let go of "his favorite

---

[29] *Missale Romanum ex decreto Sacrosancti Oecumenici Concilii Vaticani II instauratum, auctoritate Pauli Pp. VI promulgatum.* Editio typica altera (Vatican City: Typis Polyglottis Vaticanis, 1975) 488; *Missale Romanum ex decreto Sacrosancti Oecumenici Concilii Vaticani II instauratum, auctoritate Pauli Pp. VI promulgatum, Ioannis Pauli Pp. II cura recognitum.* Editio typica tertia (Vatican City: Typis Vaticanis, 2002) 508. English translation from *The Roman Missal, Revised by Decree of the Second Vatican Ecumenical Council and Published by Authority of Pope Paul VI: The Sacramentary, Approved for Use in the Dioceses of the United States of America by the National Conference of Catholic Bishops and Confirmed by the Apostolic See: English Translation Prepared by the International Committee on English in the Liturgy* (Collegeville, MN: Liturgical Press, 1985) 407.

[30] *The Annotated Book of Common Prayer*, ed. J. H. Blunt (New York: E. P. Dutton, 1916) 372–73.

[31] J. W. Legg, "On Some Ancient Liturgical Customs Now Falling into Disuse," in *Essays on Ceremonial by Various Authors*, ed. V. Staley. The Library of Liturgiology & Ecclesiology for English Readers 4 (London: De La More Press, 1904) 74–75; cf. U. Berlière, "La Prône *dans* la liturgie." *Revue bénédictine* 7 (1890) 97–104, 145–51, 241–46.

idea," though without admitting he had been wrong. In a book published in 1969, the same year as the newly-reformed Order of Mass, Jungmann "acknowledged the rightful place of prayer to Christ, rooted in the New Testament, alongside prayer through Christ in the presidential prayers of the Roman liturgy."[32] He never acknowledged, however, that his history of the *Kyrie* was doubtful on several points, and the alterations he favored remain in the Roman Missal even now, celebrated by millions of unsuspecting people every single day. Thus it is important to show not only that Jungmann was wrong, but why—how faulty methodology and presuppositions brought him to the wrong conclusions.

It is true, of course, that we now have access to many primary and secondary sources that were unavailable in Jungmann's time. This makes it easier to find and evaluate evidence that was unknown or misunderstood when Jungmann was writing, even though he was undeniably well-informed about the bibliography available to him. But there was also a fatal flaw in Jungmann's conception of what he was doing. Jungmann saw himself as engaged in "historical theology." As he practiced it, this meant that one reads liturgical texts with an eye toward discerning the underlying theological principles. By definition these principles are timeless; only their historical expression is subject to variation across time and culture. Thus Jungmann's influential article on "The Defeat of Teutonic Arianism" comes with this apologia: "The present outline is designed to encourage younger men to undertake more detailed work, the aim of which would be to make the minutiae of historical study serve a higher theological purpose: the discernment of what is an essential possession in religious life, and what the passing fashion of an age."[33] By themselves, that is, the historical data amount to minutiae: what is really important is the "theological purpose." Indeed the failure to perceive the "essential" core

---

[32] Fischer, x, referring to Jungmann, *Christian Prayer through the Centuries*, trans. J. Coyne (New York: Paulist Press, 1978) 14–17. Translation of *Christliches Beten im Wandel und Bestand* (Munich: Ars Sacra, 1969). For some developments since Jungmann's time see J. F. Baldovin, "The Body of Christ in Celebration: On Eucharistic Liturgy, Theology, and Pastoral Practice," in *Source and Summit: Commemorating Josef A. Jungmann, S.J.*, ed. J. M. Pierce and M. Downey, 49–61 (Collegeville, MN: Liturgical Press, 1999) especially 55–57.

[33] Jungmann, "The Defeat of Teutonic Arianism," 2.

principles was the bane of both liturgy and liturgical scholarship prior to Jungmann's generation.

> Liturgy ran the risk of becoming a subject for rubrical antiquarianism, an aesthetic show-piece. Historical studies of the liturgy seemed to be a matter for archaeologists. It is no accident—and in a way it is reasonable—that the great dictionary which was begun in 1907 by Cabrol and Leclercq and which was not completed until 1953, associates liturgy and Christian archaeology: *Dictionnaire d'Archéologie chrétienne et de Liturgie*. And what can happen in science can happen also in life. Even today we can still regard liturgy as something of merely archaeological interest. A person who is not well-versed in church matters might easily attend the pontifical liturgy and be quite fascinated by the precisely ordered patterns of movement, by the richness of the vestments and furnishings, by the dignity of the singing; and yet the whole thing could strike him as a work of art from the past. He might leave the house of God saying—ambiguously—"ancient culture."[34]

But there is another, unacknowledged idea at work here. How would anyone—"well-versed in church matters" or not—get the impression that the liturgy is "an aesthetic show-piece," "something of merely archaeological interest," "a work of art from the past" that is somehow unworthy of "the house of God"? According to Jungmann, one would arrive at this misapprehension by paying too much attention to the wrong things, the non-textual or ceremonial aspects of the celebration: "the precisely ordered patterns of movement," "the richness of the vestments and furnishings," "the dignity of the singing." It is only by reading the texts (which in those days required being "well-versed" in church Latin) that one can achieve a correct understanding of what the liturgy really is or should be. Jungmann saw the liturgical tradition, therefore, as something like an onion of three layers. Hidden at the center are the unchanging, timeless truths. These are expressed in the middle layer, the historically changeable texts. The message of the texts, however, is obscured by the outer layer, the non-textual elements of movement, vestments, furnishings, and singing. This outer layer is the most outdated, but paradoxically very resistant to change. Nevertheless it must be trimmed back so that the eternal truths at the center can shine through. This leaves the liturgical expert in a dire pre-

---

[34] Ibid., 91.

dicament, torn between a professed respect for the wholeness of the liturgical tradition and an inner conviction that the true inner message is being missed.

> It is always necessary, therefore, to observe and recognize in liturgy, the law of continuity. And this not merely from psychological considerations, out of regard for those who will take part in nothing and count nothing valid which is not of long-standing custom. Of its nature, liturgy is conservative. Man is caught up in constant change, but God never changes and His revelation too, which is committed to the Church, and the scheme of Redemption, given in Christ, is always the same. Prayer and worship are a constant flowing back and homecoming of the souls of restless, wavering men, to the peace of God.
> And so, even the forms through which God has been glorified in the past, take on a kind of sanctity. They are consecrated by God like a votive offering which must not be taken away from the sanctuary once it is given. Religious sentiment is very much disinclined to change liturgical forms except for very grave reasons.
> But like every living organism, the liturgy has to adapt itself to the present conditions of life. As a rule this is achieved by silent growth: but there are times of almost complete standstill, and times of stormy advance.[35]

These times of standstill and storm were, of course, Jungmann's own times. With the Missal of Pius V, issued in 1570 after the Council of Trent, "a period of standstill was inaugurated," so that, by the time of Pius X in the early twentieth, "A jerk—more than one jerk—was clearly necessary."[36] These jerks were supplied by the Liturgical Movement, which Pius X was the first pope to recognize officially.

Now the problem with Jungmann's onion-like model is that it turns history inside out. Theologically one might say that eternal truths become incarnated in historical texts. But from a historical perspective, liturgies develop in the opposite order: action is primary, then text, then theology. Human beings do not begin with timeless principles, then formulate texts, and finally add ceremonies. "The assumption that belief is primary and action a secondary expression of it is peculiar to certain phases of Western thought and thus ethnocentric if built

---

[35] Ibid., 91–92.
[36] Ibid., 92, 93.

into a definition" of ritual, since it relies on "Western, rationalist assumptions packed into the notion of belief."[37]

What, after all, does modern Christian liturgy have in common with the worship of the first disciples? For the most part it is only the actions, such as immersing in water, anointing with oil, laying on hands, breaking bread, taking the cup. If any psalms or extant hymns or prayer texts were associated with these actions, we do not know which ones or how. The four eucharistic institution narratives in the New Testament may well have developed within a liturgical context, but development did not stop when they were written down. No premodern church celebrated the Eucharist by simply reading one of the New Testament accounts and adding ceremonial actions to it. The continuity with what Jesus did is in the actions of taking bread, blessing, and breaking, more directly than in the texts. Even the Lord's Prayer comes in two recensions, which the New Testament places in two different narrative contexts, as a unit of teaching rather than an account of worship. In liturgical use, even the more developed Matthean form has had to be expanded by the addition of introductions and conclusions, something that was beginning to happen as early as the *Didache*.[38]

Historically speaking, theology comes last. The systematizers and commentators and reformers appear on the scene after the actions and texts are already in place, once the need is beginning to be felt for interpretation or improvement. Theology itself tells us this: "*Lex supplicandi legem statuat credendi*—The *lex supplicandi* founds and constitutes the *lex credendi* and is therefore primary for Christian theology."[39]

---

[37] R. L. Grimes, "Victor Turner's Definition, Theory, and Sense of Ritual," in *Victor Turner and the Construction of Cultural Criticism: Between Literature and Anthropology*, ed. Kathleen M. Ashley (Bloomington, IN: Indiana University Press, 1990) 141–42.

[38] *Didache* 8, in *The Apostolic Fathers*, ed. and trans. Bart Ehrman. Loeb Classical Library (Cambridge: Harvard University Press, 2003) 1:428–31. See also R. F. Taft, *A History of the Liturgy of St. John Chrysostom. 5. The Precommunion Rites*. OCA 261 (Rome: Pontificio Istituto Orientale, 2000) 129–54; Jeffery, *Translating Tradition*, 41.

[39] A. Kavanagh, *On Liturgical Theology: The Hale Memorial Lectures of Seabury-Western Theological Seminary, 1981* (New York: Pueblo, 1984) 134. Kavanagh's distinction between primary and secondary theology is not unrelated to the historical distinction between liturgical texts and liturgical theory. For a

Jungmann himself exemplified this process, seeing a long tradition before him which needed to be put right. Had he been more of a historian, he might have noticed that theology is actually the most transitory of all factors in liturgical history, precisely because it arises at later stages of development than actions and texts. The Carolingian reform, the Gregorian reform, the Reformation, the Counter-Reformation, and the Liturgical Movement were not serial returns to the same unchanging ideal. Each had its day, offering new solutions to new problems, until it was finally undone by the next wave of reform. Each time some texts were changed, and fewer actions, but both text and action tended to outlive the reformers' explanations of what they "really" meant.

It is true, of course, that a given action may be of more recent origin than a given text. A text may give rise to an action, just as an action may give rise to a text. But in general the actional dimension as such is both more basic psychologically and more primordial historically, for the same human reasons that "actions speak louder than words." In a sense every liturgical text is a liturgical act—an act of reciting or proclaiming, of entreating or rejoicing or affirming. That is why the conventional approaches to textual criticism don't always work with liturgical texts,[40] because the essential factor in the transmission of a liturgical text is what people do with it. And just as there are techniques for tracing the historical transmission of texts over time, so there are ways to trace the history of liturgical actions. One starts by looking for evidence of movements or gestures, and of emotional or experiential states. Ritual objects and spaces, imagery and music—the dreaded "archaeological" side of liturgy—have their own forms of historical continuity, which (properly understood) can lead us reliably through gaps in the textual evidence. It was because the reformers of Jungmann's generation could not "read" the non-semantic languages of ritual that they produced a liturgy so top-heavy with theological verbiage that it is very difficult to perform effectively.[41] But their

---

range of summary treatments of the *"lex orandi, lex credendi"* theme, see D. W. Vogel, *Primary Sources of Liturgical Theology: A Reader* (Collegeville, MN: Liturgical Press, 2000) 10–11, 52–53, 55–58, 96–97, 120–24, 152–53, 168–69.

[40] P. Jeffery, *Re-Envisioning Past Musical Cultures: Ethnomusicology in the Study of Gregorian Chant.* Chicago Studies in Ethnomusicology (Chicago: University of Chicago Press, 1992) 45.

[41] Jeffery, *Translating Tradition*, 109–18.

tone-deafness did more than cause pastoral problems; it also produced erroneous scholarly constructions of liturgical history which, in the case of the *Kyrie eleison*, then became the basis of a liturgical innovation that was misrepresented as a return to origins.

The correct way to proceed is to begin at the other end, asking not "What did *Kyrie eleison* originally mean?" but "How was it originally used?" The *Kyrie* was from the beginning associated with specific actions and emotions, uses of space and music. When these nonverbal aspects of liturgy are kept in the foreground, it becomes possible to see relationships among texts that would be missed or misconstrued when viewed through textual criteria alone. It will also become possible to see the theologians at work over time, each generation bringing order and clarity where before there had been only inarticulate action and ambiguous text—but each generation at the same time setting up potential conflicts for the theologians of the future.

THE USES OF *ELEISON*

Emotional Connotations

Historically, the word *eleison*—the second person singular, first aorist imperative active of *eleeō*—was used in emotional situations of entreaty or supplication. Persons making the entreaty would be in a state of great anxiety because they were utterly powerless to act on their own behalf. The person being asked was in complete control of the situation, and therefore utterly free to grant or withhold the favor. Petitioners could not hope to bargain, or persuade by means of argument; their only hope was to make their request so abjectly that the more powerful person would be moved to feel mercy or compassion. Thus the word is used in Homer when Lycaon begs Achilles not to kill him (*Iliad* 21:74), when Leiodes and Phemius beg Ulysses not to kill them (*Odyssey* 22:312, 344), when Hector's parents tearfully implore him not to fight Achilles (*Iliad* 22:59, 82), and when Hector's father comes to Achilles, at the risk of his own life, to plead miserably for a chance to ransom the body of his son (*Iliad* 24:503).[42]

The word *eleison*, of course, could also be addressed to gods in a ritual context. Thus in a hymn of the seventh century B.C.E., preserved by Strabo, Zeus is asked: "And have mercy on the Smyrnaeans . . . re-

---

[42] These and many similar incidents are discussed in F. S. Naiden, *Ancient Supplication* (Oxford: Oxford University Press, 2006).

member, if ever the Smyrnaeans burnt up beautiful thighs of oxen in sacrifice to thee."[43] Similarly, in a mock religious ceremony in a play of Aristophanes: "Come, I entreat you, have mercy on their voice."[44]

The anxious, pleading quality of *eleison* is particularly clear in an ancient description of a divination ritual—a text Jungmann knew.[45] It was written by Epictetus, a Stoic of the first or second century, and preserved by his student Arrian. As a Stoic, Epictetus was condemning the practice of divination on the grounds that we already know which courses of action should be chosen as good or rejected as evil, and that the emotional aspect of the ritual is unseemly for a rational person.

> From an unseasonable regard to divination, we omit many duties. For what can the diviner see, besides death, or danger, or sickness, or, in short, things of this kind? . . . Have I not a diviner within, who has told me the essence of good and evil . . .? What further need, then, have I of the entrails, or of birds?. . . .
>
> What, then, is it that leads us so often to divination? Cowardice; the dread of events. Hence we flatter the diviners. . . . The consequence of this is that they play upon us.
>
> What, then, is to be done? We should come without previous desire or aversion: as a traveller inquires the road of the person he meets, without any desire for that which turns to the right hand, more than to the left: for he wishes for neither of these; but that only which leads him properly. Thus we should come to God, as to a guide. Just as we make use of our eyes: not persuading them to show us one object rather than another; but receiving such as they present to us. But now we hold the bird with fear and trembling: and, in our invocations to God, entreat him; "Lord have mercy upon me [*Kyrie eleison*]: suffer me to come off safe." You wretch! Would you have any thing then, but what is best? And what is best but what pleases God? Why do you, as far as in you lies, corrupt your judge and seduce your adviser?[46]

---

[43] From a hymn to Zeus by Callinus (seventh century B.C.E.), quoted in Strabo, *Geography* 14.1.4 (first century B.C.E.). M. L. West, *Iambi et elegi Graeci ante Alexandrum cantati*. 2 vols. (Oxford: Clarendon Press, 1992) 2:48.

[44] Aristophanes, *The Peace* 400 (fifth century B.C.E.).

[45] *The Mass of the Roman Rite*, 1:334 n. 3.

[46] Epictetus, *On Divination* 2.7.1–3. Translation adapted from *The Works, Consisting of His Discourses, in Four Books, Preserved by Arrian, the Enchiridion, and Fragments*, trans. Elizabeth Carter. 4th ed. (London: F. C. and J. Rivington,

The Addressee of Eleison

The Epictetus text seems to be the earliest one in which *eleison* is used with the vocative *Kyrie*. It is easier to find instances where the verb was used with *Despota* ("Master"). In the second-century erotic novel *Leucippe and Clitophon* by Achilles Tatius there is an episode in which the protagonist, clinging to a piece of his wrecked ship during an ocean storm, cries out "Have mercy, Master Poseidon! [*Eleison Despota*]." Later in the book a noble woman who has unjustly been sold into slavery by a disgruntled suitor throws herself in chains at the feet of her mistress, with a plea that begins, "Have mercy on me, lady [*Eleison me despoina*], woman to woman."[47] The female equivalent of *Kyrie* is used in a bilingual early Christian example, the passion of Saint Perpetua. The father says it when he comes to her in prison, begging her to relent from her Christian commitment so as to escape martyrdom.

> He came up to me to discourage me, saying, "Daughter, have mercy [*miserere/eleison*] on my grey hairs. Have mercy on your father, if I am worthy to be called father by you. . . ." . . . [T]hrowing himself at my feet he no longer called me "daughter" but "mistress" [*dominam/kyrian*].[48]

Still, *Despota*, rather than *Kyrie*, seems to have been the usual form of address for earthly potentates, even though royal personages were certainly addressed as *Kyrie* and *Domine* in other contexts.[49] In the

---

1807) 1:182–84. On Stoic views of emotion, see L. C. Becker, "Stoic Emotion," in *Stoic Traditions and Transformations*, ed. S. K. Strange and J. Zapko, 250–75 (Cambridge: Cambridge University Press, 2004); T. Brennan, "Stoic Moral Psychology," in *The Cambridge Companion to The Stoics*, ed. Brad Inwood, 257–94 (Cambridge: Cambridge University Press, 2003).

[47] *Leucippe and Clitophon* 3.5.4, 5.17.3, 5.26.2, trans. John J. Winkler in B. P. Reardon, ed., *Collected Ancient Greek Novels* (Berkeley: University of California Press, 1989) 211, 241; see also 47–48.

[48] O. von Gebhardt, ed., *Acta Martyrum Selecta: Ausgewählte Märtyreracten und andere Urkunden aus der Verfolgungszeit der christlichen Kirche* (Berlin: Duncker, 1902) 69–70; Herbert Musurillo, ed., *The Acts of the Christian Martyrs* (Oxford: Clarendon Press, 1972) 112–13.

[49] A. Alföldi, *Die monarchische Repräsentation im römischen Kaiserreiche* (Darmstadt: Wissenschaftliche Buchgesellschaft, 1970) 209–12; W. Dittenberger, ed., *Orientis Graeci inscriptiones selectae: Supplementum sylloges inscriptionum Graecarum* (Leipzig: S. Hirzel, 1903; repr. Hildesheim: Georg Olms, 1960)

story of 2 Kings 6:26, as retold by Josephus, a woman whose son has been killed seeks justice from the king of Israel. "Now when a certain woman cried out 'Master, have mercy' [*Despota eleison*] he was angered, thinking she was about to beg for food or the like . . ."[50] A romance of Alexander the Great describes ". . . the Egyptians with supplicating voices entreating Alexander, both 'Have mercy, O Master [*Eleison, O Despota*], on your former fatherland,' and 'do not be angry at your servants forever.'"[51]

An interesting contrast between human and divine lords was made in the following incident, recorded by the Roman historian Cassius Dio. The year was 217, and the emperor Macrinus Augustus had just appointed his son Diadumenianus to the rank of Caesar. At a horse race to celebrate the son's birthday (September 14) the populace raised a protest.

> The crowd, because they could obscure their identity at the contest and by their numbers, gained the greater boldness, raised a loud cry at the horse-race . . .; they uttered many lamentations, asserting that they alone were destitute of a leader, destitute of a king; and they invoked the name of Zeus, declaring that he alone should be their leader and uttering aloud these words: "As a Lord [*Kyrie*] you were angry, as a father have mercy on us [*eleison*]."[52]

In this case, the crowd's cry seems to have been an ironic inversion of an imperial ceremony. Its arrangement in two parallel phrases, "As a Lord, . . . as a father . . .," suggest the rhythmic, alternately-chanted slogans that were used as imperial acclamations.[53] In some respects,

---

628–29. A prefect is called *Kyrios* in Oxyrhynchus Papyrus 37, in *The Oxyrhynchus Papyri* 1, ed. B. P. Grenfell and A. S. Hunt (London: Egypt Exploration Fund, 1898) 80–81.

[50] Josephus, retelling of 2 Kings 6:26 in *Antiquitates* 9.64 (first century C.E.).

[51] H. Engelmann, ed., *Die griechische Alexanderroman* (Meisenhiem: A. Hein, 1963) 226.

[52] Cassius Dio, *Historiae romanae*, ed. U. P. Boissevain (Berlin: Weidmann, 1901) 3:424. Translation adapted from H. B. Foster in *Dio's Annals of Rome Translated from the Greek* (Troy, NY: Pafraets Book Company, 1905–1906) 6:55.

[53] M. V. Anastos, "*Vox Populi Voluntas Dei* and the Election of the Byzantine Emperor," in *Christianity, Judaism and Other Greco-Roman Cults: Studies for Morton Smith at Sixty* 2: *Early Christianity*, ed. Jacob Neusner. Studies in Judaism

these can be compared to the rhythmic and rhyming cheers that modern sports fans shout to encourage their favorite teams. But the hippodrome, the arena for horse races, was a space presided over by the emperor. Whatever went on there counted as court ceremonial, which was why so much space is devoted to the hippodrome in the tenth-century *De caerimoniis* of Constantine VII Porphyrogenitos.[54] Thus the protesters of 217, taking advantage of the anonymity provided by the size of the crowd, seem to have expressed their displeasure with Diadumenianus by adapting the genre of imperial acclamation, redirecting to Zeus the loyalty they denied to Diadumenianus.

One reason this episode is of interest is because the word *Kyrios*, when applied to Christ, may also have been regarded as a subversion of an imperial title. Paul's slogan *Kyrios Christos* (Rom 10:9, 1 Cor 12:3) might have originated as a defiant Christian retort to the *Kyrios Kaisar* that Polycarp was pressured to say by the Roman police chief. However, Polycarp himself did not reply to this with *Kyrios Christos*, even though he did invert the Roman official's "Away with the atheists!" by pointing to "the entire crowd of lawless Gentiles in the stadium," instead of his own group of Christians.[55] On the other hand, it has also been argued that the Christian use of *Kyrios* for God and Jesus has more of a Jewish Aramaic than a Hellenistic background.[56] Nevertheless, I suspect it is significant that when Jesus is addressed with *Kyrie*

---

and Late Antiquity 12/2 (Leiden: E. J. Brill, 1975) 140–42, 245–54, 318–33; A. Cameron, *Circus Factions: Blues and Greens at Rome and Byzantium* (Oxford: Clarendon Press, 1976); G. Horrocks, *Greek: A History of the Language and its Speakers*. Longman's Linguistics Library (London: Longman, 1997) 254, 256–61. See also E. Kantorowicz, *Laudes regiae: A Study in Liturgical Acclamations and Medieval Ruler Worship* (Berkeley: University of California Press, 1946).

[54] There is an unfinished edition and translation in *Constantin VII Porphyrogénète: Le livre des cérémonies*, ed. and trans. Albert Vogt. 2 vols. in 4. Collection Byzantine (Paris: Société d'édition "Les Belles lettres," 1935–39).

[55] *Martyrdom of Saint Polycarp, Bishop of Smyrna*, 8, in *The Apostolic Fathers*, ed. and trans. Bart Ehrman. Loeb Classical Library (Cambridge: Harvard University Press, 2003) 1:376–79.

[56] Brief discussion and bibliography in J. A. Fitzmyer, "Pauline Theology," in *The New Jerome Biblical Commentary* (Englewood Cliffs: Prentice Hall, 1990) par. 82:52–54, pp. 1394–95. On the other hand, see D. Zeller, "New Testament Christology in its Hellenistic Reception," *New Testament Studies* 47 (2001) 312–33.

eleison in the New Testament, the petitioner also uses a royal title, "Son of David" (Matt 9:27, 15:22, 17:15, 20:31 and parallels).

In considering the relationship of the Christian *Kyrie* to imperial acclamations, one should not be misled by the frequent use of the word "acclamation" in post-Vatican II liturgiology, where it is applied to all the short texts spoken or sung by the congregation. This usage goes back no farther than the works of Joseph Gelineau.[57] Before the council, "acclamation" was never used as a technical term in Christian liturgy, except for texts like the Byzantine *polychronia*, which are historically descended from the acclamations of imperial court ceremonial. Even if the use of *Kyrios* as a christological title owes something to the ancient imperial cult, the Christian liturgical *Kyrie eleison* does not seem to be descended directly from royal ceremonial.

Penitential Rites?

In the Septuagint we find *eleison* addressed to God under a variety of titles, including *Kyrie* and *Despota*. It is most familiar in the penitential psalms, where of course it represents a translation from Hebrew. Elsewhere in the Septuagint, however, *eleison* is used without penitential implications. In the deutero-canonical books (written in Greek, or at least in Hellenistic times) *eleison* tends to occur in the prayers uttered by pious Jews when the survival of their people is threatened. The connotation is one of anxious desperation, not personal guilt over sin. Though Baruch 3:2 does have a penitential theme, "Hear, O Lord, and have mercy, for we have sinned before you" (NRSV), the other texts ask for mercy on the Jews while attributing the iniquity and lawlessness to their enemies.[58]

Anxiety and guilt combine in the Christian apocryphal *Acts of John*, after the apostle says a prayer (addressed to "God" without specification) that destroys a pagan temple—but even here the guilt is motivated by anxiety.

> And while John was saying this, of a sudden the altar of Artemis split into many pieces, and all the offerings laid up in the temple suddenly

---

[57] E.g., J. Gelineau, *Voice and Instruments in Christian Worship: Principles, Laws, Applications*, trans. Clifford Howell (Collegeville, MN: Liturgical Press, 1964) 40, 69, 84, 163, 171–72, 174.

[58] Sirach 36:1 (*Despota*), 11 or 14 (*Kyrie*; verse numeration varies); Judith 6:19; 3 Mac 6:12.

fell to the floor and its glory was shattered, and so were more than seven images; and half the temple fell down, so that the priest was killed at one stroke as the pillar came down. Then the assembled Ephesians cried out, "[There is but] one God, [the God] of John! [There is but] one God who has mercy upon us; for thou alone art God! We are converted, now that we have seen thy marvellous works! Have mercy on us, O God, according to thy will, and save us from our great error!" And some of them lay on their faces and made supplication, others bent their knees and prayed; some tore their clothes and wept, and others tried to take flight.[59]

Prior to its appearance in Christian liturgy, therefore, *Kyrie eleison* expressed the anxious entreaty of a powerless individual addressing an all-powerful lord. The petitioner could do nothing on his own to influence events in the desired direction, so that he was literally at the mercy of whatever the lord chose to do about the request. But this did not necessarily mean that the petitioner had done anything wrong, or needed to acknowledge guilt or sin. That meaning only occurs sometimes.

THE CHRISTIAN LITURGICAL *KYRIE*

Egeria, the Earliest Source

The earliest attestation of *Kyrie eleison* in a Christian liturgical context does not suggest that it originated in psalmody, court ceremonial, or acts of penitence. It implies neither the contrition of the penitential psalms nor fealty to a king. This is Egeria's description of the liturgy in Jerusalem in the years 383–84.[60] There it is part of an already elaborate sequence of liturgical actions, including prayers, blessings, dismissals, and processions. Egeria's remarks need to be read carefully, however, for every subsequent use of *Kyrie eleison* is already implicit in her description—with the glaring exception of the Penitential Rite in the Vatican II Mass.

---

[59] *Acts of John* 42, from *New Testament Apocrypha*, 2: *Writings Relating to the Apostles*, ed. E. Hennecke and W. Schneemelcher, trans. R. McL. Wilson (Louisville, KY: Westminster John Knox, 1992) 188.

[60] My translation follows the Latin text in *Journal de voyage: Itinéraire*, ed. P. Maraval. SC 296. Corrected ed. (Paris: Cerf, 2002) 238–41. On the date see 27–39.

The description begins in the church of the Anastasis ("Resurrection"), which housed a cave that was venerated as the actual tomb of Jesus. Since it is Vespers, the people have brought candles and lanterns, which are lighted from the flame of the oil lamp that burns permanently inside the tomb.

> Now at the tenth hour [i.e., around 4 p.m.], which they call here "licinicon" (we, on the other hand, say "lucernare"), the whole multitude gathers in the same way [as for the other services] at the Anastasis. All the lanterns and candles are ignited, making an endless light. However the flame for lighting the candles is not carried in from outside, but is brought out from inside the Cave—that is from behind the railings, where an oil lamp always shines night and day.

Psalms related to the theme of light or evening were sung, along with antiphons (whatever Egeria meant by that term). Plausibly the singing included Psalm 140/141, which had an important role in the Vespers rite in later Jerusalem sources.[61] Only after this had gone on for awhile did the bishop and clergy enter, signaling the transition from the monastic to the cathedral Office, hence the singing continued after their arrival. It is not clear whether Egeria's expression "hymns and antiphons" signifies a change from the "psalms and antiphons" that were sung before the bishop appeared.

> Lamplighting psalms as well as antiphons are said for some time. Then the bishop is sent for, and he comes down and sits on a raised seat, and likewise the presbyters also sit in their places. Hymns and antiphons are said.
> 5. And at the point where they have all been said according to the customary practice, the bishop rises and stands in front of the railing, that is, in front of the Cave.

The deacon calls out the names, apparently of everyone present. At each name the children call out *"Kyrie eleison."*

> And one of the deacons makes the commemoration of individuals, as is the customary practice. And every time the deacon says the name of an

---

[61] P. Jeffery, "The Sunday Office of Seventh-Century Jerusalem in the Georgian Chantbook (Iadgari): A Preliminary Report." *Studia Liturgica* 21 (1991) 61–62, 73.

individual, very many children stand, responding every time "Kyrie eleison," though we say "Have mercy, Lord." Their voices are endless.

What does "Their voices are endless" mean? The Latin is *"quorum uoces infinitae sunt."* Some translators have taken this to mean "Their voices are very loud."[62] Others think it refers to the large number of children whose voices are heard.[63] Since the word "vox" can also mean "sound," it is also possible that Egeria is referring to many repetitions or echoes of *Kyrie eleison.*[64] Non-commital translations have also been made.[65] I would translate it in parallel with Egeria's earlier statement that "All the lanterns and candles are ignited, making an endless light" (*incenduntur omnes candelae et cerei et fit lumen infinitum*): just as the great number of lights makes an overwhelming impression, so does the large number of children shouting or singing *Kyrie eleison* over and over again (*semper pisinni plurimi*) each time the deacon calls out a name. The impression is that *Kyrie eleison* is interminable: endlessly repeated by more children than one can count, infinite both temporally and spatially.

Why did Egeria repeat the *Kyrie* in Latin? "'Kyrie eleison,' though we say 'Have mercy, Lord.'" Here too I would draw a parallel, this time with her earlier translation, "which they call here 'licinicon' (we say 'lucernare')." In each case, was Egeria identifying the unfamiliar

---

[62] *Egeria's Travels*, 3rd ed., ed. J. Wilkinson (Warminster: Aris & Phillips, 1999) 143. Compare: "et leurs voix font un bruit extraordinaire," in *Journal de voyage*, ed. H. Pétré. SC 21 (Paris: Cerf, 1948) 193; "e le loro voci fanno grande rumore," in *Pellegrinaggio in Terra Santa*, ed. P. Siniscalco and L. Scarampi. 4th ed. (Rome: Città Nuova Editrice, 2000) 132.

[63] Compare "their voices are legion," *Diary of a Pilgrimage*, ed. George E. Gingras. Ancient Christian Writers 38 (New York: Newman Press, 1970) 90; "the many little boys who are always standing by, answer with countless voices," *The Pilgrimage of Etheria*, ed. M. L. McClure and C. L. Feltoe. Translations of Christian Literature, series 3: Liturgical Texts (London: Society for Promoting Christian Knowledge, n.d.) 47.

[64] Cf. "le loro voci riecheggiano infinitamente," *Pellerinaggio in Terra Santa: Itinerarium Egeriae*, ed. Nicoletta Natalucci. Biblioteca Patristica (Florence: Nardini, 1991) 161.

[65] Cf. "deren Stimmen zahllos sind," in *Itinerarium, Reisebericht, mit Auszügen aus Petrus Diaconus, De locis sanctis, Die heiligen Stätten*, ed. G. Röwekamp, with D. Thönnes. Fontes Christiani 20 (Freiburg: Herder, 1995) 229; "leurs voix sont innombrables," *Journal*, ed. Maraval, 241.

Greek expression with the familiar Latin one? If so, her text provides evidence that her Latin audience also had lamplighting services, and said Kyrie eleison in Latin. Or does her need to translate the Greek terms show that the practices themselves were unfamiliar in the West? In that case the text would be evidence for the exact opposite thesis: that her Latin-speaking audience did not have lamplighting or any form of *Kyrie eleison*. I think Egeria's compatriots back home did know a Latin form of the *Kyrie*, since what Egeria gives is not an exact literal translation ("Domine miserere"), but inverts the order of words ("Miserere Domine"). There is some supporting evidence that "Miserere Domine" (rather than "Domine miserere") was used liturgically in the fourth-century West.[66]

When the deacon has finished calling out names, everyone gets involved. Then the bishop blesses the catechumens.

> 6. And at the point where the deacon has completely said all the things he has to say, first the bishop says a prayer and prays for all. And so they all pray, both the faithful and the catechumens together. Next, the deacon raises his voice, [announcing] that every catechumen, wherever he stands, should bow his head. And so the bishop, standing, says the blessing over the catechumens.

Then the same pattern is followed for the dismissal of the faithful: a prayer, the diaconal command to bow heads, a blessing.

> Next a prayer is made, and the deacon raises his voice once more and reminds each one of the faithful to bow his head where he is standing. Next the bishop blesses the faithful, and so the dismissal is done at the Anastasis. And they begin to come up to the bishop individually to his hand.

[66] See the hymn *Miserere Domine, miserere Christe*, by Marius Victorinus (d. after 363), in *Opera* 1, ed. P. Henry and P. Hadot, 290–93. Corpus Christorum Ecclesiasticorum Latinorum 83 (Vienna: Hoelder-Pichler-Tempsky, 1971); reprinted in SC 68 (Paris: Cerf, 1960) 628–33. J. Jungmann, "Marius Victorinus in der karolingischen Gebetsliteratur und im römischen Dreifaltigkeitsoffizium," in *Kyriakon: Festschrift Johannes Quasten*, ed. P. Granfield and J. Jungmann, 2:691–97 (Münster: Aschendorff, 1970). An anti-Arian tract attributed to Augustine (but seemingly of the sixth century) seems to say that the Greeks, the Latins, and the Goths all said the *Kyrie* in their own languages, addressing it to the one *homoousion* of the Trinity (PL 33:1163).

When "they begin to come up to the bishop individually" the service is officially over, and the people are looking for private individual blessings. These are accomplished by the bishop's hand, perhaps placed on the head or on the cheek.[67] It is also possible, but not stated, that each lay person kissed the bishop's hand, as is done following some Eastern Christian celebrations today.

The worship is not finished, however. There is a procession from the Anastasis to the Cross, that is to an open courtyard adjoining Golgotha, the site of the crucifixion. In subsequent centuries a cross stood on the site; it would seem that it was already there in Egeria's time. Once in the courtyard, the double sequence of prayer and blessing is performed again.

> 7. And afterwards the bishop is conducted with hymns from the Anastasis to the Cross, and all the people will go too at the same time. When he has arrived there, first he makes a prayer, next he blesses the catechumens. Next another prayer is made, next he blesses the faithful.

It still isn't over. The entire group moves next to a place "behind the Cross." This may refer to a small chapel behind Golgotha, or it may refer to the large basilica, known as the Martyrium, in which the small chapel stood.[68] In either case, the same things are done "behind the Cross" that were done in the courtyard ("before the Cross").

> And after this once more both the bishop and the whole crowd will go once more behind the Cross, and there once more the same thing is done as [was done] before the Cross. And in the same way one approaches

[67] See the suggestions of McClure and Feltoe, *The Pilgrimage*, 46 n 2. The "coming up" to the bishop's hand in such dismissal ceremonies also underlies the origin of the sacrament of confirmation, according to A. Kavanagh, "Confirmation: A Suggestion from Structure." *Worship* 58 (1984) 386–95; repr. in *Living Water, Sealing Spirit: Readings on Christian Initiation*, ed. M. E. Johnson, (Collegeville, MN: Liturgical Press, 1995) 148–58. Here too the liturgiological focus on texts, rather than actions, has led to distortions in the reform of the confirmation rite, since "its [original] historic structure, integrity, and purpose [are] no longer detectable even by trained eyes and minds" (395; repr. 1995, 158).

[68] See the drawing in *Egeria's Travels*, rev. ed., ed. Wilkinson, 45. Compare *Itinerarium*, ed. Röwekamp, 56–57.

the bishop to his hand as at the Anastasis. In this way both before the Cross, and behind the Cross.

Egeria makes clear that this triple dismissal with processions was celebrated every evening.

> But very many huge glass lanterns hang everywhere, and there are very many tall candlesticks, both before the Anastasis and also before the Cross, as well as behind the Cross. Therefore all these things are finished by twilight. This procedure takes place in this way every day for six days, at the Cross and at the Anastasis.

Elsewhere she says that on Sunday (which she calls the seventh day) "the same thing is done according to the daily practice" (25.4). Similar accounts of the daily hours (24.2-3 and 25.3-4), seem to be briefer descriptions of the same procedure. That would mean that at Lauds, Sext, and None, the dismissals were carried out in much the same way, but without all the lamps and candles which were specific to the evening lucernare service.

Thus any pilgrim who observed the liturgical rites in Jerusalem would have observed, indeed taken part in, all the following activities several times every day.

1. The singing of psalms, hymns, and antiphons.

2. A solemn entry by the bishop and other clergy, after which the singing continues.

3. A deacon calling out names of people to be prayed for.

4. Children endlessly responding "Kyrie eleison" to the deacon.

5. A "prayer for all" said by the bishop, followed by the entire congregation, baptized and unbaptized, praying in unity.

6. A diaconal command for everyone to bow his head, followed by the bishop's blessing, after which everyone has been dismissed.

7. A procession with singing to a place where Golgotha, and the cross standing on it, can be seen.

The entire subsequent history of the *Kyrie* (apart from the post–Vatican II Penitential Rite!) is largely summed up in these seven elements—though they are variously recombined, modified, and mixed with other elements of disparate origin, such as the lamps of Vespers. But they remain identifiable.

The Litē

The complex rites Egeria described—psalmody, episcopal entrance, litanies, dismissals, processions to the cross—were not limited to Jerusalem, though they may have originated there. Traces of comparable practices can be found in the early liturgical books of both Constantinople and Rome; in both places the procession to the Cross was replaced by a procession to the baptistery, though at Rome the Lateran baptistery was dedicated to the Holy Cross.[69] However, the closest and most recognizable modern descendent of Egeria's dismissal rite is the *litē* procession, which takes place after Vespers on certain days in the Byzantine rite. Since the Byzantine Office is partly derived from the Palestinian monastic tradition, it is a close relative, indeed an indirect descendent, of the urban rite of Jerusalem that Egeria witnessed. Here are portions of one example, representing the Melkite or Byzantine-Arab tradition. Following upon the psalmody and hymnody of the Office, it incorporates four of the seven elements described by Egeria, combined with an element Egeria did not have: the blessing of bread that commemorates the early Christian Agape meals. First, the deacon calls out the names of people present, along with other intentions to be prayed for (Egeria's element 3). The choir, which is actually divided into two choirs, responds with multiple repetitions of *Kyrie eleison* (element 4).

> . . . *Then the Deacon delivereth the censer to the sexton, and lifteth the end of his girdle [stole] with his right hand, saying in a loud voice:*

[69] For Constantinople, the collects for the dismissals and the stations of the processions can be found in M. Arranz, *L'Eucologio constantinopolitano agli inizi del secolo XI: Hagiasmatarion & Archieratikon (Rituale & Pontificale) con l'aggiunta del Leiturgikon (Messale)* (Rome: Editrice Pontificia Università Gregoriana, 1996) 73–80. For the old cathedral Vespers of Rome see the appendix to Ordo Romanus 27, in *Les Ordines Romani*, ed. M. Andrieu, 3:364–66; J. Brooks-Leonard, *Easter Vespers in Early Medieval Rome: A Critical Edition and Study* (Ph.D. diss., University of Notre Dame, 1988) 49. Interestingly, this text says that the collects in the baptistries should be said "always without Kyrieleison," as if one would assume otherwise. Perhaps this is related to the fact that in the Breviarium Romanum preces beginning with *Kyrie eleison* were said before the collect on fast days only.

156

Have mercy upon me, O God, according to the multitude of thy mercies. Of thee we ask; grant and have mercy.

Right choir: Lord, have mercy (*three times*).

Deacon: And again we pray for our Bishop (N.) and all our brethren in Christ.

Left choir: Lord, have mercy (*three times*).

Deacon: And again we ask for mercy, life, safety, sound health, and the salvation of the servants of God who offer this holy offering (*mentioning them by name*), and for all other Orthodox Christians of true worship, for their visitation, their forgiveness, and the remission of their sins.

Right choir: Lord, have mercy (*three times*).

Deacon: And again we ask for the preservation of this holy church, this city, and all other cities and towns, from famine, destruction, earthquakes, flood, fire, and the sword; from the surprise attacks of foreign tribes, civil wars, and sudden death. We pray that our good and philanthropic God, in pity, mercy, and compassion, turn away from us all destruction that riseth against us, deliver us from his just threat, and have mercy upon us.

Then the two Choirs chant alternately, Lord, have mercy (*forty times, of ten times each*).

Deacon: And again we pray that the Lord God hear the voice of our supplication, though we be sinners, and have mercy upon us.

The two Choirs then chant, Lord, have mercy (*three times*), slowly, first one Choir then the other, and the third time, the two together.

Then the priest sums up with a prayer for "all the earth" (Egeria's element 5); indeed the intentions listed by the deacon have already covered almost every conceivable human situation.

Priest: Grant to us, O God our Saviour, O hope of all the earth and of those who are far at sea, thy kindness, O Lord, and be lenient towards our sins, and have mercy upon us; for thou art a compassionate and philanthropic God, and to thee do we address glory, O Father, [Son, and Holy Spirit, now and ever, and unto ages of ages.]

Choir: Amen.

The trinitarian doxology here is the first indication of who, exactly, is being addressed. After this is a command to bow the head (Egeria's element 6). The prayer that follows is initially addressed to Christ, but it includes another list of names, this time of the saints whose intercession is invoked.

Priest: Peace be unto you all.

Choir: And unto thy spirit also.

Deacon: Let us bow our heads to the Lord.

Choir: To thee, O Lord.

Priest: O most merciful Master, the Lord Jesus Christ our God, by the intercessions of our all-pure Lady, the everlastingly virgin Theotokos Mary, and by the might of thy precious enlivening Cross, and by the petitions of the incorporeal heavenly powers, of the honoured Prophet and glorious Forerunner John the Baptist, of the honourable saints, of all the all-praised Apostles, of the glorious saints, of the Martyrs of good victory, of our righteous, God-mantled fathers, of Saint (N.), Patron of this church, of Saint (N. *whose celebration we observe today*), of the two righteous saints, grandparents of Christ, Joachim and Anne, and of the rest of thy saints, let our petitions be acceptable to thee; grant us the forgiveness of our sins; cover us with the shadow of thy wings; drive away all enemies and adversaries; and preserve our lives, O Lord; have mercy upon us and upon thy world, and save our souls; for thou art good and the Lover of mankind.[70]

The next example, from the Slavonic tradition, reveals more Egerian elements. There is a bit of a procession (7), at least for the priest and deacon, preceded by candles and accompanied by the singing of canticles (1). The deacon recites a list of petitions, which this time includes the names of the saints (3). The choir responds many times with *Kyrie eleison* (4).

> But sometimes (especially on the Eve of a Great Feast) there followeth the Litiyá, that is, the Petitions of Fervent Devotion.
>
> When there is a Litiyá, the Priest and Deacon, preceded by taper bearers, come together to the end of the Temple opposite the Sanctuary, while the Choir is singing the Canticles (Stichíry Litíyiny) of the Temple or of the Feast.
>
> Then the Deacon saith, aloud, the following Prayer:
> O God, save thy people, and bless thine heritage. Visit thy world with mercy and bounties; exalt the horn of Orthodox Christians, and send down upon us thy rich mercies. Through the prayers of our all-undefiled Lady, the Birth-giver of God and ever-virgin Mary: through

---

[70] *Divine Prayers and Services of the Catholic Orthodox Church of Christ*, ed. and trans. S. Nassar (Brooklyn: Syrian Antiochian Orthodox Archdiocese of New York and All North America, 1961) 79–81; for the completion of the trinitarian doxology see 23.

the might of the precious and life-giving Cross: through the protection of the honourable Bodiless Powers of heaven; of the honourable, glorious Prophet, Forerunner and Baptist, John; of the holy, glorious, and all-laudable Apostles; of our Holy Fathers, great Hierarchs and Oecumenical Teachers, Basil the Great, Gregory the Theologian and John Chrysostom; of our Holy Father Nicholas, Archbishop of Myra in Lycia, the Wonder-worker; of our Holy Fathers Methodius and Kyril, Evangelizers of the Slavs; (of our Holy Fathers of All-Russia, Wonder-workers, Peter, Alexis, Jonah, Philip); of the holy, glorious, right-victorious Martyrs; of our reverend and God-bearing Fathers, the holy and righteous ancestors of God, Joachim and Anna; of Saint N. (*the Patron Saint of the Temple*); and of all thy Saints: We beseech thee, O all-merciful Lord, give ear unto us sinners, who make our supplications unto thee, and have mercy upon us.

Choir: Lord have mercy. (*40, usually 12, times.*)

Here follow the petitions for the Ruler of the Land and for all the Authorities according to the elements and nationalities of which the Parish is constituted.

Furthermore we pray for our Holy Synod (or Patriarch); for our Bishop (or Archbishop, or Metropolitan), N.; and for all our brethren in Christ; and for every Christian soul that is afflicted and weary in well-doing, in need of God's mercies and succour; for the protection of this holy Temple, and for those who abide therein; for the peace and quietness of the whole world; for the welfare of God's holy Churches; for the salvation and assistance of our fathers and brethren who, with diligence and in the fear of God, do labour and serve; for those who are absent and abroad; for the healing of those who lie in sickness; for the repose, refreshment, blessed memory and remission of sins of all our devout fathers and brethren, Orthodox believers, departed this life before us, who here, and in all the world, lie asleep in the Lord; for the deliverance of captives; and for our brethren who are taking part in these ministrations; and for all who minister and have ministered in this holy Temple, let us say:

Choir: Lord, have mercy. (*8, usually 12, times.*)

Furthermore we pray that he will preserve this city and this holy Temple, and every city and land from pestilence, famine, earthquake, flood, fire, the sword, the invasion of enemies, and from civil war; and that our good God, who loveth mankind, will be graciously favourable and easy to be entreated, and will turn away from us all the wrath stirred up against us, and deliver us from all his righteous chastisement which impendeth against us, and have mercy upon us.

Choir: Lord, have mercy. (*3 times.*)

Furthermore we pray that the Lord God will hearken unto the voice of petition of us sinners and show mercy upon us.

Choir: Lord, have mercy. (*Thrice.*)

In this case it is the priest who lists the names of individuals to be prayed for (3), though he does it silently. The prayer that follows also has a trinitarian doxology.

> *Then the Priest maketh mention, secretly, of whomsoever he will, both of the living and of the dead.*
>
> *Priest, aloud:* Hear us, O God our Saviour, the hope of all the ends of the earth, and of those who are far off upon the sea; and show mercy, show mercy, O Master, upon us sinners, and be merciful unto us. For thou art a merciful God and lovest mankind, and unto thee we ascribe glory, to the Father, and to the Son, and to the Holy Spirit, now, and ever, and unto ages of ages.
>
> *Choir:* Amen.

As usual the deacon commands the assembly to bow their heads (6). The prayer after it is addressed to Christ, but includes also the saints once again.

> *Priest:* Peace be with you all.
>
> *Choir:* And with thy spirit.
>
> *Deacon:* Let us bow our heads unto the Lord.
>
> *Then, as all bow their heads, the Priest reciteth the following Prayer, so that all may hear:*
>
> O most merciful Master, Lord Jesus Christ our God, through the prayers of our all-undefiled Lady, the Birth-giver of God and ever-virgin Mary (*and thence [the list of saints] as in the preceding prayer, ending with*): and of all thy Saints: Make our prayer acceptable; grant us remission of our transgressions; hide us under the shadow of thy wings; drive far from us every foe and adversary; make our life peaceful, O Lord. Have mercy upon us and upon thy world; and save our souls: forasmuch as thou art gracious and lovest mankind.[71]

---

[71] *Service Book of the Holy Orthodox-Catholic Apostolic Church: Compiled, Translated, and Arranged from the Old Church-Slavonic Service Books of the Russian Church and Collated with the Service Books of the Greek Church,* ed. I. F. Hapgood. 4th ed. (Brooklyn: Syrian Antiochian Orthodox Archidiocese, 1965) 11–12.

Between them, these two examples of the *litē* exhibit all but one of Egeria's seven elements. The missing one is the solemn entrance of the bishop. In time, though, we will have examples of that too.

The Incessant Kyrie

Egeria's element 4, endless repetitions of *Kyrie eleison*, survives in some places as a kind of abbreviation or commemoration of dismissal rites resembling the *litē*. Thus in the book Jungmann called "the Byzantine Breviary," actually the *Horologion*, we often find a triple *Kyrie* following a unit of psalmody (element 1), and twelve or forty repetitions at the end of the Office hour in a position analogous to the dismissal (6) or *litē* procession (7) described by Egeria.[72] In the Ambrosian rite of Milan, too, a triple *Kyrie* is sung after the psalmody at each hour of the Office, after the Magnificat at Vespers, after the Gloria in excelsis at Mass, and often after the exchange "*Dominus vobiscum* R̅: *et cum spiritu tuo*." A twelvefold *Kyrie* is sung at the end of Vespers during Holy Week, and various other multiple repetitions occur at other places.[73] Three or twelve repetitions of *Kyrie* are also prescribed in an

---

[72] Ὡρολόγιον περιέχον [sic] τὴν ἡμερονύκτιον ἀκολουθίαν μετὰ τῶν συνήθων προσθήκων [Book of Hours containing the daily/nightly order with the customary prayers; in Greek] 2nd ed. (Rome: Grottaferrat Press, 1937): for triple *Kyries* following units of psalmody see pp. 21, 26, 33, 41, 138, etc. Forty repetitions of *Kyrie* are called for at the ends of Mesonyktikon (pp. 32, 61), Terce (158), Mesorion (164), Sext (173), Mesorion (180), Typika (191), None (211), Vespers (232), Great Compline (255, 264, 271); twelve repetitions at Mesonyktikon on Saturdays (58), at the beginning of Orthros (p. 62) and Great and Little Compline (237, 280), in Lent at the ends of the little hours (Terce 159, Sext 175, Typika 191), the beginning and end of None (204, 211) and Great Compline (237, and at the end of Vespers (233); three repetitions at the end of Prime (141) and Little Compline (293).

[73] See "De versu Kyrie eleison," chapter 12 of the Rubricae Generales in front of the *Breviarium Ambrosianum S. Carolo Archiepiscopo editum, Andrea C. Ferrari Archiepiscopo denuo Impressum*. 2 vols. in 4 (Milan: Cogliati, 1902); *Manuale Ambrosianum ex codice saec. XI olim in usum Canonicae Vallis Travaliae*, ed. M. Magistretti. 3 vols. in 2. (Milan: Moepli, 1904–5; repr. Nendeln, Liechtenstein: Kraus, 1971) 399–418, 430–58 and throughout; W. C. Bishop, *The Mozarabic and Ambrosian Rites: Four Essays in Comparative Liturgiology*, ed. C. L. Feltoe. Alcuin Club Tracts 15 (London: Mowbray; Milwaukee: Morehouse, 1924) 101–14; *Liber vesperalis juxta ritum sanctae ecclesiae Mediolanensis* [ed. G. Sunyol] (Rome: Desclée, 1939) 845–47.

appendix to the sixth-century Gallican monastic rule of Aurelian of Auxerre (PL 68:393-96). The Coptic Office has forty-one near the end of each hour.[74]

There is no indication that any of these numbers—three, twelve, forty, forty-one, and so on—were regarded as "'mystical' numbers," as Jungmann had it. They do not represent the Trinity, the twelve apostles, the forty days in the desert, or any other such thing. It is actually innumerability or infinity that is being represented, as Egeria said. Thus I would refer to this genre as the "incessant *Kyrie*." The unceasing character is particularly evident in the Byzantine rite feast of the Universal Exaltation of the Precious and Live-Giving Cross on September 14. Egeria's element 7, the procession to Golgotha, has become a procession *with* the Cross, accompanied by five hundred repetitions of *Kyrie eleison*.[75] In medieval Constantinople, the patriarch held up a relic of the True Cross while the people repeated *Kyrie eleison* one hundred, then eighty, then sixty times.[76] Even without a cross, a sixth-century description of the monastic Night Office on Mount Sinai mentions almost five hundred repetitions, spaced at different points throughout the service, but with three hundred at the end.[77]

Litanies and Litany Texts

The biggest difference between Egeria's rite and our two forms of the Byzantine *litē* is that, in the *litē*, the deacon has a lot more to say. Besides listing the names and calling on the congregation to bow their heads, he also pronounces a sequence of intentions to be prayed for: "for mercy, life, safety, sound health, and the salvation of the servants

[74] O. H. E. Burmester, *The Egyptian or Coptic Church: A Detailed Description of Her Liturgical Services and the Rites and Ceremonies Observed in the Administration of Her Sacraments*. Publications de la Société d'Archéologie Copte: Textes et Documents (Cairo: Société d'Archéologie Copte, 1967) 96–107.

[75] *The Festal Menaion*, trans. Mother Mary [Sonia Hambourg Bessarab] and Kallistos Ware. The Service Books of the Orthodox Church (London: Faber and Faber, 1969) 153–55.

[76] J. Mateos, ed. *Le typicon de la Grande Église. Ms. Sainte-Croix n°. 40, Xᵉ siècle*. 2 vols. OCA 165–166 (Rome: Pontificium Institutum Orientalium Studiorum, 1962–63) 1:28–31.

[77] R. F. Taft, *The Liturgy of the Hours in East and West: The Origins of the Divine Office and its Meaning for Today*. 2nd rev. ed. (Collegeville, MN: Liturgical Press, 1993) 198–99, 274–75.

of God . . . for the preservation of this holy church, this city, . . . from famine, destruction, earthquakes, flood," and so on, with *Kyrie eleison* as the choral or congregational response.

Lists of this kind are what modern Western Christians usually mean by the word "litany." However the word originally designated not a text but an act. In Homer, the verb *litaneuō* meant "entreat" or "implore" (*Iliad* 9, 581; *Odyssey* 7, 145), as the verb and its corresponding noun *litaneia* also do in the Septuagint (Ps 44[45]:13; 2 Mac 3:20, 10:16), though the word does not occur in the New Testament (but see Ignatius's *Epistle to the Romans* 4.2: "implore Christ about me"). *Litaneia* could serve as a technical term for an act of pagan worship. Thus in a papyrus of the first century B.C.E. an Egyptian priest wrote to his sister about scheduling a *litaneia* "with the children" (*syn tois paidiois*).[78] Though the children's involvement naturally reminds us of Egeria, there is no information about what texts may have been said at this Egyptian ritual, or whether it included the words *Kyrie eleison*, and we should probably imagine this *litaneia* not as a text but as a ritual, a supplication, perhaps a procession. "Procession" is, in fact, what the word *litania* means in its earliest Christian uses: the Latin text of an imperial decree of 3 March 396, preserved in the Theodosian Code (16.5.30.1) and later in the Justinian Code (*Codex Justinianus* 1.5.3),[79] an epistle of the Council of Ephesus of 431,[80] and a report on

[78] "Lysimachus to his sister Taariusis, greeting. It has been decided for me not to go down until the 25th, and as the lord [κύριος] god Seknebtunis wills I will go down freely. But you [would be] acceptable to me [if] with the children concerning the litany [λιτανήας] . . . if from good fortune . . . the children and . . . if I go down. And take care of yourself so as to remain in good health. Good-bye. [The] 12th [year], Choiak 20." Tebtunis papyrus 284, published in B. P. Grenfell et al., eds., *The Tebtunis Papyri* 2 (London: Henry Frowde, 1907), 43. Their translation seems not to appreciate the relationship between the children and the litany ("supplication") since it introduces an ellipsis that does not correspond to any gap in the text. Unfortunately, there is enough papyrus missing already to make it unclear what the ritual was like or what role the children played in it.

[79] *Codex Iustinianus*, ed. Paul Krueger. Corpus Iuris Civilis, 11th ed. (Berlin: Weidmann, 1954) 2:51.

[80] *Acta Conciliorum Oecumenicorum* (Berlin: Walter de Gruyter, 1914–) 1/1/2, p. 65, 1.29.

the Council of Tyre of 518.[81] Thus it would seem that Christian litany processions and their texts are indebted to two pre-Christian antecedents: the phrase *Kyrie eleison*, and a supplication ritual (whatever that was) in which children took a significant role. It is not clear whether the two had any connection prior to their merger in Christianity.

But if Egeria gives no indication that the Jerusalem deacons recited litany texts, we know that they existed in her time, for such texts occur in book 8 of the *Apostolic Constitutions*, which is thought to represent a liturgical tradition from Antioch, not far from Jerusalem, in the 380s.[82] There the ordination rite of a bishop leads into a Eucharist by way of a five-stage dismissal rite, each with its own distinctive litany. The first one is for the catechumens, with the faithful responding *Kyrie eleison* after each intention by the deacon. After that the catechumens are told to stand up, and the deacon pronounces a few more intentions, beginning with a theme of peace:

> "Rise up, ye catechumens, beg for yourselves the peace of God through His Christ, a peaceable day, . . . Dedicate yourselves to the only unbegotten God, through His Christ. Bow down your heads, and receive the blessing."
>
> But at the naming of every one by the deacon, as we said before, let the people say, "Kyrie eleison," and let the children say it first.

A blessing by the newly-ordained bishop follows, "And after this, let the deacon say: Go out, ye catechumens, in peace."[83]

Similar diaconal litanies and episcopal prayers are said over the energumens (people possessed by the devil), the photizomenoi (more advanced catechumens who are preparing for baptism), and the penitents (baptized Christians who are on probation because they have committed serious sins), but neither the litany nor the command to depart mentions "peace." Then the deacon warns that no one may remain who is not one of the faithful; then he tells the faithful to kneel: "let us earnestly beseech God through his Christ." Again we have that emotional note of

---

[81] Ibid., 3, p. 81, 1.14.

[82] *Les constitutions apostoliques,* trans. M. Metzger (Paris: Cerf, 1992) 16.

[83] *Apostolic Constitutions,* 8.6.8–14, in *Les constitutions apostoliques 3: Livres VII et VIII,* ed. M. Metzger. SC 336 (Paris: Cerf, 1987) 154–57; *Constitutions of the Holy Apostles,* trans. J. Donaldson. The Ante-Nicene Fathers 7 (Edinburgh: T&T Clark; Grand Rapids: Eerdmans, 1989) 483.

earnestness. The longest litany of all is recited, corresponding to the Prayer of the Faithful, beginning with "Let us pray for the peace and happy settlement of the world," and ending with "Let us pray for every Christian soul," though only the local bishops are cited by name. The newly-ordained bishop says a long prayer, which is followed by the kiss of peace, then the eucharistic anaphora. After the Amen the bishop greets the faithful again with "The peace of God be with you all," and the deacon leads another litany, "on account of the gift which is offered to the Lord God," praying for all churches, for the faithful departed, and "for the good temperature of the air, and the perfect maturity of the fruits." After communion there is another litany, a long prayer by the bishop, a blessing, and at last the dismissal, "Depart in peace."[84]

In *Apostolic Constitutions* 8, morning and evening prayer also end with the same five-stage dismissal as in the eucharistic liturgy. Even the litany texts are the same, so that the *Constitutions* author states that he will not bother repeating them (8.35, 37, 40). But because there is no Eucharist and the faithful are really dismissed, a few more petitions are added to the litany of the faithful. In the evening these include prayers "for the angel of peace" and for "an evening and a night of peace"; in the morning they include one "for his angel of peace." After the bishop's prayer the deacon tells the faithful to "bow down for the laying on of hands." The bishop says a blessing, which doesn't sound quite like Egeria's description ("they begin to come up to the bishop individually to his hand"). Finally the deacon says "Depart in peace." There is another supplemental litany for use at commemorations of the dead.[85]

Though we do not know that Egeria heard litany texts like these, such texts did develop in the church of Jerusalem, and in the later form of its eucharistic rite, the Liturgy of St. James. The Jerusalem form of the litany for the faithful was known as the *synaptē, katholikē,* or *Katholikon* (συναπτή καθολική), echoing Egeria's statement that the bishop "prays for all."[86]

[84] Metzger (1987), 157–215, trans. Donaldson, 483–91.

[85] Metzger (1987), 246–59, trans. Donaldson, 496–98.

[86] B. Outtier and S. Verhelst, "La Kéryxie catholique de la liturgie de Jérusalem en géorgien (Sin. 12 et 54)." *Archiv für Liturgiewissenschaft* 42 (2000) 41–64. S. Verhelst, *Les traditions judéo-chrétiennes dans la liturgie de Jérusalem, spéciale-ment la Liturgie de saint Jacques frère de Dieu.* Textes et études liturgiques/Studies in Liturgy 18 (Leuven: Peeters, 2003) 105–70, finds fascinating evidences of Jewish background in this text and the *ektenē,* but not for *Kyrie eleison* itself.

Alongside this theme of universality, it shares two other textual themes with the litanies of the *Apostolic Constitutions*: the theme of anxiety or earnestness associated with *Kyrie eleison*, and the theme of peace which comes from the dismissal context and the kiss of peace. There are also two important differences. The Jerusalem *Katholikon* includes a list of saints, "that through their intercession the Lord may have mercy on us."[87] These appear to replace the names of the people who were prayed for in Egeria's rite. More interestingly, the litanies in *Apostolic Constitutions* 8 are addressed "to the only unbegotten God, through His Christ," following the subordinationist christology peculiar to this work, in which all prayers are addressed to God, through Christ, in the Holy Spirit.[88] In Jerusalem, on the other hand, the *Katholikon* was addressed to the Lord without distinction. These differences are even more interesting when we compare the so-called anaphora of St. Gregory, where the prayers and the litanies are addressed directly to Christ.[89] It appears that in this case the Jerusalem litany is the most archaic, retaining a certain lack of specificity as to who is being addressed. In the *Apostolic Constitutions* and the anaphora of St. Gregory, on the other hand, theologians have been at work, revising the litany to make it mean what they knew, no doubt, it was really supposed to mean.

TYPES OF LITANY TEXTS

The Standard Byzantine Types

With the passage of time we find that litany texts have become common in many liturgical traditions. Once the texts are relatively fixed we can identify specific types of litanies. We also find a tendency for litany texts to move around, appearing in parts of the liturgy that did not have litanies before. Examining how the texts are used, however, enables us to isolate two principles that account for most of the

---

[87] Ibid., 58–59.
[88] See J. Jungmann, *The Early Liturgy to the Time of Gregory the Great*, trans. Francis A. Brunner. Liturgical Studies 6 (Notre Dame: University of Notre Dame Press, 1959) 188–95, especially 191; *Constitutions Apostoliques*, trans. Metzger (1992) 25–26.
[89] A. Gerhards, *Die griechische Gregoriosanaphora: Ein Beitrag zur Geschichte des eucharistischen Hochgebets*. Liturgiewissenschaftlichen Quellen und Forschungen 65 (Münster-Westfalen: Aschendorff, 1984) 247–49.

movements. Both principles can be traced back to Egeria's rite. First, a litany may be associated with a procession (Egeria's elements 2 and 7). Second, a litany may mark the transition from psalmody to prayer (elements 1 and 3–5). The second pattern can also occur partially, with the litany closing off psalmody without prayer, or introducing prayer without psalmody.

These patterns are seen most clearly in the Byzantine Eucharist, descended as it is from the cathedral rite of Constantinople, where there are three major types of litany texts. The most familiar, since it now stands at the beginning of the eucharistic liturgy, is the *synaptē* (εὐχὴ συναπτή), meaning "prayer linked together."[90] However, it originally stood at the Prayer of the Faithful, between the dismissal of the catechumens and the kiss of peace; thus it begins by praying for "the peace from above," for which reason it is also called *eirenika*. A shorter form, known as the little *synaptē*, serves as the deacon's way of introducing collects said by the priest or bishop.[91] Another type of litany, the *aitēseis* ("requests"),[92] is often appended to the *synaptē*. Like the litany used to dismiss the faithful from the morning and evening Offices in *Apostolic Constitutions* 8, its most notable request is "for an angel of peace, a faithful guide and guardian of our souls and bodies." The major difference is in the congregational response. Every request in the *synaptē* is answered by *Kyrie eleison*, but only the first few requests in the *aitēseis* have this response; the rest are answered by "Grant, Lord (παράσχου κύριε)."

The third type of Byzantine litany, the *ektenē*, retains most clearly the character of anxious entreaty. Its original context was the penitential procession, often held on the anniversary of an earthquake or other terrifying event. The basic pattern was simple enough: the psaltists would sing the processional troparion until they arrived at a station, or stopping place on the processional route. On reaching this point they would finish their singing with the Gloria Patri, and the deacon would lead the *ektenē*. Then the psaltists would start the

[90] Mateos, *Le typicon*, 2:297, 320.

[91] R. F. Taft, *Beyond East and West: Problems in Liturgical Understanding*. 2nd rev. and enlarged ed. (Rome: Edizioni Orientalia Christiana, 1997) 193–96.

[92] R. F. Taft, *The Great Entrance: A History of the Transfer of Gifts and Other Pre-anaphoral Rites of the Liturgy of St. John Chrysostom*. 2nd ed. OCA 200 (Rome: Pontificium Institutum Studiorum Orientalium, 1978) 311–49.

troparion again, and the procession would move out to the next station.[93] The more fervent tone of this litany is evident throughout the text. It begins "Let us all say with our whole soul, and with our whole mind let us say: Kyrie eleison," but the congregation or choir answers every petition by saying *Kyrie eleison* three times, rather than only once. At the end, the congregation would often repeat the *Kyrie* nine or twelve times, from which the *ektenē* derives its name "insistent supplication" (ἐκτενὴς ἱκεσία, *ektenēs hikesia*) or the Great *Kyrie eleison*.[94] There are also abridged forms of *ektenē*, however, sometimes led by the patriarch himself, and emphasizing prayer for the bishops or the emperor,[95] or for the dead. An example of the latter occurs already in the sixth-century life of Saint Eutychius of Constantinople (PG 86:2381).

In Constantinople, where processions throughout the city were frequent, a more elaborate ritual developed for use at stations or stopping places: the Office of the three antiphons. A very similar structure was used to form the daily Office of Terce-Sext, celebrated only during Lent. The major functions and associations of the three litany types can be seen clearly in these two parallel ritual shapes (see table).

In the stational Office, that is, the abridged *ektenē* or *synaptē* with *aitēseis* marks the end of the psalmody; the full *ektenē* after the readings signals the resumption of the procession. In Terce-Sext the end of the psalmody is marked with the *synaptē*, and the end of the readings with the *ektenē*, while the *synaptē* combined with the *aitēseis* stands at the dismissal. In the processional Office, the patriarch is already present, whereas in Terce-Sext he enters during the third antiphon, and the trisagion that would normally mark his arrival is replaced by a proper troparion.

The associations and functions of the litanies in these two Offices illuminate the introduction of litanies at various places in the Byzantine Eucharist. The *aitēseis* are said in the Byzantine Eucharist after the Great Entrance. In that position they seem to be an importation from the Liturgy of the Presanctified, which was originally a Communion

[93] Mateos, *Le typicon* 1:212–13.

[94] J. Mateos, *La célébration de la parole dans la liturgie byzantine: Étude historique*. OCA 191 (Rome: Pontificium Institutum Studiorum Orientalium, 1971) 148–56; *Le typicon* 2:293.

[95] Mateos, *Le typicon* 2:202–03, 296–97.

stational Office of three antiphons	Terce-Sext
three antiphons (i.e., psalms with refrains)	three antiphons
	bishop's entry during third antiphon
short *ektenē* ("habitual prayers")	
or *synaptē* with *aitēseis*	*synaptē*
or trisagion or troparion	troparion replacing trisagion
responsorial psalms and readings	responsorial psalms and readings
ektenē, and procession starts up again	*ektenē*
	synaptē with *aitēseis*
	dismissal
(Mateos, *Le typicon* 1:4–9, 18, 62–63, 146–47, 370–71; 2:200–3, 284; cf. Arranz, *L'Eucologio constantinopolitano,* 70–72)	(Mateos, *Le typicon* 2:4–5, 323; Arranz, *L'Eucologio constantinopolitano,* 57–65)

Table. Litanies in two short Offices compared

service appended to a Vespers, following the dismissal *aitēseis*.[96] The *aitēseis* occur again in the Byzantine Eucharist as part of the preparation for Communion, where they serve to expand what was originally a prayer for the acceptance of the gifts.[97] The *ektenē* entered the Eucharist after the gospel, paralleling its location after the readings in the two types of Office.[98] The most complicated history belongs to the *synaptē*, which appears to have come into the Eucharist as a litany for the Prayer of the Faithful, following the dismissal of the catechumens, just before the transfer of gifts accompanied by a psalm chant and subsequently by the Cherubimic hymn. A remnant of it still exists at this point in the Slavonic text.[99] The reason it withered at this location was because, by the ninth century, it was also being performed near the

[96] Taft, *The Great Entrance,* 311–49; *Beyond East and West,* 224–25.

[97] Taft, *The Precommunion Rites,* 85–103.

[98] Mateos, *La célébration,* 148–73; Taft, *Beyond East and West,* 216–17.

[99] Mateos, *La célébration,* 29–33, 159–60; Taft, *Beyond East and West,* 209–10; *Service Book,* ed. Hapgood (as in note 71), 93–94.

beginning of the Eucharist. The originally processional Office of three antiphons was being used routinely to open the Mass, with the Little Entrance taking place at the third antiphon. The *synaptē* followed between the entrance and the trisagion. About the eleventh century the *synaptē* moved again, to the very beginning of the liturgy, a position paralleled in later forms of the Office of three antiphons, where the bishop was already present at the beginning.[100]

The most extravagant use of litanies in a Eucharist can be seen in the latest form of the Greek Liturgy of St. James, the Mass rite of Jerusalem. Since the Office of three antiphons never became attached to the beginning of this liturgy, the first litany occurs between the Little Entrance and the trisagion. It resembles the *synaptē*, opening "In peace let us pray to the Lord." Another litany, resembling the *ektenē* ("Let us all say: Lord have mercy") comes between the Alleluia and the gospel. The *katholikē synaptē*, preserving the traditions of Egeria's prayer for all, appears to stand for the Prayer of the Faithful, though it is placed later: just before the anaphora, following the Great Entrance, the Creed, and the Kiss of Peace. After the anaphora, the intercessions, and the diptychs, another *synaptē*-like litany introduces the Our Father. Twelve repetitions of *Kyrie eleison* are said after the response to the Sancta Sanctis, a short *synaptē* at the thanksgiving after communion, but only one *Kyrie* at the dismissal.[101]

Non-Greek Litany Texts

As the litany concept was exported into languages other than Greek, we can observe developments in new directions, expanding on one of the traditional themes at the expense of others. Thus in the Syriac form of the Liturgy of St. James, the numerous litanies of the Greek form have been much reduced, often to no more than one or three repetitions of *Kurillīson*.[102] However the diptychs, which are read by

[100] A. Strittmatter, "Notes on the Byzantine Synapte." *Traditio* 10 (1954) 107–08; Mateos, *La célébration*, 29–31; idem, *Le typicon* 2:200–201; Taft, *Beyond East and West*, 208–10.

[101] *Liturgies Eastern and Western, being the Texts Original or Translated of the Principal Liturgies of the Church* 1: *Eastern Liturgies*, ed. F. E. Brightman "on the basis of the former work by C. E. Hammond" (Oxford: Clarendon Press, 1896; repr. 1965) 34–39, 44–49, 58–59, 62–63, 65–67). [No other volumes published.] Repr. with the title *Eastern Liturgies* (Piscataway, NJ: Gorgias Press, 2002).

[102] *Liturgies*, ed. Brightman, 74, 77, 88, 108.

the deacon simultaneously with the priest's intercessions after the anaphora, have acquired the *Kurillīson* as congregational response,[103] and the name *Katholikon* (*Kathulīkī*) survives for a similar list which is read during the fraction, leading into the Our Father.[104] Thus by conflating the litany with the reading of the diptychs, something of the original Jerusalem practice of naming names and praying for all was preserved, while other aspects of the litany receded.[105] In the East Syrian Eucharist, on the other hand, where the diptychs were read before the anaphora,[106] the litanies seem to have gravitated instead to the Prayer of the Faithful, but also retained the function of preparing for dismissal. As a result, the *kāruzūtha* (from the Greek word for "proclamation") includes texts resembling the *synaptē* and *aitēseis*, which bracket a further series of petitions, each answered by "Amen." All this is followed by a blessing with heads bowed, a dismissal of the unbaptized, the handwashing and transfer of the gifts, the Creed, and only then the diptychs, the peace, and the anaphora.[107]

The Armenian rite stayed closer to the Jerusalem model of frequent litanies. The Eucharist preserves an *aitēseis*-like litany with blessing and dismissal before the Great Entrance, a litanic form for the diptychs which (however) precede rather than coincide with the priest's

[103] Ibid., 89–95; *Anaphoras: The Book of the Divine Liturgies according to the Rite of the Syrian Orthodox Church of Antioch*, ed. A. Y. Samuel, trans. Murad Saliba Barsom (Lodi, NJ, by the editor, 1991) 107–22, includes the *Kyrie* responses that are not present in Brightman.

[104] *Liturgies*, ed. Brightman, 97–99. *Anaphoras*, ed. Samuel, 123–26, has the "angel of peace" *aitēseis* at this point.

[105] The practice of reading actual names from ivory diptychs during the anaphora of a James-like Eucharist seems to have survived in the Greek-speaking church of Sant'Agata dei Goti in Rome as late as the reign of one of the early popes Hadrian (eighth or ninth century). See J.-M. Sansterre, "Où le diptyche consulaire de Clementinus fut-il remployé à une fin liturgique?" *Byzantion* 54 (1984) 641–47, pl i–ii; M. Gibson, *The Liverpool Ivories: Late Antique and Medieval Ivory and Bone Carving in Liverpool Museum and the Walker Art Gallery* (London: HMSO, 1994) 19–22 and plates VIIIa–VIIIb.

[106] R. F. Taft, *A History of the Liturgy of St. John Chrysostom*. vol. 4: *The Diptychs*. OCA 238 (Rome: Pontificium Institutum Studiorum Orientalium, 1991) 56–58, 71–75.

[107] Brightman, *Liturgies*, 262–71; Mateos, *La célébration*, 171; S. Jammo, *La structure de la messe chaldéenne du début jusqu'à l'anaphore: Étude historique*. OCA 207 (Rome: Pontificium Institutum Studiorum Orientalium, 1979) 125–56.

intercessions, and a *synaptē*-like litany introducing the Lord's Prayer.[108] An interesting feature of the Mashtots', or Rituale, preserves the memory that the dismissals in Jerusalem involved a procession to Golgotha. Several sacramental celebrations end with a dismissal or final blessing, which the deacon introduces with a text that begins "By the holy Cross let us beseech the Lord . . ." The priest replies with *Kyrie eleison* three times, then says a "Prayer of the Cross."[109] Thus the Armenian rite emphasizes the Cross theme, the West Syrian rite the reading of names, the East Syrian rite the themes of dismissal and the general Prayer of the Faithful.

In the Slavic world it was the anxious ethos of the *ektenē* that came to the fore. For though the Slavonic rite retains all the Byzantine litany types, in Slavonic they are all called *ekténiya*, even the *synaptē* and *aitēseis*. It was also the insistent character of the *ektenē* that impressed the Gallican council of Vaison, which met on 5 November 529 to produce the first datable Western reference to the *Kyrie*:

> And whereas both in the Apostolic See, and also through all the oriental and Italian provinces, the sweet and particularly salubrious custom has been introduced, that Kyrie eleison is said very frequently and with great emotion and compunction, it has pleased us also, that in all our churches this so holy custom be introduced, through a propitious God, both at Matins and at Masses and at Vespers.[110]

Indeed the *ektenē* model seems to dominate in the oldest litanic Latin texts, which are known as preces. Many of the earliest preces can be assigned to one of two types. A preces text found in the Irish Stowe missal and elsewhere, whose title *Deprecatio Sancti Martini pro populo* appears to signal Gallican origin, begins like the *ektenē*: "Let us all say, from our whole heart and mind," with the response "Lord, hear and have mercy" in Latin. A text preserved in Frankish-Gallican sources opens similarly, with the simpler response "*Domine miserere.*" Other Franco-Gallican texts open by recalling the second line of the Byzantine *ektenē*: "Lord, almighty God of our fathers," and have *Kyrie eleison* in Greek for the response. Indeed, the Stowe missal litany is placed be-

---

[108] Brightman, *Liturgies*, 428–30, 440–46.

[109] *Rituals of the Armenian Apostolic Church* (New York: The Armenian Prelacy, 1992) 17, 53–54, 63, 68–69, 97, 119, 197.

[110] Council of Vaison in Gaul (529); CCSL 148A:79.

fore the Gospel of the Mass, like the *ektenē* in the Liturgy of St. James, while the Franco-Gallican texts are preserved as processional chants. On the other hand, there are also allusions to the peace theme associated with the *synaptē*. The litanies that begin with "Let us all say" and have a Latin response (Stowe and the first Franco-Gallican text) also ask for the peace from above (*Pro altissima pace*). The last three petitions of the Stowe litany have the response "grant, Lord, grant— *Praesta, Domine, praesta*," recalling the *aitēseis*, though the angel of peace is not mentioned.[111]

The rite of Milan, which exhibits many oriental features, came closer to maintaining the distinction between *synaptē* and *ektenē*. It has two preces texts, which are sung on alternate Sundays of Lent, replacing the Gloria at Mass. One begins like the *ektenē*, "Let us all say: Kyrie eleison. Lord almighty God of our fathers: Kyrie eleison." The other touches on the *synaptē* theme of peace, but refers to the *ektenē* more clearly: "Supplicating for the gift of forgiveness and of divine peace, from our whole heart and from our whole mind we pray you: Domine miserere."[112] Both of the Milanese texts end with a triple *Kyrie*, as the Gloria in excelsis and the Office psalmody also do. Since the late Middle Ages this has often been taken as equivalent to the *Kyrie* in the Roman Mass, but I believe incorrectly: it is a Milanese way of concluding psalms and long chants, perhaps serving also to introduce the collect that often followed.[113]

The Mozarabic Preces

The most original corpus of Latin preces is found in the Mozarabic rite, where they were used at Lenten Masses (between the Old Testament

---

[111] These are the texts designated Irl[1], FG[1], and FG[2] in P. de Clerck, *La "Prière universelle" dans les liturgies latines anciennes: Témoignages patristiques et textes liturgiques*, Liturgiewissenschaftliche Quellen und Forschungen 62 (Münster: Aschendorff, 1977) 146, 190, 216–18. For Irl[1] see also *The Stowe Missal: MS. D II 3 in the Library of the Royal Irish Academy, Dublin*, ed. G. F. Warner. HBS 31–32 (London: [Henry Bradshaw Society], 1906–15; repr. Suffolk: Henry Bradshaw Society/Boydell Press, 1989) 2:6–7.

[112] These are M[2] and M[1] in de Clerck, *La "Prière universelle,"* 205–14, 166–65. See also *Missale Ambrosianum duplex (Proprium de tempore) Editt. Puteobonellianae et Typicae (1751–1902)*, ed. A. Ratti and M. Magistretti (Milan: R. Ghirlanda, 1913) 136, 121–22; *Missarum iuxta ritum sanctae ecclesiae Mediolanensis*, [ed. G. Sunyol] (Rome: Desclée, 1935) 116–17, 105–9.

[113] Thus I disagree with much of de Clerck, *La "Prière universelle,"* 282–91.

and New Testament readings), throughout the Office on penitential days, and in the burial service. Many of them are metrical, some abecedarian or acrostic, some even make use of rhyme.[114] A wide variety of responses were used, such as *Et miserere* and *Quia peccavimus tibi*. Some of these texts were evidently used in the Gallican rite also.[115] It is in the Mozarabic tradition, more than elsewhere, that we find preces in which a penitential theme is emphasized. However, this is not a rootless innovation as in the Vatican II Mass, but grows out of traditions going back to Egeria, for during Lent the Mozarabic rite retained the custom of actually dismissing the penitents after the gospel of the Mass.[116] It is therefore not surprising that the preces used at these dismissals also emphasized themes of penitence, with refrains like *obliviscere peccata nostra* ("forget our sins"), *iam miserere peccavimus tibi* ("have mercy now, we have sinned against you") and *Averte iram tuam a nobis* ("Avert your anger from us").[117] Some of the petitions in these preces are explicitly addressed to Christ, while others are not.[118]

The penitential theme merges with the cross theme at None on Good Friday, at the service corresponding to the Roman Adoration of the Cross. In the Mozarabic rite the penitents were repeatedly told to kneel, pray, and stand up again. The deacon cried *Indulgentia* ("Forgiveness!"), and the clergy and people were told to repeat it "not more

[114] W. Meyer, *Die Preces der mozarabischen Liturgie*. Abhandlungen der königlichen Gesellschaft der Wissenschaften zu Göttingen, Philosophisch-Historische Klasse, new ser. 15, no. 3 (Berlin: Weidmann, 1914).

[115] *The Bobbio Missal: A Gallican Mass-Book (MS. Paris Lat. 13246)*, ed. E. A. Lowe and A. Wilmart. 3 vols. HBS 53, 58, 61 (London: Harrison and Sons, 1917–24) 2:66; M. Huglo, "Les 'preces' des graduels aquitains empruntées à la liturgie hispanique." *Hispania Sacra* 8 (1955) 361–83; C. Rojo and G. Prado, *El canto mozárabe*. Biblioteca Central: Publicaciones del Departamento de Música 5 (Barcelona: Diputación provincial, 1929) 74–75. For a comprehensive list of Gallican preces, see M. Huglo et al., "Gallican chant," in *The New Grove Dictionary of Music and Musicians* 9:458–72. 2nd ed. (London: Macmillan; New York: Grove's Dictionaries, 2001) 469.

[116] *Liber misticus de Cuaresma: (Cod. Toledo 35.2, hoy en Madrid, Bibl. Nac. 10.110)*, ed. José Janini; studio paleográfico por el Prof. Anscari M. Mondó (Toledo: Instituto de Estudios Visigótico-Mozárabes, 1979) 7, 13, 17, 20, 22, 31, 33, 47, 54, 60 (dismissals); 29, 41, 47, 54, 62 (*Kyrie* repetitions); 111, 113–14 (not said at Easter Office and Mass).

[117] Ibid., 25, 37, 47, 49, 28, 43.

[118] Ibid.; compare 14, 25, 37, 49 vs. 28, 43, 53.

than three hundred times" according to one MS, not more than seventy-two times in another. Then the deacon began a preces-type litany, to which *Indulgentia* was the response. A prayer followed, then two hundred more repetitions of *Indulgentia*. The preces was resumed, then another prayer. Psalm 50 (*Miserere*) was sung, in some places with *Indulgentia* as part of the refrain; another hundred *Indulgentia* and the preces was completed.[119] Thus the strong penitential tone of these texts grows directly from the merger of the Egerian dismissal theme with the cross theme.

Indeed the Good Friday service was treated as a kind of climax, and the rest of Mozarabic Lent was structured to build up to it. When the penitents were dismissed at the Lenten Sunday Masses, following the preces there were repetitions of *Kyrie eleison*, which increased in number as Lent proceeded from three to five to seven.[120] The dismissals are no longer mentioned between Easter and Pentecost, however, when even the *Kyrie* at the end of the Office was omitted.[121] The two most remarkable Mozarabic preces occur in the latter half of Lent, corresponding to Roman Passiontide: they are written as if spoken by Christ himself, addressing the Father on behalf of sinners. Here is the beginning of one of them:

> See, Lord, my humility, for the enemy has arisen.
> [Response:] Have mercy, Father, justly, and grant forgiveness to all.
> Sent by the Father I came, to seek the lost and redeem captives; a dread
> ful people handed me over. Have mercy, Father, . . .
> Foretold by the prophets I was born of a virgin; I assumed the form of a
> servant to collect the dispersed; hunters seized me. Have mercy,
> Father, . . .[122]

These texts obviously look forward to the great celebration of infinite forgiveness that was the Mozarabic Good Friday, a rite which, because

[119] Ibid., 88–94. Compare *Le Liber Ordinum en usage dans l'église wisigothique et mozarabe d'Espagne du cinquième au onzième siècle*, ed. M. Férotin. Monumenta Ecclesiae Liturgica 5 (Paris: Firmin-Didot, 1904; repr. Farnborough: Gregg, 1969) 200–202; *Antifonario visigótico mozárabe de la Catedral de León*, ed. L. Brou and J. Vives. Monumenta Hispaniae Sacra, Serie Liturgica 5/1 (Barcelona and Madrid: Consejo Superior de Investigaciónes Cientificas, 1959) 272–77.

[120] *Liber Misticus*, 29, 41, 47, 54, 62.

[121] Ibid., 111, 113–14.

[122] Ibid., 40; see also 53.

of its emphasis on the cross, was itself an enacted memory of the ancient Jerusalem liturgy.

The Roman Preces

The most interesting of all the Latin preces texts is the self-described *Deprecatio Gelasii*, not only because it is ascribed to a named author and an early pope (Gelasius, 492–96), but because its relationships to other texts raise a host of questions about the early Roman liturgy. On the one hand, the *Deprecatio* begins like the Greek *ektenē*, "Let us all say: Lord hear and have mercy," but this is followed immediately by an invocation to the Trinity with no Eastern precedents: "The Father of the only-begotten, and the Son of God the unbegotten Father, and the Holy Spirit of the Lord, with faithful souls we invoke." Gelasius, or whoever the author was, seems to have wanted to establish at the outset that the entire Trinity was being addressed. The response varies, depending how one interprets the different manuscripts: *Dominus miserere, Dominus exaudi et miserere* ("Lord, hear and have mercy"), even *Domine miserere et miserere*. The only manuscript that contains music notation is also the only one to give the response in Greek: *Kyrie eleison*. In the nonmusical manuscripts there are four petitions at the end which ask for an angel of peace, and have the response *Praesta, Domine, praesta*, clearly referring to the *aitēseis*.[123] But the most unexpected feature of the *Deprecatio Gelasii* is the fact that its petitions oddly parallel the Orationes solemnes of Good Friday, even mentioning Jews and heretics along with those more typically prayed for.[124] It is as though the *Deprecatio* was composed to provide a litanic replacement for the Solemn Orations, which were once said more often than on Good Friday alone. Bernard Capelle theorized that Pope Gelasius had in fact done just that; moreover that the *Deprecatio*, moved to the beginning of the celebration, was eventually cut down to form the familiar *Kyrie* of the Roman Mass.[125] Jungmann accepted

---

[123] De Clerck, *La "Prière universelle,"* 168–73.

[124] Compare the texts of the two in de Clerck, *La "Prière universelle,"* 126–29 and 170–73.

[125] B. Capelle, "Le Kyrie de la messe et le pape Gélase." *Revue bénédictine* 46 (1934) 126–44; repr. in *Travaux liturgiques* 2:116–34 (Louvain: Centre liturgique, Abbaye du Mont César, 1962); see also G. G. Willis, *Essays in Early Roman Liturgy*. Alcuin Club Collections 46 (London: S.P.C.K., 1964), 1–48, especially 19–28; de Clerck, *La "Prière universelle,"* 282–95.

this,[126] without noticing that, if it were true, it would mean that the *Kyrie* of the Roman Mass was originally trinitarian, not christological. But in fact the *Kyrie* of the Roman Mass was not created by shortening the *Deprecatio Gelasii*.

THE LITANY OF SAINTS

By far the most important of the Latin litanies is the litany of saints. It is named for its most distinctive feature, the long lists of saints' names, with the response to each being usually "pray for us" (*ora pro nobis*), sometimes "intercede for us," or another response. Before and after the saints' names are various invocations of the Trinity and lists of things to be prayed for. The listing of names, of course, recalls the Byzantine *litē*; some texts of the *synaptē* also exhibit a tendency to multiply saints' names after the commemoration of the Virgin Mary at the end.[127] One tenth-century English source, a private prayerbook rather than a book for the liturgy, gives the litany of saints in Greek, as if it were of Eastern origin. This seems to be a retroversion of a Latin text from Rome, not an importation from the East. Indeed it is textually similar to the eighth-century Latin litany that Jungmann misread.[128]

[126] Joseph Jungmann, *Public Worship*, trans. Clifford Howell, S.J. (London: Challoner Publications, 1957) 109.

[127] A. Strittmater, "Notes on the Byzantine Synapte." *Traditio* 10 (1954) 56, 59–65; Mateos, *La célébration*, 155.

[128] *London, British Library MS. Cotton Galba A. xviii*, in *Anglo-Saxon Litanies of the Saints*, ed. M. Lapidge. HBS 106 (London: [Woodbridge: Boydell], 1991) 172–73. I agree with the arguments in E. Bishop, "The Litany of Saints in the Stowe Missal," in *Liturgica Historica: Papers on the Liturgy and Religious Life of the Western Church* (Oxford: Clarendon Press, 1918; repr. 1962) 137–64, that this and related texts came to England from Rome. Lapidge (ibid., 13–25), on the other hand, argues that the Greek text was brought from Antioch to Canterbury by Theodore of Tarsus. Though the argument is ingenious, it does not distinguish Antiochene evidence (e.g., the *Apostolic Constitutions*) from the evidence of Jerusalem (e.g., the Liturgy of St. James) and other Eastern centers. It also does not consider all the evidence for early Roman processional litanies that I will mention in this article. Even if the wording of certain phrases is suggestive of Greek origin (Lapidge, 181–89), this does not preclude the singing of litanies of the saints in Greek or Latin in Roman processions of Pope Gregory's time. The manuscript reading *"tin hamartias,"* indeed, suggests confusion between the Latin liturgical plural *"peccata"* and the Greek (and Latin) New Testament singular.

Since the litany of saints is essentially a list, its text was easily varied from one locality to another, depending on the selection of saints' names and other material at the beginning and end.[129] Some recensions had their own names: thus St. Angilbert's Ordo for St. Riquier (ca. 800) mentions four different types of litany text: "laetaniam generalem," "Gallicam," "Italicam," and "Romanam."[130] The most familiar is the type called *Letania gallica*: after the initial *Kyrie eleison, Christe eleison, Christe audi nos*, and so on, the members of the Trinity are invoked in turn, *Pater de caelis, Deus, miserere nobis. . . ."* Next comes the list of saints, with the response *ora pro nobis* after each name. After that come petitions resembling those of the preces; some request deliverance from various calamaties, and are answered with the response *libera nos Domine* ("deliver us O Lord").[131]

In liturgical usage, the litany of saints was a processional litany, associated particularly with the Rogation days.[132] The Greater (or "Roman") Rogation took place on 25 April, which coincidentally was also the feast of St. Mark. The origin of this rogation is traditionally ascribed to Pope Gregory the Great (590–604), who, according to the

[129] For studies and editions of some texts see M. Coens, "Anciennes litanies des saints." *Recueil d'études bollandiennes*. Subsidia Hagiographica 37 (Brussels: Société des Bollandistes, 1963) 129–322; J. Hennig, "Studies in Early Western Devotion to the Choirs of Saints." *Studia patristica* 8, Texte und Untersuchungen 93 (1966) 239–47; E. B. Garrison, "Saints Equizio, Onorato, and Libertino in Eleventh- and Twelfth-Century Italian Litanies as Clues to the Attribution of Manuscripts." *Revue bénédictine* 88 (1978) 297–315.

[130] *Institutio Sancti Angilberti abbatis de diuersitate officiorum (800–811)*, ed. K. Hallinger et al. Corpus Consuetudinum Monasticarum 1: Initia Consuetudinis Benedictinae: Consuetudines Saeculi Octavi et Noni, ed. K. Hallinger (Siegburg: Franz Schmitt, 1963), 298; on differences see also Kantorowicz, *Laudes regiae*, 35–43.

[131] For the *Litania italica*, see B. Opfermann, "Litania italica: Ein Beitrag zur Litaneigeschichte." *Ephemerides liturgicae* 72 (1958) 306–19. A wide range of texts is published in Coens, "Anciennes litanies."

[132] On the history of the Rogation days see D. De Bruyne, "L'origine des processions de la chandeleur et des rogations à propos d'un sermon inédit." *Revue bénédictine* 34 (1922) 14–26; P. Siffrin, "Rogazioni," in *Enciclopedia cattolica* 10 (1953) 1084–86; G. Démaret, "Les rogations." *Revue grégorienne* 14 (1929) 122–29, 168–79, 218–28.

Gallican historian Gregory of Tours,[133] responded to a plague in the year 590 by commanding the clergy and laity to assemble in the seven districts of Rome, holding processions and "crying Kyrie eleison through the streets of the city."[134] This account, however, seems to be a later interpolation into the text of Gregory of Tours, actually based on processions held during the reign of Pope Gregory II (715–31).[135] Nor does the text place these processions on April 25, despite the claims of medieval writers (see, for instance, Honorius Augustodunensis in PL 172:680-81). There may be some relationship to the Robigalia, a pagan agricultural festival that formerly took place the same day.[136] Gregory I did order twice-weekly litany processions against times of trouble,[137] indicating that he was familiar with the kind of procession that became typical of the Rogation days.

The Lesser or Gallican rogations, also known as the minor litanies, were celebrated on the three weekdays preceding Ascension Thursday (the following week in the Ambrosian rite, to avoid fasting before Ascension in opposition to Matthew 9:15). A sermon of Avitus, bishop of Vienne (d. 518), attributes the origin of these rogations to his predecessor Mamertus,[138] but a canon preserved in the collection of Regino states that all the Gallican bishops assembled at Vienne instituted the

[133] See his *Libri Historiarum X*, 2nd. ed., ed. B. Krusch and W. Levison. Monumenta Germaniae Historica: Scriptores Rerum Merovingicarum 1/1 (Hannover: Hahn, 1951) 477–81.

[134] O. Chadwick, "Gregory of Tours and Gregory the Great." *Journal of Theological Studies*, old series 50 (1949) 38–49.

[135] Ibid.

[136] T. J. Talley, "Roman Culture and Roman Liturgy," in *Rule of Prayer, Rule of Faith: Essays in Honor of Aidan Kavanagh, O.S.B.*, ed. N. Mitchell and J. F. Baldovin, 18–31 (Collegeville, MN: Liturgical Press, 1996) 26–29.

[137] *Registrum* 11.31, in *S. Gregorii Magni, Registrum Epistularum*, ed. Dag Norber. 2 vols. CCSL 140–140A (Turnhout: Brepols, 1982) 2:919–20; see also 1096, 1102–4. M. McCormick, *Eternal Victory: Triumphal Rulership in Late Antiquity, Byzantium, and the Early Medieval West* (Cambridge: Cambridge University Press; Paris: Editions de la Maison des Sciences de l'Homme, 1986) 242–43.

[138] Avitus of Vienne, *Alcimi Ecdicii Aviti Viennensis Episcopi, Opera quae supersunt*, ed. Rudolf Peiper. Monumenta Germaniae Historica: Auctorum Antiquissimorum 6/2 (Berlin: Weidmann, 1883) 108–12.

practice to counteract an attack by wolves.[139] The pre-Christian Ambarvalia may also form part of the background for the minor litanies. Besides the Rogation days, processions with the litany took place on many occasions: leading from the baptismal font to the Mass at the Easter and Pentecost vigils, on designated weekdays during Lent, and before the stational Masses, as the bishop and people went in procession, carrying crosses, from the church of the collecta to the church where Mass would be celebrated.[140] Processions with litanies would also take place in time of drought, earthquake, famine, or other calamity. Processional antiphons would often be sung before the litany; the texts usually expressed the people's sorrow for their sins.[141] Some forms of the litany of saints had special functions. The Commendatio Animae, recited over a dying person, tended to begin with the *Kyrie eleison, Christe audi nos,* and *Salvator mundi, adjuva eum,* with a particular emphasis on Old Testament saints. There are some similar examples in Greek sources.[142] Another special form, the Laudes regiae, continued the tradition of the old imperial acclamations, and thus included many petitions for the emperor, the king, the pope, the bishop, and other persons of importance. The Laudes regiae often began with texts that recall imperial acclamations: *Christus vincit, Christus regnat, Christus imperat*—"Christ conquers, Christ reigns, Christ commands," and the response to each saint's name was frequently *Tu illum adjuva*—

---

[139] The canon "Cum exigentibus peccatis" in Regino of Prüm, *De synodalibus causis et disciplina ecclesiasticis* 1.280, ed. F. G. A. Wasserschleben (Leipzig: F. G. A. Wasserschleben, 1840; repr. Graz: Akademische Druck, 1964) 131.

[140] R. Hierzegger, "Collecta und Statio: Die römischen Stationsprozessionen im frühen Mittelalter." *Zeitschrift für katholische Theologie* 60 (1936) 511–54; G. G. Willis, *Further Essays in Early Roman Liturgy.* Alcuin Club Collections 50 (London: S.P.C.K., 1968) 9–16.

[141] Some processional antiphons are edited, with music and bibliography, in M.-N. Collete, *Le répertoire des rogations d'après un processional de Poitiers (XVIᵉ siècle)* (Paris: Éditions du Centre National de la Recherche Scientifique, 1976).

[142] S. J. P. Van Dijk, "Commendatio Animae." *New Catholic Encyclopedia* 4:8–9 (New York: McGraw Hill, 1967); A. Baumstark, "Eine Parallele zur Commendatio Animae in der griechischen Kirchenpoesie." *Oriens Christianus,* new ser. 4 (1915) 298–305; F. Halkin, "Une litanie des saints dans un office grec pour un mourant," in *Corona gratiarum: Miscellanea patristica, historica et liturgica Eligio Dekkers OSB XII lustra complenti oblata* 2:51–59. Instrumenta patristica 11 (Bruges: Sint Pietersabdij, 1975).

180

"You help him."[143] Laudes were sung at many services in which the bishop or king took part, particularly at pontifical Mass, where they immediately followed the *Kyrie*. At Beauvais they were also found joined to the *Ite Missa est* (PL 143:865-66).

The singing of the *Kyrie* by children seems to have generalized, in the West, to make the litany of saints a chant especially for the laity. As early as 799 a church council decreed that the people should sing *Kyrie eleison* during processions.[144] In medieval Rome a midnight procession on the feast of the Assumption departed the Lateran *cum letania* and *concurrente populo*—with the people running alongside a famous icon of Christ, carried by the clergy. Upon reaching the steps of St. Mary Minor they paused for a rite that resembles the Byzantine feast of the Cross, but also maintained the traditional emotionality of the litany, "with the whole chorus of men and women kneeling humbly before it and striking their breasts. With one voice they say a hundred *Kyrie eleison*, a hundred *Christe eleison*, again another hundred *Kyrie eleison*, and having shed tears and prayers they go the direct way by St. Hadrian to St. Mary Major."[145]

At times the litany seems to have served as a lay substitute for the more complex chants. In a tenth-century Palm Sunday procession, the schola sang the processional antiphons but the "lay boys" sang only *Kyrie eleison*.[146] The twelfth-century Roman Pontifical directed that, at a procession during the blessing of a church, the women and children were to sing *Kyrie eleison* while the clergy sang the responsory *Erit mihi dominus*.[147] Honorius in his *Gemma animae* (PL 172:550) wrote that

---

[143] Kantorowicz, *Laudes Regiae*; B. Opfermann, *Die liturgischen Herrscherakklamationen im sacrum Imperium des Mittelalters* (Weimar: H. Böhlaus Nachfolger, 1953); J.-M. Hanssens, "De laudibus carolinis." *Periodica de re morali, canonica, liturgica* 30 (1941) 280–302; 31 (1941) 31–53.

[144] F. Zagiba, "Die irisch-schottische Mission in Salzburg im 8. Jahrhundert und die Anfänge der Choralpflege in den Alpenländern." *Kirchenmusikalisches Jahrbuch* 41 (1957) 1–3.

[145] *Le Pontifical romano-germanique du dixième siècle*, ed. C. Vogel and R. Elze. 3 vols. Studi e Testi 226, 227, 269 (Vatican City: Biblioteca Apostolica Vaticana, 1963–72) 2:138.

[146] Ordo Romanus 50, in *Les Ordines Romani* = Andrieu 5:176.

[147] *Le Pontifical romain au moyen-age*, ed. M. Andrieu. 4 vols. Studi e Testi 86, 87, 88, 99 (Vatican City: Biblioteca Apostolica Vaticana, 1938–41) 1:186. See also *Le Pontifical romano-germanique*, ed. Vogel and Elze, 1:168.

the people respond to the bishop's sermon with *Kyrie eleison*, but the clergy with the Credo. In the thirteenth century, the *Rationale divinorum officiorum* of Durandus reported that a *Kyrie* was sung during or after the Credo in some dioceses.[148] If this *Kyrie* was the remnant of a dismissal litany, it may have been a Gallican vestige, for the early Roman Mass seems to have had the dismissal before communion.[149]

The popularity of *Kyrie eleison* among lay people helps to explain the emergence of specialized litanies, notably the ones addressed exclusively to the Virgin Mary, with the saints' names replaced by such Mariological titles as *Virgo virginum, Mater purissima, Regina angelorum*—"Virgin of virgins, Mother most pure, Queen of Angels."[150] The most famous such Marian litany is the so-called *Litaniae Lauretanae* or Litany of Loreto, named for the Italian village where a venerated house was reputed to have been the Virgin's own, miraculously transported from Palestine by angels.[151] By the sixteenth century similar litanies had developed for other objects of medieval devotion, such as the Holy Spirit and the Holy Eucharist; the post-medieval centuries added litanies to Saint Joseph and the Sacred Heart.[152] *Kyrie eleison* was also common as a refrain in vernacular songs, both sacred and secular. The German songs known as "Leisen," apparently from *eleison*, in-

---

[148] Durandus of Mende, *Rationale Divinorum Officiorum* 4.25.14, ed. A. Davril and T. M. Thibodeau. 3 vols. Corpus Christianorum, Continuatio Mediaeualis 140–140B (Turnhout: Brepols, 1995–2000) 1:367. For possible Mozarabic parallels see also *Liber Misticus* 29, 41, 45, 47, 54, 62.

[149] Jungmann, *The Mass of the Roman Rite*, 341.

[150] G. G. Meersseman, *Der Hymnus Akathistos im Abendland*. 2 vols. Spicilegium Friburgense 2–3 (Freiburg: Universitätsverlag, 1958–60) 2:214–56.

[151] G. Nitz, "Lauretanische Litanei," in *Marienlexikon*, ed. R. Bäumer and L. Scheffczyk, 4:33–44 (St. Ottilien: EOS Verlag, 1992). For medieval translations into vernacular languages see M. A. van den Oudenrijn, "Die 'Frati Armeni' und die Lauretanischen Litanei." *Le Muséon* 64 (1951) 279–92; W. Schleussner, "Zur Entstehung der Lauretanischen Litanei." *Theologische Quartalschrift* 107 (1926) 254–67.

[152] B. F. Musser, *Kyrie Eleison: Two Hundred Litanies with Historico-Liturgical Introduction and Notes* (Westminster: Newman Bookshop, 1944); C. Plummer, *Irish Litanies: Text and Translation*. HBS 67 (London: Harison & Sons, 1925; repr. Woodbridge: Boydell Press, 1992); L. Gougaud, *Les saints irlandais hors d'Irlande*. Bibliothèque de la revue d'histoire ecclésiastique 16 (Louvain: Bureaux de la Revue, 1936) 194–95.

clude the tenth-century *Petruslied*[153] and the chorale *Christ ist erstan-den*.[154] In French such a song is called a *Kyriole'* or *Kyrielle*.[155] A Kyrie refrain is also found in one of the oldest surviving songs in English, the twelfth-century carol *Crist and Sainte Marie* of St. Godric.[156]

The Litany and the Kyrie

At its most basic, the litany of saints was a processional chant. Recognizing this permits us to see why Jungmann was wrong about the litany at the Paschal Vigil. It did not originate by adding names of saints to an originally christological Mass *Kyrie*—to suppose that it did is to ignore the way the text was used in liturgical action. In the oldest Roman sources the litany simply accompanies the procession to the font, then back to the altar.[157] The *Kyrie* of this Mass grows out of the litany, not the other way around. That the Mass *Kyrie* derives from the litany of saints more generally, not only at the Paschal Vigil, is clear from what Gregory the Great himself says:

> But Kyrie eleison we neither have said nor do say as it is said by the
> Greeks, because among the Greeks all say [it] simultaneously, but among

---

[153] H. Hucke, "Die Neumierung des althochdeutschen Petruslieds," in *Organicae Voces: Festschrift Joseph Smits van Waesberghe* (Amsterdam: Instituut voor Middeleeuwse Muziekwetenschap, 1963); E. Petzet and O. Glauning, *Deutsche Schrifttafeln des IX. bis XVI. Jahrhunderts aus Handschriften der K. Hof- und Staatsbibliothek in München* 1 (Munich: C. Kuhn, 1910; repr. Hildesheim: Georg Olms, 1975) 1, pl 9 and facing page. On other similar songs see O. Ursprung, *Die katholische Kirchenmusik*. Handbuch der Musikwissenschaft [9] (Potsdam: Athenaion, 1931) 98–102.

[154] W. Lipphardt, "'Christ ist erstanden': Zur Geschichte des Liedes." *Jahrbuch für Liturgik und Hymnologie* 5 (1960) 96–114; idem, "'Laus tibi Christe'— 'Ach du armer Judas': Untersuchungen zum ältesten deutschen Passionslied." *Jahrbuch für Liturgik und Hymnologie* 6 (1961) 71–100.

[155] Jeffery, *Re-Envisioning Past Musical Cultures*, 74.

[156] J. B. Trend, "The First English Songs." *Music and Letters* 9 (1928) 120–23.

[157] *Liber sacramentorum Romanae aeclesiae ordinis anni circuli (Cod. Reg. lat. 316 / Paris Bibl. Nat. 7193, 41/56) (Sacramentarium Gelasianum)*, ed. L. C. Mohlbert et al. Rerum Ecclesiasticarum Documenta, Series Maior: Fontes 4 (Rome: Herder, 1960) 72. Ordo Romanus 11 in Andrieu, *Ordines Romani* 2:444–45, Ordo Romanus 24, 27, 28, 28A, 29, 30A, 30B, 31, 32, 33 in Andrieu, *Ordines Romani* 3:295–96, 360–61, 405, 408–9, 421, 423–24, 444–45, 457, 472, 474, 501, 504, 522–23, 532. *Le Pontifical romano-germanique*, ed. Vogel and Elze, 2:101, 108–10.

us it is said by the clerics, it is responded by the people. And as many times also Christe eleison is said, though among the Greeks it is not said in any way. But in the daily masses we omit the other things that ought to be said; we say only Kyrie eleison and Christe eleison, so that we may be occupied a little longer [*paulo diutius*] in these voices of supplication.[158]

Those who say, with Jungmann,[159] that Gregory was describing the abbreviation of "a litany of eastern origin," such as the *Deprecatio Gelasii*, are discounting Gregory's own testimony that Rome did not follow the East, and they are once again ignoring the dimension of action and practice. In the Eastern litanies, and in the Western preces, "all say [*Kyrie eleison*] simultaneously," that is in response to the petitions sung by the deacon. But in the Roman practice according to Gregory, *Kyrie eleison* was said by the clerics, then repeated by the people; the same was done with *Christe eleison*, not used in the East at all.

What Gregory was describing was the original way of performing the litany of saints. From the first *Kyrie eleison* onward, each petition was normally doubled: that is, it was stated entire by the clerical cantors, then repeated in full by the assembly. That is the method indicated in the Tridentine editions of the Missal and *Caeremoniale Episcoporum* on all occasions when the litany was officially part of the liturgy: Paschal Vigil, Rogation days, ordinations. The alternation between clergy and people during processions has a plausible precedent in the marching songs of the Roman army, which also involved back-and-forth repetitions between two groups.[160] Earlier sources, however, sometimes indicate more than two repetitions: in the late eighth-century Ordo Romanus 24, the litanies of the Easter vigil were to be said seven times, then five, then three.[161] Medieval liturgical books

---

[158] Gregory I, *Registrum* 9.26, ed. Norberg, 2:587.

[159] Jungmann, *Public Worship*, 109.

[160] Jungmann, *Mass of the Roman Rite*, 1:335 n. 13; A. Alföldi, *Die monarchische Repräsentation im römischen Kaiserreiche* (Darmstadt: Wissenschaftliche Buchgesellschaft, 1970) 81–83; M. V. Anastos, "*Vox Populi*," 200; McCormick, *Eternal Victory*, 162, 242–49, 343–44, 352–60; C. Gnilka, "Ein Zeugnis doppelchörigen Gesangs bei Prudentius." *Jahrbuch für Antike und Christentum* 39:58–73; repr. in Christian Gnilka, *Prudentiana 2, Exegetica*, 170–91, 558–62 (Leipzig: K. G. Saur, 2001); Flavius Cresconius Corippus, *In laudem Iustini Augusti minoris*, ed. and trans. Averil Cameron (London: Athlone Press, 1976), 57, 100, 173.

[161] *Ordines Romani*, ed. Andrieu, 3:296.

often present three distinct litany texts for this purpose, entitled *"litania septena," "quina,"* and *"terna."*[162] Going by the extant sources, I suspect it was this practice of multiplying litany petitions that prompted the need for the prior of the schola in Ordo Romanus 1 to watch the pontiff in case "he wants to change the number of the litany."[163] Today it is the simple or responsive method of singing the litany that is most familiar. Each petition is performed only once: the cantor(s) sing(s) *Pater de caelis Deus* and the people respond *miserere nobis*—or rather the vernacular equivalent. This type of performance was originally associated only with lesser liturgical or paraliturgical functions, however. So far as strictly Roman liturgical regulations are concerned, the simple method was first authorized for the Forty Hours devotion in the Clementine Instruction of 1731.[164] Only in the 1950s, with the expanding trend to simplify the rubrics, was the simple method permitted on Holy Saturday and Rogation days as well.[165]

Among the early sources, the performance practice is most clearly seen in descriptions of the ordination rite. The litany was sung while the candidate(s) lay prostrate, between the Epistle and the Gospel (more specifically between the Gradual and the Alleluia) of the Mass,

---

[162] *Institutio Sancti Angilberti*, 295; Coens, "Anciennes litanies," 317–18; Van Dijk, "The Litany"; M. Coens, "L'origine corbéienne du psautier de Zurich Car. C 161 d'après ses litanies." *Analecta Bollandiana* 69 (1951) 114; A. F. Addeo, "Liber Missalis Ecclesiae Sancti Michaëlis Archangeli Terra Nicosiae in Sicilia." *Ephemerides Liturgicae* 69 (1955) 236–54; A. Gwynn, "The Irish Missal of Corpus Christi College, Oxford." *Studies in Church History* 1:47–68 (London: Nelson, 1964); H. Schmidt, ed., *Hebdomada Sancta*, 1:294 (Rome: Herder, 1956); 2:861–66 (Rome: Herder, 1957). On performance methods see *Le Pontifical romain*, ed. Andrieu, 2:568; *Pontifical romano-germanique*, ed. Vogel and Elze, 2:108–9.

[163] *Ordo Romanus 1*, ed. Andrieu, 2:84.

[164] A. Fortescue, *The Ceremonies of the Roman Rite Described*, ed. Rev. J. B. O'Connell. 5th ed. (London: Burns Oates and Washbourne, 1934) 390–91. One does find the simple responsive method in medieval laudes regiae litanies, e.g. *Pontifical romain*, ed. Andrieu, 2:375, 402.

[165] Compare Fortescue, as above, 350, 361, 368, with Fortescue, *The Ceremonies of the Roman Rite Described*, ed. Rev. J. B. O'Connell. 12th rev. ed. (London: Burns & Oates, 1962) 306, 321, 337. Compare the first English edition of *The Liber Usualis with Introduction and Rubrics in English, edited by the Benedictines of Solesmes* (Tournai: Desclée, 1934) 756–59, 835–59; with the last (1963), 776V–776W, 776EE–776GG, 835–59.

a position comparable to the *ektenē* in the Liturgy of St. James. The prostration itself seems to expand on the actions of kneeling and head-bowing associated with the dismissal litanies so common in the East. The earliest sources say that the Roman ordination litany was begun or intoned by the schola, the choir of young clerics. Later sources add the clarification that what the schola sang was repeated by the assembly, or a choir representing the assembly.[166] That the litany was seen as equivalent to the *Kyrie* is clear from the fact that ordination Masses originally had no *Kyrie* as such: the Introit was followed immediately by the Gloria,[167] though there could also have been a processional litany earlier on, as the bishop and people processed to the church where the ordination was held.[168] It is only in the later ordines, of Frankish origin, that there is a distinct *Kyrie* movement in the Ordinary of the Mass, unconnected to the litany.[169] Even so, something of Gregory's original method survived up to Vatican II, in the way the ninefold *Kyrie* was alternated between the celebrant and the server or ministers.[170]

The processional litany of saints seems to have acquired a more specific usage in the city of Rome, where it was used to mark the approach or arrival of the procession at its destination. We can see this in Ordo Romanus 20, which describes the procession to St. Mary Major on the feast of the Purification (February 2). The processional antiphon *Exsurge Domine* (textually unrelated to the feast) was sung by the schola (i.e., the boys' choir) and then repeated by the clergy. "But when they approach the atrium of the church of the Holy Mother of God, the pontiff signals the schola that the litany may be said, repeating it three times each [*repetentes ter vicissim*]." The Romano-Germanic Pontifical, on the other hand, prescribes an evidently non-Roman

---

[166] See the pontifical of Durandus in *Pontifical romain*, ed. Andrieu, 3:354; *Pontificale Romanum: Editio princeps* (1595–1596), ed. M. Sodi and A. M. Triacca. Monumenta Liturgica Concilii Tridentini (Vatican City: Libreria Editrice Vaticana, 1997) 39 no. 79.

[167] Ordo Romanus 34 in Andrieu 3:605, 612–13. Ordo Romanus 35, 35A, 35B in Andrieu 4:36–37, 44, 73–74, 101, 105.

[168] Ordo Romanus 36 and 38 in Andrieu 4:196, 197, 200, 202–3, 268–69.

[169] Ordo Romanus 37A, 37B, and 39 in Andrieu 4:236–37, 251–53, 284.

[170] See "Ritus Servandus in Celebratione Missae" IV.2–3 in the front of any Tridentine edition of the *Missale Romanum*. Compare H. Goussen, "Die georgische 'Petrusliturgie.'" *Oriens Christianus*, new series 3 (1913) 8.

practice: the schola sings antiphons related to the feast the entire way, even while entering the church. Yet then we are told, "But according to the Romans, when they approach the atrium of St. Mary, litanies are to be done. When these are finished before the altar, and the pontiff has entered the sacrarium, the schola begins *Suscepimus* . . ., the introit antiphon."[171]

Again, in the Major Rogation procession described in Ordo Romanus 21, the schola sings an Introit antiphon while the pontiff enters the church of the collecta. But when the procession leaves this church, it is led by "paupers from the orphanage, with a painted wooden cross, crying Kyrie eleison . . ." When that litany is finished nothing is sung, until "approaching the first church they begin the litany. And while they will have said the litany at the doors of the church, the pontiff enters." He says a prayer after this litany is completed, then "signals the choir that another antiphon may be said." When they finally arrive at the stational church, the pontiff and the deacons go into the sacrarium, "and the schola completes the litany within the presbyterium." Following the Introit, sung when the pontiff's procession emerges to begin the Mass, there will be no *Kyrie* in the Mass that day. Ordo Romanus 22 prescribes the same procedure for the stations on Lenten weekdays, and Ordo Romanus 38 does the same for Ember Saturdays: "But approaching the church, at the pontiff's signal, the schola intones the litany, singing until it reaches the choir [section of the church]." The Introit follows, but there is no *Kyrie*, for the pontiff immediately says the collect.[172] In the Ambrosian Rogations, too, it appears that repeated *Kyries* were sung at the entrance of each church, both to begin the litany as the procession departed and to end it when the next church on the route was reached.[173] Thus the litany of saints in the Stowe Missal, which begins a Gallicanized or Celticized form of the

[171] *Pontifical romano-germanique*, ed. Vogel and Elze, 2:10.

[172] *Ordines Romani*, ed. Andrieu 3:248–49, 259–60; 4:267–68.

[173] *Manuale Ambrosianum ex codice saec. XI olim in usum Canonicae Vallis Travaliae*, ed. M. Magistretti. 3 vols. in 2 (Milan: Hoepli, 1904–05; repr. Nendeln, Liechtenstein: Kraus, 1971) 3:245–68. Some confusion has been caused by the rubric "Kyrie eleison is not said" at the arrival of the Mozarabic Palm Sunday procession in *Antifonario*, ed. Brou and Vives, 247, but comparison with 271, 280 will show that this has to do with chants related to the Ambrosian psallentium, wherein three *Kyries* accompany the Gloria Patri; see *Manuale Ambrosianum* 3:3–4 and throughout.

Roman Mass, should be seen as one of the Roman elements: a fairly typical way of beginning the Mass upon arriving at the church.[174]

The general practice seems to have been that the Introit antiphon specifically accompanied the movements of the pope, whereas the litany or the *Kyrie* marked the arrival of the entire procession, though it was begun at the pope's signal. As a result the two do not always occur in a fixed order; the litany might precede the Introit, but if it did it was not restarted after the Introit—unless, as at ordinations, there was another reason to recite a litany. Thinking of the *Kyrie* as the chant of arrival helps to explain some other Roman practices: for example, it was at the *Kyrie* that the acolytes, having reached at the altar, put down their candles.[175] The Old Roman "Golden Vespers" of Easter week, the last vestige of the purely cathedral Office in Rome, began with the choirboys singing *Kyrie eleison* at the crucifix in St. John Lateran, while the clergy assembled and took their places.[176] Most interestingly, recognizing that the *Kyrie* is the arrival chant makes it possible to explain why the bishop of Rome sang a morning hymn, the Gloria in excelsis, before he did anything else—even before bothering to greet the people. Like Egeria's bishop, he had arrived during the singing of the psalms and canticles of the (morning) cathedral Office, and then had the honor of intoning the final canticle. Only after that did he actually begin the Mass, by greeting the people with "Pax vobis" and then proceeding to the collects.[177] The privilege of intoning the Gloria remained an episcopal prerogative until well into the Middle Ages.[178]

The traditional Roman Office, as codified in the *Breviarium Romanum*, is a rather monastic type of Office, emphasizing the weekly recitation of the full psalter in what is known as the Cursus Romanus.

---

[174] Bishop, "The Litany of Saints"; M. Coens, "L'origine corbéienne," 110; *Stowe Missal*, 2:3, 14 (the second leaf has been misplaced and bound within the diptychs). It is true, of course, that the Stowe Missal is a portable book for private Mass; the litany at the beginning is a reflection of the processional litany that began the Roman Mass, not a prescription for an actual procession with a choir.

[175] Ordo Romanus 1, Andrieu 2:84.

[176] Ordo Romanus 27 appendix, Andrieu 3:362–63; Brooks-Leonard, *Easter Vespers*, 32–33, 288–97.

[177] *Le Pontifical romain*, ed. Andrieu, 3:651.

[178] Jungmann, *The Mass of the Roman Rite*, 1:356–57.

That is because, in Rome, responsibility for the liturgy rested largely on the monasteries that served each of the basilicas. The Roman Cursus Monasticus, used in Benedictine monasteries, is a close relative, but follows the different psalter arrangement outlined in the Benedictine Rule. The original, unmonasticized cathedral Office of the Roman rite virtually disappeared, except for the special Golden Vespers during Easter week. Hardly any evidence survives to tell us what the Roman morning Hour was like, but if the Gloria was indeed the final canticle, that would parallel the usage at Milan and Constantinople, where the cathedral Office is much better documented.[179] In the Gallican Mass, on the other hand, the priest walked in during the chanting of the Antiphona ad Praelegendum, then greeted the people with "*Dominus sit semper vobiscum.*" If the celebrant was a bishop, he intoned the Trisagion (often an episcopal arrival chant in Constantinople), after which three boys sang *Kyrie eleison* "with one mouth." Then the morning canticle followed, in this case the Benedictus (Luke 1:68-79), and finally the readings were begun.[180]

There is, however, one bit of peculiarly Roman evidence, overlooked until now: the earliest rite for consecrating a newly-elected bishop of Rome. It begins with the first five of Egeria's seven elements: (1) the singing of Office psalms, (2) a solemn entry, (3-4) a litany, (5) prayers. "They sing psalms according to custom. The [newly-]elected [pontiff] proceeds from the secretarium with seven candle-bearers and goes to the confession [i.e., the tomb of Saint Peter]. And after the litany the bishops and priests go up to the chair together." Three of the suburbicarian bishops say prayers and anoint the new pontiff, while deacons hold a gospel book over his head. "After this the archdeacon gives him the pallium. Then he ascends to the chair and gives the peace to all the priests and says *Gloria in excelsis Deo.*"[181]

In the twelfth-century Roman Pontifical, this simple rite has been converted into the beginning of a Mass, and so it has been misunderstood

---

[179] *Manuale Ambrosianum* 3:415–16; Mateos, *Le typicon* 2:289. Bishop, *The Mozarabic and Ambrosian Rites*, 106–7; in one case the Te Deum was used, 118.

[180] *Expositio antiquae liturgiae gallicanae*, ed. E. C. Ratcliff. HBS 98 (London: Henry Bradshaw Society [Chichester: Regnum Press], 1971) 3–5; K. Gamber, *Ordo antiquus Gallicanus: Der gallikanische Messritus des 6. Jahrhunderts.* Textus Patristici et Liturgici 3 (Regensburg: Pustet, 1965) 17.

[181] Ordo Romanus 40A and 40B, ed. Andrieu 4: 297, 307–8; compare Ordo Romanus 36 in 4:202–5.

ever since.[182] The psalmody has become the Introit. The newly elected pope still proceeds from the sacrarium with seven candle-bearers, but now also with "bishops and cardinals and other clergy, dressed for a solemn rite. And they come to the confession of blessed Peter and, having done the litany there, ascend together in equality [*pariter*] to the altar." The prayers and consecration take place and the pallium is given. The pope still gives the peace to all, but only after each one has kissed his foot. After that he begins the Gloria, "and so the Mass is carried out in order."[183] The one thing that has not changed, even by the twelfth century, is the litany. Rather than the familiar ninefold *Kyrie*, it is still a litany, sung as the procession arrives at the confession of Peter's tomb.

CONCLUSION

And so, in recognizing the litany of saints as the Roman arrival chant, we finally arrive at the origins of the *Kyrie eleison* in the Ordinary of the Mass. The procession has been a long one. The documented history of the *Kyrie eleison* begins in pre-Christian rituals of divination, where it expressed the worshiper's anxiety about a future he did not know, in the presence of a deity he could not control. At some undetermined point, *Kyrie eleison* was combined with the *litania*, a pre-Christian rite of supplication in which children had an important role. All Christian uses of *Kyrie eleison* prior to Jungmann can be seen to grow out of a common matrix: the dismissal rite observed by Egeria at the Office in Jerusalem. The singing of psalms, hymns, and antiphons was interrupted by a solemn entry of the bishop and clergy, but then resumed. Then a deacon called out the names of people to be prayed for. Children endlessly responded *Kyrie eleison* to the deacon. The bishop then said a "prayer for all," followed by the entire congregation praying in unity. The deacon commanded all present to bow their heads for the bishop's blessing, then everyone was dismissed in groups: first catechumens, then faithful. Following that were processions with singing to the open courtyard before Golgotha, then to another place "behind the Cross." At both stations the dismissal was celebrated again.

---

[182] Thus K. Richter, *Die Ordination des Bischofs von Rom: Eine Untersuchung zur Weiheliturgie*. Liturgiewissenschaftliche Quellen und Forschungen 60 (Münster: Aschendorff, 1976) 13–41, assumes that a "Weihemesse" is being described.

[183] *Le Pontifical romain*, ed. Andrieu, 1:249–50; 2:369–74.

The closest thing to Egeria's practice still in use today is the *litē*, which takes various forms when it is celebrated at the end of Vespers in the Byzantine rite. The practice of reciting the names of individuals to be prayed for has not completely disappeared, but it is often replaced by the names of saints to be prayed to. The infinite repetitions of *Kyrie eleison* survive especially on the feast of the Holy Cross, which also retains elements of Egeria's processions to Golgotha.

Fully developed litany texts contemporary with Egeria appear in the *Apostolic Constitutions*, book 8, where they are used at similar dismissals of the worshipers in five groups (catechumens, energumens, photizomenoi, penitents, faithful), both at the Office and at Mass. The participation of children is noted, as is the theme of earnest insistence, continuing the pre-Christian worshiper's sense of helplessness and anxiety. The dismissal aspect, and the fact that the litany of the faithful led into the kiss of peace, have also given rise to the theme of praying for peace, which was not evident in Egeria. The most developed form of the eucharistic liturgy of Jerusalem, the Greek Liturgy of St. James, contains a number of litanies at various points, including one, the *Katholikon*, which in particular preserves the Egerian theme of praying for all.

In the rite of Constantinople, three major types of litany text coalesce around three of the major themes: the most general prayer for all in the *synaptē*, the dismissal particularly in the *aitēseis*, the procession and the theme of incessant insistence in the *ektenē*. The migration of these litanies to various parts of the eucharistic rite seems to be inspired by the ways they are used in the Office, particularly the Liturgy of the Presanctified, the Lenten Office of Terce-Sext, and the stational Office of three antiphons. The last two are not unlike Egeria's rite in that they combine psalmody and ceremonial entrance with litanic prayer, dismissal, and procession.

Beyond the Greek world, the emphases vary. In the West Syrian Eucharist the litany became associated with the reading of names at the diptychs, in the East Syrian with the Prayer of the Faithful. The Armenian Rituale preserved the theme of the Cross, while the insistent character of litanic prayer made the deepest impression on the Slavs. The Latin litanies of the preces type also favor the *ektenē* model, though some of them also refer to the prayer for peace in the *synaptē*. The Western *Deprecatio Gelasii* seems to have been written with reference to the Solemn Prayers of Good Friday.

To whom are all these litanies addressed? Most of them do not clearly distinguish which member or members of the Trinity are being called upon. Historically, this would make sense, since *Kyrie eleison* itself has a background in pre-Christian worship. In places where there was a specific theological agenda, however, the reference has been sharpened by anonymous liturgical editors. Thus the litanies of the *Apostolic Constitutions* are clearly addressed to the Father, those of the Liturgy of St. Gregory to the Son, the *Deprecatio Gelasii* to the entire Trinity. In the West, special forms of the litany of saints were addressed to the Holy Spirit, the Eucharist, the Virgin Mary, and so on. The most complex developments occur in the Mozarabic rite, where the preces were particularly associated with dismissals of the penitents during Lent. Some of these preces are addressed to Christ and some not; requests for forgiveness of sins predominate, producing the only litanic texts that significantly resemble the Penitential Rite of the Vatican II Mass, but clearly rooted in dismissal rites that look back to the time of the *Apostolic Constitutions*. Even in the Mozarabic context, however, one finds no clear sense that *Kyrie eleison* was regarded as originally or primarily addressed to Christ. In fact, as Easter approaches passion themes become more prominent in Mozarabic Lent, so that we even have two preces that are addressed to the Father from the mouth of the suffering Jesus. All this culminated on Good Friday, where the Adoration of the Cross was combined with a service featuring the penitents. The word *Indulgentia*, substituting for *Kyrie eleison*, was used as a response to the preces, but also repeated hundreds of times on its own, recalling the incessant *Kyries* at Eastern services honoring the Holy Cross.

The true history of the *Kyrie* in the Roman Mass is to be traced through the litany of saints, sung at processions to stational Masses, Rogations, ordinations, and the procession to and from the font at the Paschal Vigil. With its long lists of saints, this litany retains the tradition of reciting names, and the Roman use of processional crosses may recall something of Egeria's procession to Golgotha. The individual petitions were typically doubled, alternated between the clerical cantors and the people, as Pope Gregory described. However, the petitions could also be tripled or said as many as seven times, depending on the pope's signal to the choir.

As a processional chant, the litany of saints marked the arrival of the group at an intermediate or final destination. Thus the position of the litany varied in relationship to the processional and Introit antiphons, depending on the processional route. We see its original function in the earliest form of the ordination rite for the bishop of Rome, which is much like the Office Egeria saw. The new pontiff entered during the psalmody, in a clerical procession led by seven candles. With the other bishops and priests he stopped at the confession or tomb of St. Peter for the litany, then proceeded up to his seat. There he was ordained, exchanged the peace, and had the honor of intoning the final canticle, the Gloria in excelsis. The opening of the Roman Mass followed a similar model: the pope's entrance procession was marked by the Introit. The litany was sung upon arrival at the altar area, where the confession would be in a Roman basilica. The candles and other processional paraphernalia were put in their places. The pope intoned the Gloria, then greeted the people and said the collect. If the purpose of liturgical reform were simply to restore each element to its original shape, that is how the Mass would begin today. Instead we have something that looks more like the Mozarabic Good Friday, an assembly of sinners begging for forgiveness—but its only historical precedent is the twentieth-century Dialogue Mass, in which the congregation said the clergy's preparatory prayers along with the servers.

As historical scholarship, Jungmann's error doesn't matter much. He misunderstood the origins of the *Kyrie*, partly because he was working at a time when less was known about the Mass and Office than today, partly because of his methodology, which privileged theological interpretation over textual history, and textual history over the history of non-textual phenomena, reversing the chronological order in which action, text, and theology usually develop. But all historians are fallible, and in time their mistakes get corrected—as someday my own will. The real problem is that Jungmann's mistake has been enshrined in the worship of millions of Catholics as the alleged Roman Rite, reputedly shorn of its medieval accretions and restored to what it was in "the world of the Fathers." There it joins numerous other fanciful recreations, concocted when well-intentioned scholars used anachronistic theology to fill gaps in the record of textual history, while shunting aside the historical record of liturgical action and performance. It would have been more prudent to work in the opposite direction, beginning with the non-textual and culminating with the theology.

From a purely pastoral perspective, what should we do now? There's an argument for simply leaving things as they are, rather than forcing the liturgy to change with every new scholarly wind. The changes that have already been made since Vatican II demonstrate the risks that the People of God always take on, whenever its scholars are given leeway to start changing the liturgy around, as they are permitted to do every few centuries. But it would be unfortunate to learn this lesson so well that we feel helpless to amend obvious and relatively recent mistakes made by the incautiousness of the generation before us.

The Penitential Rite of the reformed Mass has attracted a lot of controversy on several grounds. Placing it after the readings, roughly where the dismissals are in the liturgies of the East, would at least make a certain theological sense, by making the congregation's confession of a sin a response to the message proclaimed in the Word of God. However, such an arrangement would have to be based on Eastern models, contradicting Gregory's position that Rome does not follow the East. A different case could be made that the Penitential Rite should be reserved for use at communal penance services. Following Mozarabic precedent, it might be especially appropriate for the Adoration of the Cross on Good Friday, which is not of Roman origin anyway, and where it could replace texts that appear to blame the crucifixion on the Jews. A radical suggestion for the beginning of Mass? Put it back the way it was: psalmody (not hymnody) to accompany the entrance procession, a litany or *Kyrie* music as the procession arrives in the sanctuary and the ministers position themselves for worship, personal prayers of preparation for the clergy on reaching the foot of the altar. When everything is ready the litany stops, then the presider leads the entire assembly in singing a canticle appropriate to the time of day. Then he greets everyone, says a prayer, and the readings begin. Why not? Stranger things have been tried.

Part 2

Piety, Devotion, and Song

It is not simply in the phraseology of the prayers of public worship that we find trinitarian and christological expressions of faith. They are also found in the wider piety and devotional practices of the churches as well as in congregational song. The Armenian tradition is one still little known to Western scholars, and much about its formative centuries is still shrouded in mystery. Daniel Findykian examines some medieval liturgical commentaries of the Armenian tradition, revealing how they witness to its understanding of the mystery of Christ and thus form a complement to better-known dogmatic, creedal, and canonical sources. The prayer known by and used by all Christians is the Lord's Prayer, which is not generally associated with either trinitarian doctrine or christology. Kenneth Stevenson shows otherwise, and examines how the Lord's Prayer in the interpretations of Augustine, Maximus, Lancelot Andrewes, and Karl Barth relate to the teaching about the Trinity and the person and work of Christ. It was Karl Barth, in his *Church Dogmatics*, who pointed out that *Theotokos*, the devotional title of Mary proclaimed by the Council of Ephesus, said less about Mary than about the one to whom she gave birth. Maxwell Johnson suggests that the title *Theotokos* is not simply doctrinal but devotional, and far from taking the place of the human mediating role of Christ, as Jungmann suggested, is its devotional foundation. Further, this term was used at a much earlier date than has hitherto been accepted. John Witvliet considers how the Trinity undergirds and pervades integrating aspects of liturgical celebrations in the Reformed tradition, with an eye on liturgical piety. Christians also praise God in song, and song usually belongs to the community in a way that liturgical texts do not. Stephen Marini takes a look at the hymns of Isaac Watts. Marini examines how, in a latitudinarian age when the doctrine of the Trinity and Christ's divinity were being challenged, the doctrine has expressed in the influential eucharistic hymns from the English Dissenting tradition.

Chapter 8

Christology in Early Armenian Liturgical Commentaries

Michael Daniel Findikyan
Saint Nersess Armenian Seminary

One of the features of the Armenian Rite that must be considered truly distinctive is the relative wealth of medieval allegorical commentaries that have come down to us dealing with various liturgical services and books. Besides commentaries on the Divine Liturgy, a genre known to all ancient Christian cultures, the Armenians add more than a dozen commentaries on the daily Office, several on the Lectionary, and two early allegories on the ritual of dedicating a church, all of these unknown or practically unknown in other Eastern rites.[1] To the extent that these works have been explored, they have been utilized by scholars primarily as sources documenting the historical evolution of the liturgical services that they adumbrate.[2] On the other hand,

---

[1] For a survey of the Armenian liturgical commentaries see A. Renoux, "Les commentaires liturgiques arméniens," in *Mystagogie: Pensée liturgique d'aujourd'hui et liturgie ancienne. Conférences Saint-Serge XXXIXe semaine d'études liturgiques*, ed. A. M. Triacca and A. Pistoia (Rome: C.L.V.-Edizioni liturgiche, 1993) 276–308. Renoux lists eight distinct commentaries on the Daily Office (*Žamergut'iwn*), but several of these exist in a number of different versions, which, if not philologically independent, must be considered self-standing exegetical works. See Step'anos Siwnec'i. *The Commentary on the Armenian Daily Office by Bishop Step'anos Siwnec'i (d. 735)*, ed. M. D. Findikyan. OCA 270 (Rome: Pontificio Istituto Orientale, 2004) 312–18, 515–16.

[2] For example, Step'anos, *The Commentary*; M. Findikyan, "The Armenian Liturgy of Dedicating a Church: A Textual and Comparative Analysis of Three Early Sources." OCP 64, no. 1 (1998) 75–121; R. F. Taft, "The Armenian Liturgy: Its Origins and Characteristics," in *Treasures in Heaven: Armenian Art, Religion, and Society. Papers delivered at the Pierpont Morgan Library at a Symposium*

these expositions, dating from the eighth through the fourteenth centuries, have yet to be adequately studied from a more properly theological perspective, which is what their authors forthrightly claim to be their genuine purpose.[3] I submit what follows as a preliminary attempt at just such an investigation.

What strikes the reader of these commentaries above all is their unabashedly christological focus.[4] Investigations into the Armenian Church's stance during the christological controversies, and more recently in the context of the modern ecumenical movement, have tended to focus exclusively on medieval creedal formulae, synodal pronouncements, and dogmatic treatises.[5] A more nuanced appreciation for the overtly christological allegorical methods of Armenia's many medieval liturgical interpreters might well serve to sharpen our understanding of the Armenian Church's traditional view of Christ and of his redemptive work for mankind.

As a preliminary study, I shall limit the present inquiry to two contemporary Armenian exegetes from around the year 700 C.E., Step'anos of Siwnik' (d. 735) and Grigoris Aršaruni (d. ca. 729). For reasons that are not entirely clear, and perhaps by pure coincidence, the period of a century or so surrounding this date gives rise to a sur-

---

Organized by Thomas F. Mathews and Roger S. Wieck, 21–22 May 1994 (New York: The Pierpont Morgan Library, 1998) 13–30; G. Winkler, "The Armenian Night Office I: The Historical Background of the Introductory Part of *Gišerayin Žam* [Night Office]." *Journal of Armenian Studies* 1 (1984) 93–113; idem, "The Armenian Night Office II: The Unit of Psalmody, Canticles, and Hymns with Particular Emphasis on the Origins and Early Evolution of Armenia's Hymnography." *Revue des études arménienne* 17 (1983) 471–551; H.-J. Feulner, *Die armenische Athanasius-Anaphora: Kritische Edition, Übersetzung und liturgievergleichender Kommentar.* Anaphorae Orientales 1, Anaphorae Armeniacae 1 (Rome: Pontificio Istituto Orientale, 2001).

[3] The exception is Claudio Gugerotti's theological analysis of Nersēs Lambronac'i's twelfth-century commentary on the Divine Liturgy; see *L'interazione dei ruoli in una celebrazione come mistagogia: Il pensiero di Nersēs Lambronac'i nella "Spiegazione del Sacrificio"* (Padua: Edizioni Messaggero Padova, 1991).

[4] See Renoux's observations apropos ("Les commentaires," 307).

[5] N. Garsoïan (*L'église arménienne et le grand schisme d'orient* [Louvain: Peeters,1999]), whose approach is representative, surveys the entire history of previous scholarship, and is to be consulted for the most complete bibliography on the subject.

prising number of liturgical commentaries practically throughout the Christian East. In Armenia, Step'anos's work on the Daily Office spawns an entire family of related commentaries, several of them attributed to the great Catholicos Yovhan Ōjnec'i (d. 728).[6] In Constantinople, the famous commentary on the Byzantine Divine Liturgy by Patriarch Germanus (d. ca. 730) is from this period.[7] As for the Syriac realm, we have the commentaries attributed to John of Dara (d. 824) about a century later,[8] and probably around this time the anonymous author of the so-called *Expositio officiorum*.[9] A bit earlier we have a commentary on the Office by Gabriel Qatraya bar Lipah (ca. 615),[10] and one by his contemporary and probably his relative, Abraham.[11] In the West, Amalarius of Metz (d. ca. 850) emerges as a somewhat later

---

[6] I analyze these works and their attribution in "The Liturgical Expositions Attributed to Catholicos Yovhannēs Ōjnec'i: Problems and Inconsistency," in *The Armenian Christian Tradition: Scholarly Symposium in Honor of the Visit to the Pontifical Oriental Institute, Rome, of His Holiness Karekin I, Supreme Patriarch and Catholicos of All Armenians, December 12, 1996.* OCA 254 (Rome: Pontificio Istituto Orientale, 1997) 125–73. Cf. Step'anos, *The Commentary*, 219–79.

[7] Germanus I of Constantinople, *Ecclesiastical History and Mystical Contemplation* [Ἱστορία ἐκκλησιαστικὴ καὶ μυστικὴ Θεωρία], in St. Germanus of Constantinople, *On the Divine Liturgy*, trans. Paul Meyendorff (Crestwood: St. Vladimir's Press, 1984). Cf. R. Bornert, *Les commentaires byzantins de la Divine Liturgie du VIIᵉ au XVᵉ siècle*. Archives de l'Orient chrétien 9 (Paris: Institut français d'études byzantines, 1966) 125–80.

[8] John of Dara, *De oblatione*, ed. Jean Sader. CSCO 308–9, Scriptores Syri 132–33 (Louvain: Secrétariat du CorpusSCO, 1970); trans. by Baby Varghese, *Commentary on the Eucharist*. Moran Etho 12 (Kerala, India: St. Ephrem Ecumenical Research Institute, 1999).

[9] R. H. Connolly, ed., *Anonymi auctoris Expositio officiorum ecclesiasticorum, Georgio Arbelensi vulgo adscripta*. CSCO Scriptores Syri 91–92 (Paris: C. Poussielgue, 1911–15); CSCO 64, 71–72, 76 (Louvain: L. Durbecq, 1954). Most scholars now reject the attribution of this work to Bishop George of Arbel. Connolly's "rough" English translation has recently been published as *A Commentary on the Mass by the Nestorian George, Bishop of Mosul and Arbel*, ed. Robert Matheus (Vadavathoor, Kottayam, India: Pontifical Oriental Institute of Religious Studies, 2000). See S. Jammo, *La structure de la messe chaldéenne du début jusqu'à l'anaphore: Étude historique.* OCA 207 (Rome: Pontificium Institutum Orientalium Studiorum, 1979) 49–50.

[10] See Jammo, *La structure*, 26–27 and below.

[11] See ibid., 49.

Western exponent of this quasi-movement. As further justification for the limits that I have set for my inquiry, it should be noted that in both the Armenian and Byzantine realms later mystagogical authors—for Armenia, the commentaries on the Divine Liturgy by Xosrov Anjewac'i (tenth century)[12] and Nersēs Lambronac'i (twelfth century);[13] for Byzantium, Nicholas Cabasilas's fourteenth-century *Commentary*[14]—depart, in significant yet differing ways, from earlier methodological and thematic models.

THE VERY BEGINNING: ADAM AND EVE

We begin with Bishop Step'anos Siwnec'i's early eighth-century *Commentary on the Daily Office*, the first complete liturgical commentary in Armenian.[15] Step'anos's *Commentary* became the origin and model for a prolific lineage of commentaries on the daily Hours of prayer. At least three distinct recensions of Step'anos's seminal work have been identified, which, each in its own way, updated and revised the original work according to the stylistic and theological preferences of a particular editor, as well as the specific exigencies of that editor's times.[16] The daily Liturgy of the Hours therefore inspired tremendous literary creativity in Armenia, for reasons that are not yet entirely evident. While similar works are known from this period in the Syriac world, the only Greek commentary on the Daily Office was composed by Symeon of Thessalonica (d. 1429) much later, in the early fifteenth century.[17]

As we shall see, Step'anos's procedure in interpreting the daily Hours of prayer is the key to uncovering his overall allegorical method. Step'anos is very systematic in his interpretation of the

---

[12] Xosrov Anjewac'i, *Commentary on the Divine Liturgy*, trans. S. Peter Cowe (New York: St. Vartan Press, 1991). Cf. Renoux, "Les commentaires," 299–303.

[13] Nersēs Lambronac'i, *Explication de la Divine Liturgie*, trans. Isaac Kéchichian, S.J. Recherches 9 (Beirut: Dar El-Machreq Éditeurs, 2000); see Gugerotti, *L'interazione dei ruoli*, and Renoux, "Les commentaires," 303–5.

[14] Nicholas Cabasilas, *A Commentary on the Divine Liturgy*, ed. J. M. Hussey and P. A. McNulty (London: S.P.C.K., 1960). Cf. Bornert, *Les commentaires*, 215–44.

[15] For my critical edition, English translation, and study see footnote 1.

[16] See *Commentary*, ed. Findikyan, 312–17.

[17] *Treatise on Prayer: An Explanation of the Services Conducted in the Orthodox Church*, trans. Harry Simmons (Brookline, MA: Hellenic College Press, 1984).

Hours. Be it Matins, Vespers, Compline, or any other daily service, the author always proceeds in two steps: first he explains at length the rationale for praying at the given hour; second, he goes through the order of the service, interpreting in sequence its constituent prayers, hymns, and rituals.[18] Step'anos's interpretations, in both parts, are highly allegorical, but his use of allegory is quite coherent and systematic, as we shall see.

What strikes the reader of Step'anos's *Commentary* from the outset is the centrality of the story of salvation as an organizing principle for each chapter, and for the work as a whole. Step'anos interprets each prayer-hour of the day—Night/Morning, the Third Hour, the Sixth Hour, the Ninth Hour, the Evening Hour, and the Rest Hour—squarely in the context of Christ's liberation of humanity from captivity to Satan. Curiously, Step'anos conceives of mankind's fallen state exclusively in terms of the story of the fall of Adam and Eve, an episode that the author recounts, with remarkable variety, in each chapter of the *Commentary*.[19] All of the daily Hours begin with a retelling of the story of Adam and Eve's fall from Paradise, and conclude with their restoration as a result of the redemptive acts of Christ. This topos is the organizing principle and theme of Step'anos's interpretation of the services at those Hours.[20]

[18] In some cases, such as the services of the Third, Sixth, and Ninth Hours—the so-called Little Hours—and the Sunrise Office, Step'anos is satisfied only to give the rationale. This is probably because in his time these services were still in an embryonic state of development and use, consisting, perhaps, of little more than a Psalm and a prayer. See *Commentary*, 405–29.

[19] The Armenians were intrigued by the story of Adam and Eve; this is shown by the vast corpus of apocryphal writings on the protoplasts preserved in Armenian, many of them original Armenian compositions. For an introduction to the texts and bibliography see *Armenian Apocrypha Relating to Adam and Eve*, ed. M. E. Stone (Leiden/New York/Köln: E. J. Brill, 1996); M. E. Stone, "Adam, Eve and the Incarnation." *St. Nersess Theological Review* 2 (1997) 167–79; idem, *A Concordance of the Armenian Apocryphal Adam Books* (Leuven: Peeters, 2001); and *Literature on Adam and Eve: Collected Essays*, ed. G. Anderson, M. Stone, J. Tromp (Leiden/Boston: Brill, 2000).

[20] Only the unique Armenian Sunrise Hour is interpreted without reference to Adam and Eve. Step'anos's exposition of this nascent service develops instead an allegory of Christ as the light of the world. Step'anos also handles differently the Sunday Third-Hour office, which is none other than the Eucharistic Synaxis or Liturgy of the Word. *Commentary*, 96–97, 138–39, 436.

Because this thematic scheme is so central to our author's theological method, it is worthwhile to cite one example at length. The third chapter of his *Commentary* deals with the Night and Morning Hours, which, in Step'anos's time and venue were conducted as one composite Office that began in the middle of the night and continued through morning. An introductory paragraph, perhaps provided by a later editor, lists the various biblical canticles, diaconal proclamations, and presbyteral prayers that comprise this combined Office, asking why "the holy and universal church of Christ" conducts them. Step'anos's explanation is as follows:

> God eternal established everything; visible, I say, and invisible natures. These, Scripture teaches us, were brought into existence by the Word from nothing. And later he created with his hands the royal image in honor of his own lordship, having further esteemed the ignoble substance by drawing [it] into heaven, into dominical glory, which is [to say that he created man] according to [his] image and according to [his] likeness. Accordingly, he commands [man] to conduct himself worthily so that proceeding by his own willful steps he might grasp the mystery that has been set before [him].
>
> At this point [the first man] was struck down with the glee of the evil one, for he wished to usurp the unreachable height itself, and calamity befell him for this intolerable [deed]. For his heart craved [Satan's] counsel, and progress was feigned. And therefore, dragged as if by chains into the depths of ignorance, he was driven to fashion his destroyer. For which, induced by the yoke, and totally seized by perdition unto death, he inherited the outer darkness. . . (3.2–3; 128–29)

Recounting in vivid and dramatic terms the story of Adam and Eve's downfall, Step'anos then proceeds to Christ's redemption, narrated against the backdrop of the story of the prodigal son:

> But this having transpired this way, the Father, in his love for mankind, could no longer endure the triumph of the destruction of his image. Rather, he "went ahead," according to the prophetic proclamation, [and] embraced and kissed the one returning from the swine-paths of idolatry, ordering him to be arrayed in a robe of glory and a ring, in order to renew man by the birth of his Son, [born] of the holy Virgin, so that the evil one would be idled, having found nothing among [God's] own earthly ones.

Then he gives in sacrifice the great heifer that cannot be sacrificed, his immortal Son and Word, whereby he calls the universe to the wedding feast, to renew the elements by such a dispensation. . . . Every Sunday we celebrate anew, visibly, the same mystery of the valor of our Lord, and the abolition of death, and [the mystery] of our salvation. This [we celebrate] also every day (3.3-4; 90-91, 129).

Here, then, is Step'anos's rationale for the Night/Morning Office: it is none other than the mystery of mankind's salvation in Christ, narrated exclusively with reference to Adam and Eve. The root of sin and of all tribulation is Satan, the "Adversary," the serpent in paradise. For Step'anos, all vexation attached to the human condition is traceable, if not strictly chronologically or historically, to that primordial cataclysm, which, according to this theologian, must necessarily, therefore, be the point of departure for proper comprehension of salvation, of God's mercy, of the daily Hours, of the Bible, of the Lectionary, and of daily life with its trials and perturbations.

So pervasive and eloquent is the paradigm of Adam and Eve for establishing and grounding his theology that Step'anos not once uses the word "sin" (*mełk'*) in his commentary. Here is a characteristic that we find also in a mystagogical work of Step'anos's contemporary, Grigoris Aršaruni. Grigoris was the founder of a genre which, as far as I know, is unique to the Armenians, a mystagogical interpretation of the Lectionary.[21] Sometime after 706 C.E. he composed an allegorical commentary on the Psalms and Scripture readings appointed from Epiphany to the Sunday following Pascha according to the old Armenian Lectionary of Jerusalem.[22] In Grigoris's commentary Satan is omnipresent, but almost exclusively in terms of Adam and Eve in Paradise. That is the cause of all trouble. "When one reads the *Commentary*," writes Léon Froidevaux, Grigoris's modern editor, "One is struck by the disproportion between the references to the Fall from paradise, and references to daily faults, between what we call 'original sin' and 'daily sin.' The former reappears constantly, the second appears only at the end . . . and that with great discretion" (liv–lv).

---

[21] Grigoris Aršaruni, *Commentaire du Lectionnaire*, trans. L. M. Froidevaux (Venice: St. Lazare, 1975); see Renoux, "Les commentaires," 278–82.
[22] See A. Renoux, ed. *Le codex arménien Jérusalem 121.* 2 vols. Patrologia Orientalis 35/1, 36/2 (Turnhout: Brepols, 1969–71).

That these interpretations are soundly biblical should surprise no one. Step'anos himself confesses, at the outset of his commentary, that his foray into liturgical mystagogy came about only after he had already applied himself to biblical exegesis: "Now having strolled along, and examined the old and new commandments of God, and having plucked flowers from the spiritual springs of the word as a subject for the preparation of my composition, I also composed this testament on the meaning of the prayer-hours, which are conducted night and day in the church of Christ" (*Commentary* 4; 86, 122).

Nor is it unusual that our authors' interpretations should fall strictly within the context of salvation history. Step'anos admits this explicitly at several points in the *Commentary*. Toward the end of his exposition, in the introduction to his rationale for the Evening Hour, he writes: "By progressing through the prayer hours, which are arranged according to the acts of the dispensation consummated by God by means of the cross, we have harvested them all like the flowers of the pastures, or the precious gems from the treasuries of the kingdom, storing them up as sublime profits for our souls. A crown has been brought to us, purity throughout all the years" (10.2, 155).

Now when Step'anos mentions "the acts of the dispensation consummated by God by means of the cross" he is referring specifically to the historical events of salvation as a single integral mystery. This, I believe, is highly significant. Step'anos reveals the *historia* of redemption in each hour. He finds that the acts of the dispensation are organized by the Hours of the day, making reference to the few indications of a particular hour in the Scriptures, and by chronological extrapolation and allegory. Stepanos's thesis is that the prayers appointed for various Hours must have as a referent the hours at which "the acts of the dispensation" actually took place. One way or another, as he peruses the daily Office, Step'anos manages to narrate the mystery of salvation history based on events that, according to Scripture, took place at the hour under consideration.

In his commentary on the Third Hour, for example, Step'anos scours the Scriptures to list all of the significant events of redemption that, either explicitly or implicitly, took place at that hour. His rationale for this particular Office, consequently, lists the following events that presumably took place at the third hour: Adam's deception by the serpent; Jesus' crucifixion; the coming of the Holy Spirit upon the apostles in tongues of fire; and Christ's second coming (6.3–4; 97–98, 139–40). Evidently Step'anos has no qualms about using a degree of editorial license in asserting, for example, that Adam was deceived at the third hour, or that Christ will come again at the same hour, events for which the Scriptures provide no chronological reference. Only Mark, moreover, places Christ's crucifixion at the third hour (Mark 15:25). No matter. "Regarding all of this," Step'anos writes at the end of this chapter, "we say that at this third hour the first man fell, whereupon he rose and received beneficence. Thus rightly do [we] take heed, at this hour of prayers, by beseeching the Holy Spirit to lead [us] to the land of goodness" (6.4; 98, 140).

Nor does our author find it in any way problematic, in his rationale for the Sixth Hour, which again narrates salvation history in its entirety from Adam to the Second Coming, to assert, with no further comment, that the crucifixion took place at the sixth hour. "Consequently," he writes, "The prayers of [the Sixth Hour] were rightly appointed in the church as a commemoration of the economy of Jesus Christ, our Lord, who liberated [us] from suffering by suffering, and saved [us] from darkness by darkness" (8.5; 107, 152).

Step'anos's method is no different in his rationale for the Office of the Ninth Hour. Once again the entire story of salvation is retold beginning with Adam. The first man blamed Eve for the couple's transgression and they were expelled from Paradise; the dove returned to Noah with the olive branch "toward evening"—close enough to the ninth hour for the author's purposes; Christ's blood was spilled; and the laws written in the prophets were fulfilled and completed (11.4; 115–16, 161).

Of course scripturally-based justifications for praying at set times of the day go back to ancient times and become commonplace in patristic literature East and West. Authors such as Clement of Alexandria (d. ca. 215), Origen (d. ca. 254), Tertullian (d. after 220), Cyprian of Carthage (d. ca. 258) and others cite various passages from Scripture to support the concept of praying at fixed hours. But in general, the expositions of these and other authors amount to little more than an inventory of otherwise disparate proof-texts from Scripture with little or no attempt at theological synthesis. Origen provides an example of such a rationale in his treatise, *On Prayer*:

And Peter, going up to the housetop to pray about the sixth hour, at which time also he saw the vessel let down from heaven, let down by the four corners, gives an example of the middle of the three times of prayer spoken of by David before him: In the morning you shall hear my prayer; in the morning I will stand before you, and will look upon you (Ps 5:3). The last of the three is indicated in the words, "the lifting up of my hands like an evening sacrifice" (Ps 140:2). But not even the time of night shall we rightly pass without such prayer, for David says, "At midnight I rose to praise you for the judgments of your justice" (Ps 118:62), and Paul, as related in the Acts of the Apostles, at midnight together with Silas at Philippi prayed and sang praises unto God, so that the prisoners also heard them (Acts 16:25).[23]

By contrast to Origen and others, Step'anos weaves together, with great creativity, the relevant scriptural passages into a unified narrative of salvation history. The church thus prays at the third hour, for example, not merely because it is the hour of Adam's deception by the serpent; nor because Jesus was crucified at that hour according to Mark; nor because it was the hour of the Holy Spirit's descent upon the apostles in the upper room; but rather because the mystagogue is able to perceive in his selection of biblical incidents the one mystery of salvation in Christ. Step'anos does not correlate the selected incidents according to classical typology. He does not imply any real causal or temporal relationship between the biblical events and the church's Hour of prayer. In other words, there is no chronological, horizontal continuum connecting the selected moments in sacred Scripture. Step'anos sees these events rather as interconnected, or better, as superimposed. In Step'anos's distinctive eschatological view, time collapses into a single day, or rather a single hour. The temporal separation between the past, the present, and the future evaporates so that the moments of salvation history and the moments of the church's prayer coalesce.

In his rationale for Vespers, Step'anos, following his now familiar pattern, lifts out of the Bible the following incidents that took place around the eleventh hour of the day, when the Evening Office was conducted: Adam and Eve's collapse into utter despair after the Fall; the giving of the covenant to Abraham; Christ's burial and descent

---

[23] *Treatise on Prayer*, ed. E. G. Jay (London: S.P.C.K., 1954), 114–15, cited in R. F. Taft, *The Liturgy of the Hours in East and West: The Origins of the Divine Office and Its Meaning for Today* (Collegeville, MN: Liturgical Press, 1985) 16. Similar examples by Tertullian, ibid., 17–18. Cyprian also lists various biblical events associated with the Hours of prayer, linking them in a moralizing way. Ibid., 19–20.

into Hades; and his post-resurrection appearance to the assembled apostles on the first day of the week (see John 20:19). These events are, of course, successive scenes in the story of mankind's salvation in Christ. But Step'anos understands these moments as mutually referential. No time span separates the eleventh hour today with its evening prayers from the eleventh hour of Abraham's day, nor from the hour of Christ's burial. The mystery of salvation in Christ is eternally operative in one, integral, eschatological "today." Thus can Step'anos conclude that the purpose of the Evening Office is to "supplicate the all-merciful God . . . for the downfall of [our] souls and for [Adam], according to the mystagogy of the night. For both [the prayers] of the morning and of the evening have one objective" (10.7; 111–12, 156). By praying the Evening Office, we participate in the mystery of salvation.

We find the very same technique throughout Grigoris Aršaruni's commentary on the Lectionary. For example, describing why readings from Job are appointed for the Fridays of Great Lent, Grigoris writes:

> In this way, this reading has entirely dissolved the condemnation of the man, and renewed him in his first life by means of Christ's passion. And because Adam was wounded by the tree and exiled from Paradise on Friday, it is also on Friday that the Savior, by his own wounds, healed him on the cross, and the thief entered Paradise. Rightly does the church appoint on Fridays the lections from Job, filled with suffering by Satan, following the example of the blows received by the first man himself, and by his sons, and by the creatures who were corrupted with him.[24]

RECIPROCITY AND COMPLEMENTARITY OF "TYPES"
When Step'anos and Grigoris read the Bible from this distinctive eschatological perspective, drawing into their eternal worldview the concrete ingredients of the liturgy, a new relationship emerges between old and new, one that is not simply causal or proleptic but reciprocal and complementary. Step'anos's conception of Christ's redemptive works transcends time. When, in Step'anos's view, all history collapses into one eternal "today," then there is no longer any temporal gap between Adam and Christ, or between Christ's redemptive activity and our liturgy. Step'anos expresses this eschatological reality by showing how Christ's activity in some way complements

---

[24] *Commentaire du Lectionnaire*, ed. Chérubin Tcherakian (Venice: St. Lazar, 1964) 132.

Adam's. Again in his commentary on the Third Hour, Step'anos affirms that at this hour Adam ran to the tree while Christ ran to the cross; Adam fell while Christ was lifted up; Adam walked "impudently" to the tree, while Christ's feet were nailed, outstretched on the cross (6.3; 97–98, 139–40). Similarly at the Ninth Hour, "In the very place where [Adam] heard [the words] 'You shall return to the dust,' the robber's ear heard, 'Today you shall be with me in paradise'" (9.3; 108–9, 153–54). At the hour that Adam was expelled, Christ paved the way to the tree of life.

I believe that our authors' purpose in constructing these pairings, which Robert Murray calls "comparison-series,"[25] is more than a display of rhetorical virtuosity or poetic prowess. Like the hours of the day, all events in salvation history are complementary and multivalent. In their commentaries, Step'anos and Grigoris are intent on proclaiming and celebrating the eternal and universal reality of the mystery of salvation. Moreover, by grounding the liturgy in this eschatological vision of the *historia* of redemption, our authors imply that the faithful who participate in the liturgy ipso facto participate with Christ in the sacramental work of salvation.

INTERPRETATION OF LITURGICAL UNITS
We have seen how Step'anos interprets all biblical events that explicitly or by implication occurred at the same hour as being connected trans-temporally in the divine scheme of salvation, and as eschatologically linked to the Hours of the daily Office. Our authors' approach to interpreting the concrete elements of the liturgy is identical. In the second part of each chapter of his *Commentary* Step'anos moves through the liturgical ordo from beginning to end, and repeatedly uncovers the integral mystery of salvation either in successive individual liturgical elements or in series of liturgical structures. To illustrate, let us return to the author's commentary on the Evening Office. Step'anos begins his discussion of the liturgical ordo by making a series of comparisons with the structure and meaning of the beginning of the Morning Office. The details of this somewhat unwieldy comparison (*Commentary*, 474–75) are not as important for the present purposes as Step'anos's assertion that "both [the prayers] of the morning and evening have

---

[25] *Symbols of Church and Kingdom: A Study in Early Syriac Tradition* (New York: T & T Clark, 2004) 42, 51–53.

one objective" (10.7; 156). In other words, the story of salvation is revealed equally in the Morning and the Evening prayers.

Following this comparison Step'anos sets out to interpret the primary liturgical units of Vespers, beginning with Psalms 139–141.[26] By plucking words and phrases from these three psalms, and weaving them together with his own words, the author retells the *historia* of the fall and of redemption. The resulting passage reads awkwardly because the author has knit together nine phrases from the Armenian version of Psalms 139–141. Nevertheless, he manages to read the mystery of salvation from selected words in the evening psalms:

> Save [me] (Ps 139:1) from the devil who sharpened [his] tongue like a serpent's poison (Ps 139:3), and laid a trap to thwart our journey to the supernal life (Ps 139:5). This is why it asks [God] to be a shelter in the day of battle (Ps 139:8). For the devil also endeavored, near hell (Ps 140:7), to stab us, who stood back from Christ because of the stone of the downfall (Ps 140:6). But they themselves shall fall into the same. But allow those who trust in you (Ps. 140:8) to pass through this fiery wall (Ps 140:10) to be with you in the paradise of repose, Lord, who pulled me out of the eternal prison (Ps 141:1), so that I might arrive at the land of the paradise of good things. (10.8; 112, 156–57)

After this passage Step'anos takes up the next three elements in the order of Vespers: Psalm 85,[27] the ancient vesperal hymn, "O Joyous Light," and a presbyteral supplication. In the words of these liturgical units, he perceives once again traces of the mystery of salvation in Christ:

> Give ear, O Lord (Ps 85:1), and give strength to this your servant and to [your] hand-maiden, and show me the sign (Ps 85:15) of your cross of protection, so that the multitude of the demons that hate me, having seen it, might be put to shame (Ps 85:16). By this means, those who have been nurtured in Christ's holiness by his mystical resurrection have

---

[26] In Step'anos's time, as today, Psalms 139–141 are preceded, in Armenian Vespers, by Psalm 85. Step'anos reverses this sequence in order to emphasize a certain point of his comparison of Matins and Vespers. This distortion of the liturgical ordo is exceptional in his commentary, which otherwise respects the sequence of the services. See *Commentary*, 474–75.

[27] See preceding note.

praised the light of the uncreated and ineffable triple union [allusion to the hymn "O Joyous Light"] more than the glimmer of created things" (10.9; 112, 157–58).

And so he continues through the Office, uncovering the story of salvation over and over again encoded in the words and rituals of the Vespers ordo. The *Trisagion*, too, at the conclusion of Vespers, "contains the one mystery of salvation" (10.10; 112–13, 158).

Step'anos follows precisely the same procedure throughout his commentary, and, for that matter, in his very interesting commentary on the old Armenian service of Dedicating a Church.[28] Moving systematically through this highly ritualized service, Step'anos finds the mystery of redemption veiled in the details of the rite, and manifested not once but many times in the service, in a variety of guises. The lowering of the altar table from the elevated bema and its removal outside the church represents "the almighty king lower[ing] himself from the paternal bosom to save us captives."[29] The three refrains accompanying Psalms 119–121 comprise yet another complete representation of the divine economy: the prophets crying out for salvation; mankind beseeching the incarnate Lord for the salvation of fallen human nature, which was granted through the Lord's suffering; and the earthly ones praising their redemption together with the spiritual ones.[30] As the altar table is carried in procession into the sanctuary Psalm 117 is repeated thrice: first with a gentle melody, then with a robust melody, then again in a gentle melody. This, Step'anos writes, is because: "First the forefathers, offering their entreaties to the Father, described the weight of their perils. But when the Word became man and until his second coming, the faithful supplicated the Son with robust voice, saying, 'Open for us the gate of mercy' before our afflictions. And again with a gentle voice they enter the church with the altar table. This is for those who were born through the Holy Spirit as heirs of God on the

[28] Step'anos, *Commentary on the Daily Office*, ed. S. Amatuni (Etchmiadzin: Press of the Holy See, 1917) 71–78. For a comparative-liturgical and historical study of this office see Findikyan, "The Armenian Liturgy of Dedicating a Church: A Textual and Comparative Analysis of Three Early Sources." OCP 64, no. 1 (1998) 75–121.

[29] Step'anos, *Commentary*, ed. Amatuni, 72. Findikyan, "The Armenian Liturgy," 82–83.

[30] Step'anos, *Commentary*, ed. Amatuni, 72–73.

eighth day in the end times, in the supernal city of the spiritual Jerusalem."[31] Over and over again, as Step'anos walks through the service, salvation is revealed in an infinite variety of manifestations.

No different is the approach of Grigoris Aršaruni in his Commentary on the Lectionary. Instead of the liturgical elements of a church service, Grigoris detects and composes the story of salvation from within the succession of Scripture readings indicated in the Armenian Lectionary for the days from Epiphany to the Sunday following Easter. Without entering too deeply into the details of Grigoris's curious and somewhat convoluted allegorical scheme,[32] suffice it to note his relentless effort to uncover "the mystery of salvation in Christ" (xorhurd p'rkut'ean K'ristosiw) from within "the mystery of the lections of salvation" (xorhurd p'rkut'ean ənt'erc'uacoc'n), phrases that appear in practically every chapter of the commentary.

To cite but one example, chapter 14 of Grigoris's work begins with the following heading: "How the lections and the psalms of the Wednesdays and Fridays of Lent, arranged together, beshadow the same mystery of salvation in Christ for the man and the woman, which they conduct at Epiphany and at Easter."[33] Grigoris's rationale proceeds in a manner remarkably similar to that of Step'anos. Grigoris culls lines, phrases, and subjects from the lections, weaving them together to create a narrative of salvation history. Thus the readings assigned by the old Armenian Lectionary of Jerusalem for the first Wednesday of Lent begin with "the suffering of the race of women caused by the machinations of the Evil One," and conclude with "the hope of Christ's salvation."[34] Wherever he turns, Grigoris's rationale for the selection of readings appointed on a given day or period of the liturgical year amounts to a manifestation of salvation in Christ following Adam's fall from grace. Grigoris freely selects characters,

[31] Ibid., 74.

[32] Grigoris presents a curious vision of redemption in which the salvation of Adam/man is distinguished from that of Eve/woman. The former is associated with the Feast of Nativity-Theophany (a single feast in the Armenian Rite) and the latter with Easter. This polarization determines his entire allegorical scheme and is the central organizing principle of his commentary. See Tcherakian's edition, XLV–LVI, for a discussion of Grigoris's theology.

[33] Grigoris, *Commentaire du Lectionnaire*, 16:119.

[34] Ibid., 120. Cf. Renoux, *Le Codex*, 239.

phrases, and other key words drawn from the Scripture readings to use as building blocks for his synthetic theology.

Two significant features are to be noted from the peculiar liturgical hermeneutics of Step'anos and Grigoris. First, the story of salvation history, whatever its form, wherever it is uncovered, is always unified and inclusive. The reader does not encounter isolated or detached reflections on one moment of salvation history, on, for example, the creation, or Christ's burial. Manifestations in the liturgy (or the lectionary) of scenes from the divine economy are always integrated within a complete representation of the mystery of salvation. Second, the story is found numerous times within the liturgical structures of a given service, or, in the case of Grigoris, in a given rationale or argument.

This is particularly noteworthy because the tendency in Byzantine liturgical commentary was quite different. Schultz and Taft have both shown that the tendency in Byzantine liturgical commentary was toward a gradual disintegration, or, as Schultz calls it, a "reification" of what was once a unified vision of salvation in Christ.[35] Beginning with Patriarch Germanus of Constantinople's *Commentary on the Divine Liturgy*, which exhibits some influence from the earlier commentary of Theodore of Mopsuestia, the individual components of the liturgy come to reflect or "image forth" specific, discrete moments in Christ's earthly ministry. Ultimately, by the time of Nicholas of Andida's eleventh-century *Protheoria*, the liturgy represents the entire course of salvation history from beginning to end.[36] Successive elements of the liturgy become successive scenes in a single, grand portrayal of salvation history. By the fourteenth century this fragmentation had progressed to the point that Nicholas Cabasilas could write: "The whole celebration of the mystery is like a unique portrayal of a single body, which from beginning to end preserves its order and harmony, so that each ceremony, each prayer, adds something to the whole. Thus, the opening chants symbolize the first phase of the work of redemption; the readings from Scripture and the other liturgical acts which follow represent the second period."[37]

---

[35] See H.-J. Schultz, *The Byzantine Liturgy: Symbolic Structure and Faith Expression*, trans. Matthew J. O'Connell (New York: Pueblo, 1986) 69. See below for Taft's assessment.

[36] See Bornert, *Les commentaires*, 181–213; Schultz, *The Byzantine Liturgy*, 77, 90.

[37] Cabasilas, *A Commentary*, 52–53.

We find no such fragmentation in our early Armenian commentaries, and nothing like it in later authors. While Step'anos and Grigoris reveal in the liturgy and in the Lectionary depictions of salvation history and the heavenly liturgy, for them the whole mystery of salvation history is discernable in any given liturgical movement, moment, rite, or object, and in every one. Therefore, in the course of the liturgy one does not perceive a single chronological succession of frames or scenes from salvation history (or the heavenly liturgy), but repeated epiphanies or signs of the entirety of salvation proclaimed not once *in toto*, but many times, over and over again.

This kind of integrated perspective, according to Taft, represents an earlier outlook, in which the liturgy was understood as "an anamnesis of the total mystery that is Christ in its present efficacy, the eternal intercession before the throne of God, of Christ our high priest."[38] As for the superimposition of symbols, Taft writes, *a propos* of Byzantine liturgical hermeneutics:

> The problem of later medieval liturgical allegory consists not in the multiplicity of systematically layered symbols, such as we find [in Germanus] and in patristic exegesis. The later one-symbol-per-object correspondence results not from the tidying up of an earlier incoherent primitiveness, but from the decomposition of the earlier patristic mystery-theology into a historicizing system of dramatic narrative allegory. All levels—Old Testament preparation, Last Supper, accomplishment on Calvary, eternal heavenly offering, present liturgical event—must be held in dynamic unity by any interpretation of the Eucharist. To separate these levels, then parcel out the elements bit by bit according to some chronologically consecutive narrative sequence, is to turn ritual into drama, symbol into allegory, mystery into history.[39]

It is precisely this "dynamic unity" that our Armenian mystagogues seem to have achieved, whatever one might say about the liberties they take with the biblical text to do so.[40] One can only conclude that

---

[38] See "The Liturgy of the Great Church: An Initial Synthesis of Structure and Interpretation on the Eve of Iconoclasm." *Dumbarton Oaks Papers* 34–35 (1980–81): 45–75.

[39] Ibid., 73.

[40] Note Renoux's critical assessment of Grigoris's commentary: "Cet appel à la typologie, à partir de laquelle fleurit aussi fréquemment un allégorisme débridé, se retrouve tout au long du *Commentaire*. Ce recours constant (excessif?)

their approach to liturgical interpretation reflects a broader sensibility. The mystery of Christ is to be found everywhere in the Bible, in the liturgy, in the architecture and furnishings of a church building, and presumably elsewhere. The function of mystagogy for these authors is not merely to elucidate a text or ritual for better comprehension by the faithful; it is rather to discern, to proclaim, and therefore to celebrate the truth and actuality of the mystery of Christ, "the great mystery of our salvation."

ANTIOCH OR ALEXANDRIA?

An obvious question presents itself: where did these Armenian theologians learn this approach to liturgical hermeneutics? Modern scholars, at least the relatively few that have occupied themselves with the genre of liturgical commentary, have generally tended to analyze this literature using categories adopted from the field of patristic exegesis. Bornert,[41] Schultz,[42] Taft,[43] and Mazza[44] have therefore sought to locate the allegorical approaches of the classic fourth-century mystagogies, as well as the Byzantine liturgical commentaries, within the framework of the conventional Antiochene-Alexandrine exegetical gamut. The last two decades have witnessed increasing skepticism regarding the legitimacy of these categories as applicable to any author after the fourth century, or even as mutually exclusive categories at all.[45] Be that as it may, the study of the abundant body of Armenian commentaries on the Bible is not yet even in its infancy because the vast majority of

---

aux figures bibliques, à propos de chaque péricope liturgique, l'oblige aussi à des rapprochements pointilleux des textes scripturaires; ces recherches ne débouchent pas sur une nourissante presentation du mystère du salut pour que l'on puisse parler de mystagogie" ("Les commentaires," 306).

[41] R. Bornert, *Les commentaires*, esp. 47–82.

[42] H.-J. Schultz, *The Byzantine Liturgy*.

[43] R. Taft, "The Liturgy of the Great Church."

[44] E. Mazza, *Mystagogy: A Theology of Liturgy in the Patristic Age*, trans. Matthew J. O'Connell (New York: Pueblo, 1989).

[45] A helpful summary and discussion may be found in B. Nassif, "'Spiritual Exegesis' in the School of Antioch," in *New Perspectives on Historical Theology: Essays in Memory of John Meyendorff*, ed. Bradley Nassif (Grand Rapids: Eerdmans, 1995) 343–77. See also the relevant articles and bibliography in C. Kannengiesser, *Handbook of Patristic Exegesis: The Bible in Ancient Christianity*. 2 vols. (Leiden and Boston: Brill, 2004) 165–269.

these precious sources for Armenian theology and exegesis remain locked away in manuscript depositories, waiting to be edited and studied.[46] One of the few scholars to venture an assessment of the allegorical procedures used by the Armenian biblical commentators is Peter Cowe. In his fine edition of Xosrov Anjewac'i's tenth-century commentary on the Armenian Divine Liturgy, Cowe appealed to conventional categories when he wrote:

> It is true that the Alexandrine anagogical approach to the liturgy, viewing it as a manifestation of the soul's ascent from the material to the spiritual realm, was already familiar in Armenia. The late fifth-century Ps-Dionysian corpus is cited in florilegia of the early seventh century and translated in full a century later . . . [Yet] instead of emulating the Dionysia[n] formula of introducing the subject by a general definition of what constitutes a sacrament, outlining (rather succinctly) the peculiarities of the rite and then expatiating on its mystical dimensions, Xosrov opts for an unabashedly textual orientation . . . this then was the Armenian classroom approach to biblical commentary.[47]

Elsewhere, Cowe asserts that "although christologically the Armenian Church developed a closer affinity with Alexandria, its exegetical perspective was indelibly molded by Antiochene principles."[48]

Clearly, our two authors' fascination with Christ and with the *historia* of his redemptive mission reveal them to be no strangers to the so-called Antiochene school of exegesis, with its emphasis on the chronological progression of salvation history, unveiled by means of types and antetypes. "So great is the mystery of divine worship which was prefigured in Christ," Step'anos writes, "that the truth is contained in the place of the shadowed ones; in the priests, I say, and in the various victims of sacrifices, by which the children of the Hebrews worshipped in order to gain entrance into the sanctuary . . ." (*Commentary* 9.2; 107–8, 153). Similarly, in another place he writes that with the coming of Christ "the depths [of the mystery] were revealed. The

---

[46] Many of them are listed in E. Petrosyan and A. Ter-Step'anyan, *S. Grk'i hayeren meknut'yunneri matenagitut'iwn* [Bibliography of the Armenian Commentaries on the Holy Bible] (Erevan: Hayastani Astvacašnč'ayin Ěnkerut'yun, 2002).

[47] Xosrov, *Commentary*, 53.

[48] Ibid., 52.

darkness of ignorance was dissipated at the completion of time" (9.3; 108, 153). Step'anos's commentary on the Sunday Third Hour Office, which is nothing else but the eucharistic Liturgy of the Word, is entirely occupied with the high priesthood of Christ and the eternal sacrifice of Christ to the Father as presented in the Epistle to the Hebrews, favorite themes of Antiochene-inspired authors.

Neither are our authors ignorant of the spiritualizing tendencies of the Alexandrian school. Step'anos envisions the Daily Office as a "most pleasing ascent" to "the divine heights" (10.13; 114, 160). His explanation of the Midday Hour interprets it as an elevation to the heavenly liturgy: "The Word made for us a road like [that] chiseled into the rifts of the valleys, gradually ascending from the olive groves to the mountain of divine doctrine to be near the Word of life, so that we might fix our attention and thoughts on mindfulness to that place where the temple of God is, and where the heavenly ones now, once again, officiate their feasts and truths; where [there is] no grief and no sorrow, but perpetual rejoicing by the rays of the ineffable light" (8.2; 105, 150–51).

Step'anos's mystagogy, however, is not so easily squeezed into conventional Antiochene or Alexandrian categories of exegesis, exhibiting, as it does, features characteristic of both. Furthermore, some of the allegorical procedures used consistently by Step'anos and Grigoris are not readily identifiable with approaches used by authors whom we routinely place in one school or the other. We have to look elsewhere for analogous hermeneutic systems.

The art historian Thomas F. Mathews, in collaboration with Avedis Sanjian, recently published a superb, interdisciplinary examination of the fifteenth-century illuminated Armenian manuscript known as the *Glajor Gospel (UCLA arm. 1)*, devoting particular attention to the iconographic program and characteristics of the miniatures it contains.[49] In examining the distinctive artistic representation of the various biblical scenes, Mathews sought to make connections with contemporaneous Armenian commentaries on the gospels. He discovered that the exegetical method of the authors he read was strongly reminiscent of the theological approach of St. Ephrem the Syrian, which Mathews labeled "symbolic synecdoche, or part-for whole symbolism." Mathews writes:

[49] T. F. Mathews and A. K. Sanjian, eds., *Armenian Gospel Iconography: The Tradition of the Glajor Gospel.* Dumbarton Oaks Studies 29 (Washington: Dumbarton Oaks Research Library and Collection, 1991).

It would be unfair to call this method allegorical. The correspondences [Ephrem] traces are not exactly types and antetypes; the realities are too close to be separable in such artificial categories. For Ephrem Christ already existed in the Old Testament, and Yahweh's revelations of himself to the patriarchs were manifestations of Christ's form. Sacred history takes on a kind of transparency, in which everything is foreseen and planned from the beginning and everything belongs to a single pattern. . . Since all of Christ's life and death is a single grand act of man's salvation, each individual event in his life somehow contains and reveals the whole. Thus . . . in making mud to cure the blind man, Christ is said to be recreating Adam out of the mud of the earth, but this time it is the second and redeemed Adam;[50] or, in appearing transfigured before his disciples Christ is manifesting his coming resurrection, which in fact involves the restoration of redeemed man to paradise. In this way Ephrem describes each part of Christ's life as if it stands for and encapsulates the entire work of salvation. No Gospel event is to be seen as an isolated incident; all is interrelated, as if all of history were simultaneous.[51]

Ephrem's imagination is attracted not so much to traditional "types" and "antetypes" but rather to what he calls, *râzê* (mystery-symbols). This oft-cited excerpt from Ephrem's *Hymns on Virginity* is representative of his approach:

> In every place, if you look, his symbol [*râzâ*] is there,
> and wherever you read, you will find his types.
> For in him all creatures were created
> and he traced his symbols on his property.
> When he was creating the world,
> he looked to adorn it with icons of himself.
> The springs of his symbols were opened up to run down
> and pour forth his symbols into his members.[52]

[50] See, for example, Ephrem the Syrian, *Commentaire de l'Évangile concordant, version arménienne*, ed. L. Leloir. CSCO 137, Scriptores Armeniaci 1 (Louvain: Imprimerie Orientaliste L. Durbecq, 1953) 299–300.

[51] T. F. Mathews and A. K. Sanjian, eds., *Armenian Gospel Iconography*, 82.

[52] *Hymns on Virginity* 20 in *Ephrem the Syrian—Hymns*, trans. Kathleen McVey (New York: Paulist Press, 1989) 41–42; 348–49. Cf. S. Brock, *The Luminous Eye: The Spiritual World Vision of Saint Ephrem* (Kalamazoo: Cistercian Publications, 1992) 55–56; *Selected Prose Works*, trans. E. G. Mathews Jr. and J. P. Amar, ed. K. McVey. The Fathers of the Church 91 (Washington: Catholic

For Ephrem, the significance of sacred Scripture lies not only in its narrative of the divine economy. The multitude of people, objects, places, dates, numbers, and events in the Bible are not only constituents of the story of mankind's salvation, they are also *râzê*, mutually referential signs pointing to the mystery of Christ. Sidney Griffith writes that the *râzê* "may point forward from Nature and Scripture to Christ, who in turn reveals his Father to the eye of Faith, or they point from the Church's life and liturgy back to Christ, who in turn reveals to the faithful believer the events of the *eschaton*, the ultimate fulfillment of all creation in the economy of salvation."[53] He adds, "Ephraem the exegete canvassed the scriptures in search of the *râzê*, which in the ensemble of them would disclose the whole economy of salvation, as it found its focus in the passion, death and resurrection of Christ."[54]

Here is a passage from Ephrem's *Commentary on the Diatessaron*, a work that first came to light in its seemingly ancient Armenian translation.[55] Commenting on Jesus' miracle at Cana, Ephrem perceives within the details of the story "symbols" (*râzê*) revealing the essence of the Gospel:

> Now from that water [Jesus] made wine so that he might liken it to his conception and birth, demonstrating how they came to be. He called for six urns to give testimony to the one Virgin who gave birth to him. The urns, contrary to their customary usage, conceived and gave birth to wine; and they would never give birth to more. In this way the Virgin conceived and gave birth to Emmanuel, and never again to any other. The birth from the urns transformed smallness into greatness and poverty into excess; water into sweet wine. But here [the birth from Mary transformed] greatness into poverty and glory into ignominy. These basins were [used] for the purification of the Jews; but into them our Sav-

---

University of America Press, 1994) 49; R. Murray, "The Theory of Symbolism in St. Ephrem's Theology." *Parole de l'Orient* 6/7 (1975–76): 1–20., 5; Ephrem, *Commentaire*, ed. Leloir, 31.

[53] Kannengiesser, *Handbook*, 2:1418.

[54] Ibid., 2:1419.

[55] Though the authenticity of the Armenian version has recently been questioned, E. G. Mathews judges it "to be on the whole genuine Ephrem, although later accretions have no doubt crept in" ("The Armenian Literary Corpus Attributed to Ephrem the Syrian: Prolegomena to a Project." *St. Nersess Theological Review* 1, no. 2 [1996] 154).

ior poured the teaching of his doctrine to show that he had come according to the path of the Law and the Prophets, and [to show] that everything would be transformed by his teaching, like water into wine.[56]

The eschatological superimposition and reciprocity of every moment and action in salvation history is a characteristic of Ephrem's worldview. Sebastian Brock writes: "Ephrem perceives a detailed pattern of complementarity between the processes of fall and restoration: all the individual details of the Fall are reversed, so that we are presented with a series of contrasted types, with Adam/Christ and Eve/Mary as protagonists. Salvation history can thus be described as a process of healing which extends both back to the reaches of primordial time, and down to the depths of the fallen human state."[57]

Edward G. Mathews observes the same phenomenon, among others, in Ephrem's portrayal of Christ's crucifixion. "At the very moment Christ was pierced with the lance there were removed from the Garden of Eden the cherub that had been placed there and the sword that he had wielded to prohibit anyone's reentry. It was at that moment that access into Paradise became possible once again for humanity."[58]

Here is precisely the approach taken by Step'anos Siwnec'i and Grigoris Aršaruni in their interpretations of the Armenian Daily Office and the Lectionary. Instead of the words of Sacred Scripture, Step'anos takes as his point of departure the raw materials of the Daily Office:

[56] Ephrem, *Commentaire*, ed. Leloir, 5.7:110. The translation of the Armenian version is mine.

[57] Brock, *The Luminous Eye*, 89. Besides Brock's excellent survey of Ephrem's theology and "spiritual world view" there are now several other useful introductions to Ephrem's exegetical procedures: Kannengiesser, *Handbook*, 2:1399–1421; *Selected Prose Works*, ed. McVey, 45–56; *Hymns on Paradise*. intro. and trans. by Sebastian Brock (Crestwood: St. Vladimir's Seminary Press, 1990) 7–75; *Hymns*, trans. McVey, 3–48. These should be consulted alongside several earlier works: Murray, *Symbols of Church and Kingdom*; L. Leloir, *Doctrines et methods de S. Ephrem d'après son Commentaire de l'Evangile concordant*. CSCO 220 (Louvain: Secretariat du CorpusCSO, 1961); and idem, "Symbolisme et parallelisme chez Ephrem," in *À la rencontre de Dieu: Mémorial Albert Gelin* (Le Puy: X. Mappus, 1961) 363–74.

[58] *Selected Prose Works*, 54, analyzing a collection of Ephremic texts presented by Robert Murray, "The Lance Which Reopened Paradise." OCP 39 (1973) 224–34.

the words of the psalms, prayers, diaconal proclamations, and hymns; the accoutrements of liturgy: vestments, lamps, bread, wine, baptismal font, Book of the Gospels, incense; gestures: bowing, standing, processing, elevating, giving glory; numbers, patterns, and sequences. For Step'anos, encoded in any one of these particles of the Daily Office is the entire, trans-temporal "grand act of man's salvation" in Jesus Christ waiting to be decoded and articulated.[59] Grigoris does exactly the same thing with the readings of the Lectionary, their sequence, and association with the various feasting and fasting days of the liturgical year; their content: figures, plot lines, numbers, geographical indicators—all of these are ripe for harvesting as building blocks of a synthetic narrative of salvation history.

These building blocks are not really "types" or "antetypes" in the classical sense, terms that Step'anos and Grigoris never use. By contrast, as we have seen above, in these Armenian exegetical writings the reader persistently encounters the Armenian word *xorhurd* (and derivatives), which perfectly renders the Syriac *râzâ*. These "mysteries" are Hours of the day, the Scripture readings, the concrete words and gestures of the liturgy, the words and actions of Christ. Wherever they look Step'anos and Grigoris turn up signs or "mysteries" of the divine economy. Indeed, Thomas Mathews asserts that St. Ephrem's exegetical method became "decisive for the development of native Armenian exegesis,"[60] whether practiced by scribes writing biblical commentaries, or by artists painting manuscript illuminations.[61]

This "symbolic synecdoche," a method for perceiving and articulating the mystery of Christ encoded everywhere in the Bible and in the liturgy, is a creative theology. The purpose is not historiographic precision, nor is it strict, literal clarification of a given text, ritual, or other object, but a manner of creative, speculative theological reflection. Inspired, it seems, by St. Ephrem,[62] some of whose works were trans-

---

[59] See *Commentary*, 519–20.

[60] T. F. Mathews and A. K. Sanjian, eds., *Armenian Gospel Iconography*, 82.

[61] "What the commentator did in parsing and embroidering a passage the painter did in illustrating it, not resting content with simply retelling the story in pictures but forging images that would direct the viewer in how to interpret the story" (ibid., 2). I would add that theologians did much the same thing in interpreting the liturgy.

[62] Though the approach is surely not unique to him. Later Syriac authors, perhaps inspired by Ephrem, likewise apply "symbolic synecdoche." A metri-

lated very early and circulated widely in Armenia,[63] our early commentators sought the mystery of Christ—the totality of the Gospel message—everywhere and in everything.

Salvation for them was not a future abstraction to be pondered, nor was it merely a past event to be recalled, but an objective reality which they found already perceptible in daily life, especially in the celebration of the church's liturgy. There the people of God not only connect anamnetically with the historical events of salvation, but actually participate in them with Christ, sacramentally.

All of this may be quite contrary to our modern sensibilities, and quite contrary to the critique of modern scholars, who are quick to dismiss anything but the most literal forms of patristic exegesis and liturgical mystagogy as misguided and irrelevant, if not simply naïve. And yet it seems that the Armenian authors we have considered have a rather different understanding of "theology," of "mystagogy," than we modern, enlightened scholars. For them, theology *is* christology. Much more than "fides quaerens intellectum," the discipline of theology is the proclamation and the celebration of the utter reality and radical ubiquity of the mystery of Christ; of God with us.[64]

---

cal homily *(memra)* of Jacob of Sarug (d. 708) recited at the end of the Syriac Liturgy of St. James reads: "Where Zion set up the Cross to crucify the Son / There grew up the tree that gave birth to the Lamb. Where nails were driven in the Son's hands / There Isaac's hands were bound for an offering…" (A. Y. Samuel, ed. and trans., *Anaphoras of the Ancient Rite of the Syrian Orthodox Church of Antioch* (Lodi, NJ: A.Y. Samuel, 1991) 148.

[63] A substantial corpus of works attributed to St. Ephrem survives in Armenian. These, traditional scholarship holds, were translated into Armenian very early by the fifth-century creator of the Armenian alphabet and his school. E. G. Matthews, "The Armenian Literary Corpus" has cast a shadow of doubt over the authenticity of most of these works, with the exception of the *Commentary on the Diatessaron*, the *Hymns on Nicomedia*, and the *Kc'urtk'* [*Madrāšê*].

[64] Cf. Kannengiesser, *Handbook*: "Religious thought, or 'theology' then rightfully consists in the contemplation of the *raze*, the 'mystery symbols' in which God reveals the truth about himself and the world to human beings" (2:1417).

Chapter 9

Christology and Trinity:
Interpreting the Lord's Prayer

Kenneth Stevenson
Bishop of Portsmouth

In 1952 Ernst Lohmeyer's major study of the Lord's Prayer appeared posthumously in the original German, *Das Vater-Unser*; an English translation by Gregor Smith followed thirteen years later in 1965.[1] Lohmeyer realized, perhaps even more than other scholars of his time, that to study the Lord's Prayer exclusively from the point of view of New Testament scholarship is a limited exercise. The Prayer belongs to a lengthy tradition of interpretation and use, which, in Lohmeyer's case, was richly illuminated by his ease with early patristic writings. Along with the rest of the tradition, these writings contribute to how the Prayer is used and interpreted as the prayer of Christ to the Father in the power of the Spirit.

In that christological and trinitarian sense, the Pauline texts referring to the spirit of adoption which enables us to cry "Abba! Father!" (Rom 8:15, Gal 4:6) keep recurring in writers across the centuries when the opening petition of the Prayer is being explained. Yet Lohmeyer himself, toward the end of his study, takes the risk of suggesting that there is no precise definition in the New Testament of the community to which the Lord's Prayer is given: "the praying community seems to have no clear distinguishing marks."[2] The Christian Church has been

[1] Ernst Lohmeyer, *The Lord's Prayer* (London: Collins, 1965).

[2] Lohmeyer, *The Lord's Prayer*, 285; see also W. D. Davies and D. C. Allison, *The Gospel according to St Matthew*, Critical and Exegetical Commentary Series (Edinburgh: T&T Clark, 1988) 1:590–617 (bibliography, 621–24), and C. F. Evans, *St. Luke* (London: S.C.M., 1990) 441–80; for a recent view that regards the Prayer as originally composed in Greek, not Aramaic, with Matthew's (longer) text antedating Luke's—which he suggests was for liturgical-

using and explaining the Prayer from the very beginning of its mission, at times attempting to restrict its use to the baptized. But there is a built-in tension about the character of that community, which is to be seen in the contexts of the two versions contained in the New Testament.[3] In Matthew's Gospel it comes exactly halfway through the Sermon on the Mount (Matt 6:9-13): the Prayer embodies the teaching of Jesus in what has sometimes been described as the greatest sermon ever preached. But it is not in the form of a homily for a self-defined "Christian community"; rather, it takes the form of an address delivered in the open air, to the world, with all the ambiguities that this might entail about ownership, response, stage of faith. Then in Luke's Gospel, straight after the scene with Martha and Mary, and before the disciples are taught about putting their faith into practice, they find Jesus praying, and they ask him for specific guidance—which he proceeds to provide (Luke 11:2-4).

However much we may, rightly and understandably, load the Lord's Prayer with christological and trinitarian teaching, its New Testament origins inevitably tell us of a different context: not one to which we should anachronistically aspire in some way to "return." Many are the views of scholars, preachers, and other writers down the ages on such questions as exactly who can say this Prayer, and when, and what its overall shape conveys, as well as the multiple meanings of some of its petitions. In the face of such an array we have chosen Augustine, Maximus the Confessor, Lancelot Andrewes, and Karl Barth, in the interests of comprehensiveness. Each one of them, in a particular way and in a particular liturgical context, has contributed to the tradition of interpretation of the Lord's Prayer in relation both to christology and Trinity.

---

catechetical use—see H. B. Green, *Matthew: Poet of the Beatitudes,* Journal for the Study of the New Testament Supplement Series 203 (Sheffield: Academic Press, 2001) 77–91, and Appendix A, 293–99 (on the Lucan text).

[3] See K. W. Stevenson, *The Lord's Prayer: A Text in Tradition* (London/Minneapolis: S.C.M./Fortress, 2004) 17–24, and nn. 237–38, for a discussion of recent scholarship, of which the literature is considerable; in addition to this study in relation to the Prayer's use and interpretation, see also idem, "The Lord's Prayer in Tradition," *Ecclesia orans* 21 (2004) 301–22.

In 394 Augustine wrote his treatise on what he was the first to call "the Sermon on the Mount."[4] This work demonstrates a preoccupation with exegesis that was never to leave him. Everything that he writes or preaches subsequently on the Lord's Prayer is derivative from this main, seminal work, which itself may have resulted from some kind of preaching ministry while he was still a young presbyter.[5]

In many ways much of his basic treatment of the Prayer as he goes through it verse by verse builds on what we know of the North African tradition of writers such as Tertullian and Cyprian. He takes care, like them (and many others), to provide quotations from the New Testament to explain the Prayer as an expression of the teaching of Christ, and in that sense christological (e.g., John 6: 27, 41, on "daily bread").[6] Augustine's principal contribution is the extent to which he deliberately espouses a comprehensive interpretation, one based on a fundamental structure of three heavenly petitions (the name, the kingdom, and the will) followed by four earthly ones (daily bread, forgiveness, temptation, and evil). Augustine is the first to take such a firm line about the sevenfold shape of the Prayer, which has other consequences to which we shall return. Like Tertullian and Cyprian, he insists at the start that to address God as "Our Father" is the privilege of the baptized, of those who have been given the spirit of adoption; he goes out of his way to distinguish the Christian from the Jew in the intimate and at the same time corporate way in which we can address God (*sermone Domini,* 2.4.15). When it comes to the individual petitions, Augustine deliberately goes for rich variety: the kingdom is to be understood in four different ways, encompassing our partial ex-

---

[4] *De sermone Domini in monte* (= *sermone Domini*) 2.4.15–11.38) ed. A. Mutzenbecher, CCSL 35 (Turnhout: Brepols, 1967); English translation in NPNF 1/6 (Edinburgh: T&T Clark, 1996) 38–47; see also the important study by M. Jackson, "The Lord's Prayer in Saint Augustine," in *Studia patristica* 27, ed. E. A. Livingstone (Louvain: Peeters, 1993) 311–21.

[5] See Stevenson, *The Lord's Prayer,* 77–84, and nn. 249–50.

[6] On Tertullian, see *Opera,* part 1, 255–74, ed. E. Dekkers et al., CCSL 1 (Turnhout: Brepols, 1954) 255–74, and Stevenson, *The Lord's Prayer,* 28–32, n. 239; on Cyprian, *Opera,* part 2, 90–113, ed. M. Simonetti and C. Moreschini, CCSL 3A Turnhout: Brepols, 1976) 90–113, and Stevenson, *The Lord's Prayer,* 32–35, n. 239; see also A. Stewart-Sykes, ed. and trans., *Tertullian, Cyprian and Origen: On the Lord's Prayer* (New York: St. Vladimir's Seminary, 2004).

perience on earth as well as the final kingdom at the end of time (*sermone Domini*, 2.5.20-21); daily bread refers to our daily physical needs, our daily spiritual needs, as well as the Eucharist (and he takes a gentle sideswipe at the Christian East for not, apparently, having a daily celebration) (*sermone Domini*, 2.7.25-27); the petition for the forgiveness of sins Augustine in later sermons goes so far as to claim is a daily renewal of baptism,[7] an idea that will have had its own impact on ordinary piety. The temptation-petition brings us face to face with an unstable textual tradition, both in terms of gospel texts and liturgical usage (not invariably the same thing in the early Latin West); this Augustine inherited and contributed to, by trying to distance God from being seen as the direct agent of the experience, with his favored *ne inferas* (do not bring us).[8] Unlike his two North African predecessors, he insists that "evil" is to be comprehensive—not exclusively the devil (as in Eastern traditions of interpretation), but impersonally "every evil" as well (this comes to be echoed in the Latin rite's embolism at Mass).[9]

All these points are to be found in his later writings on the Lord's Prayer, whether the letter to Proba and her companions after the fall of Rome in 410, the four pre-baptismal sermons preached around 412, or the *Encheiridion* or doctrinal handbook written around 421–423. Their repetition is noticeable, often to the point of direct verbal parallels and the use of the same Scripture texts.[10] From all this the Lord's Prayer

---

[7] Sermons 213.8 and 261.10, in *The Works of St Augustine: Sermons*, part 3, 6:145–46, and 7:213 (New York: New City Press, 1993); Latin texts in PL 38:1064–65 and 1207; Augustine does not mention this in his exposition of the Sermon on the Mount; see *sermone Domini* 2.8.28–29.

[8] *Sermone Domini*, 2.9.30–34; see also T. van Bavel, "'Inferas-inducas': à propos de Mtth 6, 13 dans les oeuvres de saint Augustine," *Revue bénédictine* 69 (1959) 348–51, although he overlooks the difference between the gospel text and the liturgical text (cf. *De dono perseverentiae* 6.12, in PL 45:1000).

[9] *Sermone Domini*, 2.9.35, and Stevenson, *The Lord's Prayer*, 101–102; see Jean Deshusses, *Le sacramentaire grégorien*, Spicilegium Friburgense 16 (Fribourg: Ed. Universitaires, 1971) 91; see also Stevenson, *The Lord's Prayer*, 253–54, n. 50; on the East, cf. n. 20.

[10] Letter 130 to Proba, in *Confessions and Letters*, NPNF 1/1 (Edinburgh: T&T Clark, 1994) 465–66; Latin text in PL 33:494–507; Sermons 56–59 in *Works* 3/6, 95–131; Latin texts in PL 38:377–402; *Encheiridion* 7 (*On the Creed and Lord's Prayer*) 115 (Matthew's version), and 116 (Luke's version), in NPNF 1/3

emerges with a weight of pastoral application, clearly intended as the daily prayer of all Christians, hence its place in catechesis; but from the evidence, recited alone by the priest at Mass, though obviously "followed" by the congregation as they listen to its recitation between the eucharistic prayer and communion.[11]

As if this massive, comprehensive edifice were not enough, Augustine goes on to apply the seven petitions in two particular directions, which reflect his exegetical concerns at the time. Neither appears in his other writings, and, as we shall see, it was some time before later writers adopted either of them. The seven petitions are taken to correspond to the seven gifts of the Spirit (Isa 11:2-3) and to the first seven of the Beatitudes (Matt 5:3-9), which provides a scheme as follows:

> fear of the Lord/poverty of spirit/heavenly fatherhood;
> piety/meekness/kingdom;
> knowledge/mournfulness/the will of God;
> might/thirsting after righteousness/daily bread;
> counsel/merciful/forgiveness;
> understanding/ purity of heart/temptation;
> and wisdom/peacemaking/deliverance from evil (*sermone Domini*,
> 2.38-39).

It is an ingenious ensemble; it involves starting at the end of the list of spiritual gifts and working backward, and then reading off the seven opening categories of beatitude, leaving out the persecuted and those who are reviled. For Augustine the number seven is the key, and all else fits around it. Why? To go for the gifts of the Spirit would echo the prayer used at the giving of the spiritual seal in Milan just after coming from the font at baptism: Augustine would have experienced exactly this at his own baptism at the hands of Ambrose, but we have no evidence for the practice in North Africa, or indeed elsewhere.[12] Here is a heightened pneumatology, an application of the internal life

---

(Edinburgh: T&T Clark, 1993) 238–39 and 274; Latin texts in PL 40:234, 285–86, and 286.

[11] Stevenson, *The Lord's Prayer*, 99; see also in general R. F. Taft, "The Lord's Prayer in the Eucharist: When and Why?" *Ecclesia orans* 14 (1997) 137–55.

[12] See Ambrose, *De sacramentis* 3.2. 8–10, and *De mysteriis* 6.41–42, in *Des sacrements, des mystères*, ed. B. Botte, SC 25bis (Paris, Cerf, 1994) 96, 140, 178; and Stevenson, *The Lord's Prayer*, 80.

of the Prayer to the gifts of God in the Holy Spirit; moreover, the very attitudes of people whom Jesus declares "blessed" are brought into its eloquently reticent ambit, providing a way of turning the Prayer in specific terms toward following Christ. As it happens, it is not until the seventh century, with Isidore of Seville, that the gifts of the Spirit are again taken up, reflecting Carolingian trinitarian concerns as well as the sheer weight of Augustine's influence; and not until the ninth century, with Rabanus Maurus, that the Beatitudes once more enter the scene, although in a different arrangement. Subsequent medieval writing and preaching build even more on Augustine's sevenfold foundations.[13]

MAXIMUS THE CONFESSOR

If Augustine's youthful christological and trinitarian interpretations of the Lord's Prayer are at different stages explicit and implicit, Maximus the Confessor in his maturity is overtly so on both counts. His brief but concise *Commentary on the Our Father*, written for a friend, comes before the Monothelete controversy in which he became involved in 634 and which led to his exile. His *Mystagogy* on the Eucharist, written for a monastic setting, contains a short paragraph on the Prayer, described as the "symbol of adoption," as distinct from the creed, the "symbol of faith," both of which are terms with strongly baptismal overtones; in some ways this short piece is a kind of summary of the other work. Both the *Commentary* and the *Mystagogy* appear to date from ca. 628–630.[14]

In the *Commentary* Maximus shows himself more structuralist than other Eastern writers. Like others, Augustine included, he uses biblical

---

[13] See Isidore, *De officiis ecclesiasticis* 1.15.3–5, in PL 83:753, and Stevenson, *The Lord's Prayer*, 91; Rabanus Maurus, *Commentarium in Mattaeum* 2, in PL 107.821–23, and Stevenson, *The Lord's Prayer*, 119–20.

[14] Maximus, *Selected Writings*, trans. G. C. Berthold, Classics of Western Spirituality (New York: Paulist Press, 1985) 99–119, nn. 119–125 (= SW, followed by page ref.); Greek text in *Opuscula exegetica duo*, ed. P. Van Deun, Corpus Christianorum: Series Graeca 23, (Turnhout/Leuven: Brepols/University Press, 1991) 27–73. See *Mystagogia* 18 for his treatment of the Creed; Greek text in PG 91:696 (Lord's Prayer), 695 (Creed); both the *Commentary* and the *Mystagogia* are discussed in Stevenson, *The Lord's Prayer*, 59–61, 244, n. 26; see also the important study by N. Russell, *The Doctrine of Deification in the Greek Patristic Tradition* (Oxford: Oxford University Press, 2004) 267–70.

quotations to earth the Prayer in the gospel. The Prayer consists of seven parts, and this is signaled at the start. The first is the invocation of the heavenly Father. This approach differs from Augustine (with whose writings he was probably familiar, though he was not influenced by them) and the patristic and medieval West, where seven petitions result from treating temptation and deliverance from evil as separate. Maximus, by contrast, follows Eastern tradition, which tends to draw them together. One of the consequences of this is that in the Eastern eucharistic liturgies, when there is an embolism (in every rite except the Byzantine), its opening words refer not to deliverance from evil but to temptation, and it usually ends with a doxology of some kind. In the case of the liturgy used by Maximus (the Byzantine rite), there was no embolism, only the doxology ("the kingdom, the power and the glory") said by the celebrant alone. The doxology's first appearance in writings on the Lord's Prayer is in John Chrysostom's homilies on Matthew's Gospel, which he delivered in Antioch as a presbyter in 390; it came to be expanded, as in subsequent Byzantine rite practice, to refer to the Trinity.[15] Maximus will have known of this

---

[15] See John Chrysostom, *Hom. in Mat.* 19.10, in NPNF 1/10:136–37; Greek text in PG 57:282; see also Stevenson, *The Lord's Prayer*, 49–51, and 69; for the eucharistic liturgies, see F. E. Brightman, *Liturgies Eastern and Western*, 2: *Eastern* (Oxford: Clarendon Press, 1896) 58–60 (Greek James: Lord's Prayer by congregation, an embolism and the doxology by celebrant, 99–100; Syriac James: Lord's Prayer by congregation, embolism with its own doxology, by celebrant, 135–36; Greek Mark: Lord's Prayer by congregation, embolism and the doxology by celebrant, 181–82; Coptic Mark: Lord's Prayer by congregation, embolism with its own doxology by celebrant, 234–35; Ethiopic: Lord's Prayer with the doxology by congregation; no embolism; the introduction and prayer following are about worthy reception of Holy Communion, 295–96; Church of the East: Lord's Prayer with the doxology, both by congregation, followed by embolism that also includes the words of the doxology: it is also recited by the congregation, in full, presumably with doxology, as part of the thanksgiving prayers after Communion, see 303, 339–40; Basil and John Chrysostom, *Barberini 336*: Lord's Prayer by congregation, the doxology by celebrant; no embolism, 444–45; Armenian: Lord's Prayer by congregation, embolism and doxology by celebrant). With the exception of *Barberini 336*, Brightman's texts come from a later date; the Syrian Orthodox rite appears to have lacked the Lord's Prayer as late as the time of James of Edessa (ca. 633–708), for which see B. Varghese, *The Syriac Version of the Liturgy of St. James* (Cambridge: Grove, 2001) 43; on the Coptic rite, see G. J. Cuming, ed., *The Liturgy of St. Mark*, OCA

liturgical use of the doxology, but it does not appear in his *Commentary*.

Moreover, instead of Augustine's Platonist scheme of heavenly and earthly petitions, in Maximus we encounter a different and more anagogical approach. What lies behind this is Maximus's interpretation of deification (*theōsis*) as expressed in 2 Peter 1:4, a text used much by Eastern writers, but sharpened considerably by him, as Norman Russell shows in his recent study. For Maximus, it is about the *kenōsis* of the divine Son bringing about the *theōsis* of the human person. Thus the opening petition claims our place as adopted children, and the rest of the Prayer leads the believer to the salvific goal of *theōsis*. The seven parts of the Prayer thus correspond to the seven mysteries of the new dispensation: "theology," the opening invocation, contemplating God; "adoption in grace," the hallowing of the name; "equality of honor with the angels," the kingdom; "participation in eternal life," the will; "the restoration of nature inclining toward itself to a tranquil state," daily bread; "the abolition of the law of sin," forgiveness; and "the overwhelming of the tyranny of evil which has dominated us by trickery," protection from temptation and the evil one. This kind of overall shape (but no more) is comparable to Cyril of Alexandria's preaching on the Lukan text of the Prayer.[16]

It will be seen straightaway that Maximus does not rely on exegetical methods in order to elaborate his scheme. Nor does he draw christology or the Trinity into his discussion as he goes along. Instead he comes at both from the very beginning, each petition leading to the next: "Our Father" directs us "to honour the consubstantial and superessential Trinity,"[17] for "we sanctify his name on earth," hence the necessity of praying for God's will in the life of discipleship.[18] When it comes to the kingdom, Maximus alludes to the manuscript variant in Luke's version of the Prayer (Luke 11:2) mentioned by Gregory of Nyssa, on whom he depends elsewhere in his treatment; "may your

---

234 (Rome: Pontificium Institutum Studiorum Orientalium, 1990) 50–52 (early texts), 137–38 (commentary); see also Stevenson, *The Lord's Prayer*, 247, n. 46; cf. n. 12 on the Roman rite.

[16] SW 102–3; cf. *Sancti Cyrilli Alexandrini Commentarii in Lucam, pars prior.* CSCO 140: Scriptores Syri 70 (Louvain: Dubecq, 1953) 194–217; Stevenson, *The Lord's Prayer*, 55–56.

[17] SW 106; cf. 103–10.

[18] SW 107.

Holy Spirit come upon us and purify us."[19] Our sense of corruption is therefore a prelude to our desire to do the will of God, which is part of the struggle we face as human beings trying to be faithful and responsive disciples, in following Christ, whose will was at one and the same time totally free and obedient to the Father.[20] To do that will means seeking God, which in turn leads us in the search for daily bread, the Bread of Life, which is spiritual, as Origen taught, and not material, as Gregory of Nyssa insisted.[21] It is not explicitly eucharistic, so no all-embracing Augustinian interpretation here! Forgiveness is the fruit of "spiritual detachment," detachment from our own sins.[22] Forgiveness, therefore, is inextricably linked to temptation and evil, as a forgiving soul is more likely to resist the former and recognize the latter for what it really is. Maximus ends with an ascription of glory and praise to the Trinity.[23]

In Maximus's time in most of the East, the Prayer was used at the Eucharist (from the late fourth/early fifth centuries on), figured prominently in baptismal catechesis, and was embedded in the daily Offices. As Nicholas Madden points out,[24] the key to Maximus's *Commentary* on the Prayer is his structure, which is about the progression of the soul from invocation to victory over the evil one. Unlike any other writer, even the medieval Western commentators at their

[19] SW 107; cf. 106.

[20] SW 112.

[21] SW 113–15; see *Origen: Prayer, Exhortation to Martyrdom*, trans. J. J. O'Meara, Ancient Christian Writers 19 (New York: Paulist Press, 1954) 92–102 (27.1-13); Greek text in PG 11:505–09; *St. Gregory of Nyssa: The Lord's Prayer; The Beatitudes*, trans. H. C. Graef (New York: Newman Press, 1954) 63–65 (Sermon 4); Greek text in PG 44:1168–69; see also Russell's remarks on Origen's exposition of the Lord's Prayer (*The Doctrine*, 142–43), where the theme of *theōsis* is present, but less systematically worked out.

[22] SW 115–16.

[23] SW 116–18.

[24] "The Commentary on the Pater Noster: An Example of the Structural Methodology of Maximus the Confessor," in *Maximus Confessor: Actes du Symposium sur Maxime le Confesseur, 2–5 Septembre, 1980*, ed. F. Heinzer and C. Schonborn, Paradosis 27 (Fribourg: Presses Universitaires, 1982) 147–55; on the influence of Maximus on subsequent liturgical commentaries, see R. Bornert, *Les commentaires byzantins de la Divine Liturgie du VIIe au XVe siècle*, Archives de l'Orient chrétien 9 (Paris: Institut français d'études byzantines, 1966) 123–24, and passim thereafter.

most ingenious, Maximus bases that progression on the internal unity of the Prayer, where the moment one reaches a particular stage, one is on to the next. Near the conclusion Maximus writes: "the aim of the prayer should direct us to the mystery of deification." This is the summit of all christological and trinitarian aspiration: not the obliteration of all that is human, but adding to fallen nature what is divine, namely the eternal grace of the God who stoops to raise us to new life in him. Worship is thus seen as an essential ingredient in the work of salvation history, a revelation in itself. The whole of Maximus's discussion is suffused with an Orthodox trinitarian christology, reflecting his theological priorities as well as the liturgical and doctrinal language of his time. The nearest we come to such an explicit trinitarianism in the West at this time is in Ildephonsus of Toledo, whose *Remarks concerning Baptism* suggests that the Prayer is addressed to the whole Trinity, but he says no more; he is simply not in the same league as Maximus.[25]

LANCELOT ANDREWES

In 1611, the Authorized (King James) Version of the Bible appeared. Lancelot Andrewes, by then Bishop of Ely, had a direct hand in its production as chairman of the group dealing with the opening books of the Old Testament. In the same year Andrewes had published in a small format a series of nineteen sermons on prayer and the Lord's Prayer.[26] These had probably been delivered at Pembroke Hall, Cambridge, about twenty years earlier, when as a young theologian he was a public catechetical preacher, an important role at the time, as Ian Green has pointed out. The published version is entitled *Scala Coeli* (Ladder of Heaven), which Marianne Dorman suggests is a deliberate attempt to point to prayer as the way toward heaven (not the "Scala

---

[25] Ildephonsus, *Annotationes de cognitione baptismi* 133–35, in PL 96:166–67; Stevenson, *The Lord's Prayer*, 91–92.

[26] Lancelot Andrewes, *Sermons* 5:362–476 (= S, followed by number and page reference); in addition to Stevenson, *The Lord's Prayer*, 181–82, see idem, *Abba Father: Understanding and Using the Lord's Prayer* (Norwich: Canterbury Press, 2000) 168–74. The principal study of Andrewes's theology is V. Lossky, *Lancelot Andrewes, the Preacher (1555–1626): The Origins of the Mystical Theology of the Church of England* (Oxford: Clarendon Press, 1991); see also I. Green, *The Christian's ABC: Catechisms and Catechizing in England c. 1530–1740* (Oxford: Clarendon Press, 1996) 147, 201–3; and 479–507 (on the Lord's Prayer in general).

Coeli" indulgence Henry VII gained for Requiem Masses in his new chapel in Westminster Abbey in 1500).[27] Andrewes serves a useful purpose in our discussion as he links the other three figures, Augustine, Maximus, and Karl Barth. A man of considerable learning, he was at one and the same time widely read in the Eastern fathers (as Nicholas Lossky has demonstrated) and a child of the Latin patristic West, as well as being an obvious product of the Reformation.

Why should he preach so many sermons on prayer? He is, in effect, following a patristic tradition, instanced by Tertullian, Cyprian, and others, of dealing first with the theology of prayer, and then with the text of the Lord's Prayer. The first six sermons are therefore introductory. In them Andrewes, a pastor of souls, has to defend the need for set prayers, against radical Puritans who either wanted to replace the Book of Common Prayer with an English version of the Genevan Service Book, or else with something even simpler.[28] The Prayer Book in Andrewes's day directed that the Lord's Prayer be recited twice at the daily Offices (at the start and later on), once at the (daily) Litany, and twice at the (usually quarterly, but sometimes monthly) Eucharist (at the start, and immediately after Communion). Such a lavish, medieval-style provision was the target of supporters of more emphatically Reformed worship. Calvin's liturgy only used the Prayer once at morning service, in connection with intercession; this sometimes took the form of a paraphrase, adapting medieval devotional practice. The Prayer never had any special place in connection with Communion. Andrewes follows Augustine and Luther in dividing the Prayer into seven petitions; he therefore rejects Calvin's espousal of the Eastern sixfold scheme, which drew temptation and deliverance together. Moving in the direction of Maximus, however, he regards the Prayer as consisting of one heavenly (the invocation of the name) followed by

[27] See M. Dorman, *Lancelot Andrewes: A Perennial Preacher of the Post-Reformation English Church* (Tucson: Iceni Books, 2004) 70, where she cites E. Duffy, *The Stripping of the Altars: Traditional English Religion 1440–1580* (New Haven: Yale University Press, 1993) 375f. The Westminster connection is strengthened when one considers that Andrewes was Dean from 1601–1605; in that capacity he took part in such prominent occasions as Queen Elizabeth I's funeral, and James VI of Scotland's coronation as James I of England, both in 1604.

[28] See K. Stevenson, "Richard Hooker and the Lord's Prayer: A Chapter in Reformation Controversy," *Scottish Journal of Theology* 57 (2004) 39–55, for a discussion of this issue; see also Stevenson, *The Lord's Prayer*, 179–84.

six earthly petitions; and he follows Luther's scheme, for kingdom, will, and bread are about the need for good things, whereas forgiveness, temptation, and evil are about the removal of wrong things. Unlike all other prayers, which are "the prayers of nature," the Lord's own is "the prayer of charity."[29]

Andrewes is a strongly trinitarian and christocentric preacher. One of his mannerisms is to focus on the three persons of the Godhead near the start. This he does in the third sermon, whose text is James 1:16-17: God is Light (1 John 1:5); Christ is the Light of the World (John 8:12); and the Holy Ghost came to the apostles in tongues of fire (Acts 2:3). As he slowly goes through the Prayer in the remaining sermons, his pneumatology comes to the fore: the Spirit works on our understanding in our will, for God is our Father, and we are reborn, through the Savior's blood, bearing the stamp of the sons of God, as temples of the Holy Spirit. Here is a combination of an Augustinianism that is unready to accept too easily a reconciled world immediately, and a confidence in the divinization in which we share as adopted children who can address God as "Our Father." "There must be an imitation, and we must set ourselves forward to our heavenly country."[30]

His fertile mind follows Augustine in offering as comprehensive an interpretation as possible. But he goes further. In a sermon devoted entirely to "in earth as it is in heaven," he identifies these words not just with the doing of the will but the hallowing of the name and the coming of the kingdom as well, citing "the ancient fathers" in support.[31] This requires some explanation. Though himself unaware of

---

[29] S 7, 369.

[30] S 8, 379.

[31] S 12, 405 (not noted in Stevenson, *The Lord's Prayer*, 181); cf. *The Preces Privatae of Lancelot Andrewes*, ed. and trans. by F. E. Brightman (London: Methuen, 1902) 281.31 (and 386, where Brightman refers to the start of S 12, and also to the *Catechism of the Council of Trent*); for the other sources, see J. Carmignac, *Recherches sur le "Notre Père"* (Paris: Letouzey and Ané, 1969) 112–17; for Origen see *Prayer*, trans. O'Meara, 88; for the *Opus imperfectum* see PG 56:712; for Meister Eckhart, see *Tractatus super Oratione Dominica*, ed. E. Seeberg (Stuttgart-Berlin: W. Kohlhammer, 1936) 115–18, where Seeberg cites what he regards as authentically Chrysostom, 115; for Cajetan see *In quattuor evangelia et Acta apostolorum commentarii* (Lyon: J. and P. Prost, 1639) 33; for the Trent Catechism see *Catechismus ex decreto Concilii Tridentini*, (Rome: In aedibus Populi Romani, apud Paulum Manutium, 1566) 314, where phraseology

Andrewes's writings, Jean Carmignac has drawn attention to a minority tradition of interpretation, first found in Origen's discourse *On Prayer*; thereafter in the *Opus Imperfectum* on Matthew's Gospel attributed to John Chrysostom, and therefore invested with his authority (but now regarded as the work of an early-fifth-century Arianizing bishop in the Danube province of the Eastern Empire); Meister Eckhart; Cajetan's 1527 commentaries on Matthew and Mark (Luke and John followed in 1528); and then in the *Catechism of the Council of Trent* (1566), but only in the early editions. Of these authors Andrewes could not know of Origen's work on prayer (it did not come to light again until 1686); he will certainly have known Ps-Chrysostom and regarded it as authentic, and therefore of some importance (this is presumably what he means by "the ancient fathers"); he is unlikely to have known of Eckhart's work; he could well have known Cajetan (some of whose other works are known to have been in Andrewes's own library; he would have respected Cajetan as a Catholic Reformation eirenicist of sorts); and as a post-Reformation catechist he could have been aware of the Trent catechism. In any case, however, multiple levels of meaning were always grist to Andrewes's mill, and here he is as good as his word, for in the layout of the Lord's Prayer in his book of private devotions, the words "in earth as it is in heaven" stand alone, in order to make exactly this point explicit. It is interesting to note how in 1881 the Cambridge scholars B. F. Westcott and F. J. A. Hort took the same view of the structure of the Prayer on linguistic grounds, and they have been generally followed by New Testament scholarship since.

Over the thorny question of "daily bread" Andrewes suggests that all four ancient languages are correct: it is "daily" as in the Latin; it is "for our substance" as in the Greek; it is "to relieve hunger" as he interprets the Syriac ("the bread of our need"); and it is also "meet for our meals," which he takes to be a Hebrew rendition. It is thus both material and spiritual, but he refrains from interpreting it eucharistically, al-

---

similar to Cajetan's is used, e.g., in the repetition of *"sicut in coelo et in terra"*; for the removal of this interpretation from later editions of the Trent Catechism, see Carmignac, *Recherches*, 113, n. 13; see also B. F. Westcott and F. J. A. Hort, *The New Testament in the Original Greek* (London and Cambridge: Macmillan, 1881) 2:320; as Carmignac notes (114), this is followed by C. Gore, *The Sermon on the Mount* (London: Murray, 1896) 124; in fact, Gore notes this same teaching in the Trent Catechism, but is slightly cautious about this interpretation ("refers probably to all the three preceding clauses").

though he comes near to it in one of the short paraphrases on the Prayer in his private devotions ("give angels' food unto eternal life").[32] Similarly with forgiveness, he hammers home the importance of mutuality, the distinction between forgiving (which we can do) and forgetting (which we can't), and the fact that "Christ having penned this petition . . . returns to the same matter" (i.e., after giving the Prayer in the Sermon on the Mount).[33] He neatly distinguishes between not committing evil (temptation) and not experiencing it (deliverance).[34] Although the Prayer Book did not begin to adopt the concluding doxology until the revision in 1662, it was widely known and used by Anglicans, not just because it appeared in Erasmus's text, nor because Calvin favored it (though that would have helped), but because preachers like Andrewes were aware of its presence in the Eastern liturgies. So Andrewes rounds off this lengthy series by ascribing the kingdom to Christ, the power to the Holy Spirit, and the glory to God the Father.[35]

KARL BARTH

Barth's exposition of the Lord's Prayer is to be found in a series of seminars that he gave comparatively late in his career at Neuchâtel University between 1947 and 1949, when they were published in French; an English translation appeared in 1952.[36] Whereas Luther

---

[32] S 13, 420–21; cf. *Preces Privatae*, 284.4.

[33] S 15, 438–40.

[34] S 17, 450.

[35] S 18, 413; for Calvin on the doxology, see *Institutes of the Christian Religion*, ed. J. T. McNeill and F. L. Battles, Library of the Christian Classics, 21 (Philadelphia: Westminster Press, 1961), 3.20.47, pp. 915–16; the doxology was not directed in the Prayer Book until 1662, but only in the first recitation at morning and evening prayer, in the second recitation at the Eucharist, in the thanksgiving after childbirth, and in the (new) form of service for use at sea, for all of which see F. E. Brightman, ed., *The English Rite* (London: Rivingtons, 1915) 132–33, 156–57, 696–97/704–7, 882–83, and 906–8; among the contributory factors to the growing popularity of the doxology in the Elizabethan period was Alexander Nowell's influential catechism, published in various editions from 1570 onward, for which see *A Catechism by Alexander Nowell* (Cambridge: Cambridge University Press, 1853) 202–5.

[36] Karl Barth, *Prayer and Preaching* (London: S.C.M., 1964); see also idem, *Prayer: 50th Anniversary Edition with Essays by I. John Hessellink, Daniel Migliore, and Donald K. McKim*, ed. D. Saliers (Westminster: John Knox Press, 2002) (= KB, followed by page ref.); mention also needs to be made of Barth's uncompleted

gave the Prayer a central place in almost every service, Calvin's position was, as we have seen, more reserved: he saw it as a quotation from Scripture, a guide to all prayer rather than a liturgical text, and therefore occupying a significant place in the 1541 Geneva Catechism.[37] Geneva, Heidelberg, Scotland as a whole, and other centers of Reformed Christianity soon proved conservative enough to resist its exclusive use in paraphrase form as the intercession at the Sunday service. By Barth's time it had long been not only the central prayer of the catechism, to be learnt by heart and recited both privately on one's own and domestically with others, but it had become an accepted public possession of Reformed Church worship. Don Saliers describes Barth's overall treatment as a "synoptic" view of the two great Reformation figures, Luther and Calvin.[38]

Barth's opening words describe the church in terms that echo Calvin himself as "those who are gathered by Jesus Christ,"[39] and he goes straight into adoptive sonship "by thy Word, by thy Spirit,"[40] which is accomplished "at Christmas, on Good Friday and at Easter and which is made effective at our baptism."[41] Here is a nuanced form of the trinitarian theology that is taken to be implicit in those opening words, and a genuinely liturgical theology drawing together the birth, death, and resurrection of Christ, carefully spread through the church year, which many of the Reformers themselves had been so keen to abolish. Barth then applies his "analogy of faith" by insisting that "when we call God our Father, we are not using symbols, but are experiencing

---

treatment of the Lord's Prayer, a fragment of a longer projected work, in *The Christian Life* (Edinburgh: T&T Clark, 1981) 233–71; see Stevenson, *The Lord's Prayer*, 163–67, and nn. 263–64 (on Calvin), and 205–7, and 270 n. 20 (on Barth). The literature both by and on Barth is prodigious, but for the main themes of his work, see *Karl Barth: Studies in Theological Method*, ed. Stephen Sykes (Oxford: Blackwell, 1979); T. F. Torrance, *Karl Barth* (Edinburgh: T&T Clark, 1990); and M. Higton and J. McDowell, eds., *Conversing with Barth* (Aldershot: Ashgate, 2004).

[37] See T. F. Torrance, ed. and trans., *The School of Faith: The Catechisms of the Reformed Church* (London: Clarke, 1959) 44–51.

[38] KB xi.

[39] KB 22; cf. "we must daily desire that God gather churches unto himself" (*Institutes* 3.20.42, p. 905).

[40] KB 23.

[41] KB 24.

the full reality of the words 'father' and 'son.'"[42] The urgency of this reality has the effect of turning the fatherhood and sonship we experience in this life into pale shadows of God's fatherhood of us his children for "we are not surrounded by nothingness. The doctrine of Sartre and Heidegger is not true, for it sinks back into paganism."[43]

Following Calvin rather than Luther, he sees the Prayer made up of six petitions, but following Luther he regards it as the action of Christ in us now, which means that "we must take our part in God's action."[44] Thanks to Barth and others, eschatology became a far stronger feature on the landscape of theological writing (and praying) throughout the twentieth century; this elicits from him a mild rebuke toward both Luther and Calvin on their interpretations of "your kingdom come."[45] For Barth, an enthusiast for the Lukan variant mentioned by Gregory of Nyssa and Maximus, the kingdom and the Spirit are inextricably linked: "if one prays for the coming of God's kingdom, one prays also that the Holy Spirit may come within us."[46] This must be something quite different from "the perfect Church" that he suspects even the two great Reformers saw lying behind the fulfilment of this petition. Following both Luther and Calvin, he regards daily bread not as eucharistic but "the earthly symbol of God's grace."[47] Forgiveness is a necessity, a prelude to living what Migliore calls the "theology of freedom."[48] This is the air Barth breathes into the Prayer, for as with Augustine and Calvin, temptation includes not only daily experience but the final temptation, of being parted from God.[49] Barth's "theology of freedom" leads into the doxology, which (like Calvin) he sees as part of the Prayer, "because the kingdom, the power and the glory belong to God, and not the Devil, sin, death or hell."[50]

---

[42] KB 25.

[43] KB 33.

[44] KB 30; on the shape of the Prayer, see *Institutes* 3.20.42, p. 898), and *Luther's Works*, ed. U. Leupold (Saint Louis: Concordia, 1956), 21:145–46 (Sermon on the Mount); Stevenson, *The Lord's Prayer*, 158–68, and 262–64, nn. 18–22.

[45] KB 31.

[46] KB 40; for Gregory, see *The Lord's Prayer*, trans. Graef (as in note 17), 52–54 (Sermon 3); Greek text in PG 44:1157–60; for Maximus, see SW, 107.

[47] KB 47; cf. *Institutes* 3.20.44, pp. 907–10, and *Luther's Works* 21:146–47.

[48] KB 96.

[49] KB 63.

[50] KB 65.

CONCLUSION

First, each of these four writers brings his own approach to the church's universal prayer. Augustine and Maximus both stress the "boldness" with which we can dare to call God our Father, echoing the liturgical introductions at the Eucharist in the North African and Greek rites. This also appears in Andrewes, although the introductory words that survived from the Sarum Mass in the 1549 *Prayer Book* were dropped in 1552 (and remained absent in 1662; they reappeared in twentieth century revisions).[51] Robert Taft has argued for the three-fold "unit" of introduction, Prayer, and embolism in the patristic East and West as an indication of the need to include the Prayer as a novelty that required some justification, fleshing out its meaning and focus. The introduction may reflect a need to point to this Prayer's uniqueness—and here one wants to echo Andrewes's distinction between "the prayers of nature" and "the prayer of charity." There may, too, be a practical reason: when the Prayer is introduced it enables all the worshipers to join in with those unique opening words—that are often left (to the considerable irritation of some) to the liturgical president when they are absent.[52] Barth, however, a more faithful son of the Reformation than Andrewes, needs no introductory words. He exudes a confidence that they are being prayed and made real by Christ whenever they are uttered: they can never be no more than "mere words," and in that sense the Prayer is implicitly christocentric from start to finish.

Second, the Lord's Prayer is both trinitarian and christological. But to what extent? Both dimensions lie between the lines of those two

---

[51] Texts in F. E. Brightman, *The English Rite* 2:640–41, 696, 704–07; see Stevenson, *The Lord's Prayer*, 175–77, and 265, n. 30; for the 1764 Scottish Episcopal rite, see J. Dowden, *The Annotated Scottish Communion Office* (Edinburgh: Grant, 1884) 17.

[52] See above n. 15; see also Taft, "The Lord's Prayer in the Eucharist" (as in n. 11). Jungmann draws attention to the "oration" style of the Roman embolism: see *The Place of Christ in Liturgical Prayer* (London/Dublin: Chapman, 1965) 122; see also G. Wagner, *Der Ursprung der Chrysostomusliturgie* (Münster: Aschendorff, 1973) 122–25, for discussion of the introductory prayer in the Liturgy of John Chrysostom. The exception in the East is Syriac St. James, where after the introductory prayer the celebrant goes straight into the opening words; the congregation only joins in at "hallowed be your name" (Brightman, *Liturgies Eastern and Western*, 100).

opening words, "Our Father," once they are understood as claiming adoption as God's own children. The process of interpretation immediately raises the sheer impossibility of driving a wedge between a New Testament exegesis of "what the prayer originally meant" and the "living text" of the Prayer in the life of the church.[53] That also includes biblical quotations, especially words from Jesus in the Gospels, in order to expound its meaning. The Lord's Prayer brings us face to face with liturgical theology from the very start, and in its wake comes a rich *Wirkungsgeschichte*—a history of interpretation, echoed in recent developments in biblical scholarship, for example in the commentary on Matthew's Gospel by Ulrich Luz.[54] Particular preachers and writers may well go on to invest other parts of the Prayer with more explicitly trinitarian and christological applications, some of them exegetical, like those of Augustine and Andrewes, others more systematic, like those of Maximus and Barth.[55] We can also note the recurrence of the "Lukan variant" in the kingdom petition in Maximus and Barth, to bring a further emphasis to the work of the Spirit, which meets Maximus's understanding of *theōsis* as applied overall to the Prayer. There is, too, the strand of interpretation that applies "on earth as in heaven" to the hallowing of the name and the coming of the kingdom as well as the doing of the will. This position was not taken by Augustine (who suspected Origen), nor by Maximus (for whom it might have undermined his particular notion of the Prayer's shape),

---

[53] See D. C. Parker, "'As Our Saviour Taught Us . . .': The Lord's Prayer," in *The Living Text of the Gospels* (Cambridge: Cambridge University Press, 1997) 49–76.

[54] See Ulrich Luz, *Matthew 1–7: A Commentary*, trans. W. C. Linss (Edinburgh: T&T Clark, 1990) 367–89.

[55] Although Augustine's sevenfold symbolism of the gifts of the spirit and the Beatitudes was influential throughout the middle ages (see Stevenson, *The Lord's Prayer*, 117–50), it does not survive into the Catechism of the Council of Trent, for which, see *Catechismus*, 306–59; see also J. A. McHugh and C. J. Callan, eds. and trans., *Catechism of the Council of Trent for Parish Priests* (New York: Wagner, 1923); this does not, however, mean that it was expunged from popular teaching, for which see, for example, Robert Bellarmine, *Disputationes christianae fidei adversus huius temporis haereticos: De bonis operibus* (Cologue: Agrippa Gualter, 1619), 5:1146–48 ("de numero et ordine petitionum orationis dominicae"), where he not only expounds Augustine's sevenfold scheme but also mentions his "three heavenly, four earthly" structure, and takes Calvin to task for his sixfold structure, which Bellarmine knows comes from the East.

nor by Barth (whose French and German versions of the Prayer would have made it difficult in any case); but it was championed by Andrewes. On such a basis not only is the first part of the Prayer brought together yet more closely into a unity, but the work of the Spirit is identified in the name-hallowing and kingdom-proclaiming that are part of the Christian life.

Third, there is the matter of the overall shape of the Prayer. In those first three petitions the Lord's Prayer locates the Christian in the life of God, which is where we should begin. As so many commentators have remarked, were we to try to invent our own prayer we would inevitably begin with something like "daily bread." The name, kingdom, and will of God provide the basis on which to pray the rest of the Prayer in ways that locate the Christian in time, with bread for today, forgiveness for yesterday, and protection from temptation and evil in the future. It is no coincidence that when we are praying about ourselves the difficulties of interpretation really begin to surface, such as over what sort of bread (Augustine, alone among the four to experience daily Communion, alone provides an explicitly eucharistic view), what kind of forgiveness (Calvin and his followers, Barth included, naturally recoil against medieval penance), and how to put into words the relationship between a sinful, fallen world and the providence of God (hence all those wrestlings with temptation and evil). But for all these subtle variations, writers such as Augustine, Maximus, Andrewes, and Barth nonetheless draw the work of Christ into the narrow confines of this unique Prayer, with Maximus providing the most explicitly overall trinitarian focus.

Fourth, we come to the question, to whom does the Prayer belong? Our authors vary somewhat in their response, Augustine and Maximus maintaining that it belongs to the baptised only, and Andrewes and Barth placing much more emphasis on the catechizing of Christians growing up with it. The question of ownership, however, is posed in a different way at a time soon after Augustine's death. In mid-fifth century Ravenna, Peter Chrysologus preached on the Lord's Prayer no fewer than six christocentric homilies (more have survived from him than from anyone else in antiquity, Augustine included) to those preparing for baptism.[56] His approach is far removed from Augustine,

---

[56] *Collectio Sermonum*, ed. A. Olivar, CCSL 24A (Turnhout: Brepols, 1981) 402–5 (67), 406–11 (68), 412–18 (69), 420–23 (70), 424–28 (71), and 429–33 (72);

whose exegesis he would have thought too comprehensive; from Maximus, whose anagogical interpretation he would have found too subtle; from Andrewes, whom he would have found too contrived; and indeed from Barth, whom he would have regarded as lacking in specific focus on the seven petitions, where one, pithy interpretation each time is sufficient. In this latter respect Peter was rather like most ordinary preachers down the ages. He did admit, however, as a matter of concern to some (though not, it seems, to himself), that among his congregations were people who were not (yet) going to be baptized. While receiving unsolicited "comment" about changes in religious practice is the stock-in-trade of the episcopal office in any age, such a breakdown of what we often call the *disciplina arcani* does bring us face to face with a community where already in antiquity the boundaries surrounding the use of the Prayer are somewhat negotiable.

Fifth, there is the question of what impact these writers had. Augustine's youthful exposition of the Sermon on the Mount, in all its devastating clarity, is replicated in his subsequent preaching and writing; apart, that is, from his treatment of the Beatitudes and the sevenfold gifts of the Spirit, which, as we have seen, had to await Carolingian take-up. His thought dominated subsequent teaching about the Prayer in the West, influencing Luther as well as Anglicans such as Andrewes. Maximus, writing in his maturity, stands in the tradition of previous Greek writers such as Gregory of Nyssa, but produces a uniquely anagogical approach, within a new framework, in a sublime, effortless style, whose influence was to prove of a lasting nature, not least through its inclusion in the *Philokalia* of Saint Nicodemus and Saint Macarius (which gives far more space to the writings of Maximus than anyone else), first published in Greek in 1752.[57]

---

those that comment on use of the Prayer by people not to be baptized are 67.11, 68.3, 11, 69.6, 70.3, and 72.2; in addition to Stevenson, *The Lord's Prayer*, 87–89, see idem, "The Six Homilies on the Lord's Prayer of Peter Chrysologus," in *Studia Liturgica Diversa*, ed. M. E. Johnson and L. E. Phillips (Oregon: Pastoral Press, 2004) 65–70; on the question of the presence of non-catechumens in the congregation (noted by Taft, "The Lord's Prayer in the Eucharist," 151, n. 72) see 67; for a corrective against an over-romantic view of the "discipline of the secret" see J. Day, "Adherence to the Disciplina Arcani in the Fourth Century," in *Studia Patristica* 35 (Louvain: Peeters, 2001) 266–70.

[57] For an English translation, see *The Philokalia*, ed. and trans. G. E. H. Palmer et al. (London: Faber and Faber, 1981) 2:285–305.

Andrewes as a young catechist influenced a generation of Cambridge undergraduates with his preaching, which the (comparatively recent) invention of printing brought to a wider audience in 1611, fortified by subsequent improved editions in 1642 and 1843. In many respects these sharp, well-arranged sermons lack none of the theological depth of his better-known productions, but lack their complexity. Barth, on the other hand, delivered a series of university seminars in post-Second World War Neuchâtel that echoed his theological priorities—of the kingdom, the otherness of God, and the accessibility of divine grace, delivered with verve and directness. The lectures were immediately published in French and English. In 2002, they reappeared in a revised English translation, together with a series of commemorative essays to mark the fiftieth anniversary of the first English edition.

Finally, each one of these works has an oral origin, except the short treatise by Maximus, although that in all probability resulted from his teaching ministry. More recently the computer and the Web site have placed the Prayer—and its interpreters—still more in the public domain, rendering any restrictive aspiration about the Prayer's ownership even more problematical. A recurring feature, too, of twentieth-century scholarship has been to alert us to the deeply Jewish setting in which this unique Prayer was brought to birth,[58] which begins to pose other questions about its use. That messy, risky world is but one more example of the challenges before us to create imaginative ways of expressing our trinitarian, christocentric faith through the words that our savior Christ continues to teach us.[59]

[58] Noted as long ago as 1925, in specific terms, by W. O. E. Oesterley, *The Jewish Background of the Christian Liturgy* (Oxford: Clarendon Press, 1925) 151–54.

[59] Emphasized repeatedly by Jungmann, *The Place of Christ*, 127, and 145–46.

Chapter 10

Sub Tuum Praesidium: The Theotokos in Christian Life and Worship before Ephesus

Maxwell E. Johnson
University of Notre Dame

Thanks in large part to Joseph Jungmann,[1] treating the question of the *Theotokos* as a christological-doctrinal issue with little or no attention to its wider context or possible pre-history has become common. A summary statement by Elizabeth Johnson in her recent book illustrates this point:

> [T]he school of Alexandria argued for a stronger, ontological form of union in which the divine Son of God personally united himself to human nature. While safeguarding the unity of natures in the person of Christ, this notion tended to dilute his humanity, seeing it as somehow mixed with or swallowed up by transcendent divinity. In this school, the passionately preferred title for Mary was *Theotokos*, or God-bearer, meaning that she was the mother of the one who is personally the Word of God. Although the essence of the controversy was christological, the marian title itself bore the brunt of the dispute. When the Council of Ephesus in 431 opted for the title *Theotokos*, it spread like wildfire, keeping its original form in the East and being transmuted into the more colloquial "Mother of God" in the West. According to most scholars, the impetus from this council allowed the development of the marian cult to go public in the church. Although discourse about Mary had been in play to express christological truths, it opened up the later trajectory where attention was focused on Mary herself.[2]

---

[1] Joseph Jungmann, "The Defeat of Teutonic Arianism and the Revolution in Religious Culture in the Early Middle Ages," in *Pastoral Liturgy* (New York: Herder and Herder, 1962) 1–101.

[2] Elizabeth Johnson, *Truly Our Sister: A Theology of Mary in the Communion of Saints* (New York: Continuum, 2003) 117–18.

While it affirms the christologically dogmatic importance of the official acceptance of the *Theotokos* doctrine by the Council of Ephesus, such an overly dogmatic or conciliar approach to the issue may have inherent methodological dangers. That is, such an approach has led on occasion to a circular manner of reasoning in which it is assumed that the presence of the word "Theotokos" in a text is a hermeneutical key serving as a criterion for dating that text, or a portion thereof, to a time *after* Ephesus. While surely in some instances the term was added to or interpolated into a text after Ephesus, the question of the origin of the title would seem to be of great importance for historical and liturgical-theological scholarship. Is the title *Theotokos* only doctrinal, and not devotional and/or liturgical in emphasis, before it emerges as a particular dogmatic term, a development out of the church's *lex orandi* broadly understood? Are we dealing here with a development that constitutes a "revolution" in doctrine, piety, and devotion, or one which, like many other elements in the immediate post-Constantinian ecclesial context, is an instance of evolution, consistent with what went before? In what follows these questions will be addressed briefly under three headings: (1) the term *Theotokos* before Ephesus, (2) popular devotion to Mary before Ephesus?, and (3) the earliest liturgical feast of Mary-*Theotokos*.

THE TERM *THEOTOKOS* BEFORE EPHESUS

In *Mary Through the Centuries: Her Place in the History of Culture*, Jaroslav Pelikan notes not only that the origins of the term *Theotokos* are obscure, though "an original Christian creation," but also that "the first completely authenticated instances of the use of this title came from the city of Athanasius, Alexandria. Alexander, [Athanasius's] patron . . . referred to Mary as Theotokos in his encyclical of circa 319 about the heresy of Arius."[3] That it is also a common term in the writ-

---

[3] Jaroslav Pelikan, *Mary through the Centuries* (New Haven: Yale University Press, 1996) 57. While Pelikan is surely correct in noting that the title *Theotokos* was "a term of Christian coinage" and not borrowed from pagan use, in the world of early Christianity devotion to mother goddesses like Isis, whose cult is first testified to also in Alexandria (see T. Klauser, "Rom und der Kult der Gottesmutter Maria," *Jahrbuch für Antike und Christentum* 15 [1972] 120), or to "mothers of the gods," such as the shrine to the Μήτηρ θεῶν in pre-Christian Constantinople (see N. Constas, "Weaving the Body of God: Proclus of Constantinople, the Theotokos, and the Loom of the Flesh," *Journal of Early Chris-*

ings and theology of Athanasius himself is confirmed by a word search in the *Thesaurus Linguae Graecae* (hereafter, TLG) which reveals that, together with numerous spurious attributions, *Theotokos* appears four times in his *Orationes tres contra Arianos,* once in his *Vita Antonii,* three times in *Expositiones in psalmos,* and at least once in *De incarnatione Verbi Dei.*

Although both Alexander and Athanasius use the term in an overall anti-Arian context, it is not used in its later sense to defend a particular christological assertion about the unity of natures or personhood in Christ, which is certainly the meaning of the term at Ephesus. In his encyclical letter to Alexander of Constantinople, Alexander writes only that Christ "bore a body not in appearance but truth, derived from Mary the Mother of God [ἐκ τῆς Θεοτόκου Μαρίας],"[4] and in *De incarnatione* Athansius writes: "The Word begotten of the Father from on high, inexpressibly, inexplicably, incomprehensibly and eternally, is He that is born in time here below of the Virgin Mary, the Mother of God [ἐκ παρθένου Θεοτόκου Μαρίας]."[5] In both cases it would seem that the term is used as little more than an honorific title for Mary. That is, an apparent anti-docetic defense of Christ's humanity ("not in appearance but in truth") and the temporal birth of the Word do not need to be demonstrated or defended by the term *Theotokos* since a simple reference to the Virgin Mary without an additional title would have been sufficient.

In his compelling 1989 essay, "Le titre Θεοτόκος avant le concile d'Ephèse,"[6] Marek Starowieyski provides an impressive list of fourth-century and early (pre-Ephesine) fifth-century authors where the title appears. In addition to Alexander and Athanasius this list also includes the Synod of Antioch; Arius of Alexandria; Eustathius of An-

---

tian Studies [1995] 174 n. 21), was part of the overall cultural landscape. That such a cultural context would be influential in shaping popular Marian piety, beginning rather early in the history of the church, should not surprise us any more than a modern Guadalupan scholar would be surprised to discover that pre-colonial Náhuatl devotion to the goddess *Tonantzin* in Mexico somehow continued in popular devotion to the Virgin of Guadalupe in the sixteenth century and beyond.

[4] PG 18:568; translation from Pelikan, *Mary,* 237.

[5] *De incarnatione* 8, PG 26; translation from W. Jurgens, ed., *Faith of the Early Fathers* 1 (Collegeville, MN: Liturgical Press, 1970) 340.

[6] In *Studia Patristica* 19 (Berlin: Academie Verlag, 1987) 236–42.

tioch; Eusebius of Caesarea; Asterius Sophistes; Hegemonius; Julian the Apostate; Titus of Bostra; Basil the Great; Cyril of Jerusalem; Apollinaris of Laodicea; Gregory Nazianzen; Gregory of Nyssa; Eunomius; Diodore of Tarsus; Didymus the Blind; Epiphanius; Antiochus of Ptolemais; Severian of Gabala; Theophilus of Alexandria; Theodore of Mopsuestia; Nilus of Ancyra; various pseudonymous treatises attributed to Athanasius, Chrysostom, and Ephrem the Syrian; and Ambrose of Milan, cited as the first to use the term "Mater Dei" in the Latin Church.[7] Since this list includes Orthodox, Arian, Arianizing, Apollinarist, and anti-Apollinarist authors, Starowieyski rightly concludes that:

> [L]e terme est employé, meme s'il ne s'accorde pas avec leur christologie respective. Ce titre n'a donc pas de repercussions sur leur théologie ni leur théologie sur le titre. . . . Les texts proviennent d'Egypte—certainement le plus grand nombre, de Palestine, du Syrie, de Mésopotamie, d'Arabie, d'Asie Mineure. Leur emploi est donc general dans toute la region de la Mediterranée. En prenant en consideration le contexte, on constate que le titre Θεοτόκος n'est employé que comme une simple appellation, á l'exception des textes de la fin du IVe siècle (ibid., 238).

In the first quarter of the fourth century, therefore, i.e., about one hundred years before the Council of Ephesus, the term *Theotokos* had become—or was becoming—a common title for the Virgin Mary. How far does its use go back before this?

Some contemporary biblical scholars would put the idea, if not the title, back into the New Testament infancy narratives, where Elizabeth's designation of Mary as "Mother of my Lord" (Luke 1:43) may well mean "Mother of Yahweh!"[8] Similarly, Ignatius of Antioch says in his letter to the Ephesians that "our *God*, Jesus the Christ, was conceived by Mary by the dispensation of God."[9] By the beginning of the third century the word Μήτηρ in reference to Mary was starting to appear in an abbreviated form (*MP*) as a *nomen sacrum* in New Testament

---

[7] For the full list and texts see ibid., 237–38.

[8] See C. K. Rowe, "Luke and the Trinity: An Essay in Ecclesial Biblical Theology," *Scottish Journal of Theology* 56 (2003) 1–26. My thanks to Bryan Spinks for directing me to this reference.

[9] Ignatius, *Ephesians* 18, emphasis added. See also, ibid. 7 and 19.

papyri,[10] and at the end of the third and beginning of the fourth century the word may have appeared in a lost treatise of Pierius (d. 309) called Περὶ τῆς Θεοτόκου,[11] and in a fragment attributed to Peter of Alexandria.[12]

Starowieyski also includes in his list the anaphora called Egyptian or Alexandrian Basil (hereafter, EgBAS), one of our earliest surviving eucharistic prayers, often dated in the first part of the fourth century. While much of the extant text is available only in the later Bohairic Coptic dialect, the Sahidic version edited by J. Doresse and E. Lanne also contains this important text from the intercessions:

> Since, Master, it is a command of your only-begotten Son that we should share in the commemoration of your saints, vouchsafe to remember, Lord, those of our fathers who have been pleasing to you from eternity: patriarchs, prophets, apostles, martyrs, confessors, preachers, evangelists, and all the righteous perfected in faith; especially at all times the holy and glorious Mary, Mother of God; and by her prayers have mercy on us all, and save us through your holy name which has been invoked upon us.[13]

The Armenian version of Basil (hereafter, ArmBAS) includes the names of John the Baptist and Saint Stephen the Protomartyr after "the Mother of God, the holy Virgin Mary"; it does not ask for mercy by her prayers—or by anyone else's—but refers simply to all the saints who are remembered or commemorated in the Eucharist.[14]

---

[10] A. H. R. E. Paap, *Nomina Sacra in the Greek Papyri of the First Five Centuries* (Leiden: Brill, 1959) 15. My thanks to Lawrence Hurtado for directing me to this reference.

[11] J. Quasten, *Patrology* 2 (Westminster: Newman Press, 1953) 112.

[12] Fragment 7, PG 18:517B.

[13] Text in J. Doresse and E. Lanne, *Un témoin archaïque de la liturgie copte de saint Basile* (Louvain: Publications universitaires, 1960), and J. R. K. Fenwick, *The Anaphoras of St. Basil and St. James: An Investigation into Their Common Origin*, OCA 240 (Rome: Pontificio Istituto Orientale, 1992) 26; translation in R. C. D. Jasper and G. Cuming, *Prayers of the Eucharist: Early and Reformed*. 3rd rev. ed. (Collegeville, MN: Liturgical Press, Pueblo, 1987) 72.

[14] For the text in Armenian with German translation see Erich Renhart, ed., "Die älteste armenische Anaphora: Einleitung, kritische Edition des Textes und Übersetzung," in *Armenische Liturgien: Ein Blick auf eine ferne christliche Kultur*, ed. E. Renhart and J. Dum Tragut. Heiliger Dienst, Ergänzungsband 2

We must proceed here with caution. In her study of the intercessions in the anaphora of John Chrysostom (hereafter, CHR), Gabriele Winkler has argued, based on early anaphoral sources (i.e., Strasbourg papyrus, *Apostolic Constitutions* 8, and Cyril [John] of Jerusalem's *Mystagogical Catechesis* 5), that the anaphoral commemoration of the saints evolved from listing only categories of saints (patriarchs, prophets, apostles, and martyrs) to naming specific saints only later with Mary herself added as a result of the christological controversies.[15] In CHR the "commemoration" is part of the anamnesis/offering, and not the intercessions, and reads: "We offer you this reasonable service also for (ὑπὲρ) those who rest in faith, . . . especially our all-holy, immaculate, highly glorious, Blessed Lady, Mother of God and ever-Virgin Mary."[16] Robert Taft has written of this "Theotokos ekphonesis" that it is "but the incipit of the now defunct diptychs of the dead. Its interpolation into both the [Byz] Basil and Chrysostom Anaphoras occurred under Patriarch Gennadius I (458–471), at the command of Emperor Leo I (457–474), an innovation provoked by Patriarch Martyrius (459–470) of Antioch's refusal to grant Mary the Theotokos title."[17]

(Graz/Salzburg, 2001) 172–73. Although since H. Engberding's magisterial study (*Das eucharistische Hochgebet der Basileiosliturgie: Textgeschichtliche Untersuchung und kritische Ausgabe*. Theologie des Christlichen Ostens. Texte und Untersuchungen [Münster in Westf.: Aschendorff, 1931]), most contemporary liturgical scholarship has viewed EgBAS as the earliest extant version of the Basilian anaphoral tradition, Gabriele Winkler has drawn attention to the importance of ArmBAS, and has suggested a Syrian rather than Cappadocian origin for this widespread and influential eucharistic prayer. See her article, "On the Formation of the Armenian Anaphoras: A Preliminary Overview," in *Worship Traditions in Armenia and the Neighboring Christian East*, ed. Roberta Ervine (New Rochelle, NY: forthcoming). See also idem, "Zur Erforschung orientalischer Anaphoren in liturgiegleichender Sicht II: Das Formelgut der Oratio post Sanctus und Anamnese sowie Interzessionen und die Taufbekenntnisse," in *Acts of the International Congress: Comparative Liturgy Fifty Years after Anton Baumstark (1872–1948), Rome, 25–29 September 1998*, ed. R. F. Taft and G. Winkler. OCA 265 (Rome: Pontificio Istituto Orientale, 2001) 407–91.

[15] "Die Interzession der Chrysostomusanaphora in ihrer geschichtliche Entwicklung," OCP 36 (1970) 309ff.

[16] Translation from Jasper and Cuming, *Prayers*, 133.

[17] Robert Taft, "Praying to or for the Saints? A Note on the Sanctoral Intercessions/Commemorations in the Anaphora," in *Ab Oriente et Occidente (Mt 8, 11): Kirche aus Ost und West: Gedenkschrift für Wilhelm Nyssen*, 439–55 (Erzabtei

We should note the expansion of *Theotokos* in ByzBAS and CHR with the addition of several honorific adjectives (i.e., "all-holy, immaculate, highly blessed [glorious], Blessed Lady") in relation to EgBAS, ArmBAS, as well as Syrian Basil[18] and the Antiochene Syriac anaphora called the Twelve Apostles (hereafter, APsyr), which has a close familial relationship to CHR. The pertinent text from APsyr reads: "Especially therefore let us make the memorial of the holy Mother of God and ever-Virgin Mary," and, after listing apostles, prophets, and saints, continues in a manner akin to EgBAS, "by whose prayers and supplications may we be preserved from evil, and may mercy be upon us in either world."[19] Interestingly, without referring to the *Theotokos* the author of *Mystagogical Catechesis* 5:9, in describing the commemoration of patriarchs, prophets, apostles, and martyrs in the fourth-century Jerusalem anaphora, includes the phrase "that at their prayers and intervention God would receive our petition," demonstrating that already in the fourth century reference to the intercessory prayer of the saints, such as we see in EgBAS and APsyr, is appearing in eucharistic euchology. Indeed, the addition of *Theotokos* to *Mystagogical Catechesis* 5:9 would give us something remarkably similar to the commemoration in EgBAS.

While we must be cautious about the possibility of Egyptian liturgical evidence for the use of the term *Theotokos*, the fifth-century Byzantine historian Socrates provides the following information about Origen of Alexandria: "Origen . . . in the first volume of his *Commentaries* on the apostle's epistle to the Romans, gives an ample exposition of the sense in which the term *Theotokos* is used. It is therefore obvious that Nestorius had very little acquaintance with the treatises of the ancients, and for that reason . . . objected to the word only; for that he does not assert Christ to be a mere man, as Photinus did or Paul of Samosata, his own published homilies fully demonstrate."[20] Unfortunately, the Greek text of Origen's *Commentary on Romans* is lost, and Rufinus's Latin translation omits any reference to the term in the

---

St. Ottilien: Eos Verlag, 1996) 440. See also Taft, *A History of the Liturgy of St. John Chrysostom*, 4: *The Diptychs*. OCA 238 (Rome: Pontificio Istituto Orientale, 1991) 100–102.

[18] H. Engberding, "Das anaphorische Fürbittgebet der syrischen Basiliusliturgie." *Oriens Christianus* 50 (1966) 16.

[19] Translation from Jasper and Cuming, *Prayers*, 128.

[20] Translation in NPNF 2/2, 171.

section of chapter 1 where it may once have been present. In her recent critical edition of this commentary, *Der Römerbriefkommentar des Origenes*, Caroline P. Hammond Bammel indicates in the notes where the term may have occurred in Origen's comments on 1:3-4, Christ as both Son of God and Son of David in the flesh.[21]

Besides the reference in Socrates—who, in the words of Johannes Quasten, is both "objective and sincere"[22] if lacking in theological interest—*Theotokos* appears in at least two fragments of Origen's writings usually considered authentic. According to the TLG the term occurs three times in *Fragmenta in Lucam* (not surprisingly, all in the context of Luke 2) and once in *Selecta in Deuteronomium*, making as many as five possible references to the *Theotokos* in Origen's writings. As Starowieyski notes, while theologians often contest this evidence, patristics scholars generally accept it.[23]

At least from the first quarter of the fourth century on, then, the term *Theotokos* was a common title for the Virgin Mary, one that cut across ecclesial lines as well as the boundaries of what might be called orthodoxy and heresy. While the term itself is hard to document before the third century, Mariological interest was certainly fostered by Justin Martyr and Irenaeus of Lyons in their theology of Mary as the "New Eve,"[24] as well as by Marian narratives like the mid-second to early-third century *Protoevangelium of James*. Hence, it would not be surprising to find this title in some third-century theological discourse. Indeed, the fact that fourth-century authors of such diverse christological positions can employ the term strongly suggests a common, earlier, and shared history of the term.

POPULAR DEVOTION TO MARY BEFORE EPHESUS?

Recent scholarship on the acceptance of the title *Theotokos* at Ephesus suggests that it was both liturgical and devotional in use. We have seen that no undisputed evidence exists for its appearance in liturgical usage, but must ask if it was devotional in nature, that is, rooted in popular piety.

---

[21] *Der Römerbriefkommentar: Kritische Ausgabe der Übersetzung Rufins, 1–3*, ed. Caroline P. Hammond Bammel (Freiburg in Breisgau: Herder, 1990) 56.

[22] J. Quasten, *Patrology* 3 (Utrecht/Antwerp: Spectrum, 1966) 533.

[23] Starowieyski, "Le titre," 237: "Ce témoignage contesté souvent par le théologiens, est généralement accepté par les patrologues."

[24] See Pelikan, *Mary*, 39–52.

In the past scholars tended to denigrate or even dismiss "popular religion" as mere superstition, as vestiges of paganism, reflecting a form of belief and practice among the "unenlightened" lower than the official religion of the elite. Modern scholarship has been willing to embrace a broader view, including as theological and liturgical sources the religious lives and practices of the poor, women, and others. In the United States and Latin America today this occurs especially among Latino-Hispanic theologians where such *religiosidad popular* has increasingly moved from the periphery to the center of theological thought and reflection.[25] To understand the Christian faith, and even its liturgical expressions, among Hispanic-Latinos today we must attend to this popular religion and its diverse contexts and meanings.

If contemporary Hispanic-Latino theology has made the case for the study of the popular faith of specific groups within contemporary Christianity, the same sensitivity has increasingly been shown by scholars of early Christianity. Peter Brown's important work on the cult of the saints in the Latin West represents a significant scholarly shift. Brown argues convincingly that the real history of the early church is to be read in the development of the popular practices and beliefs associated with the cult of the martyrs and later saints at their shrines, practices shared by the intellectual elite and others in the

[25] On "popular religion" or popular piety in general, see the *Directory on Popular Piety and the Liturgy: Principles and Guidelines* from the Congregation for Divine Worship and the Discipline of the Sacraments (Rome: Vatican City, 2001). For discussion of and various approaches to popular religion in an Hispanic-Latino context see R. S. Goizueta, *Caminemos con Jesús: Toward a Hispanic/Latino Theology of Accompaniment* (Maryknoll, NY: Orbis Books, 1995); O. Espín, *The Faith of the People: Theological Reflections on Popular Catholicism* (Maryknoll, NY: Orbis Books, 1997); A. García-Rivera, *St. Martín de Porres: The "Little Stories" and the Semiotics of Culture* (Maryknoll, NY: Orbis Books, 1995); and A. de Luna, *Faith Formation and Popular Religion: Lessons from Tejano Experience* (Lanham: Rowman and Littlefield, 2002). On the resurgence of popular religion in other contexts see P. Malloy, "The Re-Emergence of Popular Religion among Non-Hispanic American Catholics," *Worship* 72 (1998) 2–25, and M. Driscoll, "Liturgy and Devotions: Back to the Future?" in *The Renewal That Awaits Us*, ed. E. Bernstein and M. Connell (Chicago: Liturgy Training Publications, 1997) 68–90. See also M. Johnson, *The Virgin of Guadalupe: Theological Reflections of an Anglo-Lutheran Liturgist*. Celebrating Faith: Explorations in Latino Spirituality and Theology (Lanham: Rowman and Littlefield, 2002).

church in spite of their differing intellectual facilities.[26] Similarly, in the recent *Festschrift* for Paul F. Bradshaw, Robert Taft writes of the turn his own work has taken, saying that "in so doing I have, in a sense, been responding to my own appeal, made years ago, that we 'integrate into our work the methods of the relatively recent *pietá popolare* or *annales* schools of Christian history in Europe' and study liturgy not just from the top down, i.e., in its official or semi-official texts, but also from the bottom up, 'as something real people did.'"[27]

Cyrille Vogel[28] once noted that until the middle of the second century ancient burial inscriptions reveal that Christians prayed both *for* and *to* deceased Christians, whether they were martyrs or not, a point underscored also by Taft in a recent essay.[29] Such prayer *for* deceased baptized Christians as part of the *communio sanctorum*, of course, is highly consistent with CHR where, as we have seen, prayer is made *for* (ὑπὲρ) the *Theotokos* and the saints, and ArmBAS, where the *Theotokos* and the saints are simply commemorated at the Eucharist.[30] The Roman *canon missae* is striking in this regard since in its *Communicantes* the assembly merely prays in "communion" with and "venerates the memory" (*et memoriam venerantes*) of Mary (called *Genetricis Dei et Domini nostri Jesu Christi*) and the saints, and in the *Nobis quoque peccatoribus* asks for our admission into the company of the apostles and martyrs.

At the same time, by the end of the second century prayer to the martyrs, or at least asking for their intercession, even with regard to exercising the office of the keys, was becoming a common Christian practice. So, for example, the late-second or early-third-century North

---

[26] P. Brown, *The Cult of the Saints: Its Rise and Function in Latin Christianity* (Chicago: University of Chicago Press, 1981) 12ff.

[27] "The Order and Place of Lay Communion in the Late Antique and Byzantine East," in *Studia Liturgica Diversa: Essays in Honor of Paul F. Bradshaw*, ed. M. E. Johnson and L. E. Phillips (Portland: Pastoral Press, 2004) 130.

[28] "Priére ou intercession? Une ambiguïté dans le culte paléochrétien des martyrs," in *Communio Sanctorum: Mélanges offerts à Jean-Jacques von Allmen* (Geneva: Labor et Fides, 1982) 284–89.

[29] Taft, "Praying to," 439–55. See also M. Kunzler, "Insbesondere für unsere allheilige Herrin . . . ," in *Gratias Agamus: Studien zum eucharistischen Hochgebet*, ed. A. Heinz and H. Rennings, (Freiburg/Basel/Wien: Herder, 1992) 227–40.

[30] See note 14 above.

African *Passion of St. Perpetua and St. Felicitas* describes a vision of the martyr Saturus who sees Perpetua and himself after their martyrdom being appealed to by his bishop Optatus and a presbyter Aspasius. This vision is well summarized by Frederick Klawiter:

> In a vision Saturus saw himself and the other martyrs transported to paradise after death. They were carried by angels to a place whose walls were made of light. Upon entering they heard voices chanting endlessly in unison, making but one sound: "Holy, holy, holy." As the martyrs stood before a throne, angels lifted them up to kiss an aged man of youthful countenance, who touched their faces with his hand. Then they were commanded to go and play. They went out before the gates and saw their bishop Optatus and the presbyter Aspasius approaching them. Optatus and Aspasius were apart from one another and very sad. Throwing themselves at the feet of Perpetua and Saturus, they said: "Make peace between us, for you departed and left us thus." Perpetua and Saturus embraced them and began to talk to them; however, they were interrupted by angels who scolded the bishop and presbyter, instructing them to settle their own quarrels and advising the bishop about shepherding his flock. The angels thought that Perpetua and Saturus should be allowed to rest [*refrigerare*], and, in addition, it was time "to close the gates" [*claudere portas*] . . .[31]

While this vision may be interpreted as opposing the invocation of martyrs to exercise the office of the keys after death, Klawiter is certainly correct in noting that the text says that "Saturus and Perpetua 'were very moved and embraced' (*moti et conplexi sunt*) the bishop and presbyter. Evidently, they were not displeased that the two had come to them for a resolution." And, further, "The reasonable view is that Perpetua and Saturus had departed by death before Aspasius and Optatus were able to approach them in order to receive peace. Thus, this situation compelled the bishop and presbyter to approach them *through prayer* after Perpetua and Saturus had died."[32]

Similarly, in an often neglected passage in his *De oratione*, Origen not only witnesses to but actually advocates prayer to the saints

[31] F. C. Klawiter, "The Role of Martyrdom and Persecution in Developing the Priestly Authority of Women in Early Christianity: A Case Study of Montanism." *Church History* 49/2 (1980) 258–59. The text in question is *Passio SS. Perpetuae et Felicitatis* 12–13.

[32] Ibid., 259 and n. 29, emphasis added.

saying: "[I]t is not foolish to offer supplication, intercession, and thanksgiving also to the saints. Moreover, two of them, I mean intercession and thanksgiving, may be addressed not only to the saints but also to other people, while supplication may be addressed only to the saints if someone is found to be a Paul or a Peter so as to help us by making us worthy of receiving the authority given them to forgive sins."[33]

Scholars have often dated the famous short Marian prayer, usually called by its Latin title, *Sub tuum praesidium*, to the same third-century context.

> To your protection we flee, holy Mother of God [*Theotokos*]:
> do not despise our prayers in [our] needs,
> but deliver us from all dangers,
> glorious and blessed Virgin.[34]

Used liturgically in the Coptic, Greek, and Ambrosian Rites (for which the evidence is no earlier than the fifth and sixth centuries), and in the Roman Rite (for which evidence is no earlier than the seventh), the somewhat corrupted Greek version of this text in the manuscript published by C. H. Roberts in 1938 has been viewed as third-century or even earlier:

```
    . πο . [              ]
    ευσπλα[γχνὲ παρθενε ?]
    κατ αφε[σιν αμαρτιων ?]
    θεοτοκε: τα[ς εμας ?]
  5 ικεσιας: μη παρ-
    ειδης εμ περιστασει
    αλλ εκ κινδυνου
    ρυσαι ημας"
    μονη δε[
 10 ηρυλου [
```
        5. 1. παρίδης.   6. 1. ἐν.[35]

---

[33] Origen, *De oratione* 14.6; translation in *An Exhortation to Martyrdom*, . . ., trans. Rowan Greer. The Classics of Western Spirituality (New York: Paulist Press, 1979) 111–12.

[34] Translation from the Latin by Kilian McDonnell, "The Marian Liturgical Tradition," in *Between Memory and Hope: Readings on the Liturgical Year*, ed. Maxwell E. Johnson (Collegeville, MN: Liturgical Press, 2000) 387.

[35] See ibid. See also P. F. Mercenier, "La plus ancienne prière à la sainte Vierge: le *Sub tuum Praesidium*." *Les questions liturgiques et paroissiales* 25 (1940)

Arguments against a third-century date focus on the presence of the term *Theotokos*, reasoning that since the term must be later, the text cannot be earlier. Even if the text of *Sub tuum praesidium* is no older than the early fourth century, it remains the earliest Marian prayer in existence—unless the greetings to Mary of the angel and Elizabeth (Luke 1) are already Christian hymn texts themselves—and testifies to some kind of Marian devotional piety well before Ephesus. Indeed, in the middle of the fourth century the Emperor Julian the Apostate in his *Against the Galileans* criticized "the superstition of Christians for invoking the Theotokos."[36]

At the same time, nothing in this prayer of supplication to the *Theotokos* is inconsistent with Origen's advocation of prayer to the saints, or with his possible use of the title *Theotokos* in the third century. Also, nothing is really inconsistent between this *Sub tuum praesidium* prayer and the commemoration or intercession of the *Theotokos* in EgBAS or ArmBAS.

I believe that we should also take into account the possible shaping of early Marian devotional piety by the mid-second- to early-third-century *Protoevangelium of James*, which, as Robert Eno notes, is "unusual in that it showed some interest in and development on Mary for her own sake."[37] This apocryphal gospel, termed doctrinally "orthodox" by George Tavard,[38] (1) gives us the names of Mary's parents, Joachim and Anna; (2) defends Mary's *virginitas in partu* and even *post partum* in rather graphic detail (see note 44 below); (3) provides us with the narrative contents of what will become two Marian feasts later in the Christian East and West, i.e., her Nativity on September 8, and, when she was three-years old, her Presentation in the Temple on November 21; (4) associates her closely with the Jerusalem Temple, and describes her as a

---

33–36. Text from C. H. Roberts, *Catalogue of the Greek Papyri in the John Rylands Library* 3 (Manchester: University Press, 1938) no. 470, pp. 46–47.

[36] As quoted in Pelikan, *Mary*, 56.

[37] "Mary and Her Role in Patristic Theology," in *The One Mediator, the Saints, and Mary,* ed. H. George Anderson et al. Lutherans and Catholics in Dialogue 8 (Minneapolis: Augsburg Fortress, 1992) 164.

[38] *The Thousand Faces of the Virgin Mary* (Collegeville, MN: The Liturgical Press, 1996) 19. On the influence of the apocryphal gospels on Marian piety and iconography see I. Karavidopoulos, "On the Information concerning the Virgin Mary Contained in the Apocryphal Gospels," in *Mother of God: Representations of the Virgin in Byzantine Art,* ed. Maria Vassilaki (Milan: Skira, 2000) 67–89.

"weaver" of the purple and scarlet for the temple veil, both images that, according to Nicholas Constas, will have a great influence on the Marian theology of Proclus of Constantinople in the fifth-century controversy with Nestorius.[39] Indeed, the Virgin Mary as the "Ark" or "Tabernacle" in which the Logos made flesh dwells will be well attested in later Greek patristic literature.[40] All of this was already in place—at least in this text—by the end of the second or beginning of the third century! That this narrative somehow remained dormant for two or three centuries and then, suddenly, was "discovered" and started suggesting Marian feasts, imagery, and theology seems rather unlikely.

Perhaps in this context early Christian catacomb art should also be reconsidered. In the Roman catacombs of S. Priscilla and the Cimitero Maggiore are two famous images of a woman and young child, which tour guides today regularly describe as early representations of the Virgin and Christ Child. The art historian André Grabar, however, asks "who can provide any final solution to the puzzling scene in the catacomb of Priscilla, where one person seems to point to a star in the presence of a woman and child? And who can identify with any certainty, in the catacombs of the Cimitero Maggiore, the mother and child who appear with a monogram of Christ on either side and are flanked by two donors? Is this really the Virgin Mary, or is this some Christian woman with her child?"[41]

Whatever early hermeneutical key might have been available for interpreting such iconographic depictions of a "Christian woman with her child" would have long ago been replaced by the interpretative key provided by the Virgin and Child. And, given the overall context that appears to have been developing with regard to Marian symbols and theology, it would be surprising if the possibly third-century S. Priscilla image did not come quickly to be interpreted as Balaam or Isaiah pointing to the star of Jacob, and the woman with her child as the Virgin and Christ Child.[42]

---

[39] Constas, "Weaving the Body," 169–94.

[40] See Gary Anderson, "Mary in the Old Testament," *Pro Ecclesia* 16 (2007): 33–55.

[41] *Christian Iconography: A Study of Its Origins* (Princeton: Princeton University Press, 1968) 9. My thanks to John Klentos of the Patriarch Athenagoras Institute, Berkeley, California, for directing me to this reference.

[42] See S. Carletti, *Guide to the Catacombs of Priscilla*. Pontifical Commission for Sacred Architecture (Vatican City: Pontifical Commission for Sacred Architec-

Whatever one might conclude about Marian devotional piety in the first three centuries, by the middle of the fourth century prayers, hymns, and other texts illustrate that such devotion, and not only the title *Theotokos*, was becoming rather widespread. The following hymn, one of several *Soghyatha* included in the appendix of Edmund Beck's critical edition of the hymns of St. Ephrem, provides a Syrian example of this devotion:

> Awake, my harp, your songs
>> in praise of the Virgin Mary!
> Lift up your voice and sing
>> the wonderful history
> Of the Virgin, the daughter of David,
>> who gave birth to the Life of the World (1.1).

> This Virgin became a Mother
>> while preserving her virginity;
> And though still a Virgin
>> she carried a Child in her womb;
> And the handmaid and work of His Wisdom
>> became the Mother of God (1.20).[43]

Beck is certainly correct that this hymn should not be considered Ephrem's, but his argument is based on the presence of "Mother of God" and *virginitas in partu*, both of which he believes are of a later date. However, the title *Theotokos* was already common by this time,[44] and, as Sebastian Brock has noted, "the *soghyatha* in Beck's edition are all later than Ephrem, and are only preserved in early liturgical

---

ture, 1982) 21–23. See also A. Cameron, "The Early Cult of the Virgin," in *Mother of God: Representations of the Virgin in Byzantine Art*, ed. Maria Vassilaki (Milan: Skira, 2000) 5.

[43] *Hymnen de Nativitate (Epiphania)*, ed. E. Beck. CSCO 186, Scriptures Syri 82 (Louvain: Sécretariat du CorpusSCO, 1959) 91ff.; translation from Jurgens, *Faith*, 1:312.

[44] In the *Protoevangelium of James* (translation in *The Apocryphal New Testament*, ed. J. K. Elliott, [Oxford: Clarendon Press, 1993] 48–67) 20, Salome performs a *post-partum* gynecological examination of Mary and her hand begins to drop off as though burned with fire; this certainly confirms a prior history of *virginitas in partu*.

manuscripts, which attribute things to Ephrem with abandon!"[45] That is, the hymn above is not Ephrem's, but not because the Marian theology is necessarily later than his lifetime.

Brock himself has drawn attention to the presence of the title "Mother of God" in East Syrian liturgical texts, and to the rich poetic imagery regarding Mary in the authentic hymns of Ephrem.[46] Two examples of this, clearly reflecting the ancient patristic Eve-Mary typology, follow:

> The virgin earth of old gave birth to the Adam who is lord of the earth,
> But today another virgin has given birth to the Adam who is Lord of
>   heaven (*H. Nativ.* 1.16; p. 186).

> Adam brought forth travail upon the woman who sprang from him,
> But today she (Mary), who bore him a Saviour, has redeemed that travail.
> A man (Adam) who himself knew no birth, bore Eve the mother:
> How much more should Eve's daughter (Mary) be believed to have
>   given birth without the aid of a man (*H. Nativ.* 1:14-15; p. 187).

Ephrem relates the baptismal womb of the Jordan to the womb of Mary giving birth to Christ, and even views the incarnation of Christ as Mary's own baptism:

> O Christ, you have given birth to your own mother
> in the second birth that comes from water. . . .
> The Son of the Most High came and dwelt in me,
> And I became his mother. As I gave birth to him,
> —his second birth—so too he gave birth to me
> a second time. He put on his mother's robe
> —his body; I put on his glory (*H. Nativ.* 16.9, 11; p. 190).

> Fire and Spirit are in the womb of her who bore you,
> Fire and Spirit are in the river in which you were baptized,
> Fire and Spirit are in our baptism,
> And in the Bread and Cup is Fire and Holy Spirit (*H. Fid.* 10.17; p. 190).

---

[45] E-mail conversation with Sebastian Brock, February 14, 2005.

[46] S. Brock, "Mary in Syriac Tradition," in *Mary's Place in Christian Dialogue*, ed. A. Stacpoole, (Wilton: Morehouse-Barlow, 1982) 182–91. The texts that follow are from this essay.

On the basis of such Marian imagery, clearly reflecting an incarnational-sacramental-liturgical context, Brock says that "in actual fact, the Christological differences that separate the Syrian Orthodox, Greek Orthodox (Chalcedonian) Churches and the Church of the East do not appear to have had much affect on their attitudes to Mary. . . . Thus those who are familiar with the Byzantine tradition will find much of what Syriac writers say on the subject of Mary not unfamiliar."[47]

If this kind of poetic devotion is present in mid-fourth century Syria, developing Marian devotion and theology also have a place in Cappadocia. Gregory Nazianzen has no qualms about declaring that "if anyone does not agree that Holy Mary is the Mother of God [ἐπὶ τῆς Θεοτόκον τὴν ἁγίαν Μαρίαν], he is at odds with the Godhead."[48] In his *Oratio XXIV*, in a story about Cyprian of Antioch and the virgin Justina, he refers to a prayer of intercession offered by Justina to "the Virgin Mary, imploring her to help a virgin in danger."[49]

Similarly, Gregory of Nyssa in his treatise on *Virginity* writes that death "found at last in virginity a barrier beyond which he could not pass. Just as in the time of Mary, the Mother of God [ἐπὶ τῆς Θεοτόκου Μαρίας], the Death who had reigned from Adam until then found, when he came to her and dashed his forces against the fruit of her virginity as against a rock, that he was himself shattered against her . . ."[50]

Of special interest in this devotional context is his *Vita Gregorii thaumaturgi* where he refers to an apparition of both Mary ("the mother of the Lord") and the apostle John to Gregory the Wonderworker. This is the first reference to a Marian apparition in the history of the church.[51] Of course neither of the above references to a prayer of intercession (Nazianzen) or to an apparition of Mary (Nyssa) tells us anything

[47] Ibid., 183.

[48] *Letter to Cledonius the Priest, against Apollinaris*; translation from Jurgens, *Faith*, 2:40–41.

[49] PG 35:1181A; translation from H. Graef, *Mary: A History of Doctrine and Devotion*, 1 (New York: Sheed and Ward, 1963) 64.

[50] Translation from Jurgens, *Faith*, 44.

[51] See PG 46:912. This would explain why the TLG provides some nine references to a homily on the incarnation by Gregory the Wonderworker. This attribution, however, is not regarded as correct; see M. Jugié, "Les homélies mariales attribuées a Saint Grégoire le Thamaturge." *Analecta Bollandiana* 43 (1925) 86–95. Jugié believed the vision itself to be authentic.

about the third century, but they do "tell us . . . about the situation in the time of the writers";[52] for developing Marian devotional piety, that is what is significant.

That "there was a popular veneration for the Virgin Mother which threatened to run extravagant lengths"[53] in the fourth century is testified to by the *Panarion* of Epiphanius of Salamis (315–403 C.E.). Not only was there in existence an anti-Marian group called the *Antidicomarianites*, who denied Mary's perpetual virginity,[54] but also an extreme pro-Marian group known as the *Collyridians* (from κολλυρίς, "cakes"), a group comprised mostly of women who worshiped Mary as a "goddess," offered to her, and then themselves consumed, small cakes, and had a female priesthood. Epiphanius's critique of the Collyridians, while certainly warning against excessive Marian piety, tends to stress the subordinate role he believed that women should aspire to in the church in imitation of the passivity of Mary. Nevertheless, if he is a credible witness we see not only a developing Marian popular piety in the fourth century but that it was prevalent enough to become problematic and heretical. Thus already in the fourth century we have corroborating evidence for the statement of E. Ann Matter that "the practice of the pious often takes its own course,"[55] a maxim that will be demonstrated over and over again, especially in the later history of Marian doctrine and devotion (even unto our own day).

Perhaps, however, the best example of popular Marian piety comes in early fifth-century Constantinople, on the very eve of the controversy with Nestorius and the resulting Council of Ephesus. In his studies of the theology of Proclus of Constantinople, Nicholas Constas refers to the following event that took place shortly after Nestorius had become patriarch of Constantinople:

> Nestorius was scandalized by the devotion to the Virgin which he encountered upon his arrival in Constantinople. Nestorius was further outraged to learn that during the reign of his predecessor the empress

[52] Eno, "Mary and Her Role," 166.

[53] H. Thurston, "Virgin Mary, Devotion to the Blessed—Down to the Council of Nicaea," in *The Catholic Encyclopedia* (New York: The Encyclopedia Press, 1913) 15:459–60.

[54] *Panarion* 79. Augustine (*De haeresibus* 56, based on Epiphanius) refers to this group but not to the *Collyridians*.

[55] As quoted by E. Johnson, *Truly Our Sister*, 119.

Pulcheria [whose spiritual advisor, in fact, had become Proclus] had been permitted to receive communion within the sanctuary of the Great Church. According to one source, Nestorius, barring the empress from the chancel screen, insisted that "Only priests may walk here," to which she replied, "Why, have I not given birth to God?" "You?" he retorted, "have given birth to Satan," and proceeded to drive Pulcheria from the sanctuary. Not long after this confrontation, Nestorius publicly challenged the dignity of the Virgin Mary and began to preach against the propriety of calling her the Theotokos—the Birth-giver of God. . . . The people of Constantinople, who are said to have been passionately devoted to theological discussion, were greatly offended at this. Besides, the term had been generally accepted by the bishops of the capital from at least the time of Gregory the Theologian. Unlike the term "homoousious" . . . the title "Theotokos" was a powerfully evocative word which belonged to the language of liturgy and devotion. As a result, local resistance to Nestorius formed quickly and was actively supported, and to a certain extent orchestrated by Proclus and Pulcheria.[56]

As this event clearly demonstrates, the dogmatic decision at Ephesus was rooted not simply in the theology of the unitive personhood of Christ but, undoubtedly, was also the product of the *lex orandi* and of popular piety and devotion. As far back as 1940, P. F. Mercenier argued that: "En le defendant contre Nestorius avec l'acharnment que l'on sait, saint Cyrille ne combattait pas seulement pour une opinion ou un terme d'école, mais pour une expression et une croyance depuis longtemps consacrées par l'usage liturgique . . . Ce serait une nouvelle application de l'adage: *Legem credendi statuat lex supplicandi.*"[57] Indeed, consistent with the Marian theology of Nestorius's predecessor, Atticus of Constantinople (d. 425), who had instructed Pulcheria and her sisters, Arcadia and Marina, that if they imitated the virginity and chastity of Mary they would give birth to God mystically in their souls,[58] Pulcheria's Marian self-identification ("have I not given birth to God?") indicates that such personal or popular devotion to the *Theotokos* could even become a kind of Marian mysticism.

---

[56] Constas, "Weaving the Body," 173–75; see also *Proclus of Constantinople and the Cult of the Virgin in Late Antiquity: Homilies 1–5*, ed. Nicholas Constas. Supplements to Vigiliae Christiane 66 (Leiden/Boston: E. J. Brill, 2003).

[57] "La plus ancienne prière," 36.

[58] See Constas, "Weaving the Body," 171–72.

THE EARLIEST LITURGICAL FEAST OF
MARY-*THEOTOKOS*

The historical context of Proclus and Nestorius is also important for the history of the liturgical year since in Proclus's famous homily delivered at the Great Church of Constantinople in the presence of Nestorius, probably in the year 430, the first two words refer to "the Virgin's festival" being celebrated that day (Παρθενικὴ πανήγυρις).[59] While it is a matter of debate which Marian feast Proclus's reference intended (the Annunciation, the Sunday before Christmas, and the Sunday after Christmas have all been suggested), current scholarship has argued that the feast in question was probably the day after Christmas, December 26, 430, "a day on which the Byzantine Church continued to celebrate a 'synaxis' in honor of the Theotokos."[60] In two places in his writings Athanasius refers to the necessity of keeping a "memory" or "commemoration" (μνήμη) of Mary.[61] Because of this Jaroslav Pelikan, in line with the much earlier works of Martin Jugié[62] and Hilda Graef[63]—who both underscored the pre-Ephesine existence of a Marian "feast" on either the Sunday before or after Christmas in the East—has suggested "that evidence and his language seem to make it plausible that such a commemoration of Mary was being kept already during his time and that his argument was based upon it."[64] Such would make this Marian feast already associated with Christmas a mid-fourth-century reality; of course, Athanasius may simply be referring to the memory of Mary or, perhaps, even to the type of anaphoral commemoration we have noted above.

That the Virgin Mary should ultimately come to be commemorated liturgically in relationship to the feast of Christmas in both East and West is surely no surprise. But apart from Athanasius's use of μνήμη we have no clear evidence of such a feast prior to Proclus's homily, and it is quite possible that this feast had been instituted at Constantinople no earlier than Atticus or Sisinnius (426–427).[65] That a feast asso-

---

[59] See *Proclus*, ed. Constas, 136.

[60] Ibid., 58.

[61] *Letter to Epictetus* 4, and *Letter to Maximus the Philosopher* 3.

[62] "La première fête mariale en Orient et en Occident, l'Avent primitif." *Echos d'Orient* 26, 130 (1923) 129–52.

[63] Graef, *Mary*, 133.

[64] Pelikan, *Mary*, 61.

[65] See *Proclus*, ed. Constas, 58; see also M. Fassler, "The First Marian Feast in Constantinople and Jerusalem: Chant Texts, Readings, and Homiletic Litera-

ciated so closely with Christmas should already be known by Athanasius does not seem likely; indeed our first reference to Christmas itself being celebrated in the East is *Apostolic Constitutions* 8.33.6, usually dated today ca. 381 C.E.[66]

This does not mean, however, that no Marian feast or commemoration was in existence prior to the fifth century, and that Athanasius could not have known of its existence and celebration at Alexandria. Indeed, the oldest Marian feast is usually identified as the August 15 celebration of Mary Theotokos, with its origin in Jerusalem, and first documented in the fifth-century *Armenian Lectionary*, one of our major guides to liturgical life in late-fourth century Jerusalem. The entry in the *Armenian Lectionary*[67] reads:

> Com. MARY THEOTOKOS, at *Second Mile from Bethlehem*, 15 August
> PS + ANT: 132 (a8)
> O.T. LESSON: Isa. 7-10
> APOSTLE: Gal. 3.29-4.7
> ALL/PS: 110.1
> GOSPEL; Luke 2.1-7

Pierre Jounel summarizes the standard theory about this feast succinctly:

> The liturgical cult of Mary originated in Jerusalem, with the feast of August 15 as its foundation. Initially celebrated at the Kathisma or place where according to tradition Mary paused to rest before going on to Bethlehem, the feast was transferred, toward the end of the fifth century, to Gethsemane and the basilica where people venerated the tomb of the Virgin. The feast of Mary Theotokos thus became the feast of the Dormition of the Mother of God. At the end of the sixth century, Emperor Maurice ruled that this feast was to be celebrated throughout the empire.[68]

---

ture," in *The Study of Medieval Chant: Paths and Bridges, East and West: In Honor of Kenneth Levy,* ed. Peter Jeffery (Woodbridge/Rochester: Boydell, 2001) 29–42.

[66] *Les constitutions apostoliques,* ed. Marcel Metzger. SC 320, 329, 336 (Paris: Cerf, 1985–1987) 3:242–43.

[67] Text from A. Renoux, *Le codex arménien Jérusalem 121,* 2. Patrologia Orientalis 36 (Turnhout: Brepols, 1971) 355–57; translation from *Egeria's Travels to the Holy Land,* trans. John Wilkinson (London: S.P.C.K., 1971) 274.

[68] "The Veneration of Mary," in *The Church at Prayer 4: Liturgy and Time,* ed. A. G. Martimort et al. (Collegeville, MN: Liturgical Press, 1986) 131.

With regard to the August 15 date, however, various explanations have been offered, including taking August 15 as the date of the Kathisma's dedication, or of Jerusalem's deliberately distancing itself from Constantinople's Christmas-related Marian feast since it held out longer before succumbing to the new December 25 date for the celebration of Christ's beginnings. No one, however, has been able to offer a conclusive argument as to why August 15 became the date of this feast.

The date and contents of the feast are Walter Ray's concern in his recent Notre Dame doctoral dissertation.[69] Ray notes that a core structure, still present in the liturgical calendar of the *Armenian Lectionary,* displays what he calls a parallel "narrative framework" to a calendrical structure also found "in the pre-Christian, Essene, or proto-Essene *Book of Jubilees,*" which centered on the story of Isaac. According to Ray, in the calendar and narrative world of *Jubilees* the festival of Pentecost on 3/15 (= May 15), always a Sunday, was simultaneously the celebration of the birth of Isaac, who had been conceived by Sarah nine months earlier on 6/15 (= August 15!). Significantly, it is the Isaac-Jesus typology emerging from this tradition that occupies St. Paul's attention in his Galatian correspondence (see Gal 4:21-31). Ray writes:

> The Feast of Weeks, understood as the 15th of the third month, had particular meaning for the Jubilees calendar as the completion of the fifty days, the time of the ultimate fulfillment of covenant renewal which was both promised and foreshadowed in the birth of Isaac. In its Christian form the final day of the feast would have been remembered as the time of divine adoption of the community and the giving of the Spirit (Acts 2, Gal 4:5-6), but also the time of particular revelation of the divine sonship of Jesus in the power of the Spirit, first in light of the resurrection/ascension (cf. Rom 1:3, Acts 2:33) but also in light of his special birth (Luke 1:35). . . . We should perhaps add Christ's baptism to the list, where we again find the themes of divine sonship and the coming of the Spirit. . . . [I]n Luke-Acts both the birth and baptism of Jesus manifest the same narrative pattern as Pentecost.[70]

Jesus' own beginnings, according to Ray, whether at his conception, his birth in Bethlehem, or at what might be called his "spiritual birth" in the

---

[69] "August 15 and the Development of the Jerusalem Calendar." Ph.D. diss., University of Notre Dame, 2000.

[70] Ibid., 262.

Jordan, have clear Pentecostal connotations quite possibly stemming from an early Jerusalem Christian adaptation of this ancient Qumran-*Jubilees* calendrical and narrative tradition. And, together with all of this, a compelling reason has been given for the date of August 15.

In developing this approach Ray takes into account the fact that one of the apparent anomalies of the calendar of feasts in the *Armenian Lectionary* is the presence of the feast of the infants or "Holy Innocents" on May 18 in some manuscripts. Based on this feast in May, Bernard Botte once suggested that the Jerusalem liturgy may have once had some sort of commemoration of Christ's nativity in May as well.[71] Ray summarizes:

> The feast of the Infants in May is the remnant of the beginning of a course reading of the epistle to the Hebrews and the gospel of Matthew and of a feast of Christ's nativity coinciding with Pentecost, dated according to the fixed-date *Jubilees* calendar to May 15. This commemoration of Christ's nativity, along with the feast of Mary on August 15, understood as a commemoration of Christ's conception, and the commemoration of Christ's crucifixion at Passover, evidences a Christ cycle that mirrors an Isaac cycle in the calendar of *Jubilees*. There we read that "in the middle of the sixth month the Lord visited Sarah and did for her as he had said. And she conceived and bore a son in the third month, in the middle of the month . . . on the feast of the firstfruits of the harvest" [*Jubilees* 16:12-13]. *Jubilees* is unique in pre-Christian literature in dating the sacrifice of Isaac to the time of Passover.[72]

Ray has made a solid contribution not only to the study of the early liturgical year at Jerusalem but also to that of developing early Christian mariology. In addition to establishing a compelling reason for why August 15 should emerge as the date of a commemoration centered on the incarnation, Ray has also pushed back the possibility of a type of Marian commemoration to a very early period as well. As he himself notes, even the earlier station for the feast, two or three miles from Bethlehem, is already part of the narrative of Christ's birth in the

---

[71] B. Botte, *Les origines de la Noël et de l'Épiphanie*. Textes et études liturgiques 1 (Louvain: Abbaye du Mont-César, 1932) 9ff.

[72] Ray, "Toward a Narrative-Critical Approach to the Study of Early Liturgy," in *Studia Liturgica Diversa: Essays in Honor of Paul F. Bradshaw*, ed. M. E. Jonson and L. E. Phillips (Portland: Pastoral Press, 2004) 9.

Protoevangelium of James.[73] This would be consistent with what we have already seen; if Athanasius has any feast in mind it may be this one.

At the same time, if Ray is correct in his analysis of the origins and development of this feast, the earliest so-called Marian feast, ultimately becoming the feast of her Dormition and/or Assumption, began as an early Jerusalem commemoration of the incarnation or annunciation, nine months before a primitive celebration of Christ's nativity. In other words, the origin of even this Marian feast, like the December 26 feast in Constantinople and the much later January 1 feast in Rome, appears to be closely tied both christologically and calendrically with some type of nativity cycle.

CONCLUSION

Where does all of this leave us with regard to Marian devotion and popular piety before Ephesus and its dogmatic definition of Mary as *Theotokos*? While our conclusions must remain tentative, we can safely say that devotion to Mary *Theotokos* did not spring up out of thin air, or merely fall out of heaven, at the Council of Ephesus. Nor did it simply "spread like wild fire" only after the Council of Ephesus. Rather, such devotion is rooted in piety and devotion from at least the third century. As we have seen:

(1) The title *Theotokos*, while of course christological in a broad sense, appears as an honorific title for Mary in diverse fourth-century authors with diverse christological positions. In other words, *Theotokos* as a title for Mary does not appear to be tied originally to a particular christological position as a banner of orthodoxy, as it came to be at the Council of Ephesus. Prior to that it was simply one honorific way in which to refer to Mary.

(2) Use of the title itself, as well as our earliest Marian prayer, *Sub tuum praesidium*, may well be mid-third-century Alexandrian in origin, and Origen himself, as testified to by Socrates, may well have been the first to have used this title in theological discourse.

(3) Such use of the title and devotion to the *Theotokos*, including liturgical use in the developing anaphoral tradition, appear to be consistent with the growing development of prayer and supplication to the saints, as testified to in general by the cult of the martyrs and by Origen in particular.

---

[73] Ray, "August 15," 56ff.

(4) Already, by the beginning of the third century, the *Protoevangelium of James* reflects an interest in Mary herself and provides several Marian elements that will develop and become, ultimately, the content of theological reflection, liturgical celebration, and popular devotion in the life of the church.

(5) The earliest Marian feast on August 15, quite possibly a commemoration of Jesus' conception nine months before an earlier May 15 Jerusalem commemoration of his birth, rooted in the sectarian Jewish *Jubilees* tradition, would seem to place the origins of this feast in the earliest days of Christianity itself.

(6) Even the doctrinal controversy with Nestorius of Constantinople is not merely about doctrine. Rather, in the context of the late fourth and early fifth centuries, where Marian devotion is witnessed to not only in Egypt but in Cappadocia (Gregory of Nyssa and Gregory Nazianzen) and Syria (Ephrem) as well, the controversy is also devotional as certainly indicated by what might be called the "Marian mysticism" of Atticus, Pulcheria, and Proclus.

These points suggest strongly, I believe, that we need to view what happened after the Council of Ephesus—an increase of both liturgical and popular Marian piety and devotion, especially in the East, where the christological focus of *Theotokos* has always remained stronger than in the West—as an evolution in piety and devotion. Such piety and devotion appear to be consistent with what came before, not something radically new, revolutionary, and brought about merely by an elevated christology. That is, just as it is becoming more common to acknowledge the existence of a higher christology early in the history of the church, we may note that many elements of a rather full Marian devotion and piety are to be found rather early as well.

Chapter 11

Prism of Glory: Trinitarian Worship and Liturgical Piety in the Reformed Tradition

John D. Witvliet
Calvin Institute of Christian Worship

The doctrine of the Trinity, as Cornelius Plantinga phrases it, is "attached with conceptual gears and pulleys" to near every major theme in Christian theology.[1] It is intimately related with our understanding not only of God and Christ, but also of creation, humanity, salvation, the church, and eschatology. Elsewhere, I have distinguished five uses of the doctrine of the Trinity, each of which has implications for the theology and practice of worship.[2] These five unique strands of trinitarian discourse address different practices, problems, and theological loci. Briefly, in different contexts, the adjective trinitarian is used

1. to accent the mediation of Jesus Christ and the Holy Spirit as agents of divine grace,

2. to call for balanced and integrated interpretation of the divine economy,

3. to commend both worship and doctrine that are rooted in God's actions in history as recorded in Scripture (sometimes in contrast with terms "philosophical" or "speculative"),

---

[1] Cornelius Plantinga, "The Threeness/Oneness Problem of the Trinity." *Calvin Theological Journal* 23 (1988) 37.

[2] See John D. Witvliet, "The Trinitarian DNA of Christian Worship," *Colloquium: Yale Institute of Sacred Music* 2 (2005) 87–105; and "Trinity/Call to Worship," in *A More Profound Alleluia: Worship and Theology in Harmony*, ed. Leanne Van Dyk (Grand Rapids: Eerdmans, 2005).

4. to commend patterns for human communal life that embody or reflect the relationally robust triune life of God (especially in ecclesiology and ethics), and

5. occasionally, to call for refining definitions of the attributes or metaphors used to speak about God.

Each of these five strands of trinitarian discourse echos patristic concerns. Each is developed by theologians from across the ecumenical spectrum. Indeed, one significant feature of the doctrine of the Trinity is the way in which this single doctrine has been used to make so many different points.

Distinguishing these strands is more than an exercise in basic theological logic. It helps us see internal inconsistencies, challenging us to notice how easy it is to be enthusiastic about one of these themes while unwittingly undermining trinitarian distinctives in another. It also establishes that trinitarian worship is about much more than explicit trinitarian language in prayer openings and doxologies (the usual focus in books like this one), but rather embraces nearly every aspect of how we address God and relate to each other as worshipers.

Given the constraints of space, my aim in this essay is to explore only the first two of these themes: the triune action or mediation of God in worship, and the integration of worship with a trinitarian vision of the divine economy. Taken together, these two themes conceptualize worship in both space and time, and they offer a parsimonious plumb line by which to test liturgical practice. My goal will be to probe these themes in light of some Reformed (and Presbyterian) articulations of each, and thus to represent a Reformed voice in the ecumenical conversation of this book.[3]

---

[3] Any use of the term "Reformed tradition" in a brief essay such as this is bound to ignore significant factors in the complex mosaic of Reformed Churches, which involves not only diverse ethnic identities (South Africa African, English, Dutch, German, Hispanic, Huguenot, Hungarian, Scottish, Korean, Indonesian), but also vast differences in theology and polity represented by the bewildering mix of denominations, such as Christian Reformed Church, Orthodox Presbyterian Church, Presbyterian Church in America, Presbyterian Church—USA, the Reformed Church in America, and the United Church of Christ.

THEME I: THE TRINITARIAN GRAMMAR OF MEDIATION
The ad-per-in *Prayer Formula*

First, the doctrine of the Trinity grounds the basic grammar of Christian prayer and proclamation by conceiving of Jesus Christ and the Holy Spirit as fully divine agents whose actions enable our effective participation in worship.

Christian liturgy has historically featured two types of divine address in prayer: prayers offered *to* the Father, *to* the Son, and *to* the Holy Spirit, and prayers *to* God, *through* Christ, *in* the Spirit. This latter "to-through-in" (*ad-per-in*) pattern is a condensed summary and application of three New Testament themes. First, God the Father receives our worship, as Jesus' familiar words simply assume: "those who worship the Father . . . worship in Spirit and truth" (John 4:24).[4] Second, Jesus Christ is the One who perfects our worship. Just as Hebrew priests represented the people of Israel before God, so Jesus represents us before God: "because Jesus lives forever, he has a permanent priesthood. Therefore he is able to save completely those who come to God through him, because he always lives to intercede for them" (Heb 7:23-25). Third, the Holy Spirit is the one who prompts our prayer in the first place: "[by the Spirit] we cry, 'Abba! Father!'"; and when we are too weak to pray, "the Spirit himself intercedes for us with groans that words cannot express" (Rom 8:15, 26). These three themes are condensed into Paul's formula: "through Christ [we] have access in one Spirit to the Father" (Eph 2:18). We might call this pattern the trinitarian grammar or logic of our address to God.

Conversely, there are biblical texts that point to the trinitarian dynamics of God's address to us. First, the Father is the one who sends the Spirit to prompt us. "God has sent the Spirit of his Son into our hearts" (Gal 4:6). Second, Jesus Christ is the "content" of God's speaking to us, the "Word" who comes to us "full of grace and truth" (John 1:1, 14), "the radiance of God's glory and the exact representation of his being" (Heb 1:3). Third, the Holy Spirit prompts us to perceive and comprehend God's address: "We have received . . . the Spirit who is from God, that we may understand what God has freely given us" (I Cor 2:12). In other words, Jesus Christ and the Holy Spirit are the agents who make right spiritual perception and reception possible.

---

[4] Author's own translation.

This is a way of thinking about worship that is, we might say, "geographically complex." As Sarah Coakley explains, it suggests that prayer or worship is "one experience of God, but God as simultaneously (i) doing the praying in me, (ii) receiving that prayer, and (iii) in that exchange, consented to in me, inviting me into the Christic life of redeemed sonship."[5] In this vision, God inhabits three places in our imagination at the same time. To push the spatial metaphors: as we worship, God is at work before us, alongside us, and within us. These images are further compressed in Robert Jenson's evocative language: "The particular God of Scripture does not just stand over against us; he envelops us."[6]

It is easy to get lost in the symmetry of these trinitarian formulations and to miss the point that both revelation and response, both proclamation and prayer, are gifts of divine grace.[7] Trinitarian liturgical formulae are not simply symmetrical rhetorical flourishes to append to a prayer or sermon, but are rather shorthand acknowledgments of the mediation of Jesus Christ and the Holy Spirit that make both liturgical proclamation and liturgical prayer occasions of divine grace. In the words of Hilary of Poitiers, "God cannot be known except through God, just as God does not receive worship except through God."[8] Only God can effect perception of the revelation of God. Only God can grant communion with God. Only by the Spirit do we confess Jesus as Lord. The human self cannot achieve these lofty ends, nor can any semidivine intermediary. (Importantly, this trinitarian grammar of mediation is a doctrine of grace only if the Son

---

[5] Sarah Coakley, "Living into the Mystery of the Holy Trinity: Trinity, Prayer, and Sexuality," *Anglican Theological Review* 80 (1998) 224.

[6] Robert Jenson, *Triune Identity: God according to the Gospel* (Philadelphia: Fortress, 1982) 51.

[7] This can be seen in the titles of several books and articles that link the trinitarian theology with the doctrine of grace. See, for example, G. C. Berkouwer, *The Triumph of Grace in the Theology of Karl Barth*, trans. Harry R. Boer (Grand Rapids: Eerdmans, 1956); A. J. Torrance, *Persons in Communion: An Essay on Trinitarian Description and Human Participation* (Edinburgh: T&T Clark, 1996); and C. Schwöbel, "The Triune God of Grace: Trinitarian Thinking in the Theology of the Reformers," in *The Christian Understanding of God Today*, ed. James M. Byrne (Dublin: Columba Press, 1993).

[8] Hilary of Poitiers, *De Trinitate*, 5.20. See also R. C. Gregg and D. E. Groh, *Early Arianism: A View of Salvation* (Philadelphia: Fortress, 1981) 193.

and Spirit are not less than God—which makes it odd to suggest, as some scholars do, that the *per-ad-in* formula automatically implies an Arian vision.[9]) The trinitarian formula frees us of this pretension and this burden. Part of the pastoral significance of this theme is to restore a vision of worship that is marked by grace, not works; joy, not obligation.

Joseph Jungmann's Pastoral Concern

This trinitarian grammar for prayer is the central concern in Joseph Jungmann's *The Place of Christ in Liturgical Prayer*. One of the most tantalizing terms in that title is also one of the least explored, the word "place." The word functions metaphorically, suggesting that we conceptualize the experience of liturgy partially in spatial or geographic terms. Near the end of his book Jungmann draws on other spatial terms to explain his thesis, lamenting that "as the mediatorship and humanity of Christ recede into the background, the poor creature is confronted immediately with the overwhelming majesty of God."[10] "Recede" and "background" are also spatial metaphors, depicting God as distant or removed. They echo the spatial metaphors found throughout Scripture, vividly illustrated in the spatial language of Ephesians 2:13: "in Christ Jesus you who once were far off have been brought near." So also, the famous prepositions "to, through, in" are veiled spatial metaphors, conveying a mental picture of the spatial relationships of objects (or in this case divine persons). One way to think of Jungmann, then, is as a theological cartographer, mapping Jesus' location in our conceptualization of liturgy's divine-human encounter.

One of Jungmann's primary concerns was the link between our spatial conceptions of God and the nature of liturgical participation or piety. In the preface to the first German edition, Jungmann observed that he wrote the book, in part, "to clarify . . . the evident contrast between the older, traditional way of liturgical piety . . . and our current

---

[9] The explicit exclusion of prayers to the Father and the Son and the Spirit may well arise from Arian impulses, but the presence of *per-ad-in* prayers by themselves does not imply Arianism. Indeed, *per-ad-in* prayers reach their full potential as occasions of the grace of triune action only if the context is not Arian.

[10] Joseph Jungmann, *The Place of Christ in Liturgical Prayer*. 2nd rev. ed., trans. A. Peeler (Staten Island, NY: Alba House, 1965) 251.

forms of popular devotion."[11] Near the end of the book he concluded that to "have an educational effect on the community, to edify it, to put it into a religious frame of mind, not just for the moment but to enrich its knowledge of religion and ennoble it—all this is one of the functions of liturgical prayer inherent in its very nature."[12] In short, his aim was to restore the mediatorship of Jesus Christ firmly in the consciousness of Christian worshipers, a theme that ran through much of his work, including the translated volumes *Pastoral Liturgy, Christian Prayer through the Centuries*, and others.[13] And while other essays in this volume observe that that this pastoral concern may have blinded him to certain historical evidence, there is nevertheless significant value in this central pastoral theme. His work was the harbinger of Vatican II's concern for the "full, conscious active participation" of the faithful in the liturgical assembly. It is an example of what Ellen Charry has called the "pastoral function of Christian doctrine."[14]

Reformed Interest in Trinitarian Conceptualizations

Anyone speaking about the Reformed tradition's enthusiasm for this trinitarian grammar must begin cautiously. The Reformed tradition, after all, provided the context in which Enlightenment Deism flourished, in which Unitarianism was birthed, and in which Schleiermacher famously relegated the doctrine of the Trinity to a footnote.

[11] In the preface to the second German edition he describes the essential thesis of the book as "the evidence of the decisive influence which the Arian crisis exerted on the development, firstly of liturgical prayer and then of Western piety in general" (xiv).

[12] He went on to say, "Liturgical prayer must always remain prayer directed to God: it must be divine service and not community service, but it is intended equally to guide the community to God and fill it with the thoughts which can kindle in all hearts the same flame of true Christian prayer" (275). And again: "There is one God, who has made everything, and Jesus Christ, his only Son, has reconciled us sinners with him. If only these two doctrines, the second as well as the first, *are not only believed but inwardly grasped*, a good part of religious education is already accomplished" (277).

[13] See Jungmann, *Christian Prayer through the Centuries*, trans. John Coyne (New York: Paulist Press, 1978) 1–5, 155–69; idem, *Pastoral Liturgy* (New York: Herder and Herder, 1962) 89–105.

[14] Ellen Charry, *The Pastoral Function of Christian Doctrine* (New York: Oxford University Press, 1997).

Nevertheless, influential Reformed liturgical texts and theological treatises over nearly five centuries offer ample evidence of a common concern for this same trinitarian grammar of mediation. In the sixteenth century trinitarian concerns run deeply through the writings of Calvin and Bullinger, as well as Hyperius and Musculus. In the seventeenth and eighteenth centuries this trinitarian vision is represented well by John Owen and Jonathan Edwards. Even Protestant Scholasticism—much maligned even by some of the trinitarian theologians mentioned in this paper—offers a robustly trinitarian approach to worship. In the nineteenth century, trinitarian concerns run through the confessional theology of Charles Hodge and B. B. Warfield, as well as the Romantic thought of John Williamson Nevin.[15] In the twentieth century this trinitarian concern runs through several different streams of Reformed thought, including conservative confessionalism, Barthian neo-orthodoxy, and active contributions to the ecumenical and liturgical movements, with vivid examples in Dutch, Scottish, Swiss, French, American, and Korean communities, and now increasingly from Indonesia, East and West Africa, and beyond.[16] Reformed trinitarianism has been especially prominent in several ecumenical dialogues. The Orthodox-Reformed ecumenical dialogue, for example, focused all of its energies on the doctrine of the Trinity, including this stirring summary:

> The Reformed Churches appreciate the theological foundations of Orthodox worship and share with the Orthodox the conviction that all earthly forms of worship in the Church are a participation through the Spirit in the on-going worship which the risen and enthroned Christ, the Lamb of God, who is both "Offerer and Offering," constitutes in his own high-priestly self-presentation before the Father on behalf of all those whom he has redeemed and consecrated in union with himself.

---

[15] See R. A. Muller, *Post-Reformation Reformed Dogmatics: The Triunity of God*, 4 (Grand Rapids: Baker Book House, 2003); A. Plantinga Pauw, *"The Supreme Harmony of All": The Trinitarian Theology of Jonathan Edwards* (Grand Rapids: Eerdmans, 2002); R. Letham, *The Holy Trinity: In Scripture, History, Theology, and Worship* (Phillipsburg, NJ: P & R Pub., 2004); and P. Butin, *Revelation, Redemption, Response: Calvin's Trinitarian Understanding of the Divine-Human Relationship* (New York: Oxford University Press, 1995).

[16] See L. Vischer, *Christian Worship in Reformed Churches Past and Present* (Grand Rapids: Eerdmans, 2003).

They believe that this sharing in the worship of the Father, which Christ himself is, is the heart of the Church's Eucharistic worship and communion, and that it is from that centre that the life and the activity of the Church on earth are nourished and directed.[17]

Likewise, a recent report on Reformed-Lutheran ecumenical discussions speaks of "the Reformed emphasis on the Spirit, the trinitarian work of God, and the assembly of the faithful," where the "trinitarian fullness of the gift of the Supper" is realized because of "the Spirit's activity in lifting up the hearts of the faithful."[18] Consider three examples in more detail.

John Calvin

In the sixteenth century John Calvin's treatises and prayers express a particularly vivid trinitarian grammar of mediation. One of the clearest statements comes from a rarely studied treatise, "Summary of Doctrine Concerning the Ministry of the Word and Sacrament," which places this trinitarian vocabulary in the foreground of its explanation:

I. The end of the whole Gospel ministry is that God, the fountain of all felicity, communicate Christ to us who are disunited by sin and hence ruined, that we may from him enjoy eternal life; that in a word all heavenly treasures be so applied to us that they be no less ours than Christ's himself.

II. We believe the communication to be (a) mysterious, and incomprehensible to human reason, and (b) spiritual, since it is effected by the Holy Spirit; to whom, since he is the virtue of the living God, proceeding from the Father and the Son, we ascribe omnipotence, by which he joins us to Christ our Head, not in an imaginary way, but most powerfully and truly, so that we become flesh of his flesh and bone of his bone, and from his vivifying flesh he transfuses eternal life to us.

III. That we believe the Holy Spirit to effect this union rests on a certain ground, namely this: Whatever (a) the Father [John 14:16] or

[17] T. Torrance, ed., *Theological Dialogue between Orthodox and Reformed Churches* (Edinburgh: Scottish Academic Press, 1985) 5–6.
[18] K. F. Nickle and T. F. Lull, eds., *A Common Calling: The Witness of Our Reformation Churches in North America Today* (Minneapolis: Augsburg Fortress, 1993) 48, 47.

(b) the Son does to bring the faithful to salvation, Holy Scripture testifies that each operates through the Holy Spirit [John 15:26, 16:7]; and that (c) Christ does not otherwise dwell in us than through his Spirit, nor in any other way communicates himself to us than through the same Spirit [Rom. 8.9].

IV. To effect this union, the Holy Spirit uses a double instrument, the preaching of the Word and the administration of the sacraments.[19]

This is a vision of worship, to use Philip Butin's phrase, as "Trinitarian enactment," in which both God's coming to us in Word and Sacrament and our coming to God in praise and petition happen "in Christ, through the Spirit."[20] As Hughes Oliphant Old has repeatedly argued, "For Calvin the worship of the church is a matter of divine activity rather than human creativity."[21] Indeed, the Holy Spirit was the grammatical subject of many of Calvin's sentences about worship, preaching, and the sacraments. Calvin's acute perception of divine majesty and human finitude only serves to heighten the drama of this trinitarian movement. To use spatial terms: the greater the distance between divine majesty and human finitude, the greater the force of divine action that is required to restore communion and the greater the grace we can perceive in this movement. It is a vision of worship as a whirlwind of divine activity that the Reformed tradition has been catching up to ever since.

A significant feature of Calvin's trinitarian mapping was his stress on the human nature of the ascended Jesus as significant for the ongoing worship of the church. Drawing (remarkably) on a relational rather than Aristotelian view of space,[22] Calvin posited:

[19] John Calvin, *Calvin: Theological Treatises*, trans. J. K. S. Reid (Philadelphia: Westminster, 1977) I–IV.

[20] Philip Butin, *Revelation*, 102; idem, "Worship as Trinitarian Enactment," in *Reformed Ecclesiology: Trinitarian Grace according to Calvin: Studies in Reformed Theology and History* (Princeton: Princeton Theological Seminary, 1994) 19–27.

[21] Hughes Oliphant Old, "John Calvin and the Prophetic Criticism of Worship," in *John Calvin and the Church: A Prism of Reform*, ed. Timothy George (Louisville: Westminster/J. Knox, 1990) 234.

[22] See D. Farrow, *Ascension and Ecclesia: On the Significance of the Doctrine of the Ascension for Ecclesiology and Christian Cosmology* (Grand Rapids: Eerdmans, 1999) 174ff.

The same body, therefore, which the Son of God once offered to the Father in sacrifice, he daily offers us in the Supper as spiritual food . . . the virtue of the Spirit being sufficient to *break through* all impediments and surmount any *distance of place*. . . . Therefore in the sacred supper we acknowledge a miracle which surpasses both the limits of nature and the measure of our sense. . . . The secret virtue of the Spirit makes things *separated in space* to be united with each other, and accordingly enables life from the flesh of Christ to *reach us* from heaven.[23]

In sum, "what, then, our mind does not comprehend, let faith conceive: that the Spirit truly unites things separated in space."[24] As Douglas Farrow analyzes it: "Calvin saw that neither a Eutychian response (Jesus is omnipresent) nor a Nestorian one (absent in one nature but present in the other) will do, since either way Christ's humanity is neutralized and his role as our mediator put in jeopardy."[25] Calvin offered strong assent for a Chalcedonian Christology and insisted that the exalted Christ, in his human nature, intercedes for us in heaven. Since Calvin, the Reformed tradition has often been associated with an "Ascension christology" that stresses Jesus' ongoing work in heaven as prophet, priest, and king.

Like Jungmann, Calvin was also deeply concerned that this trinitarian vision might shape liturgical piety. The result of this trinitarian vision was, in Calvin's words, "trust in prayer, but also peace for godly consciences, while they safely lean upon God's fatherly mercy."[26] His sermons and commentaries featured extended passages addressed not primarily to scholars or pastors, but to worshipers. One of Calvin's fundamental worries—related to, but different from that of Jungmann—was that worshipers would never perceive this trinitarian activity, but have their attention instead fixed on concrete actions. If Jungmann was concerned about a theological "farsightedness" that did not perceive the "nearness" of God in Christ, Calvin was concerned

---

[23] John Calvin, "The Best Method of Obtaining Concord on the Sacraments," in *Selected Works of John Calvin*, vol. 2, ed. Henry Beveridge and Jules Bonnet, trans. Henry Beveridge (Grand Rapids: Cuttlefish, 1983) 575–78. Italics added to highlight the spatial metaphors.

[24] John Calvin, *Institutes of the Christian Religion*, 4.17.10 (Philadelphia: Westminster, 1973).

[25] Farrow, *Ascension and Ecclesia*, 177.

[26] Calvin, *Institutes*, 2.15.6.

about a spiritual "depth perception" in which the faithful did not perceive the heavenly reality "behind" or "above" their liturgical participation: "For as superstitious men foolishly and wickedly attach God to symbols, and, as it were, draw him down from his heavenly throne to render him subject to their gross inventions: [in contrast] so the faithful, piously and rightly, ascend from earthly signs to heaven."[27] And again, "[Superstition is] the disposition of the mind, when men imitate those services which are lawful and of which God approves, but keep their whole attention fixed on the outward form, and do not attend to their object or truth."[28] Note carefully: Superstition here is not pagan reliance on a wooden god. It is a sin of the mind or spirit, the failure to perceive the trinitarian cartography of liturgical action.

As critics regularly point out, Calvin's official liturgical texts are, by Orthodox, Catholic, or Anglican standards, very lean, and often do not reflect the full force of his theological writings. Yet alongside his official liturgies we must also study Calvin's sermons, lectures, and extemporaneous prayers; these are also liturgical acts, and would have represented a significant part of the experience of worship in Calvin's Geneva. Here references to the trinitarian grammar of worship abound. His goal was to help worshipers perceive the triune activity that made worship possible. Thus, worshipers would hear Calvin preach: "When then God speaks to us, by the mouth of men, then he adjoins the inward grace of his Holy Spirit, to the end, that the doctrine be not unprofitable, but that it may bring forth fruit. See then how we hear the heavenly Father: that is to say, when he speaks secretly to us by his Holy Spirit, and then we come unto our Lord Jesus Christ."[29] And they would hear Calvin pray at the conclusion of the Lord's Supper:

> Heavenly father, we offer you eternal praise and thanks that you have
> granted such a great benefit to us poor sinners, having drawn us into

[27] John Calvin, "On Genesis 33:21," in *Commentary on the Book of Genesis*, ed. and trans. John King (Carlisle, PA: Banner of Truth Trust, 2000).

[28] John Calvin, "Commentary on Isaiah 1:14" in *Commentary on the Book of the Prophet Isaiah*, vol. 1, trans. William Pringle (Grand Rapids: Eerdmans, 1979).

[29] John Calvin, "Third Sermon on Jacob and Esau," in *Ioannis Calvini opera quae supersunt omnia*, ed. Wilhelm Baum, Edward Cunitz, and Edward Reuss (Brunswick: C. A. Schwetschke, 1848) 58:54.

the communion of your Son, Jesus Christ, our Lord, whom you have delivered to death for us, and whom you give us as the meat and drink of eternal life. Now grant us also this additional benefit: that you will never allow us to forget these things; but that having them imprinted on our hearts, we may grow and increase daily in the faith which is at work in every good deed. And in this way, may we arrange and seek to live our whole life in the exaltation of your glory and edification of our neighbor, through the same Jesus Christ, your Son, who in the unity of the Holy Spirit lives and reigns with you, O God eternally. Amen.[30]

Here is a prayer that concludes with a high trinitarian doxology, reflects a trinitarian grammar of liturgical action, but also pastorally insists that we perceive ourselves as part of that trinitarian dynamic, with God "imprinting" these benefits on our hearts. As a number of commentators have argued, Calvin must be seen as one of the most ardent defenders of a trinitarian grammar of mediation in the Christian tradition.

The Torrances

In the last forty years this trinitarian grammar of worship has been explored in a particularly enthusiastic way by Scotland's quartet of Torrances (Thomas, James, Alan, and Iain), and their students. Taken together, their work offers hundreds of pages of analysis that explore this trinitarian vision of worship. Thomas Torrance sums up this work with the following definition: "In our worship the Holy Spirit comes forth from God, uniting us to the response and obedience and faith and prayer of Jesus, and returns to God, raising us up in Jesus to participate in the worship of heaven and in the eternal communion of the Holy Trinity."[31] Here again is a trinitarian vision that operates with a Chalcedonian Christology and places particular stress on the ongoing worship of Jesus in his human nature in heaven. It develops a theological trajectory that extends from patristic sources, through Calvin, through William Milligan's 1892 *The Ascension and Heavenly Priesthood of our Lord*—and is captured in the well-rehearsed line in Scottish Eucharistic liturgies that we "plead the eternal sacrifice of Jesus."[32]

---

[30] Calvin, "Form of Church Prayers," in ibid. (1867) 6:180.

[31] *Theology in Reconstruction* (Grand Rapids: Eerdmans, 1965) 250.

[32] B. D. Spinks, "The Ascension and the Vicarious Humanity of Christ: The Christology and Soteriology behind the Church of Scotland's Anamnesis and

The vision is given sharpest focus in Thomas Torrance's influential essay, "The Mind of Christ in Worship: The Problem of Apollinarianism in the Liturgy." Reflecting on the priestly office of Christ in light of Cyril of Alexandria's critique of Apollinarius, Torrance argued that Jesus' human mind is crucial in conceptualizing a trinitarian geography of worship. Jesus accomplishes perfect human worship in his humanity. Jesus, because of his full humanity, is able to represent us vicariously. Jesus is at once the perfecter and pattern of our praise. This vision of the human Jesus worshiping in heaven serves to dignify the humanity of our own offerings and to stress the sheer grace we have in participating in pure worship in Christ.[33]

Pastoral concern is crucial here, too. James B. Torrance is particularly concerned with theological schemes that correctly stress "God-humanward movement in Christ" but wrongly imply that "the human-Godward movement is still ours." He contends that this tendency functions as a liturgical Pelagianism which ignores the priesthood of Christ, such that "the only priesthood is our priesthood, the only offering our offering, the only intercessions our intercessions." This vision implies that "God throws us back upon ourselves to make our response" and ignores that "God has already provided for us that Response which alone is acceptable to him—the offering made for the

---

Epiklesis," in *Omnes Circumadstantes: Contributions towards a History of the Role of the People in the Liturgy*, ed. C. Caspers and M. Schneiders (Kampen: J. H. Kok, 1990), and J. M. Barkley, "'Pleading His Eternal Sacrifice' in the Reformed Liturgy," in *The Sacrifice of Praise: Studies on the Themes of Thanksgiving and Redemption in the Central Prayers of the Eucharistic and Baptismal Liturgies in Honour of Arthur Hubert Couratin*, ed. B. D. Spinks (Rome: C.L.V.-Edizioni liturgiche, 1981). See also W. Milligan, *The Ascension and Heavenly Priesthood of Our Lord* (London, 1892; repr. London: Macmillan, 1977).

[33] *Theology in Reconstruction*, 250. This theme echoes through J. Torrance, *Worship, Community, and the Triune God of Grace* (Downer's Grove, IL: InterVarsity Press, 1996); A. Torrance, *Persons in Communion*; and I. Torrance, "A Theological Interpretation of the Agreed Statements," in *Agreed Statements from the Orthodox-Reformed Dialogue*, ed. Lukas Vischer (Geneva: World Alliance of Reformed Churches, 1998) 25–35. For analysis of this theme, see E. M. Colyer, *How to Read T. F. Torrance: Understanding His Trinitarian & Scientific Theology* (Downers Grove: InterVarsity Press, 2001) 115–16, 263–72, and G. Hunsinger, "The Dimension of Depth: Thomas F. Torrance on the Sacraments," in *The Promise of Trinitarian Theology: Theologians in Dialogue*, ed. E. M. Colyer (Lanham: Rowman & Littlefield, 2001) 129–60.

whole human race in the life, obedience and passion of Jesus Christ." Torrance argues that this distorted view of worship is functionally unitarian, operating apart from the work on the Holy Spirit and the mediatorship of Christ.[34]

The Torrances speak frequently about the problem of substitute priesthoods. Thomas Torrance laments that "inevitably a substitute priesthood arises to mediate between us and Christ . . . in modern times, especially throughout the various Protestant Churches, this takes the form of a *psychological sacerdotalism.*"[35] Elsewhere he laments "how frequently the minister's prayers are so crammed with his own personality (with all its boring idiosyncracies!) that the worship cannot get past him in order to worship God in the name of Christ—but is forced to worship God in the name of the minister!"[36] The latest book in this vein, Graham Redding's *Prayer and the Priesthood of Christ in the Reformed Tradition*, is surely correct in noting that for many congregations today, the primary substitute priesthoods are music, the personality of its preacher or worship leader, and a variety of popular prayer techniques—all of which tend to "throw us back upon ourselves to make our response."[37] While the Torrances share with Calvin enthusiasm for the *ad-per-in* formula, their pastoral application offers a different emphasis, seeing the breakdown mostly in perceptions of the human-Godward movement of worship. In other words, the same trinitarian grammar corrects a slightly different pastoral problem than for Jungmann or Calvin.

---

[34] J. Torrance, *Worship, Community*, 18, 7, 43, also 50. Thomas Torrance is more acerbic in his description of this distortion: "Nothing could be more wrong than to reverse the movement of descent and ascent into a movement of ascent and descent for that would be to enunciate a doctrine of the ministry as Pelagian movement grounded upon an Adoptionist Christology and upon a heathen notion of atonement as act of man upon God, involving a correspondingly heathen notion of Eucharistic sacrifice" (*Royal Priesthood* [Edinburgh: Oliver and Boyd, 1955] 40).

[35] T. Torrance, *God and Rationality* (New York: Oxford University Press, 1971) 206. See also A. Torrance, *Persons in Communion*, 314.

[36] T. Torrance, *God and Rationality*, 167–68.

[37] Graham Redding, *Prayer and the Priesthood of Christ in the Reformed Tradition* (London: T&T Clark, 2003). See also D. Meeter, "The Trinity and Liturgical Renewal," in *The Trinity: An Essential for Faith in Our Time*, ed. Andrew Stirling (Nappanee, IN: Evangel Publishing House, 2002) 222.

North America

Third, the last decade has witnessed an unprecedented level of trinitarian interest in North America among parts of the Reformed tradition that often have little contact with each other—both mainline Presbyterians with an active record of participation in the liturgical and ecumenical movements, and conservative-confessional Reformed-Presbyterian voices from denominations that have not participated in broad ecumenical dialogues or in the twentieth century liturgical movement.

Among mainline voices active in the liturgical and ecumenical movements, the premier example of liturgical reform remains the 1993 *Book of Common Worship* (PCUSA). A well-celebrated service based on this book would begin with a trinitarian greeting from 2 Corinthians 13:14, include trinitarian epicleses before the reading and preaching of Scripture as well as at baptism and the Lord's Supper, feature several prayers that conclude with trinitarian doxologies, and end with a trinitarian charge and benediction. Such a service may well also include explicitly trinitarian hymns. Alert worshipers would discern that the service not only addresses prayers to the triune God, but also portrays God as the simultaneous recipient, motivator, and perfecter of worship, reflecting the trinitarian grammar of mediation. It is a spirit conveyed in several *Book of Common Worship* prayers, such as this prayer of intercession: "Gracious God, because we are not strong enough to pray as we should, you provide Christ Jesus and the Holy Spirit to intercede for us in power. In this confidence we ask you to accept our prayers."[38] Here, Christ is not merely an exemplar of good prayer, but the priest who prays on our behalf. In the *Book of Common Worship* and other

---

[38] *Book of Common Worship* (Louisville: Westminster John Knox, 1993) 103. Similar trinitarian emphases are found in the UCC *Book of Worship* (New York: Office for Church Life and Leadership, 1986), the CRC-related *Worship Sourcebook* (Grand Rapids: Calvin Institute of Christian Worship: Baker Book House, 2004), and the RCA *Worship the Lord* (New York: Reformed Church in America, 2005). The *Book of Common Order of the Church of Scotland* (Edinburgh: Saint Andrew Press, 1994) also features several of these practices, though arguably with a less thoroughgoing trinitarianism throughout. See K. Greene-McCreight, "What's the Story? The Doctrine of God in *Common Order* and the *Book of Common Worship*," in *To Glorify God: Essays on Modern Reformed Liturgy*, ed. B. D. Spinks and I. R. Torrance (Grand Rapids: Eerdmans, 1999) 99–114.

recently published service books, a trinitarian grammar of mediation is like DNA that works itself out in every part of the liturgy.

New service books have been complemented by a spate of writings by Reformed authors—with arguably more attention given to liturgy in the last decade than in the previous century or, for that matter, at any time since the 1540s. Significantly, much of this literature has probed how trinitarian worship involves much more than trinitarian flourishes at the end of prayers. It calls for explicit language throughout the liturgy, including preaching, and implicit confirmation in every aspect of the atmosphere of worship.[39] Thus, based on trinitarian logic, Donald Bruggink calls for architecture that does not give a feeling of "anxiety and nervousness" but of "response" and "serenity." Because worship is grounded in Word and Spirit, Christian worship and the space that houses it, should, says Bruggink, "reflect the peace with God" that worshipers have in Christ.[40] Thomas G. Long develops this logic of grace into an evocative metaphor for preaching, suggesting that "to be a preacher is to be a midwife. We do not create the word; we do not establish the time of its arriving; we cannot eliminate the labor pains that surround it; but we serve with gratitude at its coming and exclaim with joy at its birth."[41] And several writers speak of the grace of prayer, particularly epicletic and eucharistic praying.[42]

This trinitarian grammar has also received extensive recent study among quite a variety of conservative confessional Reformed voices, rarely represented at gatherings of the North American Academy of Liturgy or on membership rosters of the World Alliance of Reformed Churches or the World Council of Churches. Gerrit Scott Dawson

---

[39] The call for trinitarian preaching is most clear in M. Shuster, "Preaching the Trinity: A Preliminary Investigation," in *The Trinity: An Interdisciplinary Symposium on the Trinity*, ed. S. T. Davis et al. (Oxford: Oxford University Press, 1999) 357–81.

[40] Donald Bruggink, *Christ and Architecture* (Grand Rapids: Eerdmans, 1965) 446, 448.

[41] Thomas G. Long, *The Witness of Preaching* (Louisville: Westminster John Knox, 1989) 20–21.

[42] See C. D. Erickson, "The Strong Name of the Trinity," *Reformed Liturgy and Music* 19 (1985) 205–10; H. Hageman, "The Eucharistic Prayer in the Reformed Tradition." *Reformed Liturgy and Music* 22 (1988) 190–93; H. O. Old, *Leading in Prayer: A Workbook for Worship* (Grand Rapids: Eerdmans, 1995); and Vischer, "The Epiclesis," in *Christian Worship in Reformed Churches*, 30–39.

begins his *Jesus Ascended: The Meaning of Christ's Continuing Incarnation*, with a perceptive pastoral chapter diagnosing the contemporary church's "overidentification with the present age," in which life in American suburbia keeps us comfortable with a largely benign view of God and the worship of the church. He goes on to argue that the antidote to this pastoral problem is a vibrant awareness of Christ's ongoing mediation as a crucial dynamic in a trinitarian conception of worship. Likewise, Robert Letham, in his extended treatise *The Holy Trinity: In Scripture, History, Theology and Worship*, is concerned that much worship is "generally theistic" without any awareness that we live "in an atmosphere saturated by the Trinity," and Jeffery J. Meyers builds his theological explication of worship around the theme of "Trinity and Covenant Renewal Worship."[43]

Other sources confirm how pervasive the pastoral problems behind these concerns really are. In his much discussed book *Soul Searching: The Religious and Spiritual Lives of American Teenagers*,[44] the sociologist Christian Smith analyzes his large scale study of North American youth, contending that while today's youth are surprisingly religious, their operative theological vision is nevertheless one of "Moralistic Therapeutic Deism." Here the problem is not quite what Jungmann described: God is not so much perceived as distant and inaccessible but rather as close and altogether benign. A slightly different version of this pastoral diagnosis is offered by Cornelius Plantinga, who senses that the difficulty in teaching the mediation of Christ to a contemporary audience arises because many contemporary persons have no sense that

---

[43] G. S. Dawson, *Jesus Ascended: The Meaning of Christ's Continuing Incarnation* (Phillipsburg: P and R Publishing, 2004) 9; Letham, *The Holy Trinity*, 414; and J. J. Meyers, *The Lord's Service: The Grace of Covenant Renewal Worship* (Moscow, ID: Canon Press, 2003) 105–30. See also J. Frame, *Worship in Spirit and Truth* (Phillipsburg: P and R Publishing, 1996); D. G. Hart, *Recovering Mother Kirk: The Case for Liturgy in the Reformed Tradition* (Grand Rapids: Baker Academic, 2003) 102–3; M. Horton, *A Better Way: Rediscovering the Drama of God-Centered Worship* (Grand Rapids: Baker Books, 2002); and P. G. Ryken et al., eds., *Give Praise to God: A Vision for Reforming Worship: Celebrating the Legacy of James Montgomery Boice* (Phillipsburg: P and R Publishing 2003).

[44] Christian Smith, *Soul Searching: The Religious and Spiritual Lives of American Teenagers* (Oxford: Oxford University Press, 2005).

they need a mediator.[45] Despite a generation of renewed interest in trinitarian theology, it appears that Lesslie Newbigin's diagnosis is still apt: "the ordinary Christian in the Western world who hears or reads the word 'God' does not immediately and inevitably think of the Triune Being—Father, Son, and Spirit . . . [but rather] of a supreme monad."[46]

Summing Up

Several strands of Reformed theology insist on a basic trinitarian cartography for the God-human communion at the heart of worship. Worship is offered to the Father, through the Son, in the Spirit. This theological vision insists that worship is not an act of obeisance to appease a distant deity; an act of self-expression to impress a waiting God; a gift calculated to curry divine favor, or to generate, manipulate, or prevent divine activity. Worship is not an accomplishment to achieve, but a gift in which to participate. It is motivated not by fear, guilt, or shame, but by gratitude. Worship, to use an image from the Hebrew Scriptures, is more like Elijah's reception of fire from heaven on Mount Carmel than the frantic efforts of the opposing prophets to call forth the action of their gods.[47]

Yet this same basic vision needs to be applied differently in different eras. Jungmann was concerned that the trinitarian geography was too distant, with Christ, the mediator, too far away. Calvin worried that worshipers would be deaf to this trinitarian music altogether. The Torrances worry about church practice that unwittingly displaces the priesthood of Christ in our experience of prayer. North American

[45] Cornelius Plantinga, *A Place to Stand* (Grand Rapids: Board of Publications of the Christian Reformed Church, 1979) 99.

[46] Lesslie Newbigin, *The Open Secret: An Introduction to the Theology of Mission*, rev. ed. (Grand Rapids: Eerdmans, 1995) 27. This point was also acknowledged by participants in the 1984 Reformed/Anglican dialogue: "The image of God in the minds of many people in our churches is a unitary one—the solitary creator, the prime mover of the philosophers—consequently the doctrine of the Trinity has been regarded as an incomprehensible mystification of something simple" (*God's Reign and Our Unity* [London: S.P.C.K., 1984] 27).

[47] For use of the Mount Carmel narrative in discussions of worship as a graced event, see Torrance, *Worship, Community*, 50–53, and J.-J. von Allmen, *The Lord's Supper* (Richmond: John Knox, 1969) 80. See also T. G. Long, "Reclaiming the Unity of Word and Sacrament in Presbyterian and Reformed Worship." *Reformed Liturgy and Music* 16 (1982) 14–15.

pastors worry that today we have the opposite problem from Jung-mann, perceiving God as being so close that no mediator is needed.

A more extensive historical analysis would turn up examples where the formula breaks down in other ways. In some historical cases christology is too low to achieve any mediation. In other cases the Holy Spirit is virtually absent from the language of worship and the sensibility of the congregation. In others the Spirit is named as significant, but the Spirit is not identified as the Spirit of Christ. In still others worship is offered "through Jesus" but practice implies that it is offered in the power of energetic music or spiritual disciplines or intense introspection. In each case the basic trinitarian formula remains a source of prophetic challenge. It serves as a theological plumb line against which to test practice and piety, interrogating each culture, tradition, and even each congregation in a slightly different way.

THEME II: TRIFOCAL VISIONS OF THE DIVINE ACTION
Trinitarian theology as integrative

A second theme is concerned not with the mediation of Son and Spirit, but rather with how our theological imaginations hold together the works and attributes associated with Father, Son, and Spirit. "Trinitarian" here refers to an integrated vision of all divine activity. If the first theme essentially offers commentary on the church's response to Arianism, the second is commentary on the church's response to Marcion. If the first theme has to do with our spatial mapping of the divine-human relationship, the second has to do in part with our mapping of time. With a few notable exceptions, the second theme is less acknowledged in Reformed discussions of trinitarian worship despite its prevalence in systematic theology. Yet it has significant potential for addressing pressing problems in liturgical piety, given that persistent problems in liturgical piety today arise from sub-Christian views of time.

One of the most cited treatments of this theme was offered by H. Richard Niebuhr, who contended, only slightly whimsically, that Christianity might well be characterized as "an association, loosely held together, of three Unitarian religions." The first, a "unitarianism of the creator," worships "the Almighty Maker of heaven and earth, the first cause and the great designer" of the cosmos. The second, a "unitarianism of Jesus Christ" worships Jesus Christ, the source of redemption, and shows little interest in "philosophical explanations or in questions about man's place in nature." The third, predictably, a "unitarianism of the Spirit . . . looks to the reality found in the inner life rather than to the Being beyond nature or to the Redeemer in history for the fundamental principle of reality and value."[48] Niebuhr's main point is that Christians have a persistent tendency to narrow their view of God's actions and relationship to the world, and to separate, rank, and pit against each other aspects of the divine economy. In contrast, the doctrine of the Trinity calls for viewing God's actions as a comprehensive and unified whole. As Niebuhr argued, the doctrine serves as "a formulation of the *whole* Church's faith in God in distinction from the partial faiths and partial formulations of parts of the Church and of individuals in the Church." The doctrine is valuable "to correct the over-emphases and partialities of the members of the whole not by means of a new over-emphasis but by means of a synthesized formula in which all the partial insights and convictions are combined."[49] In sum, one central implication of Trinity doctrine is that the works of God, attributed as they are in scriptural narrative and the Christian tradition to Father, Son, and Holy Spirit, are not in any way disjointed or at cross purposes. The divine economy is not only unimaginably fulsome, but wondrously interrelated.

Among the many Reformed theologians to explore this theme, the Dutch theologian Arnold van Ruler is a particularly interesting example. Van Ruler's work reflects a post-Barthian appropriation of the vividly trinitarian concerns of the earlier Dutch theologians Abraham Kuyper and Herman Bavinck, whose writings are experiencing something of a renaissance in these years.[50] Van Ruler argued that all theological loci, such as soteriology and missiology, should be approached from both a "Christological" and "pneumatological" point of view.[51] In

---

[48] H. Richard Niebuhr, "The Doctrine of the Trinity and the Unity of the Church." *Theology Today* 3 (1946) 372, 374, 376.

[49] Ibid., 372, 383.

[50] Van Ruler advocated a "more catholic, that is to say, purely trinitarian way" of interpreting the divine economy, which would examine not just God's actions in Christ, but also in creation and eschatological fulfillment (*Calvinist Trinitarianism and Theocentric Politics*, trans. John Bolt [Lewiston: E. Mellen Press, 1989] 107). For Kuyper and Bavinck, see J. Bratt, ed., *Abraham Kuyper: A Centennial Reader* (Grand Rapids: Eerdmans, 1998), and H. Bavinck, *Reformed Dogmatics*, vol. 2, ed. John Bolt, trans. John Vriend (Grand Rapids: Baker Academic Press, 2004).

[51] See especially the essay, "Structural Differences Between Christological and Pneumatological Perspectives" in van Ruler, *Calvinist Trinitarianism*, 27–46.

his words: "The great synthesis of all the various elements of Christian truth is an *a priori* given in its first and proper (we could perhaps say only) dogma, the trinitarian dogma." Thus, he called for the interrelation of creation and redemption, redemption and the kingdom of glory, and creation and eschatology. These are *"the* questions," he insists, "that arise in a trinitarian theology": "it is only in a fully trinitarian framework that one is able to determine the meaning of reason, history, the state, art, and what it is to be human. To accomplish this, the doctrines of the creation and eschatology need to provide their own accents."[52] In sum, van Ruler argues for a synthetic approach where the often independent topics of creation, redemption, and eschatological fulfillment may enrich, delimit, and correct each other.

One of the most significant conceptual consequences of this synthetic approach is that redemption must be understood as a renewal of creation: "Regeneration is not a new creation (*nova creatio*) but a renewal of creation (*recreatio*)." Creation provides the context for understanding God's subsequent actions in history: "God does not create himself anew in Israel or in Jesus Christ. He [Jesus Christ] is not a new, strange God but the one who created the world. He is, thus, not estranged from the essence of things or from the depths of the human heart."[53] As Paul Fries summarizes: "Any mode of relationship which would deny, eclipse, or supersede God's creation van Ruler emphatically rejects, whether that mode be a contemporary form of Gnosticism depicting salvation as a rescue of the individual from this world or the eschatological enthusiasm for the novo creatio positing a new creation problematic in its relationship to the original creation."[54] This insistence generates a decidedly this-worldly account of divine action, salvation, and the Christian life: "It is thus characteristic of the Spirit to grasp us in our concrete reality."[55]

Of all of the underemphasized elements of the divine economy, van Ruler was most concerned to emphasize the work of the Holy Spirit. He was especially critical of Barth's christocentrism and argued for the "absolute necessity" of a vibrant and fulsome pneumatology in order

[52] Ibid., 1–2, 11, 14, 16, 19.

[53] Ibid., 32, 181, also 82.

[54] Paul Fries, "Van Ruler on the Holy Spirit and the Salvation of the Earth," *Reformed Review* 26 (1973) 123, and also "Spirit, Theocracy and the True Humanity: Salvation in the Theology of A. A. van Ruler," *Reformed Review* 39 (1986) 207–12.

[55] Van Ruler, *Calvinist Trinitarianism*, 82.

that "the imperative of a trinitarian theology would become apparent anew." He stressed the unique character of the Holy Spirit's work: "It is the Holy Spirit who, no less than the Son, is God Himself, and whose outpouring and indwelling is a new act of God of comparable significance to the incarnation."[56] He argued that a pneumatological framework makes two fundamental contributions to the structure of Christian theology: it points to the future kingdom of God as the end or goal of creation and redemption, and it compels theologians to consider the full scope of the Spirit's work inside and outside of the church. Van Ruler consistently emphasized the pluriformity of the Holy Spirit's work. An adequate pneumatic theology, he argued, points toward God's activity in all of creation.[57]

Similar themes echo in the writings of several Reformed theologians. The British theologian Colin Gunton, for example, calls for a theological vision like that of Irenaeus in which "creation, fall, redemption, and eschatology" are "thought together in their distinctness, but not separateness, and interrelatedness."[58] The South African theologian Adrio König calls for describing "salvation history in creation terminology," where redemption, the history of Israel, and Jesus Christ are each understood as a restoration of creation. He argues that this move prevents theologians from "keeping the Church and the world in separate, watertight compartments," prevents a reductionistic understanding of redemption as mere escape from the world, and challenges Christians to value, marvel at, and protect the created cosmos. König concludes: "Redemp-

---

[56] Ibid., 1, 11, 6, 60. On this aspect of van Ruler's pneumatology, see Fries, "Van Ruler," 123–35, and "Spirit, Theocracy," 206–14; J. Bolt, "The Background and Context of Van Ruler's Theocentric (Theocratic) Vision and its Relevance for North America," in *Calvinist Trinitarianism and Theocentric Politics* (Lewiston: E. Mellen Press, 1989) xxxvi; and D. Meeter, "Is the Reformed Church in America a Liturgical Church?" in *Pulpit, Table, and Song: Essays in Celebration of Howard Hageman*, ed. H. M. Elkins and E. C. Zaragoza (Lanham: Scarecrow Press, 2002) 207–32.

[57] Van Ruler contended that the Christian life is intimately linked with life in the world beyond the church. Indeed, the collection of his essays is entitled *Calvinist Trinitarianism and Theocentric Politics*. Van Ruler here is expressing a theme common in Dutch Reformed theology, that all of life is related to the sovereign rule of God.

[58] Colin Gunton, *The One, the Three, and the Many: God, Creation, and the Culture of Modernity* (Cambridge: Cambridge University Press, 1993) 158.

tion is not the repudiation of creation or the production of another, different creation, but the restoration and renewal of the original fallen creation." Redemption is not *from* this world, but *for* it.[59]

In sum, in van Ruler, Gunton, and König we discover a trinitarian method or habit of mind that seeks an integrated interpretation of the divine economy. This method highlights two particular themes: redemption as renewal of creation and the eschatological force and breadth of the work of the Holy Spirit.

An Integrative, Trinitarian Theology of Liturgy (e.g., J. J. von Allmen)

This emphasis on the comprehensive and integrated scope of God's activity has significant implications for the theology of worship. It suggests that Christian liturgy can best be understood in terms of the whole sweep of the divine economy. Christian worship—especially if it is conceived as a locus for divine action as theme one of this essay contends—is not isolated from God's actions of creation and re-creation, redemption and eschatological kingdom-building, but rather is interrelated with each.

No Reformed theologian pursued an integrated theology of liturgy as doggedly as the Swiss Reformed pastor and theologian Jean-Jacques von Allmen. Just as Gunton, van Ruler, and König approach systematic theology as a synthetic task, so von Allmen approached liturgy by examining the connections and relationships between liturgy and each aspect of divine work. Von Allmen did not write on the topic of theological methodology, and so did not comment extensively on this integrative approach. Yet important clues throughout his writings suggest that he was self-conscious about its importance. He called the Eucharist "a kind of crucible in which all the elements which constitute the gospel are combined." He suggested that "eucharistic theology . . . is a theology of complementary rather than contradictory alternatives," where one of the deadliest maladies is lack of balance and mutual interpretation: "Christian disunity threatens to isolate one particular element of the eucharistic life and make it distorted or heretical, not intrinsically, but because this particular element can no longer be completed or balanced by other elements in this life."[60] This

[59] Adrio König, *New and Greater Things* (Pretoria: University of South Africa, 1988) 145, 104–8, 144–46.

[60] Jean-Jacques von Allmen, *The Lord's Supper* (Richmond: John Knox, 1969) 9, 16–17.

integrating vision is based on an explicitly theological assumption regarding the unity of God's being and work: it is because the church worships "the One who is the same yesterday, today, and forever," and because God's work as Father, Son, and Spirit is a unified whole, that "the past, present, and future must be taken into account when a liturgical renewal is carried out."[61] Von Allmen linked this sense of the full scope of God's activity explicitly with trinitarian theology in this passage on preaching: "Christian preaching cannot therefore be understood apart from the doctrine of the Trinity: on the basis of the past work of His Son, and in the perspective of the work He is yet to do, God the Father gives us today, through the Holy Spirit, faith in the salvation which has been accomplished and hope in the salvation yet to be revealed."[62] In this way von Allmen argued that the doctrine of the Trinity is a confession of the unity and comprehensiveness of God's work, an invitation to approach liturgy in constant awareness of past, present, and future aspects of God's action.

Von Allmen developed this integrative theology of liturgy primarily in categories of time. He summed up his eucharistic theology by asserting that the Lord's Supper is the nexus "of anamnesis of the historical sacrifice of Christ, of self-dedication to Christ as the present High-Priest, and of anticipation of the messianic meal."[63] His theology of preaching began with the assertion that "preaching continues the past preaching of Jesus, and looks forward to the Word which He will speak at His return. That is why God Himself is at work at this present day, when we preach."[64] Of liturgy as a whole, von Allmen concluded, "There is a past, determinative for all time, which comes to life again in Christian worship. . . . There is also a future, determinative for all time, which finds in worship its prefiguration and the earnest of what it will be, and the absence of this too would mortally wound Christian worship."[65] Von Allmen worked, as it were, before a vast cosmic time line, the whole of which provides the interpretive framework for

[61] Ibid., 20.

[62] Jean-Jacques von Allmen, *Preaching and Congregation* (Richmond: John Knox, 1962) 8.

[63] Von Allmen, *The Lord's Supper*, 93, and also idem, "Worship and the Holy Spirit," *Studia Liturgica* 3 (1963) 129.

[64] Von Allmen, *Preaching and Congregation*, 7; also 32.

[65] Von Allmen, *The Lord's Supper*, 20.

understanding any of the constituent parts. Evoking Irenaeus, he spoke of liturgy as "a recapitulation of the whole history of salvation."

More specifically, von Allmen repeatedly returned to four aspects of the divine economy that he believed must be prominent in any integrated theology: creation; the life, death, and resurrection of Jesus; the present *missio Dei* in the world; and the eschatological kingdom of God. First, creation provides the basic framework, purpose, and goal for worship. "The divine purpose in creation," von Allmen wrote, is that humanity "should lead the entire universe in offering to the Creator a worship in which all creation would find its true fulfillment and know real peace . . . God's intention was basically a liturgical intention. . . . [Worship is] the expression of the mystery of creation!"[66]

Second, the life of Jesus Christ is "the centre of God's economy of salvation," its "obligatory point of reference," its "watershed." Von Allmen concludes: "It is of this messianic cult that the Church is both a memorial and an effective echo."[67]

Third, liturgy is intimately related to the ongoing work of the Holy Spirit in the world today. The Sunday gathering of the church is a time when the church is "expressly commissioned to be dispersed in the world, to penetrate it in every part, to live there on the Christ who has given himself to the Church, in order to make him known and loved in the world." He suggested that without a link to its apostolic function, the church "will get lost in archaism or modernism, in aestheticism or clericalism."[68] Von Allmen crystallized this point into a single metaphor: worship and work, liturgy and life are like the systolic and diastolic movements of the cardiovascular system. Balanced and integrated liturgy and mission, just like healthy cardial circulation, is the key to maintaining vitality in the life of the church.[69]

Fourth, von Allmen argued that Christian worship is irreducibly eschatological: "In summing up the process of salvation, the cult is also directed toward the future. It is not merely a representation of the death and victory of Christ, it is also an anticipation of His return and foreshadowing of the Kingdom which He will then establish." For von

[66] Von Allmen, *Preaching and Congregation*, 69–70.

[67] Von Allmen, *Worship: Its Theology and Practice* (London: Oxford University Press, 1965) 33, and (quoting Peter Brunner) 25.

[68] Von Allmen, *The Lord's Supper*, 13, 8.

[69] Von Allmen, *Worship: Its Theology and Practice*, 55, 77, 81; idem, *The Lord's Supper*, 23; and idem, "Worship and the Holy Spirit," 127.

Allmen, "Divine worship is an eschatological event. Its whole procedure is a sort of echo of the incarnation and a prefiguration of worship in heaven." The gathering is "already a participation in the worship of the Kingdom which will gather together the elect of all places and times that they may live for ever by the grace of the triune God, Father, Son and Holy Ghost, to glorify Him for ever."[70]

In sum, von Allmen's theology of liturgy is self-consciously linked with all aspects of God's action in the world. Worship "sums up the work of Him in whom God has summed up all things."[71] Thus, while von Allmen and van Ruler write with different temperaments and influences, they share (also with Gunton, König, and others) this trinitarian integrating impulse.

Pastoral Function:
Restoring Creational and Eschatological Piety and Practice
As with the mediation theme, this integrative theme also suggests ways to evaluate and deepen piety. It functions as a kind of trifocal habit of mind that is always on the lookout for distortions or disintegration. Some periods of church life suffer from otherworldliness, while some suffer from being too earthbound. Some periods tend toward conceiving of the Spirit apart from creation, some from emphasizing creation and law apart from redemption in Christ; some from obsessive concern with the details of Christ's second coming, others from almost no eschatological vision at all. In each case, a trifocal vision that insists on the unity of divine action offers, with rather elegant simplicity, a certain pastoral poise, a responsive posture to interrogate and address the strengths and weaknesses of any given cultural moment. Further, this trinitarian habit of mind also has a built-in humility about it, given that perfect synthesis is never achieved.

While Jungmann was primarily concerned with piety that viewed God as distant, many North American communities today face quite a different problem. In the celebrated words of Rabbi Abraham Heschel: "We know what to do with space but do not know what to do about

---

[70] Von Allmen, *Worship: Its Theology and Practice*, 35; idem, *Preaching and Congregation*, 32; idem, *Worship: Its Theology and Practice*, 199. See also B. Bürki, "Jean-Jacques von Allmen dans le Mouvement Liturgique." *Studia Liturgica* 16–17 (1986–87): 53–54, who identifies this theme as von Allmen's "préoccupation primordiale."

[71] Von Allmen, *Worship: Its Theology and Practice*, 102.

time."[72] Part of the contemporary problem is an obsession with the present moment. For comfortable North American worshipers and worship leaders today, the great temptation is to slip into expressions of petition, thanksgiving, and proclamation that are nearly exclusively focused on the present moment, perhaps an inevitable result of lives and churches that are content with the status quo. Part of the contemporary problem is a corresponding ambiguity or confusion about creation and eschatological fulfillment. Pastoral response calls for growth in two areas of liturgical piety: the development of a creational piety that looks back to the origins of the cosmos, and an eschatological piety that looks forward to the fullness of God's coming kingdom.[73]

All of this directly affects practice. A balanced, comprehensive, and integrated approach to the divine economy commends liturgical practices that ensure that the full scope of the divine economy is sensed and experienced by the worshiping community. It calls for a resounding "Amen" not only to the present priestly work of Christ, but also to God's gift of creation and the gift of new creation in eschatological time.

Specifically, this vision commends practices that depict the divine economy as a comprehensive and integrated whole: comprehensive hymns of praise, Scripture readings from both Old and New Testaments, the full narrative recital of divine activity in the ecumenical creeds, eucharistic prayers, and the (modest) recent revival of the Easter Vigil service even among Protestants. For example, as von Allmen

---

[72] Abraham Heschel, *The Sabbath* (New York: Farrar, Straus and Young, 1951) 4–5.

[73] H. O. Old, *Themes and Variations for a Christian Doxology* (Grand Rapids: Eerdmans, 1992) 109–10, and J.-J. von Allmen, *Worship: Its Theology and Practice,* 158–70. See also Meeter, "Is the Reformed Church," 198; A. C. Honders, "Remarks on the Postcommunio in Some Reformed Liturgies," in *The Sacrifice of Praise: Studies on the Themes of Thanksgiving and Redemption in the Central Prayers of the Eucharistic and Baptismal Liturgie,* ed. B. D. Spinks (Rome: C.L.V.-Edizioni liturgiche, 1981) 146, 147, 148; H. Hageman, "The Law in the Liturgy," in *God and the Good: Essays in Honor of Henry Stob,* ed. C. Orlebeke and L. Smedes (Grand Rapids: Eerdmans, 1975) 45; L. Briner, "Worship in the Name of Jesus: Reflection upon Cross and Resurrection as Controlling Event and Metaphor in the Worship of Christians." *Reformed Liturgy and Music* 12 (1978) 43; and H. Stob, *Ethical Reflections: Essays on Moral Themes* (Grand Rapids: Eerdmans, 1978) 61.

stressed, in the creed "the Church gives back to God in its *wholeness* that Word which He addressed to it in the Gospel; . . . that is to say that the Credo is not merely the response of the Church to the Word partially proclaimed during a particular service, but to the whole Gospel."[74] The Christian year is also an important strategy for achieving a comprehensive and integrated view of the divine economy. The Christian year, said von Allmen, "gives the faithful the opportunity to experience *the fullness* of the mystery of salvation."[75] In addition, a particularly vivid integrating practice among Protestant traditions has been four-stanza trinitarian hymns that devote a stanza to each divine person and conclude with a trinitarian doxology. Such symmetry is not essential to trinitarian worship, but it is a simple strategy for highlighting this trifocal vision.

The Lord's Supper is perhaps the place where a comprehensive yet integrated vision is most intensely focused. Thomas Long notes that while "preaching, of necessity, is selective . . . the sacrament works to place the particularities of preaching into the context of the whole mystery of resurrection faith."[76] For this reason the fullness of the divine economy is reflected not just in theologies of the Lord's Supper but also in eucharistic practice. Thus, Bruno Bürki calls churches to "imagine a Eucharist which is clearly and fully trinitarian in structure, language, and, above all, inspiration."[77] One of the greatest gains in the 1993 Presbyterian *Book of Common Worship* and the 2004 *Worship Sourcebook* is the explicitly trinitarian shape of their eucharistic prayers.[78]

---

[74] Von Allmen, *Worship: Its Theology and Practice*, 166, emphasis added.

[75] Ibid., 235, emphasis added.

[76] Long, "Reclaiming," 17. See also D. Migliore, *Faith Seeking Understanding: An Introduction to Christian Theology* (Grand Rapids: Eerdmans, 1991) 220–21; Erickson, "The Strong Name," 67; and K. B. Westerfield Tucker, "The Eucharist in the *Book of Common Worship* (1993)," *Princeton Seminary Bulletin* 16 (1995) 147.

[77] "The Lima Text as a Standard for Current Understandings and Practice of the Eucharist." *Worship* 16 (1986–87) 65. See also R. P. Byars, *Lift Your Hearts on High: Eucharistic Prayer in the Reformed Tradition* (Louisville: Westminster John Knox, 2005) 55–83.

[78] Arlo Duba notes that in the most recent compilation of prayers for the *Book of Common Worship*, attention was given to "balance the dual anamnetic dimensions of the past and the future; of the historic sacrifice of Christ (the

A comprehensive, balanced, and integrated vision of divine activity also has particular significance for the practice of liturgical prayer—an especially important theme to explore in light of the pervasiveness of extemporaneous prayer in much of Reformed and Presbyterian practice. Prayers of thanksgiving, for example, depend upon an interpretation of particular events as acts of God. As Christoph Schwöbel observes, in prayers of gratitude, "We acknowledge thereby that God is a free agent who could have acted otherwise, but who chose to act in such a way that human beings can express their gratitude for the way he has acted." The unity of the divine economy, notes Schwöbel, provides the necessary background against which "earlier events interpreted as acts of God can be used as the interpretive framework to identify other events as the acts of God."[79] Unity in the divine economy makes thanksgiving possible. That unity is naturally reflected in narratively-shaped prayers that rehearse and express gratitude both for actions long held to be divine and for recent events that are newly interpreted as divine action. This approach corrects extemporaneous prayers that reflect overconfidence in our ability to discern divine work as well as prayers that reflect a kind of agnostic refusal to attribute anything to divine action.

Similarly, intercessory prayer depends upon a confidence that God will act faithfully in the future. The past actions of God, says Colin Gunton, provide "the ground for believing that there are further divine acts to come, or that the ascended Christ is a living and active advocate with the Father, or that the Spirit works to perfect the creation." Relying on his trinitarian vision of the divine economy, Gunton continues, "If God is the one who creates and redeems through Christ and the Spirit, and is made known as such by the incarnate, crucified, risen, and ascended Jesus, then that is the one he always is. Any new action, therefore, can be expected within the framework of this eternal revela-

---

death-resurrection) and of festive, jubilant participation in the kingdom which is to come." See Arlo Duba, "Presbyterian Eucharistic Prayers," in *New Eucharistic Prayers: An Ecumenical Study of Their Development and Structure*, ed. F. C. Senn, 96–126 (New York: Paulist Press, 1987), 109, 110, and idem, "Hints for a Morphology of Eucharistic Praying: A Study of John 13:31–17:26." *Worship* 57 (1983) 376.

[79] Christopher Schwöbel, "Divine Agency and Providence," *Modern Theology* 3 (1987) 228.

tion."[80] Similarly, Adrio König contends that the unity of the divine economy means that "God may be proclaimed as the one who can do again what once he did." A doctrine of God derived from the economy points to who God is, how God acts, and therefore "what we may expect" of this God.[81] Likewise, von Allmen concluded, Christian prayers must not express any statement or wish, but "should be controlled by what we know of God's will revealed in Jesus Christ."[82] This theological point grounds the liturgical practice of linking praise and petition in fitting ways. Indeed, one liturgical correlate of the confession of the unity of the divine economy is forms of prayer (e.g., the collect) that recite divine actions as the basis for present thanksgiving and petition.

Yet in practice congregations still suffer from extemporaneous prayers that do not benefit from this theologically-grounded form, and from by-the-book praying that does not perceive the genius and pastoral significance of its forms. What is needed are criteria to highlight the strengths of historic prayer forms and to guide the practice of extemporaneous prayer. Consider, for example, the criteria implied in these evaluative questions:

1. Is a given text a prayer to the triune God that also stresses the Christ's role in perfecting the prayer and the Spirit's role in prompting it?

2. Is Christ presented not just as an exemplar of prayer, but also as mediator?

3. Does the scope of the prayer (in both thanks and petition) include all of creation and does it affirm the goodness of creation?

4. Does the prayer have eschatological momentum that expresses longing for the fullness of triune blessing?

5. Does the prayer offer thanks and blessing for the kinds of past divine activity that correspond with the kind of divine activity being asked for the petitions?

---

[80] Colin Gunton, *A Brief Theology of Revelation* (Edinburgh: T&T Clark, 1995) 80.

[81] Adrio König, *New and Greater Things*, 175–76, and *Here Am I: A Believer's Reflections on God* (Grand Rapids: Eerdmans, 1982) 160.

[82] Jean-Jacques von Allmen, "The Theological Meaning of Common Prayer," *Studia Liturgica* 10 (1976) 129.

Questions like these help to pass on the wisdom we inherit from historic sources to contemporary audiences, particularly to Reformed and Presbyterian audiences (and others in free-church or low-church liturgical traditions) who do not regularly use officially approved liturgical resources.

To summarize this second theme: trinitarian worship rehearses the full scope and unity of divine action, confident that each action is part of a unified, integrated whole. Otto Weber once argued that a deficient appropriation of the doctrine of the Trinity and an incomplete or unintegrated view of the divine economy has inevitable repercussions in prayer and spirituality: "It is only when we constantly keep the unity of God in his work in view that we can avoid an isolated 'theology of the first article,' or an isolated 'Christocentrism,' or an isolated 'Spiritualization' of theology." In fact, said Weber, "It can be said that at this point the Doctrine of the Trinity gains its most direct relationship to 'piety' . . . when the Doctrine of the Trinity falls apart or retreats in the consciousness of the Community, then piety becomes one-sided and, measured by the liveliness and the wealth of the biblical witness, is impoverished."[83] That is, at its best this trinitarian vision of worship also entails pastoral concern for piety that perceives its beauty.

Taken together, the two main themes of this paper offer an accessible plumb line by which to both comprehend and to test liturgical practice. Trinitarian worship offered to the Father, through Christ, in the Spirit conceives of God as the One who acts "before" us, "within" us, and "alongside" of us to receive, prompt, and perfect our worship—divine action in continuity with both past and future divine actions. Trinitarian pastoral concern calls for helping worshipers sense the grace, beauty, and majesty of this vision. This vision challenges the reigning assumptions and practices of each historical period in a slightly different way, guiding the pastoral and prophetic message needed in each generation.

To propose a metaphor: liturgy is the *prism* by which Christian communities perceive the fullness of the divine economy and through which communities sense the significance of each aspect of the economy for worship, doctrine, and life. It was Isaac Newton who grasped that white light was made up of the spectral colors of the rainbow. A prism is a triangular piece of clear glass that bends light as it passes

[83] *Foundations of Dogmatics*, vol. 1 (Grand Rapids: Eerdmans, 1982) 393.

through its apex, allowing viewers to see the whole spectrum. Christian liturgy is a moment in time and space in which—through word and sacrament, prayer and praise—the church, through the power of Spirit, perceives and participates in the remarkable multiplicity of perfectly unified divine action, and enjoys a foretaste of the communion of divine life. No wonder Jonathan Edwards concluded, "God has appeared glorious to me on account of the Trinity."[84]

---

[84] *Personal Narrative*, as cited in A. Plantinga Pauw, *The Supreme Harmony of All: The Trinitarian Theology of Jonathan Edwards* (Grand Rapids: Eerdmans, 2002) 1.

Chapter 12

Trinity and Christology in the Communion Hymns of Isaac Watts

Stephen A. Marini
Wellesley College

Isaac Watts (1674–1748) was the founder of English Protestant hymn-ody.[1] Miles Coverdale, Thomas Sternhold, John Hopkins, and Nahum Tate preceded Watts as versifiers of the biblical psalms, and George Wither, George Herbert, John Mason, Thomas Ken, Richard Baxter, William Barton, Joseph Stennett, and Benjamin Keach wrote original hymns before him. But Watts exceeded them all in the range, quality, and quantity of his hymns and metrical psalms. He also holds pride of place because he laid the theological and literary foundations of the evangelical poetics practiced by Charles Wesley and a host of successors to the present day.[2]

Watts's fame rests on three principal poetical works, *Horae Lyricae: Poems Chiefly of the Lyrical Kind* (1706), *Hymns and Spiritual Songs in Three Books* (1707), and *The Psalms of David Imitated in the Language of the New Testament* (1719). These immensely popular collections made Watts the most widely published Dissenting writer in eighteenth-

---

[1] I am grateful to David L. Wykes, Director of Dr. Williams's Library, London and joint Director of the Dr. Williams's Centre for Dissenting Studies, Queen Mary University of London, for commenting on an earlier version of this essay.

[2] For the development of English hymnody before Watts, see Louis F. Benson, *The English Hymn: Its Development and Use in Worship* (New York: Hodder and Stoughton, 1915) 45–107; Harry Escott, *Isaac Watts, Hymnographer: A Study of the Beginnings, Development, and Philosophy of the English Hymn* (London: Independent Press, 1962) 67–117; and J. R. Watson, *The English Hymn: A Critical and Historical Study* (New York: Oxford University Press, 1997) 57–132.

300

century Anglo-America and even gained him a modest place in Samuel Johnson's *Lives of the English Poets* (1781).[3]

In *Horae Lyricae* Watts rejected Restoration classicism and commenced his lifelong project of renewing sacred poetry. "The naked themes of Christianity," he wrote in the preface to the second edition of 1709, "have something bolder and brighter in them, something more surprizing and celestial than all the adventures of Gods and Heroes. . . . How wondrous a conquest might be obtain'd over the wild world, . . . if the . . . happy talent [of poetry] were employ'd in dressing the scenes of religion in their proper figures of majesty, sweetness, and terror."[4] In his two later works Watts developed a new system of praise for English Dissent and executed it with hymnody and metrical psalmody of a high order. In the 1709 Preface to *Hymns and Spiritual Songs* Watts declared flatly that "of all our religious solemnities, psalmody is the most unhappily managed." He rejected the Reformed dictum that only biblical songs, particularly the psalms, should be sung in congregational worship. "Many of them are foreign to the state of the New Testament," he wrote, "and widely different from the present circumstances of Christians."[5] Watts bluntly presented his "human composures" in *Hymns and Spiritual Songs* as a remedy. "The most frequent tempers and changes of our spirit, and conditions of our life, are here copied," he wrote of his own hymns, "and the breathings of our piety expressed according to the variety of our passions."[6] In *The Psalms of David Imitated* Watts took the still more radical step of remodeling the psalms for Christian worship. Seeking to make David

[3] Samuel Johnson, *Lives of the English Poets*, ed. G. B. Hill (Oxford: Clarendon Press, 1905) 3:302–11.

[4] Isaac Watts, *Horae Lyricae. Poems, Chiefly of the Lyric Kind, in Three Books*, 2nd ed. (London: J. Humfreys for N. Cliff, 1709) vi, xiv–xv.

[5] Isaac Watts, *Hymns and Spiritual Songs. In Three Books. I. Collected from the Scriptures. II. Compos'd on Divine Subjects. III. Prepared for the Lord's Supper*, 2nd ed. (London: Printed by J. H[umphreys] for John Lawrence, 1709) iii and iv. Hereafter *HSS*. The closest thing to a modern critical edition of this or any of Watts's works is Selma L. Bishop's *Hymns and Spiritual Songs, 1707–1748: A Study in Early Eighteenth Century Language Changes* (London: Faith Press, 1962). Bishop reprints the second edition (1709) and notes all textual variations from the first sixteen English editions.

[6] *HSS*, vii.

"speak like a Christian" to worshipers, he proposed to "imitate" his psalms "in the language of the New Testament."[7]

To achieve these goals Watts sought to create a consensus hymnody for Old Dissent. "I have avoided the more obscure and controverted points of Christianity," he explained in the Preface to *Hymns and Spiritual Songs*, "that we might sing [God's] praises with understanding. The contentions and distinguishing words of sects and parties are secluded, that whole assemblies might assist at the harmony, and different churches join in the same worship without offence."[8] He therefore composed his lyrics as simply as possible for maximum comprehension. "The whole book is written in four sets of metre," he wrote, "and fitted to the most common tunes. . . . The metaphors are generally sunk to the level of vulgar capacities. I have aimed at ease of numbers, and smoothness of sound, and endeavoured to make the sense plain and obvious."[9]

These elements of Watts's "renovation of psalmody" have been carefully assessed by generations of hymnologists. What has largely escaped notice, however, is that despite his insistence to the contrary, Watts's "hymns of human composure" were deeply influenced by innovative liturgical theologies and contested trinitarian doctrines.[10] Interpreters have tended to grant uncritically Watts's claim that his sacred lyrics were theologically nonpartisan, and they have accordingly failed to place them adequately in their doctrinal and historical contexts. Book III of *Hymns and Spiritual Songs* offers an especially rich example of these neglected historical, liturgical, and doctrinal influences. Watts "prepar'd" Book III "for the holy ordinance of the Lord's Supper," finding David's psalms wholly inadequate for expressing the great eucharistic themes of atoning sacrifice and faithful memorial. For Watts, the liturgical incoherence of singing non-Christian praise at

---

[7] Isaac Watts, *The Psalms of David Imitated in the Language of the New Testament and Applied to the Christian State and Worship*, in *The Works of the Rev. Isaac Watts, D.D. in Nine Volumes* (Leeds: Edward Baines, 1813) 9:33. Hereafter *PDI*.

[8] *HSS*, vii–viii.

[9] *HSS*, viii.

[10] The major scholarly treatments of Watts's hymnody are Benson, *The English Hymn*, 108–218; Escott, *Isaac Watts*, 173–217; Watson, *The English Hymn*, 133–70; and A. P. Davis, *Isaac Watts: His Life and Works* (New York: Dryden Press, 1943) 156–215. None of these works, however, interpret Watts's hymns in the context of his doctrinal writings or in the framework of Old Dissent.

302

the defining act of Christian worship demanded a new collection of sacred lyrics, so that "in imitation of our blessed Saviour we might sing a hymn after we have partaken of the Bread and Wine."[11]

Book III is by far the smallest of the three books of lyrics in *Hymns and Spiritual Songs*, containing just twenty-five hymns on the Lord's Supper and fifteen doxologies based on the *Gloria Patri*. Watts thought that "above an hundred hymns" elsewhere in *Hymns and Spiritual Songs* were appropriate and possibly even "more suitable" to the Supper than those in Book III, yet he "distinguished and set by themselves" this third group of lyrics "because there are expressions generally used in these, which confine them only to the table of the Lord."[12]

While the hymns in the first two books range across many Scripture paraphrases and "divine subjects," Book III focuses entirely on the Lord's Supper and trinitarian doxological responses to it. As such, it constitutes the most thorough address to any theological topic in Watts's entire hymnodic corpus. Book III presents Watts's evangelical theology of the Supper and a multifaceted exploration of its associated trinitarian doctrines. When placed in the context of Watts's other early writings, moreover, the communion hymns and doxologies gain further resonance as commentary on the trinitarian and christological controversies that troubled him and eventually fractured Old Dissent in England in the early eighteenth century.

In this essay I will argue that Watts's experience of those controversies crucially influenced not only the theology and imagery of individual eucharistic and trinitarian poems in Book III, but the careful structural design of its poetic sequence as well. Most importantly, Watts's distinctively pluralistic voice, presenting various positions on these essential doctrines, emerged out of his response to the growing trinitarian crisis of Old Dissent. The latitude of his response, combined with the emotional fervor with which he articulated it, enabled Watts to produce hymnody that ultimately bridged the way from Old Dissent to New Dissent in England, and from Puritanism to Evangelicalism in America.

---

[11] *PDI*, 28–29; *HSS*, xii.
[12] *HSS*, xii.

TRINITARIAN AND LITURGICAL CONTEXTS OF WATTS'S *HYMNS AND SPIRITUAL SONGS*

Watts composed *Hymns and Spiritual Songs* during a fifteen-year period that witnessed the rise of the Trinitarian Controversy in English Protestantism. While Anglican writers carried out most of the public disputation, the Controversy also powerfully influenced the Presbyterian, Independent, and Baptist communions of Old Dissent. Watts studied, ministered, and wrote hymns in this increasingly heated environment of trinitarian disputation. *Hymns and Spiritual Songs* was first published in 1707 and revised only once, in 1709. Its communion hymns and doxologies reflect Watts's experience of the early trinitarian debates at the turn of the eighteenth century.

Little is known about Watts's first encounters with these doctrines, but the Trinitarian Controversy broke out in earnest while he was a student at Thomas Rowe's Dissenting academy at Newington Green, London, between 1690 and 1693. In a letter to his brother Enoch written during this period, Watts offered succinct summaries of Arianism and Socinianism that reflect ample familiarity with these heterodox views of the Trinity.[13] The source of Watts's exploration of alternative theologies was most likely Thomas Rowe's rigorous intellectual training, which exposed him to the Enlightenment methodologies of doubt and rational certainty in Descartes, Locke, and Pufendorf. David L. Wykes has observed of Dissenting academies like Rowe's that "with respect to controversial questions of doctrine, the method of instruction adopted by the tutors involved presenting defences of both the orthodox and heterodox positions. Exposing students to the different arguments, however, encouraged some to question the very doctrines that the teaching was intended to defend. Perhaps more important than the ideas themselves was the encouragement given to the principle that students should discover the truth for themselves."[14] An annotated list of books Watts kept during these years suggests that just such an intellectual opening happened to him at Rowe's academy.

---

[13] Isaac Watts to Enoch Watts, undated (ca. 1690–1694), in George Burder, *Memoirs of the Life and Writings of Isaac Watts, D.D.* (London: J. Barfield, 1806) 110–11.

[14] David L. Wykes, "The Contribution of the Dissenting Academy to the Emergence of Rational Dissent," in *Enlightenment and Religion: Rational Dissent in Eighteenth-Century Britain*, ed. Knud Haakonssen (Cambridge: Cambridge University Press, 1996) 128.

One interpreter has concluded from this list that Watts was "shaken by the combination of scholarship and disbelief that he encountered" in his tutor's syllabus.[15]

Watts's own trinitarian ferment continued while he was employed for five years as a tutor in the household of Sir Thomas Hartopp of Stoke Newington after graduating from Rowe's academy. During these years the Trinitarian Controversy took a new direction with the publication of John Locke's *Reasonableness of Christianity* (1695) and John Toland's *Christianity Not Mysterious* (1696). These works ignited the long-smoldering problem of the compatibility of reason and revelation and openly questioned the rationality of orthodox trinitarian and christological doctrines. The works of Locke and Toland caused a theological sensation that may also have attracted the unsettled young Watts. He confided to his friend Pocyon in a 1696 letter that "when I have given my Thoughts a loose, and let them rove without confinement, I seem to have carried reason with me even to the camp of Socinus; but then St. John gives my soul a twitch and St. Paul bears me back again . . . almost to the Tents of John Calvin. Nor even then do I leave my reason behind me. So difficult a Thing it is to determine by mere Reasoning those Points which can be learnt by Scripture only."[16]

During this period of theological questioning Watts began writing the poems that would become *Horae Lyricae, Hymns and Spiritual Songs*, and *The Psalms of David Imitated*.[17] The poems continued to accumulate after Watts was ordained in 1699 as assistant to Isaac Chauncy at Mark Lane Independent Chapel, a prestigious Dissenting congregation in London. A letter of March, 1700, from his brother Enoch indicates that a large number of hymns already existed.[18] Two years later, at the age of twenty-eight, Watts succeeded Chauncy as senior pastor at Mark Lane Chapel.

Watts seems to have resolved his earlier struggles with the Trinity by the time of his ordination, but at the cost of an inward debate the vehemence of which still showed through in an account of rejecting

---

[15] W. E. Stephenson, "Isaac Watts's Education for the Dissenting Ministry: A New Document," *Harvard Theological Review* 61 (1968) 280.

[16] Isaac Watts, *Reliquae Juveniles: Miscellaneous Thoughts in Prose and Verse, In Natural, Moral, and Divine Subjects; written chiefly in Younger Years* (London: Richard Ford and Richard Hett, 1734) XLIX, 189.

[17] Davis, *Isaac Watts*, 201.

[18] Enoch Watts to Isaac Watts, March, 1700, in Burder, *Memoirs*, 110–11.

Socinianism during his "younger years" written more than twenty years after the fact. "So perverse and preposterous did their sense of the scripture appear," he wrote in 1722 of Socinians at the turn of the century, "that I was amazed how men, who pretended to reason above their neighbours, could wrench and strain their understandings, and subdue their assent to such interpretations."[19] Watts's acceptance of trinitarian orthodoxy also entailed the embrace of cumbersome and ultimately unconvincing Reformed apologetics that he came to regret. "I was led easily into scholastic forms of explication," he later recalled, "this being the current language of several centuries. And thus unawares I mingled those opinions of the schools, with the more plain and scriptural doctrine, and thought them all necessary to my faith."[20]

If Watts found Reformed trinitarian apologetics unduly arcane, however, his experience of the Lord's Supper at Mark Lane Chapel was quite the opposite. The congregation's Supper ritual consisted of a simple rehearsal of the words of institution with no eucharistic preface, and with extempore prayers over each of the elements and distribution in both kinds. A communion discourse preceded the Supper while the singing of a hymn or doxology followed it. Horton Davies interpreted Mark Lane Chapel's celebration of the Supper as "formally Zwinglian in its symbolical and memorialist interpretation, yet the special communion discourses and the prayers imply not a doctrine of the 'real absence' but of the 'Real Presence.'"[21] In such a liturgical environment Watts developed a view of the Supper that emphasized the emotional power of its memorial action to bring believers into closer communion with Christ and one another.

Meanwhile the Trinitarian Controversy continued to flare as Newtonian speculations entered the debate from the pens of Samuel Clarke and William Whiston. Clarke (1675–1729) came under the influence of Isaac Newton while a student at Caius College, Cambridge. Between

---

[19] Isaac Watts, *The Christian Doctrine of the Trinity: or, Father, Son, and Spirit, Three Persons and one God, Asserted and Proved, with Their Divine Rights and Honors Vindicated, by Plain Evidence of Scripture without the Aid or Encumbrance of Human Schemes* in *The Works of Isaac Watts, D. D. in Six Volumes*, ed. David Jennings and Philip Doddridge (London: T. and T. Longman, 1753) 6:415.

[20] Isaac Watts, *Sermons on Various Subjects* 3 (London: John Clark and Richard Hett, Emanuel Mathews, Richard Ford, 1727) x–xi.

[21] Horton Davies, *Worship and Theology in England*, 3: *From Watts and Wesley to Maurice, 1690–1850* (Princeton: Princeton University Press, 1961) 101–4.

1704 and 1707, Clarke published his Boyle Lectures under the title *Demonstration of the Being and Attributes of God*, an attack on Deism that nonetheless conceded the rationality of some of its anti-trinitarian arguments. The last of Clarke's Boyle Lectures appeared just as Watts was preparing the first editions of *Horae Lyricae* (1706) and *Hymns and Spiritual Songs* (1707). Whiston (1667–1752), Newton's successor from 1702 to 1710 as Lucasian Professor of Mathematics at Cambridge, proposed what he called a "Eusebian" anti-trinitarian doctrine in his *Sermons and Essays* (1709), for which he was expelled from the university. As Whiston's controversial views became known, Watts was writing the great prefaces for the second editions of *Horae Lyricae* and *Hymns and Spiritual Songs*, both published in 1709.[22]

The best evidence for Watts's early trinitarian and liturgical theologies comes from two sermons that he preached at the outset of his ministry. The first of these, "The Scale of Blessedness, or, Blessed Saints, Blessed Saviour, and Blessed Trinity," was published in 1721. According to Watts's note, however, it was "delivered near twenty years ago," that is, close to his ordination in 1702, and was still "very agreeable to my present sentiments on this subject."[23] "The Scale of Blessedness" is the second half of a two-part discourse on Psalm 65:4: "Blessed is the man whom thou choosest, and causest to approach unto thee, that he may dwell in thy court." Watts drew the doctrine from this text that "nearness to God is the foundation of a creature's happiness."[24] He did not mean "nearness" in the nineteenth- and twentieth-century sense of emotional intimacy with Jesus, but rather as proximity to the divine construed through the popular Neoplatonist idea of the Great Chain of Being.[25]

[22] Davis, *Isaac Watts*, 202. For a brief account of Clarke and Whiston, see Michael Watts, *The Dissenters from the Reformation to the French Revolution* (Oxford: Clarendon Press, 1978) 371–73.

[23] Isaac Watts, "The Scale of Blessedness, or, Blessed Saints, Blessed Saviour, and Blessed Trinity," *Sermons on Various Subjects*, 1 (London: John Clark, Emanuel Mathews, and Richard Ford, 1721) 400.

[24] Ibid., 349–73. This was the doctrine for both of Watts's sermons on Psalm 65:4, as stated in the first of them titled "Nearness to God the Felicity of Creatures."

[25] See Arthur O. Lovejoy, *The Great Chain of Being: A Study of the History of an Idea* (Cambridge, MA: Harvard University Press, 1936).

The first part of the sermon describes five ascending "degrees of blessedness" beginning with sinners who "are brought so near to God, as to be within the sound and call of his voice," and ending with "the blessedness of the three glorious persons in the Trinity." Believers and angels ranged in between. At the top of the scale, however, Watts distinguished between the degree of nearness to God that "the man Christ Jesus" experienced and that of the eternal Son as one of "the three glorious persons in the trinity." "The man Christ Jesus," Watts taught, was the Son's human nature, "that flesh and that soul, which were chosen by God the Father's decree, and the will of God the Son, from among all possible, and all future flesh and souls, to be made forever one with God." "The man Christ Jesus" enjoyed "a union of habitual blessedness" with God, but one that Watts described as a heightened variety of what believers also experience. "He enjoys and feels all that we enjoy and feel," Watts wrote, "and vastly more too, for he is the medium through which we approach and we enjoy [the Father]."[26]

"God the Son," however, experiences the nearness of the three persons of the Trinity to themselves as an entirely different degree of blessedness, "an inconceivable In-being and Indwelling in each other" wrapped in an absolute mystery of "delight and felicity unknown to all but the blessed three who enjoy it." Watts taught that the nearness of the Three Persons existed beyond not only human and angelic comprehension, but even that of "the man Christ Jesus." "This is a nobler union, and a more intense pleasure," he wrote, "than the man Christ Jesus knows, or feels, or can conceive, for he is a creature. These are glories too divine and dazzling for the weak eye of our understandings, too bright for the eye of angels, those morning-stars; and they, and we, must all fall down together, alike confounded."[27]

This first part of "The Scale of Blessedness" took the form of a seventeenth-century school figure on the Great Chain of Being. Hidden in its unexceptionable presentation, however, was an unusually sharp distinction between the eternal and created natures of Christ that cast his human nature as continuous with our own, to the point of dissociating "the man Christ Jesus" from "the Son of God." To assuage any doctrinal uncertainty that might ensue from such a view, Watts resorted to faith in the impenetrable mystery that was the Trinity.

[26] *Sermons on Various Subjects*, 1:379, 382.
[27] Ibid., 1:388–92, 396, 399.

Watts's approach to trinitarian issues here seems to have been motivated by his growing reaction against "scholastic forms of explication" and a concomitant search for a strictly scriptural ground of doctrinal exposition that he would pursue for the rest of his career. Even in this early attempt to parse trinitarian doctrine, Watts did not flinch from the consequences of his "evangelical" theological method. If Scripture presented different and even conflicting depictions of "the man Christ Jesus" and "the Son of God," the believer's task was to affirm them both and reject any rational doubt by affirming faith in the ultimately mysterious truths of God. In Watts's opinion, the Scripture evidence in fact entailed such multiple perspectives on the Trinity. He would insist on acknowledging them all in doctrine and celebrating them in sacred song.

In the concluding part of "The Scale of Blessedness" Watts made what would become another characteristic theological move, drawing liturgical implications and applications from his trinitarian doctrine. His reflections about nearness to and in God led him to claim that "communion with God, which has been impiously ridiculed by the profane wits of the last and the present age, is no such visionary and fantastick notion as they imagine." He began his defense of this proposition with the common social meaning of "communion," as "when two or more persons partake of the same thing. So friends have communion in one table when they dine together." By extension, "Christians have communion in one sermon, in one prayer, or one sacrament, when they join together in those parts of worship, and the saints have communion with God in blessedness, when they rejoice in the same object of contemplation and love." Watts also gave a second sense of "communion" as individual "converse with God . . . in secret, as when a Christian pours out his whole heart before God, and is made sensible of his gracious presence, by the sweet influences of instruction, sanctification, or comfort. When man speaks, and God answers, there is a sacred communion between God and man." Watts concluded that both of these senses combine in the elements of worship—prayer, the ministry of the Word, and the Lord's Supper—to produce "publick" as well as "secret" communion with God.[28]

The same linkage of trinitarian and liturgical theology informed another of Watts's early sermons, "The Doctrine of the Trinity, and the

[28] Ibid., 1:403.

Use of It." Published in 1727 but apparently also composed many years earlier, it carried another disclaimer that Watts had "never changed my belief and profession of any important part of [this divine subject], as will here appear with abundant evidence." For the sermon on the Trinity Watts took as his text Ephesians 2:18: "Through him we both have access by one spirit unto the father." He reiterated his evangelical, anti-scholastic approach, writing that "I follow'd the track of no particular scheme whatever, but have represented the sacred Three . . . in that light in which they seem to lie most open to the common view of mankind in the word of God." Rejection of "particular schemes," however, did not mean abandonment of rational argument. To the contrary, Watts saw fit to present his early trinitarian theology in no fewer than seventeen propositions upon whose orthodoxy he insisted. Again he took an open-ended position: "Both the Son and the Holy Ghost have such a communion in true and eternal godhead, as to have the same names, titles, attributes, and operations ascribed to them . . . which belong only to the true God," he wrote, "and yet, . . . there is such a plain distinction between them, as is sufficient to support their distinct personal characters and offices in the great work of our salvation."[29]

In the concluding "improvement" or "use" of this sermon, Watts applied trinitarian doctrine to liturgical theology as he had done in "The Scale of Blessedness." To work out the trinitarian "access" believers have to the Father, Watts proposed to "consider the different stations, or characters, in which the sacred Three are represented in this great and important concern of our salvation, [and] . . . our duties [of worship] to the sacred Three . . . correspondent to the stations in which the gospel places them." As he assigned a specific "character and office" to each of "the sacred Three," however, Watts began to verge toward a modalist or Sabellian view of the Trinity. The Father is "our original maker, lord and sovereign . . . the first spring of mercy, the author of all grace." More controversially, Watts defined the Son

---

[29] Isaac Watts, *Sermons on Various Subjects*, vol. 3 (London: John Clark and Richard Hett, Emanuel Mathews, Richard Ford, 1727) ix–xi, 478–487. The dating of Watts's writings is a notorious problem. Early editions of his works were incomplete and thematically arranged. The sequence of the published works was only finally determined by Davis, *Isaac Watts*, 271–78. Dating of individual items in collections like *Sermons on Various Subjects* depends on Watts's own prefatory remarks or scattered references elsewhere.

exclusively as the Mediator between God and humanity. "We must trust in him for complete salvation," he wrote, "both from sin and hell, and resign ourselves, as guilty, sinful, and perishing creatures, into his hands, and to his methods of relief." On the Spirit's "character and office," however, Watts was a bit more reticent. "We are chiefly to seek the aids of the blessed Spirit," he wrote, "from God the Father, through the mediation of his Son Jesus Christ."[30]

Running through the sermon on the Trinity was a persistent suggestion of a hierarchy of being within the godhead, reflected in the concomitant duties of worship Watts associated with the respective Persons. "The scripture generally instructs us to make God the Father the more direct object of our addresses in prayer," he wrote, "because it is he (who) sustains the supreme dignity and majesty of godhead, . . . as the prime Agent in our salvation and prime object of worship." By contrast, the Son mediates the liturgy as our intercessor with the Father. "All our prayers, and acts of worship and obedience, must be recommended to the Father by [the Son of God's] name, and through his intercession." The Spirit again occupies a clearly subordinate status. "We must ask that [the God of all grace] would assist us, by his Spirit, in all the holy and devout exercises of our souls," he taught, "and enable us to worship God the Father aright, through Jesus Christ, in all his own appointments."[31]

"The Scale of Blessedness" and "The Doctrine of the Trinity" outlined a method of theological discourse that replaced complex doctrinal and philosophical argument with "scripture evidence" and an emphasis on the human implications of the Trinity's salvific actions. Watts's central images of human relationship to the Trinity were "nearness," "approach," and "access," all aspects of the same reality whereby souls are drawn savingly to God. The best way for believers to understand the Trinity, therefore, was by the different "characters and offices" that "the sacred Three" perform for their salvation. Watts had exchanged scholastic argument for a kind of divine functionalism. In good Newtonian fashion he claimed his reasoning followed "the analytical method," but also he insisted that it was strictly "evangelical," categorically based on the Scriptures. In any case, the workings of Watts's theological method left the Trinity intact, but assigned its

---

[30] *Sermons on Various Subjects*, 3:487.
[31] *Sermons on Various Subjects*, 3:488, 490–91.

unity to the realm of absolute mystery and compromised both the equality of its Persons and the full divinity of Christ.

For Watts, believers' understanding of the Trinity's work also entailed duties of worship specific to each Person's character and office. The Father is to be praised, the Son is to be invoked as Mediator and atoning sacrifice, and the Spirit is to be called upon to aid "the holy and devout exercises of our souls." In all of these aspects, worship has both "publick" social and "secret" individual dimensions of communion, which find their supreme realization in the Lord's Supper. "At the supper of the Lord," Watts wrote in the peroration of "The Scale of Blessedness":

> when with hope and joy we receive the bread and the wine, as divine seals of the faithfulness of God's covenant, and when we transact those solemn affairs also as seals of our faith and love, and our engagements to be the Lord's, we may properly be said to hold fellowship, or communion, with him. . . . What swift advances of holiness doth the saint feel in his heart, and practice in his life, after such seasons of devotion! What glory doth he give to religion in a dark and sinful world! What unknown pleasure doth he find in such approaches to God![32]

THE LORD'S SUPPER HYMNS

Hymns and Spiritual Songs followed the strategy of Watts's early sermons, presenting doctrine in a language of "scripture faith" with as little argumentative scaffolding as possible. While that strategy may rightly be classified as evangelical in its confidence that Scripture alone makes the best case for Christian belief, it also derived, in Watts at least, from the perceived danger of "scholastic" controversy. In all of his work Watts sought to mitigate theological conflict on matters that he considered inessential for saving faith lest dispute divide the church and hinder souls from finding Christ. By 1709 the Trinity had become such a danger to Old Dissent. In this context, his remarks that *Hymns and Spiritual Songs* "avoided the more obscure and controverted points of Christianity" and "secluded the contentions and distinguishing words of sects and parties" take on new meanings.

Watts's decision to provide new communion hymns and doxologies drove his hymn project onto contested trinitarian ground. He was convinced that these genres were necessary to complete the reform of the

<hr />

[32] *Sermons on Various Subjects*, 1:405.

liturgy, yet to provide them risked conflict over trinitarian speculations, including his own. To achieve his goal Watts needed new poetic techniques and theological treatments. His native literary talent provided the poetic techniques, which lie beyond the scope of this essay,[33] but he found the theological treatments by creating in Book III a set of variations not only on Reformed eucharistic doctrine but on the Trinitarian Controversy itself. He filled his Lord's Supper poems and trinitarian doxologies with an extraordinary array of biblical imagery and diverse doctrinal nuances. When he had finished Book III, the most important liturgical dimensions of the Lord's Supper and many shades of emergent trinitarian speculation in Old Dissent had found hymnodic expression. As he promised, Watts "secluded" explicitly partisan language, and he made the extraordinary offer that "where any unpleasing word is found, he that leads the worship may substitute a better." Yet these very comments acknowledged that he had composed his lyrics in an atmosphere of contested theological opinion.

Watts commented directly on the issue of theological partisanship. "If any expressions occur to the reader that savour of an opinion different from his own," he wrote in the Preface to *Hymns and Spiritual Songs*, "these are generally such as are capable of an extensive sense, and may be used with a charitable latitude." Watts's contemporaries well knew, however, that such latitudinarian rhetoric was not theologically neutral. It entailed "charitable" openness to diverse and possibly heterodox opinions, not their exclusion. In the context of the incipient Trinitarian Controversy, Watts's call for "an extensive sense" of his "expressions" meant precisely that he intended his lyrics to give voice, however subtle, to many shades of trinitarian opinion in Old Dissent. While he marked out his own views clearly enough, Watts's genius in Book III of *Hymns and Spiritual Songs* was to set places at the Lord's table for others as well.

Three aspects of Book III most directly address trinity, christology, and the Lord's Supper: the overall structure of the book, the trinitarian and christological content of individual hymns, and the doxologies. Watts's design for his collection of communion hymns was masterful, leading the reader through a sequence of carefully placed meditations on the ordinance. Deploying the lyrics in groups of one, two, or three hymns, Watts wove together three principal themes: scriptural

---

[33] On Watts's poetical style see Watson, *The English Hymn*, 133–70.

accounts of the Supper and its types, its character as "communion with Christ and the saints," and its christological memorial of the New Covenant.

This design is worth considering in closer detail. The collection begins with the presentation of the three themes in hymns I–III. Two christological hymns follow on the atonement. Another pair addresses the Supper as communion in Watts's double sense, the first describing it socially as "a feast for remembrance," and the second expressing it individually as the believer's response to Christ's sacrifice. From christology and communion, Watts moves to trinitarian aspects of the Supper in hymns VII–X. An interlude in hymn XI addresses the Supper's liturgical action as "pardon brought to our senses," then four hymns follow on gospel tropes of the Supper such as the gospel feast in Luke 14. Hymn XVI, a christological interlude on "the agonies of Christ," leads to yet another pair of trope lyrics on the Supper as "incomparable food." The last seven Lord's Supper hymns return to Watts's doctrinal themes of communion. Hymns XIX and XX register the spiritual empowerment of believers in communion, while hymns XXI and XXII speak of the presence of Christ in the Supper, and the last three lyrics treat the Supper in an experiential and eschatological mode. Hymn XXV, the final lyric, concludes with a plea to Christ to "raise our faith to sight."

The hymnodic sequence of Book III follows Watts's homiletical principle of avoiding "scholastic" disputation. It is structured as a sermon discourse similar to "The Scale of Blessedness" and "The Doctrine of the Trinity." As in those sermons, Watts relies on simple explanatory strategies to present his doctrinal reflections on Trinity, Christ's two natures, and the Supper. The last sections of Book III provide a concluding "improvement" or "use" in the form of an exhortation on the communion of believers with Christ and one another in the Supper. A reader of Book III apprehends this tacit argument almost subliminally; it does not overwhelm the individual hymns, yet it subtly shapes the collection as a whole and gives momentum to the sustained iteration of the communion theme in the final hymns.

As the overall structure of the Lord's Supper sequence follows the homiletical style of Watts's contemporary sermons, so the individual hymns reflect the trinitarian, christological, and eucharistic positions he took in them. Several examples must suffice. Hymn IV, "Christ's dying Love; or, Pardon bought at a dear price," is the first explicitly christological lyric in Book III. It gives a dramatic account of Christ's atoning act of will, but treads softly on the vexed question of his two natures. The hymn, quite popular in the eighteenth and early nineteenth centuries, begins clearly enough with the Son's choice to aid sinful humanity:

> How condescending and how kind
> Was God's Eternal Son?
> Our Misery reach'd his heavn'ly Mind,
> And Pity brought him down.

Stanzas two and three highlight Christ's innocent suffering, but stanza four gives these somewhat uneasy lines:

> This was Compassion like a God,
> That when the Saviour knew
> The Price of Pardon was his Blood,
> His Pity ne'er withdrew.

Watts's sense that Christ did not "know the Price of Pardon" until after his incarnation and ministry widens the gap between "the Eternal Son" and "the man Christ Jesus" on Watts's "scale of blessedness" to the point of implicitly questioning Christ's divine nature. The hymn concludes with the Savior reigning in heaven and the saints receiving "repeated seals of Jesus [*sic*] dying love" in the Supper, but it leaves a nuance about the two natures that registers the unsettled state of contemporary christology when it was published. Like so many lyrics in *Hymns and Spiritual Songs*, "How condescending and how kind" is technically orthodox, but it could be read or sung with approval by Dissenters of more heterodox leanings.[34]

The cluster of hymns VII–X contains Watts's most explicit trinitarian lyrics in Book III. Hymn VIII, "The Tree of Life," compares the cross to an imagined tree of life in heaven, its "ever-smiling boughs" growing "near the Throne" and ornamented with the Son and the Spirit:

> Hovering amongst the Leaves there stands
> The sweet Celestial Dove;
> And Jesus on the branches hangs
> The Banner of his Love.

---

[34] *HSS*, III:IV, 285–86.

These homely images are hardly the stuff of sophisticated trinitarian doctrine, but through them Watts affirmed that all three Persons engage in human salvation while quietly querying their equality by locating the Son and the Spirit at a distance from the Father enthroned.

Hymn X, "Christ Crucify'd; The Wisdom and Power of God," gives extended treatment to the relations between the Father and the Son. It identifies "the Grace that rescu'd Man" as the Father's "brightest Form of Glory," drawn on the cross "in precious Blood and crimson Lines." Watts dwells on the mysterious will of the Father, "Where Grace and Vengeance strangely joyn / Piercing his Son with sharpest smart / To make the purchas'd Pleasures mine." The hymn shifts to contemplate "the sweet Wonders of that Cross" and ends with the believer longing to join the angels "to praise the Lamb, / And worship at his Father's Throne." The tenor of this hymn, in contrast to some of the others, is strongly Calvinist, understanding the economy of grace as strictly a function of the Father's mysterious will:

> Here [God's] whole Name appears compleat;
> Nor wit can guess, nor Reason prove
> Which of the Letters best is writ,
> The Power, the Wisdom, or the Love.[35]

The most famous Lord's Supper lyrics in Book III are hymns VI and VII, "The Memorial of Our Absent Lord" and "Crucifixion to the World by the Cross of Christ." Both were quite popular in the eighteenth and nineteenth centuries, and "Crucifixion to the World," better known by its first line "When I Survey the Wondrous Cross," was one of the most commonly used hymns of the twentieth century. It is widely held to be Watts's greatest hymn. Taken together the two hymns make a complete presentation of his theology of the Lord's Supper.

Hymn VI is a primer for the saints explaining why Jesus has provided the Supper and how it should be used to gain communion with him and one another. It begins with a straightforward two-stanza explanation of why believers need the Supper:

> Jesus is gone above the Skies,
> Where our weak Senses reach him not;

---

[35] *HSS*, III:VIII and X, 289–90 and 292–93.

And carnal Objects court our Eyes
To thrust our Saviour from our Thought.

He knows we are "apt to forget his lovely Face," so "to refresh our Minds he gave / These kind Memorials of his Grace." Stanza three follows the *Westminster Confession* (1646) in describing the elements as spiritual food and observes its mandate that believers partake of them both outwardly through the senses and inwardly by faith: "We on the rich Provision feed, / And taste the Wine, and bless the God." After the elements are "tasted," the spiritual action of memorial takes place, transcending sensory temptations and suffusing the soul with divine love.

> Let sinful Sweets be all forgot,
> And Earth grow less in our Esteem;
> Christ and his Love fill every Thought,
> And Faith and Hope be fix'd on him.

In the hymn's final stanza this memorial unites believers in a "publick communion" of eschatological expectation:

> Our Eyes look upwards to the Hills
> Whence our returning Lord shall come;
> We wait thy Chariots [sic] awful Wheels
> To fetch our longing Spirits home.[36]

Positioned just after "Jesus is gone above the Skies," "When I Survey" (Hymn VIII) articulates the "secret communion" of the individual believer that complements the social experience of "publick communion" treated in the preceding hymn. The first two lines, "When I survey the wondrous Cross, / On which the Prince of Glory dy'd," place the believer at the Lord's Table meditating upon the "character and office" of Christ as Mediator. The next six lines depict the believer's penitential response of renunciation of the world:

> My richest gain I count but Loss,
> And pour contempt on all my Pride.

---

[36] *HSS*, III:VI, 288.

Forbid it, Lord, that I should boast
Save in the Death of Christ my God;
All the vain things that charm me most,
I sacrifice them to his Blood.

In the eucharistic context of Book III the believer's "sacrifice" of vanity
and pride resonates as a moral *imitatio Christi*, death to the world,
which is carried through the next six lines, including the often-omitted
fourth stanza: "Then I am dead to all the Globe, / And all the Globe is
dead to me." The fifth and final stanza reiterates the believer's self-
sacrifice as a response to the Supper's memorial action: "Love so
amazing, so divine, / Demands my Soul, my Life, my All."[37]

"When I Survey" is still prominently employed as an invitation
hymn, but it has lost the eucharistic context in which it was originally
composed. Watts conceived the hymn as the believer's most intimate
response to eucharistic grace, a profoundly liturgical utterance that articulates the *Westminster Confession*'s teaching that the faithful "receive
and feed upon Christ crucified . . . as really, but spiritually, present to
the faith of believers in that ordinance, as the elements themselves are,
to their outward senses."[38]

THE DOXOLOGIES
Many other dimensions of Book III are worth considering further, especially Watts's exploration of communion's individual, social, and meta-
physical aspects in the final sections of the Lord's Supper hymns. For
trinitarian and christological issues in Book III, however, it is more essential to examine the fifteen trinitarian doxologies that conclude it. The
Puritans, and later English Independents and Presbyterians, were am-
bivalent about doxological utterance. On the one hand, the Puritans rejected the *Gloria Patri* as a relic of the Mass along with other ritual songs
including the *Magnificat*, *Benedictus*, and *Nunc Dimittis*. Yet the *Westminster Directory for the Publique Worship of God* (1645) made no reference to
either the *Gloria Patri* specifically or to doxologies in general, assigning
them to a category of liturgical indifference. After the Glorious Revolution at least some English Independents and Presbyterians began adopt-

---

[37] *HSS*, III:VII, 289.

[38] Westminster Assembly, *The humble advice of the Assembly of Divines, now by
authority of Parliament sitting at Westminster, concerning a confession of faith* (London: Company of Stationers, 1647) XXIX:VII, 51.

ing various doxologies in worship, including both the *Gloria Patri* and the final verse of the 1695 "Evening Hymn" by the Anglican Non-Juror Thomas Ken that begins "Praise God from whom all blessings flow."[39]

Watts's principal reason for writing new doxologies was to replace the *Gloria Patri* in Dissenting worship with more appropriate short hymns. He expressed the need for new doxologies characteristically as a resolution of the tension between the demands of tradition and the imperative of *ecclesia semper reformanda*. "I Cannot perswade my self to put a full Period to these Divine Hymns," he noted in Book III, "till I have address'd a special Song of Glory to God the Father, the Son, and the holy Spirit. Tho' the *Latin* Name of it, *Gloria Patri*, be retain'd in our nation from the Roman Church; and tho' there may be some Excesses of superstitious Honour paid to the Words of it, which may have wrought some unhappy Prejudices in Weaker Christians, yet I believe it still to be one of the noblest parts of Christian Worship."[40]

Adumbrating the strategy he would later use in *The Psalms of David Imitated*, Watts solved this dilemma by recasting the *Gloria Patri* "into a variety of forms" including "a plain version or a larger paraphrase to be sung alone or at the conclusion of another hymn." The growing tensions over trinitarian theology in Old Dissent, however, seem to have been another subtext for addressing "unhappy prejudices" not only about the *Gloria Patri* but also about the Trinity itself, for Watts's doxologies, like his Lord's Supper hymns, articulated many dimensions of the emerging trinitarian debate.

Also like the Lord's Supper hymns, the doxologies follow a carefully contrived structure of presentation, here a metrical and thematic one. Watts wrote four sets or "forms" of the *Gloria Patri*, two "larger paraphrases" and one "plain version" of it, each in Long (8.8.8.8.), Common (8.6.8.6.), and Short (6.6.8.6.) meters, as well as a concluding "form" in Hallelujah Meter, 6.6.6.6.4.4.4.4. These "forms" of the *Gloria Patri* addressed the same trinitarian themes Watts had offered in his sermons and the Lord's Supper hymns: the "character and office" of the Three Persons, the mystery and paradoxes of the Trinity, and the duty of worship and praise to each of "the sacred Three." This

---

[39] Horton Davies, *Worship and Theology in England*, vol. 1: *From Cranmer to Hooker, 1534–1603* (Princeton: Princeton University Press, 1970) 101–4, and vol. 2: *From Andrewes to Baxter and Fox, 1603–1690* (Princeton: Princeton University Press, 1975) 398, 458.

[40] *HSS*, III: 308.

structure captured the principal aspects of Watts's own early trinitarian theology while once again acknowledging the doctrinal controversies developing around him.

The "larger paraphrases," hymns XXVI–XXXI and XXXVIII–XXXIX, are of greatest interest, since their length of two to five stanzas permitted Watts to introduce substantive theological commentary. Hymn XXVI, the first doxology, exemplifies Watts's initial "form" of the *Gloria Patri*, stating in its first three stanzas the "character and office" of each Person, then ending with a final stanza on the Three. All four stanzas are linked by biblical water symbolism, and Watts's fine culminating image for the Trinity as "That Sea of Life and Love unknown / Without a Bottom or a Shore," is oceanic and mysterious. The second and third hymns of this first group continue the same formula of depicting each Person, but with more explicitly doctrinal definitions of their salvific roles and rather less metaphorical elevation. This group of doxologies seems thoroughly orthodox on first reading; indeed it is in every technical sense, yet an important element is missing. None of them explicitly affirms the unity of the godhead. Hymn XXVII speaks of "Th' eternal Three and One" and hymn XXVIII of "the great One and Three," but Watts pointedly does not employ the traditional formula of "Three in One." Even granting that the *Gloria Patri* itself does not use this formula, it is still plain that Watts's first "form" of "larger paraphrases" emphasizes the distinctions between the Three Persons at the expense of their unity. This position precisely followed Watts's teaching in the sermon on the Trinity and provided a liturgical entering wedge for heterodox beliefs in Old Dissent.[41]

The second set of paraphrases moves to the different, but also familiarly Wattsian, doctrinal terrain of trinitarian mystery. Hymn XXIX, the first lyric in this group, rehearses the powerful sense of trinitarian paradox and the social and individual qualities of "nearness" that Watts emphasized in "The Scale of Blessedness":

> Glory to God the Trinity
> Whose Name has Mysteries unknown;

---

[41] *HSS*, III:XXVI and XXVII, 309–10. Watts does use the phrases "Three in One" and "One in Three" later in the second and third "forms" of the *Gloria Patri*, hymns XXX and XXII, but this traditional formula appears only twice in the fifteen doxologies.

In Essence One, in Person Three;
A social Nature, yet alone.

The second and concluding stanza turns from the inherent mystery of the Trinity to the inability of creatures to comprehend it. The only appropriate response to the divine mystery, the stanza teaches, is worship and praise:

When all our noblest Powers are joyn'd
The Honours of thy Name to raise
Thy Glories over-match our Mind,
And Angels faint beneath the Praise.[42]

Another significant rhetorical omission becomes apparent in this second set of doxologies. Watts does not use the name "Holy Spirit" or "Holy Ghost" here, despite the precedent of the *Gloria Patri*. In fact, neither term appears at all in Book III. Watts prefers "God the Spirit" or simply "the Spirit." This neglect of the traditional name for the third Person cannot have been accidental. In the sermon on the Trinity Watts had already expressed doubts about whether believers should "directly address ourselves in prayer to . . . the Spirit of God." His subtle rejection of the Spirit's traditional name in the doxologies left the issue quite open while stopping short of heterodox formulation.[43]

The third set of doxologies consists of single stanza "plain versions" of the *Gloria Patri* whose theme is the worship and praise of the Trinity conceived in Wattsian terms as "honour" to "the sacred Three." Hymn XXXV is typical of this group:

Honour to thee, Almighty Three
And Everlasting One;
All Glory to the Father be,
The Spirit, and the Son.[44]

In the fourth and final group of *Gloria Patri* paraphrases, Watts addressed the themes of the previous three "forms" in four hymns cast

---

[42] *HSS*, III:XXIX, 311.
[43] *Sermons on Various Subjects*, 3:492.
[44] *HSS*, III:XXXV, 313.

in the unusual Hallelujah Meter, classically employed by Thomas Sternhold and John Hopkins for Psalm 148 in *The Whole Booke of Psalmes* (1562), known in Watts's time as the "Old Version" of the Church of England. Hymn XXXVIII, the first Hallelujah lyric, can ably stand for the whole set, and indeed for all of Book III. It is a tour de force that not only outlines the "character and office" of each of "the sacred Three" in separate stanzas, but also shifts voice in each stanza, from first-person singular to first-person plural to imperative voice, registering Watts's theology of simultaneous "publick" and "secret" communion. This splendid doxology, singled out for its excellence by its interpreters Bernard Manning and Horton Davies, adds both mystery and worship in its final stanza to synthesize Watts's entire presentation of the Trinity:

> Almighty God, to Thee
> Be endless Honours done;
> The undivided Three,
> And the Mysterious One:
> Where Reason Fails
> With all her Pow'rs,
> There Faith prevails,
> And Love adores."[45]

AFTER *HYMNS AND SPIRITUAL SONGS*

During the ten years following the second edition of *Hymns and Spiritual Songs*, Watts worked on *The Psalms of David Imitated* amid deepening trinitarian dispute in Old Dissent. Just as this metrical psalter went to press, controversy over trinitarian issues helped to fuel schism among Dissenters at the 1719 Salters' Hall Conference in London. By a narrow vote London area ministers of the Presbyterian, Independent, and Baptist denominations refused to discipline several colleagues in Exeter who stood accused of teaching Arian and Socinian doctrines. The orthodox minority walked out of the conference, demanding that the majority subscribe to the doctrine of the Trinity as defined either in the *Westminster Confession* or the *Thirty-Nine Articles* of the Church of England. The majority claimed faith in "the proper divinity of Christ,"

---

[45] *HSS*, III:XXXVIII, 313–14; Bernard Manning, *The Hymns of Wesley and Watts: Five Informal Papers* (London: Epworth, 1942) 105; Horton Davies, *Worship and Theology in England*, 3:113.

but denied ecclesiastical authority to require subscription to any particular formulation of it. At Salters' Hall, Old Dissent's observance of Westminster orthodoxy, already softening, collapsed under the majority's endorsement of Scripture alone as the standard for formulating doctrine and the Christian liberty of ministers to interpret it freely. Decades of bitter recrimination and renewed trinitarian controversy followed, marking the end of Old Dissent as a cohesive force in English Protestantism.[46]

Historians disagree about Watts's role, if any, at the Salters' Hall Conference, but within a few years he publicly enlisted with the majority. In *The Christian Doctrine of the Trinity* (1722), *Four Dissertations on the Holy Trinity* (1724), and *Three Dissertations on the Holy Trinity* (1725), Watts affirmed the Trinity as a "scripture doctrine," but denied that any particular theological formulation of it should be required as a term of communion. In these works Watts also admitted that Scripture sometimes depicted the Son and the Spirit as less than divine, even as it gave evidence for their divinity as well. He held to this characteristically open-ended position for another twenty years, but very late in his career Watts returned yet again to trinitarian and christological issues. In *A Faithful Inquiry after the Ancient and Original Doctrine of the Trinity* (1745), and *Useful and Important Questions concerning Jesus the Son of God* (1746), he advanced an Arian theology in which the Son was a spiritual being created by God before the universe. In *The Glories of Christ as God-Man Displayed* (1746), one of his last published works, Watts extended his position to include both the Son's human and divine natures in God's creating act.[47]

When New Dissent emerged in the 1730s it had become a political faction uniting orthodox and heterodox Presbyterians, Independents, and Baptists in a common quest for full religious liberty rather than an ecumenical front for Westminster orthodoxy. Remarkably, most of

[46] M. Watts, *The Dissenters*, 374–93; R. Thomas, "The Non-Subscription Controversy amongst Dissenters in 1719: the Salters' Hall Debate," *Journal of Ecclesiastical History* 4 (1953); and D. L. Wykes, "Pierce, James," in *Oxford Dictionary of National Biography*, ed. H. C. G. Matthew and B. Harrison (Oxford: Oxford University Press, 2004) 43: 449–52.

[47] All of these works are included in the first edition of Watts's works, *The Works of the late reverend and learned Isaac Watts, published by himself and now collected into Six Volumes*, eds. David Jennings and Philip Doddridge (London: T. and T. Longman, 1753).

these doctrinally diverse religious parties endorsed Watts's hymns and metrical psalms, and claimed him for their own. The same held true for British North America, where after the Great Awakening (1726–1745) Watts became the canonical poet of Evangelical Calvinists as well as the favorite of moderate Old Side Presbyterians and Old Light Congregationalists. His hymns and metrical psalms somehow provided a liturgical unity that his controversial writings, and hundreds of others like them, could not achieve. Certainly Watts's poetical skills had much to do with this outcome, but it is doubtful that literary excellence alone can account for the success of his hymns and psalms in the doctrinal turmoil that engulfed Old Dissent after 1719 in England, and Congregationalists and Presbyterians after 1740 in British North America.

Watts's interdenominational popularity at a time of deep denominational division is an extraordinary phenomenon that requires an explanation it has never fully received. One important reason for it was the liturgical canopy that Book III of *Hymns and Spiritual Songs* supplied. In his 1709 preface Watts had called for "charitable latitude" in doctrine and worship in order to "give to sincere consciences as little disturbance as possible, for, blessed be God, we are not confined to the words of any man in our public solemnities."[48] His communion hymns and doxologies defied such doctrinal "confinement" at a moment when trinitarian debates were still incipient and cordial. A decade later Old Dissent had broken apart at the Salters' Hall Conference, abruptly ending the "charitable latitude" of opinion that his lyrics had so eloquently expressed.

Watts's deep commitment to "publick" and "secret" communion in the Lord's Supper and his broad doctrinal inclusivity on the Trinity, however, enabled him to write hymns and doxologies for the Lord's Supper that satisfied emergent Arians and Socinians as well as orthodox Westminster Calvinists. Frozen in time, his diverse and nuanced liturgical lyrics of 1709 appealed later to the entire theological range of New Dissent and American Reformed communions. Isaac Watts's pluralistic hymnody of the Lord's Table gave powerful liturgical sustenance to English Dissenters and their American counterparts at a critical time of trinitarian and christological debate and ecclesiological transformation, helping them to maintain a common religious culture on their way to becoming a spiritual and ecclesial force that continues to shape our religious world today.

[48] *HSS*, III: viii.

Part 3

Some Aspects of
Contemporary Protestant Worship

Some of the earlier essays in this collection center on the current liturgies of the major world churches, such as Eastern Orthodox, Syrian Orthodox, and Roman Catholic. But what of modern Protestant worship, which is always more fluid and malleable than that of the older great churches? Though new liturgical texts have been written for many Protestant denominations, hymn singing still remains an important part of their public worship. Karen Westerfield Tucker selects ten current denominational hymnals and considers what they teach about the person of Christ, asking how they answer the question, "And you, who do you say that I am?" However, traditional hymnals jostle alongside contemporary praise and worship songs and music that comes from many newer churches, such as Vineyard churches. Lester Ruth takes a close look at the piety of some of this contemporary worship music, suggesting that the Trinity is marginal to much contemporary evangelical piety and is something that composers need to address. Another contemporary issue, mainly of the more liberal mainline denominations, is the quest for inclusive language in the wake of criticism from Christian feminist theology. This has led to the omission of much traditional trinitarian language and biblical christological titles, and the use of newer inclusive language and names. How justified is this? Is it successful, or does it undermine orthodox belief? These issues are explored by Kathryn Greene-McCreight.

Chapter 13

"But who do you say that I am?": Christology in Recent Protestant Hymnals

Karen B. Westerfield Tucker
Boston University School of Theology

In the preface to his collection *ΙΧΘΥΣ, Christ in Song: Hymns of Immanuel* published in 1869, the church historian Philip Schaff (1819–1893) observed that in the history of *lyra Christologica*, "the Church before the Reformation celebrated mainly the objective facts of Christ's life (*Christus pro nobis*); while the hymnists after the Reformation, without neglecting the festival themes, brought out more fully the subjective application of Christ's merits, and our relation to Him (*Christus in nobis*)."[1] Dividing his book into two separate yet theologically related parts, Schaff exposed in the first section—under headings from Advent to Glorification and Judgment—the work of salvation accomplished by Christ *extra nos* in his earthly ministry, a work that continues in his heavenly intercession and is to be completed at his return. In the second part, Schaff kept the work *pro nobis* alongside the work wrought *in nobis*. Here, for example, a christological approach to the justification and sanctification of humanity is illuminated poetically through the development of such themes as the love and loveliness of Christ, Christ as refuge and strength, union with Christ, and Holy Communion. To avoid any absolutist claim of historical periodization, Schaff included hymns by German- and English-language hymn writers in the first section, and Greek and Latin hymns in the second.[2]

Schaff's bipartite methodology, in its highlighting of the soteriological themes of classical Continental Protestantism, did not employ "the

---

[1] Philip Schaff, *ΙΧΘΥΣ, Christ in Song: Hymns of Immanuel* (New York: Anson D. F. Randolph, 1869) v–viii.

[2] Among the Greek and Latin writers in the section "Christ in Us" Schaff includes Clement of Alexandria, Gregory Nazianzen, Anatolius, Stephen the Sabaite, Theoctistus, Ambrose, Prudentius, Peter Damian, and Bernard.

Trinity" as a specific heading, which would have made explicit the ontological grounding of the saving work recognized and recounted in the poetry. Nevertheless the Trinity was not overlooked, for, under the heading "Incarnation" in the first part of the book, the eternally begotten Son is identified by means of hymnic articulations of the Nicene faith: laud and honor is given to the one who is the Alpha and Omega, consubstantial, coeternal with the Father and Spirit "while unending ages run."[3] Throughout the course of the book, ascriptions of praise and thanksgiving are given to the Son *in se* and for all his works, and these are summed up in a single stanza by Henry Alford, former Dean of Canterbury:

> Thou that art the Father's Word,
> Thou that art the Lamb of God,
> Thou that art the Virgin's Son,
> Thou that savest souls undone,
> Sacred sacrifice for sin,
> Fount of piety within:
> Hail, Lord Jesus![4]

By his approach to the contents of *IXΘΥΣ* (*Ichthus*), Schaff unwittingly demonstrated how the establishment of organizational structures may inadvertently proffer a particular, a nuanced, or even a peculiar christological reading. The two methods Schaff adopted, with the liturgical year for the first part, and the *ordo salutis* for the second, were established organizational schemes for Protestant hymnals in the nineteenth century as they are today. Yet these structures do not make explicit the divine relation of the Son to the Father and the Spirit—or the two interpenetrating natures of Christ (the *communicatio idiomatum*)—that can be more clearly seen by methods that follow a credal outline or a dogmatic structure. Because the organization of hymnbooks provides a system of theology for the pew, the layout of the contents, especially in denominational books, is a significant matter.[5] John Wesley, for example, identified his 1780 *Collection of Hymns for the*

---

[3] Reference is to the hymn by Clemens Aurelius Prudentius, *Corde natus ex Parentis*, translated as "Of the Father's Love Begotten" (Schaff, *IXΘΥΣ*, 43–45).

[4] Schaff, 693.

[5] For a fuller discussion on the significance of hymnal organization, see my "Congregational Song as Liturgical Ordo and Proper: The Case of English-

Use of the People Called Methodists as a "little body of experimental and practical divinity" that was intentionally arranged "according to the experience of real Christians."[6] Wesley's scheme, which still survives at least in part in hymnals of the Wesleyan and Methodist families, proved useful to the evangelical agenda of drawing attention to the *Christus in nobis*, but did not give full expression to the entire *lex credendi*.

In the remainder of this essay I will examine ten current denominational hymnals from the United States and Canada to assess their organization and hymn selection as pertains to both intended and unintended statements related to christology. A series of questions will be posed to the recent books produced by the Advent Christian Church,[7] the Anglican Church of Canada,[8] the Christian Church (Disciples of Christ),[9] the Episcopal Church (USA),[10] the Evangelical Lutheran Church in America,[11] the Presbyterian Church (U.S.A.),[12] the Southern Baptist Convention,[13] the United Church of Canada,[14] the United Church of Christ,[15] and the United Methodist Church.[16] Is the Christ portrayed exhaustively as divinity, or, conversely, is he a man divorced from divinity? Is a Nicene understanding of the Second Person conveyed? Are the two natures of the incarnate Son related in ways that respect the Chalcedonian definition? What relation is there

---

Language Hymns and Hymnals." *Studia Liturgica* 28 (1998) 102–20, especially 117–20.

[6] In *The Works of John Wesley* 7, ed. Franz Hildebrandt and Oliver A. Beckerlegge (Nashville: Abingdon, 1983) 74.

[7] *Hymns of Heritage & Hope* (Charlotte, NC: Advent Christian General Conference of America, 2001).

[8] *Common Praise* (Toronto, ON: Anglican Book Centre, 1998).

[9] *Chalice Hymnal* (St. Louis, MO: Chalice Press, 1995).

[10] *The Hymnal 1982 according to the Use of the Episcopal Church* (New York: Church Hymnal Corp., 1985).

[11] *Lutheran Book of Worship* (Minneapolis, MN: Augsburg, 1978).

[12] *The Presbyterian Hymnal: Hymns, Psalms, and Spiritual Songs* (Louisville, KY: Westminster John Knox, 1990).

[13] *The Baptist Hymnal* (Nashville, TN: Anson D. F. Randolph, 1991).

[14] *Voices United: The Hymn and Worship Book of The United Church of Canada* (Etobicoke, ON: United Church Publishing House, 1996).

[15] *The New Century Hymnal* (Cleveland, OH: Pilgrim Press, 1995).

[16] *The United Methodist Hymnal* (Nashville, TN: United Methodist Publishing House, 1989).

between the earthly work and the post-earthly work, and how are the benefits of that work to be appropriated? All this is to ask, according to an authorized corpus of song, who do we say that he is?

CHRISTOLOGICAL CLAIMS IN HYMNAL ORGANIZATION
As made evident by the hymn books compiled by Schaff and Wesley, it is difficult for one single type of organizational scheme—liturgical year, *ordo salutis*, credal outline or dogmatic structure, or experiential pattern—to carry fully and clearly the church's christological claims. Recognizing the limitations of a single plan, recent hymnal editorial committees have opted to combine methods in order to produce a theologically sensible and practically useful sequence of hymns.

All ten hymnals employ as part of their arrangement a progression of hymns according to the liturgical year, thereby marking episodes in the life of Christ, and also providing a system for confessing his person and work from the orientation of his glorious exaltation.[17] The majority of subheadings for the christological calendar are similar across the hymn books, with a variation provided by the Advent Christians who emphasize the "Second Coming" rather than the "reign of Christ" or "Christ the King." Placement of the liturgical year sequence in the overall schemes varies, but can be distilled to three general forms: liturgical year hymns placed within an overall credal structure; liturgical year hymns juxtaposed to a credal or dogmatic structure; and liturgical year hymns put adjacent to "general" hymns of differing arrangements. Each of the three forms appears to have distinct advantages and disadvantages in communicating by heading the essentials of christology.

Liturgical Year Hymns in a Credal Structure
In the first category, the liturgical year hymns are typically located under the broad heading of "Jesus Christ," and placed between those hymns meant to be addressed to or descriptive of God the Father and those to or about the Holy Spirit. Although a trinitarian claim is intended by this structure, the phraseology of some of the general headings makes a precise definition difficult. Related to this is a problem similar to one found in anaphoral construction: how simultaneously

[17] See Joseph Jungmann, "The Defeat of Teutonic Arianism and the Revolution in Religious Culture in the Early Middle Ages," in *Pastoral Liturgy* (New York: Herder and Herder, 1962) 53.

to identify the Persons of the Godhead singly without obscuring their triune coinherence, and without lapsing into either modalism or confining a Person's work to a particular phase of salvation history.

Self-defined as a non-credal church, the Disciples of Christ use as the first three general headings in their *Chalice Hymnal*: "God Beyond all Name and Form," "God Known in Jesus Christ," "God Present in the Holy Spirit." They include under the first category a few Trinity hymns that take up a sequence of stanzas successively praising the Persons of the Trinity, though these hymns are not arranged under a subhead identifying them as such (nor is there a heading "Trinity" in the topical index). Among these Trinity hymns is the standard "Come, Thou Almighty King" with the second stanza inviting the "incarnate Word"; then a text that, succumbing to modalism, over the course of four stanzas addresses "Creator God," "Redeemer God," "Sustainer God," and "Great Trinity";[18] and two texts by the recent hymn writers Tom Troeger and Ruth Duck that articulate biblical metaphors for the three Persons. In his stanza on the second Person, Troeger uses the images "Word and Wisdom, Root and Vine, / Shepherd, Savior, Servant, Lamb, / Well and Water, Bread and Wine, / Way who leads us to I AM."[19] Other than the brief identification of the Second Person as Logos and Savior, much is left to the imagination (or previous catechesis) regarding the Son as God-Man in these Trinity hymns.

Such ambiguity continues under the second general heading, "God Known in Jesus Christ," not only in the wording of the heading itself, but also in the selection of hymns. As is typical of many "Advent" and "Birth" sections of hymnals, more emphasis is given to the "boy-child" than to the Incarnate One owing to the sentimentality associated with the season and its over-familiar repertoire. The inclusion of Latin hymns such as "Creator of the Stars of Night" and "O Come, O Come, Emmanuel," and hymns from liturgical sources, for example "Let All Mortal Flesh Keep Silence" from the Liturgy of St. James, preserves a Nicene reading in these sections. Among the "Suffering" and "Death" hymns, it is again the older hymns that explicitly proclaim that it is the God-Man and not just an innocent, God-fearing man who suffers. The American spiritual "Jesus Walked This Lonesome Valley" and Brian Wren's "Here hangs a man discarded, / a scarecrow hoisted

---

[18] "Creator God, Creating Still," no. 62 by Jane Parker Huber.
[19] "Source and Sovereign, Rock and Cloud," no. 12.

high, / a nonsense pointing nowhere / to all who hurry by" convey a picture of the "man of sorrows" different from what we see in the third and fourth stanzas of Johann Heerman's "Ah, Holy Jesus":

> For me, kind Jesus, was thy incarnation,
> thy mortal sorrow, and thy life's oblation;
> thy death of anguish and thy bitter passion,
> for my salvation.
>
> Therefore, kind Jesus, since I cannot pay thee,
> I do adore thee, and will ever pray thee,
> think on thy pity and thy love unswerving,
> not my deserving.

The inclusion of a subsection "Praise to Christ" under the general heading "God Known in Jesus Christ"—and preceding the sequence of liturgical year hymns—provides, in effect, the interpretive key for what follows, and also prevents a limited understanding of who Jesus Christ is. The one who makes God known is himself to be ascribed glory and majesty and is (to continue the familiar words of Edward Perronet that are quoted in this subsection) to be crowned Lord of all. Of course it is for the benefits of his work that Christ's name is praised, and that personal and corporate appropriation is fully recognized among the hymn selections in this section.

Thus the first two general headings used in the *Chalice Hymnal* may not adequately signal the Son's identity, and even a reading of subheadings may not provide sufficient theological clarity. Two other hymnals under examination employ variations of this approach, but their methods too are not without problems. Following a pattern similar to that used in the *Chalice Hymnal*, the *United Methodist Hymnal* sets out the general headings "The Glory of the Triune God," "The Grace of Jesus Christ," and "The Power of the Holy Spirit," and locates a subsection "In Praise of Christ" immediately before the sequence of christological year hymns (from "Promised Coming" to "Resurrection and Exaltation") under the heading specifically associated with the Son. But this arrangement, while acknowledging the Three-One God, denies a specific place to the First Person, and, by distinguishing the "Triune God" from "Jesus Christ" and the "Holy Spirit," may imply that the Son and Spirit are separate from the Godhead and acknowledged only for their respective functions of providing grace and power.

The *Baptist Hymnal* does specify separate subsections for Father, Son, and Holy Spirit, but locates them under two different general headings: "God the Father" appears as a subsection under the first general heading "The Glory of God," which also includes a subsection devoted to "God's Work"; and "God the Son" and "God the Holy Spirit" are located under the broad category "The Love of God." To make this trinitarian reading even more problematic, the section "God the Trinity" is identified as a section under the heading "The Love of God" following the hymns that focus upon the Spirit. Yet the presence in the section on "God the Son" of a subsection of hymns dedicated to his praise and adoration works against a subordinationist reading thanks to texts such as F. Bland Tucker's paraphrase of the Philippian kenotic hymn ("All Praise to Thee, for Thou, O King Divine") and Delma Reno's hymn "Praise the Lord, the King of Glory" that recasts the Nicene statement with the words "With the Father thro' creation, / Heav'n and earth now sing His fame; / Hope and joy of ev'ry nation, / Life and light are in His name."[20] The *Baptist Hymnal* also utilizes an unusual subcategory in this section, "Friend," which, to press the Son's identity as God and man, locates it between hymns dealing with the Son as "Savior and Lord" and those addressing his "Return."

Hymns that amplify *Christus pro nobis* and *Christus in nobis* can be found together in sections of hymnals identified with the Trinity and with Jesus Christ, especially when the latter is organized in part according to the liturgical year. Hymns connecting the earthly and post-earthly are also found in hymnals organized along credal or dogmatic lines in those sections that focus upon the church, the *ordo salutis*, or the Christian life more broadly. It is in the sections of sacramental hymns—in the *United Methodist Hymnal* under the general heading of "The Community of Faith" corresponding to that article of the Apostles' Creed—that the ongoing benefits of Christ's work are most obviously expressed. A eucharistic hymn by the eighteenth-century English hymn writer Charles Wesley in the United Methodist collection, for example, describes a Scripture event as an ongoing reality and of continuing efficacy:

> O Thou who this mysterious bread
> Didst in Emmaus break,

[20] "Praise the Lord, the King of Glory," no. 232.

Return, herewith our souls to feed,
And to thy followers speak.

Unseal the volume of thy grace,
Apply the gospel word;
Open our eyes to see thy face,
Our hearts to know the Lord.

Of thee communing still, we mourn
Till thou the veil remove;
Talk with us, and our hearts shall burn
With flames of fervent love.

Enkindle now the heavenly zeal,
And make thy mercy known,
And give our pardoned souls to feel
That God and love are one.[21]

Liturgical Year Hymns Juxtaposed to a Credal or Dogmatic Structure

In hymnals of this organizational configuration, the first hymns of the book are sequenced according to the church year; these are then followed by hymns ordered according to a clearly identifiable systematic pattern. For example, the first 215 hymns of the United Church of Canada's *Voices United* move thematically from Advent to the Reign of Christ. The next groupings of hymns come under the general headings of "God's Creating and Redeeming Love," "The Community of Faith," "The Church in the World," and "A New Heaven and a New Earth"—categories quite similar to the overall arrangement found in the *United Methodist Hymnal*. The general heading "God's Creating and Redeeming Love" is divided into three sections—"God," "Jesus Christ," and "Holy Spirit"—with hymns of praise for each Person delineated under each section. A subsection labeled "The Triune God" comes under the section "God," and here the majority of hymns devote successive stanzas to each Person of the Godhead, typically concluding in a fourth stanza with reference to the Three as Unity. Many of the theological dilemmas arising from similar organizational configurations that have been already discussed apply here.

But a new problem appears with this scheme in that there are two principal locations for christologically-focused texts: the section identified as "Jesus Christ" and the section sequenced according to the liturgi-

<hr />

[21] "O Thou Who This Mysterious Bread," no. 613.

cal year. Are these parallel sections, or do they in effect divide the christological presentation perhaps in theologically problematic ways (e. g., incarnation and atonement emphasized in one place, Jesus as lover and friend in another)? Or is the section "Jesus Christ" primarily a catch-all for random texts that do not comfortably fit into the liturgical year template? In *Voices United*, two subsections of hymns come under "Jesus Christ": those offering praise and thanksgiving to Christ, and those that fill out the comma in the Apostles' Creed separating "born of the Virgin Mary" from "suffered under Pontius Pilate." Lyrical illustration of the Christ to whom "a thousand tongues" offer praise is balanced with metrical narratives recounting "When Jesus the healer passed through Galilee." Here the section "Jesus Christ" conveys a picture of the God-Man; nevertheless, it also must be "read" in conjunction with the liturgical year section to reveal fully why the Son is worthy of adoration.

In the case of the *Presbyterian Hymnal*, which locates the subsection "Jesus Christ" between "God" and "Holy Spirit" under the general heading "Topical Hymns," the fourteen hymns not included among those illuminating the Christian year are much more thematically eclectic, ranging from Fred Kaan's incarnation-focused "Down to Earth, as a Dove" to the African-American spiritual "Amen" that rehearses episodes in the life of Christ, William Billings' "When Jesus Wept," and Anna Bartlett Warner's childhood favorite "Jesus Loves Me." For those who use this book, the church year progression of hymns *is* the systematic instruction in christology. Even the majority of hymns focused upon praise to the Trinity are placed in this sequence (under "Trinity" in reference to Trinity Sunday), with a few others located under the less-obvious category of "Morning and Opening Hymns."

The church year sequence of hymns is likewise the main source for christology in the *Lutheran Book of Worship* which is organized under three main heads: "The Church Year," "The Church at Worship," and "The Life of Faith"; there are no separate sections devoted to lyrical exegesis of "God." Yet the christological hymns are not limited to the first section, for as might be surmised from the headings, hymns elucidating the *Christus pro nobis* can be found under "The Church at Worship"; and "The Life of Faith," with its subheads of "Justification," "Repentance, Forgiveness," "Christian Hope," and others, contains hymns that develop *Christus in nobis*.

The *New Century Hymnal* of the United Church of Christ presents a method that falls between the two major organizational patterns thus far described. Although questions have been raised both within and outside the denomination regarding the approaches to God language and textual revision taken up by the hymnal's editorial committee,[22] the committee's novel systematic sequencing of hymns avoids some of the problems of the other organizational styles. Five general headings are employed: "Hymns of Praise," "Hymns for the Christian Year," "Hymns for the Faith and Order of the Church," "Hymns for the Life and Work of the Church," "Hymns of Christian Hope." Under "Hymns of Praise" there is a section "The Holy Trinity" which is subdivided into sections focusing upon "God," "Jesus Christ," and "Holy Spirit." While it is problematic to identify "God" with the first Person alone, the listing of the Three Persons under the category "Holy Trinity" does resolve an awkwardness evident in the other collections.

The disconnection of the "Jesus Christ" hymns from those assigned under the liturgical year continues in this book, but is lessened by virtue of the first section's being principally hymns of praise—that then sets the stage for the other hymns to demonstrate the worthiness of praise. Of the ten hymnals examined, the organizational method presented in the *New Century Hymnal* provides the clearest outline of the Second Person of the Godhead in relation to his work and the human response to that work. Unfortunately the perhaps overly scrupulous concern about using the name Father and gendered language in the hymns themselves has quite muddied theologically what the table of contents in summary makes so clear.

Liturgical Year Hymns adjacent to "General" Hymns

Both Anglican books under examination take this approach in their hymnal organization, with the church year in first place within the collection. Hymns devoted to Jesus Christ fall in a general section at some distance in the book from those linked with the liturgical year—with the general hymns overall being of a more obvious systematic arrangement in the Episcopal Church (USA)'s *Hymnal 1982* than in the Anglican Church of Canada's 1998 resource. Despite the disconnect in space between the christological year hymns and those on "Jesus Christ," the two sections in both books are thematically interconnected and overlap in their presentation of the christological material, though within the latter section the rationale for their arrangement is not

---

[22] See, for example, the chapter "A Tale of Two Hymnals" in S. A. Marini, *Sacred Song in America: Religion, Music, and Public Culture* (Urbana, IL: University of Illinois Press, 2003) esp. 194–207.

overt. Effectively the two sections duplicate one another, but the separation of some into church year categories may be seen as advantageous in liturgical performance, particularly when the texts explicitly refer to the day or season in the liturgical year—as is the case with the majority of Lenten hymns. Conversely, an adaptation of Philipp Nicolai's "How Brightly Shines the Morning Star" is located in the general sections of both of these books, whereas the same text is placed either in nativity or epiphany sections in other hymnals.

The separation of "Jesus Christ" hymns into a separate category also allows for poetic exploration of complex theological themes not tidily placed within the framework of the liturgical year, and both of these books are bold in their inclusion of such hymns. Among these hymns are ones that speak in a single text to Christ as fully human and fully divine. The Canadian *Common Praise* contains a contemporary hymn that rearticulates the Chalcedonian definition stating that characteristics that can be affirmed of the human nature or the divine nature—even when in paradoxical relationship to each other—may be affirmed of the "one and the same Son and Only-begotten God the Word, Lord Jesus Christ" on account of the personal union. Appropriately this strong theological text by the late United Church of Canada minister Sylvia Dunstan is set to the original tune "Christus Paradox."

> You, Lord, are both lamb and shepherd.
> You, Lord, are both prince and slave.
> You, peacemaker and swordbringer
> of the way you took and gave.
> You, the everlasting instant;
> you, whom we both scorn and crave.
>
> Clothed in light upon the mountain,
> stripped of might upon the cross,
> shining in eternal glory,
> beggared by a soldier's toss,
> you, the everlasting instant;
> you, who are both gift and cost.
>
> You, who walk each day beside us,
> sit in power at God's side.
> You, who preach a way that's narrow,
> have a love that reaches wide.
> You, the everlasting instant;
> you, who are our pilgrim guide.

Worthy is our earthly Jesus!
Worthy is our cosmic Christ!
Worthy your defeat and victory.
Worthy still your peace and strife.
You, the everlasting instant;
you, who are our death and life.

TEXTUAL ALTERATIONS AND SHIFTING MEANINGS

It is impossible given the number of hymns contained in the ten hymnals to examine each for its contribution to the nexus of christological interpretation found between a single set of book covers. But it is possible to look at one hymn shared across all ten books that generally occurs in subsections focused upon praise and adoration of the Son (an exception is the Advent Christians who place it under "Ascension and Reign"). "Beautiful Savior," more commonly translated from the seventeenth-century German text *Schönster Herr Jesu* as "Fairest Lord Jesus," comes into English via an 1873 translation by Joseph A. Seiss. Seiss's original translation, found predominantly in hymnals of the Lutheran family, among them the *Lutheran Book of Worship*, is:

Beautiful Savior, King of Creation
Son of God and Son of Man!
Truly I'd love thee, Truly I'd serve thee,
Light of my soul, my joy, my crown.[23]

The majority of hymnals, including four of our books (the hymnals for the Advent Christian, Baptist, Episcopal, and United Methodist churches), have adapted Seiss's translation to:

Fairest Lord Jesus, Ruler of all nature,
O Thou of God and man the Son,
Thee will I cherish, Thee will I honor,
Thou my soul's glory, joy and crown.

Theologically, the text in either version conforms to both Nicene and Chalcedonian definitions, and is theologically consonant with the

---

[23] The original German is *"Schönster Herr Jesu, Herrscher aller Erden, / Gottes und Marien Sohn / Dich will ich lieben, Dich will ich ehren, / Du meiner Seele Freud und Kron."*

Johannine prologue in its appellation of Jesus as the "King of Creation" or the "Ruler of all nature."

Of particular interest here is the second line of this the first stanza, which in German reads, "Gottes und Marien Sohn," which weds the divine and human and makes the claim of human specificity. The Lutheran Seiss overlooked a literal translation for unspecified reasons; Philip Schaff, in a translation dated earlier than that of Seiss, preserves the original German, somewhat awkwardly, with the line, "Jesus, of God and of Mary the Son."[24] The text used in the United Church of Christ hymnal is the only one to reflect the original German by using the phrase "God and the blessed Mary's child," but the rest of the hymn is weakened by a decision to adjust what was considered offensive imperialist language: in particular the change of the first line to "Beautiful Jesus, head of creation" may imply to a casual user that the one addressed in the hymn is first in a line of created things.[25]

Three of the hymnals follow another translation, apparently an altered version of a text found in *Church Chorals and Choir Studies* dated 1850, that reads for the second line "O Thou of God to earth come down," which not only removes reference to the two natures of Christ and the repeated biblical assertion of him as the Son of Man, but also renders ambiguous the connection of the "fairest Lord Jesus" to God.[26] The Anglican Church of Canada's decision to insert the line "O thou the Godhead's human son" is equally problematic since numerous misreadings may result. Thus the simple adjustment of a single poetic line may make dramatically different theological assertions as to who we say that Christ is.

CONCLUSION

What may be learned by this assessment of christology exposed through the organization of hymnals? Many things could be said, but three will be mentioned here.

---

[24] Schaff, *IXΘΥΣ*, 413. Schaff, who notes that this hymn may come from the twelfth century and may have been sung by the Crusaders, uses "Fairest Lord Jesus" for the opening line.

[25] *The New Century Hymnal*, no. 44. While Colossians 1:15 calls Christ *prototokos pases ktiseos*, the next verses make it clear that he preceded all creatures as their creator.

[26] Found in the hymnals of the Disciples of Christ, the Presbyterian Church (U.S.A.), and the United Church of Canada.

First, in order to be theologically accurate in presenting an outline summary of the person and work of Christ, hymnal organizers in the future would be wise to employ a combination of the standard methods—credal or doctrinal patterns, the liturgical year, the *ordo salutis*—that then are well integrated into a single, unified construct. While not flawless, the *New Century Hymnal* is a good example of a method that works. Editorial committees should pay attention not only to ease of hymn access for liturgical usage, but also to the intentional and unintentional teaching that takes place in the sequence of hymns. For many Protestant denominations the hymnbook is their prayer book and their most frequently accessed statement of belief. In previous generations—for instance in my own Methodist tradition—persons training for the ministry used the hymnbook with its *theologia prima* as the principal source for theological instruction and reflection. Of course this raises the matter of the loss of an identifiable and usable system of organization for hymnals as print books are laid aside in favor of hymn collections on DVD, CD-ROM, and even the Internet, and isolated texts are splashed on overhead screens.

Second, it appears that old and new hymns in combination best give a full and deep presentation of christological doctrine. Hymns written from the twentieth century to the present, either in the optimistic style of the social gospel hymns or in texts that dwell on the pathos of the suffering servant, speak well to the human side of the God-Man; the text "O young and fearless prophet of ancient Galilee" is characteristic of this repertoire. Older hymns, particularly those taken from a liturgical source, often accentuate well the majesty and praise due to the triune God purely for the sake of worship. Hymns thus should be chosen with care and on balance for the hymn collections themselves. In the push to include new hymns, editorial committees must measure whether the christological perspectives presented in the old materials are adequately represented in the new. Care and balance of what might be called "lyrical theology" ought also to be considered for each gathering of the assembly for worship.

Third (and this is related to the second), writers of new hymn texts today should be encouraged for the purposes of doxology to capture in verse the principal tenets of the faith in strong and profound language. More hymns need to surface along the lines of Sylvia Dunstan's "Christus Paradox" that articulate the theological consensus of the ecumenical creeds and declarations, and thus may be shared across ecclesiastical traditions. A kind of ecumenism has existed for generations by the sharing of hymn texts across ecclesiastical lines, perhaps making hymns the original "cross-over" music. Focus upon such specifically dogmatic hymns would potentially have the additional benefit of countering the "Jesusolatry" and the narcissistic approaches that pervade the liturgical song of many Protestant churches today. Perhaps through our shared hymnody addressing *Christus in se*, *Christus pro nobis*, and *Christus in nobis*, the prayer of Christ himself may be realized: that they may all be one.

Chapter 14

Lex Amandi, Lex Orandi: The Trinity in the Most-Used Contemporary Christian Worship Songs

Lester Ruth
Asbury Theological Seminary

The last fifty years in worship have been tumultuous for Christians, even those not in the liturgical movement. Various changes have touched a wide swath of churches. Among the influential changes is the emergence of a new body of worship music known as praise choruses or contemporary worship music (CWM). For many newer churches and younger Christians, it is the only music they know.

My goal is to analyze the theological content of the lyrics that are the heart of this body of music. The particular lens for analyzing will be trinitarian. After establishing a core repertoire of CWM, I will assess these songs from several vantage points. I conclude with why this body of music is minimally trinitarian.

This trinitarian omission is ironic since most of this music's composers and users would identify themselves as conservative in theology. If they are conservative in theology—thus presumably trinitarian—what created the gap? The Christians who write and use these songs expect them to express a common relationship—even passion or intimacy—with God, not a common faith. This relationship is rooted in the heart, thus the title for this study: *lex amandi, lex orandi*. What we must love with our hearts establishes how we should pray in music.

METHOD
CWM originated in the late 1960s and early 1970s. Despite its recent origin, composers have written thousands of songs. In order to have a manageable and representative group I acquired from Christian Copy-

right Licensing International (CCLI), the major clearinghouse for the handling of royalties, lists of the top twenty-five songs for each of its twice-a-year dispersements. These lists reflect the CWM songs most used by CCLI license-holding churches in the United States, factoring in frequency of use and size of worshiping congregations, as reported by these churches. I acquired lists for each of the CCLI's first fifteen years, thirty lists, covering 1 April 1989 to 31 March 2004.[1]

Seventy-two different songs appear on these thirty lists. They constitute the base repertoire for my current study, and appear alphabetically at the end of this chapter. I determined average rankings for each song for the entire fifteen years, and to give fair consideration to more recent songs, I also calculated averages for the last five years. I calculated, too, the frequency of appearance in the twice-a-year lists, using the same two time frames, to assess which songs have appeared most consistently.

I assessed the potential trinitarian dimensions by asking these questions: Do the songs name the Trinity or all three Persons of the Trinity? Do the songs direct worship toward the Trinity as a whole or toward one of the Persons of the Trinity? Do the songs remember the activity of the divine Persons among themselves? Do the songs see Christian worship as participation in inter-trinitarian dynamics or activity? Do the songs use the character of inter-trinitarian relationships to explore a desired character for relationships among Christians, for example, unity, love, sacrifice, humility?

TRINITARIAN ASPECTS
On the whole, there are few trinitarian aspects within this body of CWM.

Naming the Trinity
Do the songs name the Trinity or all three Persons of the Trinity? None of the seventy-two songs refer to the Trinity or the triune nature of God per se. Moreover—and more surprisingly—only three songs refer to all three Persons of the Trinity: "Glorify Thy Name," "Father I Adore You," and "Shine Jesus Shine."[2] The first two of these have

---

[1] CCLI does not endorse or deny any conclusions the author draws from this data.

[2] Compare a similar review of the 362 songs produced by Vineyard Music from 1999 to 2004 in R. Parry, *Worshipping Trinity: Coming Back to the Heart of Worship* (Milton Keyes, UK: Paternoster, 2005) 143.

three verses, one each directed to the Father, Jesus, and the Spirit. The trinitarian naming in "Shine Jesus Shine" comes as the standard feature of the recurring chorus: "Shine, Jesus, shine, fill this land with the Father's glory. / Blaze, Spirit, blaze, set our hearts on fire."

Not naming the Trinity is the result of not naming the first and third Persons of the Godhead; few of the songs refer to God the Father or the Holy Spirit. With respect to God the Father, only one song in addition to the three named above speaks of God as "Father."[3] Another seven speak about the first Person of the Godhead using terms other than Father. An example is "Because He Lives," which notes "God sent His Son / They called him Jesus."[4] Sometimes these songs used alternative names for the first Person like "Holy One" ("Give Thanks") or "Most High" ("Our God Reigns"). No song uses the name "Holy Spirit," and only six refer to the Spirit.[5]

This infrequency of reference to the first and third Persons of the Trinity contrasts with the numerous times the Son of God is named. Thirty-five of the songs make reference to the second Person. Of these, twenty-seven speak of Jesus, Christ, or Jesus Christ. The other eight speak of Christ more generally as "Lord," "God," or "King," but it is clear from context that Christ is meant. For example, "Lord I Lift Your Name on High" remembers the Lord's coming, cross, and resurrection in a way that makes it clear that the "Lord" is Christ.

That clarity of reference is not present in all seventy-two songs. In order of frequency, the most used titles for the divine object of worship are "Lord" (forty-four occurrences), "God" (twenty-five occurrences), and "King" (seventeen occurrences). In twenty-six of the forty-four occurrences of "Lord" the lack of contextual clues makes it difficult to determine who this "Lord" is. In twelve of the twenty-five occurrences of "God" the lack of contextual clues obscures the specific identity of God. Except in a few cases the context makes clear that the

---

[3] "How Can We Name a Love."

[4] Others include "Jesus Name Above all Names," "Bind Us Together," and "I Stand in Awe." Only four speak of Jesus Christ as "Son of God," another factor contributing to the low trinitarian consciousness. These four are "Give Thanks," "Jesus Name Above All Names," "Because He Lives," and "Bind Us Together."

[5] "Glorify Thy Name," "Shine Jesus Shine," "You are My King," "Better is One Day," "Surely the Presence of the Lord," and "Father I Adore You."

"King" is Jesus Christ. Specificity for the divine object of worship is least in the five songs that do not use any divine title or name at all.[6]

A good way to summarize the way these songs name the Trinity or the Persons of the Trinity is to take a look at those nine songs whose purpose is to contemplate the divine name. The Christ-centeredness suggested by the review of specific names above is reflected in the Christ-focus in these nine songs.[7]

Worshiping the Triune God

The ways in which these songs name the Persons of the Trinity affect the answer to a related question: Do the songs direct worship toward the Trinity as a whole or toward one of the Persons of the Trinity? Because many more of the songs name the second Person of the Trinity, the songs are more likely to direct worship toward Christ.

Addressing worship to the Trinity as a whole or to the Holy Spirit occurs least. No song worships God for being triune. The two that worship the whole Trinity are the two structured by naming each of the Persons of the Trinity ("Glorify Thy Name" and "Father I Adore You"). Of the six that name the Spirit, only three direct worship to the Spirit, the same songs (mentioned above) that name all three Persons of the Trinity. The other three songs that mention the Holy Spirit do so in passing references to the worshiper's enjoyment of the Spirit.[8]

Worshiping the first Person of the Godhead also rarely occurs. Of the eleven songs that make clear reference to the first Person, whether as Father or by some other name, three worship the Father directly. These three include the two songs internally structured by trinitarian naming ("Glorify Thy Name" and "Father I Adore You") and the song

---

[6] "I Could Sing of Your Love Forever," "Breathe," "Above All," "Draw Me Close," and "When I Look into Your Holiness." "Above All" does commemorate Christ's crucifixion and eternal nature without naming him. "I Could Sing of Your Love Forever" refers to the "You" as "healer." "As the Deer" and "You're Worthy of My Praise" are not included because they speak (only) of the recipient as King.

[7] "Glorify Thy Name," "Lord, I Lift Your Name on High," "Jesus, Name Above All Names," "Praise the Name of Jesus," "Emmanuel," "His Name is Wonderful," "There's Something About That Name," "How Majestic is Your Name," and "Bless His Holy Name."

[8] "You are My King," "Better is One Day," and "Surely the Presence of the Lord."

with the second highest overall ranking, "Give Thanks." This latter song is exceptional since it worships the Father on the basis of trinitarian activity. One other song that distinguishes the first Person of the Trinity ("Bind Us Together") possibly addresses God the Father in petition, depending upon whether its prayer to the "Lord" has the Father in mind.[9] Whether some of the composers who speak of the "Lord" or "God" generically had God the Father in mind is difficult to tell. Given the tendency to name the second Person of the Trinity in CWM, more likely these references have Christ in mind.

Worshiping Jesus Christ is the main preoccupation in this music. Thirty-two of the thirty-five songs that refer to Christ by name or context worship him. Twelve songs worship Christ in direct prayer. The basis for worshiping Christ varies in the thirty-two songs. Eleven acknowledge Christ's divine nature, either explicitly or implicitly.[10] Several root worship in remembrance of his ministry, usually his death and resurrection.[11] Others speak of Christ's exalted status, often by piling up honorific titles; these songs are strings of Christ's titles.[12] Those that speak of Christ's exaltation often connect this status to his kingship, and occasionally to contemplation of the name "Jesus" itself. Because many more songs focus worship on Christ, the basis for worshiping the Son is more fully developed compared to the Father or the Spirit.

Remembering Trinitarian Activity

With so few of the songs naming all three Persons there is little remembrance of trinitarian activity in the corpus. Do the songs remember the activity of the divine Persons among themselves? The answer is minimally, at best. To sing of how these Persons have acted without

---

[9] "Open our Eyes Lord" is another possibility.

[10] "Awesome God," "All Hail King Jesus," "Jesus Name Above All Names," "Holy Ground," "Our God Reigns," "Emmanuel," "Here I Am to Worship," "We Will Glorify," "His Name is Wonderful," "Surely the Presence of the Lord," and "I Stand in Awe."

[11] Examples include "Majesty," "Lord I Lift Your Name on High," "You are My All in All," "You are My King," "Here I Am to Worship," "Above All," "Celebrate Jesus Celebrate," "Turn Your Eyes Upon Jesus," and especially "Our God Reigns."

[12] Examples include "All Hail King Jesus," "Jesus Name Above All Names," "We Will Glorify," and "His Name is Wonderful."

naming them is difficult. As a whole, these songs are what some call "functionally unitarian."[13]

As noted above, only three songs name and distinguish all three Persons of the Godhead. In two of these ("Glorify Thy Name" and "Father I Adore You"), the composers do not explore how the Persons interact but rather make each the object of worship. The structure of the songs implies equality between the Father, Jesus (instead of Son for metrical reasons), and the Spirit. The third, "Shine Jesus Shine," has more substance in speaking of trinitarian activity. The song is an extended petition, directed to Jesus, requesting a revealing of God's glory or light. The main petition makes Jesus the mediator of the Father's glory, and the Spirit the enabler of our participation in this glory. This song is exceptional among the seventy-two in that it implies reliance upon Christ or the Spirit to experience the Father.

A few songs refer to two Persons of the Trinity within the same song, eight the Father and the Son[14] and two the Son and the Spirit.[15] One song ("Better is One Day") appears to speak of the Father and the Holy Spirit if "living God" refers to God the Father. In the songs that discuss the Father and the Son, the strongest theme is that the Father has given the Son, whose death saves us. Six of the Father/Son songs have this theme, usually in brief references such as that the "Holy One" has given Jesus Christ his Son ("Give Thanks") or even that Jesus is the Lamb of God ("You are My All in All").[16] The two songs that explore this theme more fully come from the Suffering Servant prophecy in Isaiah 53 ("I Stand in Awe" and "Our God Reigns"). The two remaining Father/Son songs have undeveloped associations between the two. In "Jesus Name Above All Names," for example, the

---

[13] I note that those who use this phrase speak of a wider phenomenon. See, for example, J. B. Torrance, *Worship, Community and the Triune God of Grace* (Carlisle: Paternoster, 1996) 20.

[14] "Give Thanks," "Our God Reigns," "I Stand in Awe," "Because He Lives," "Bind Us Together," "You are My All in All," "Jesus Name Above All Names," and "How Can We Name a Love." "Open Our Eyes" also possibly refers to the Father and the Son.

[15] "You are My King" and "Surely the Presence of the Lord."

[16] Two other songs refer to the Lamb without amplification: "We Fall Down" and "We Will Glorify." I have not included them among those songs that speak of the Father and the Son since they refer to the "Lamb" without exploring this title.

composer speaks of Jesus as Son of God, Emmanuel, and God with us, as part of a stringing together of names and titles for Christ without explanation.[17]

The two songs that speak of Christ and the Holy Spirit make only passing reference to their relationship. In "You are My King" the singer possesses the Spirit of Jesus owing to his crucifixion and resurrection. In "Surely the Presence of the Lord" the singer feels the "sweet Spirit" as a result of the Lord Jesus fulfilling the promise of his presence.

Besides the absence of names, two factors contribute to the lack of emphasis on the activity of the Trinity. The first is a tendency to emphasize divine character traits or status but not the dynamics of the Trinity. "Shout to the Lord," for example, exults in the idea that no one can compare to Jesus as he is the singer's comfort, shelter, and tower of refuge and strength. "As the Deer," the fourth ranked song, never names God, but speaks of the song's recipient as the singer's strength, friend, brother, real joygiver, king, etc. These songs represent the strong tendency to speak of the Divine in exalted terms but not of worship of the Trinity and its activity. The second factor is the de-emphasis on God's saving activity. When God's actions are recalled, the remembrance does not put salvation in a broader meta-narrative of the specific activities of the Father, Son, and Holy Spirit within the economy of salvation. Usually the saving work is attributed to a single entity, whether God, the Lord, or Christ, and spoken of as a simple historic event.

Most of the eighteen songs that commemorate God's saving activity focus on the crucifixion and resurrection of Christ. Reference to the crucifixion, sometimes with the resurrection, occurs in fourteen songs.[18] For example, "Give Thanks" speaks of the Holy One having given Jesus Christ his Son. Only three of the songs that mention the crucifixion place it in a wider context. "Lord I Lift Your Name on

---

[17] "How Can We Name a Love" is the other. Two songs that mention Emmanuel without explanation are "All Hail King Jesus" and "Emmanuel," neither of which I include among the Father/Son songs.

[18] "Lord I Lift Your Name on High," "Here I Am to Worship," "Because He Lives," "Bind Us Together," "Turn Your Eyes Upon Jesus," "I Stand in Awe," "Our God Reigns," "Majesty," "You are My All in All," "Shine Jesus Shine," "You are My King," "Above All," "Oh How He Loves You," and "Awesome God."

High" associates it with the Christ's incarnation, cross, burial, and exaltation; "Here I am to Worship" associates creation, Christ's incarnation, crucifixion, and exaltation. Another crucifixion-remembering song, "Awesome God," makes the crucifixion the activity of the same God (Christ) who judged Adam and Eve in the Garden, brought judgment on Sodom, and is about to return.

Few of the songs explore the internal dynamics of the Trinity with respect to this limited commemoration. In the songs' economy of salvation the relationship of the Holy Spirit to Christ or to the Father is nonexistent. With respect to the dynamic between the Father and the Son, there is only the occasional passing association of Christ's saving activity to the Father.[19] This leaves even the doctrine of the atonement underdeveloped in its trinitarian aspects.

The few remembrances of God's saving activity mean that possibilities for exploring the trinitarian aspect of salvation are missed. Because this music's soteriology emphasizes salvation as personal experience, the songs do not explore possible trinitarian aspects in cosmic or ecclesial understandings of salvation. With little emphasis on present aspects of God's work, like Christ's heavenly mediation, and the Holy Spirit's saving work, God's saving activity seems to be something done in the past which now results in a personal relationship. There also is little sense of God's ongoing mission in the world and little eschatology in the songs.

Participation in the Trinity

The lack of emphasis on the internal dynamics or activity of the Trinity relates to another trinitarian deficiency. Because so few of the songs commemorate God's activity as a dynamic interplay between Father, Son, and Holy Spirit, the songs do not contemplate worship as participation in trinitarian activity.

CWM tends to objectify God as the recipient of worship so as to emphasize a distinction between the one worshiped and the worshiper. God/Christ/the Lord/the King is someone out there whom we adore as worthy of our worship. The songs speak at length of our love for God, with little sense of Christians being brought into the internal dynamic of this God's triune community. Almost all the language of relationship and activity in these songs describes the dynamic between human worshipers and the divine recipient, not the

[19] "Give Thanks," "Because He Lives," and "Bind Us Together."

relationship and activity among the Persons of the Trinity. The songs put more emphasis on worshipers' activity than on divine activity. With so little contemplation of internal trinitarian dynamics, the songs have no room to say that the worship of Christians participates in these dynamics.

In particular, there is little sense of worshipers being in Christ or Christ being in worshipers as an ecclesial reality. These songs do not reflect an understanding of worship as being the common activity of a church that is in Christ during worship. Neither do these songs represent worship as participation in Christ's action through us to the Father. The forty-one songs that are some sort of prayer provide little sense of being addressed to the Father through the Son in the power of the Holy Spirit; they mainly address Christ in prayer. Of the few that address God the Father, none speak of us addressing the Father through Christ, or the church's prayer being Christ praying through us. Nor do the songs speak of Christ's having any ongoing intercessory ministry.

The Trinity in the Church

By now one can predict the answer to the last question used to investigate the trinitarian dimensions of the most-used CWM: Do the songs use the character of inter-trinitarian relationships to explore a desired character for relationship among Christians, for example, unity, love, sacrifice, or humility? The answer is, very rarely.

These seventy-two songs have a very low consciousness of the church. Only one ("Lord Be Glorified") uses the word "church," while another ("We Have Come Into His House") has been labeled by CCLI as having a church theme. Only a handful possess a sense of God's people as community.[20] CCLI has labeled two as about fellowship: "We Have Come Into His House" and "Bind Us Together." The songs that show ecclesial consciousness are not those with the highest average use. Only "Bind Us Together" has a vision for the church derived from contemplating the triune God; it petitions the Lord for a greater measure of unity, basing the request on the triune God's nature and activity. Beyond this, the music has little to say about relationships among Christians.

---

[20] "We Bring the Sacrifice of Praise," "Holy Ground," "Our God Reigns," and, perhaps, "Joy to the World."

REASONS FOR THE ABSENCE OF
TRINITARIAN CONTENT

Acts of omission, not commission, cause the lack of a trinitarian dimension in most CWM.[21] Songwriters, marketers, and the churches choosing these songs do not value trinitarian content, or miss it if it is not included. Neither the way of composing songs, nor their promotion by the publishers, nor the way churches use them make theological concerns a priority. Few theological expectations are placed on the songs, their composers, and church musicians. Other concerns marginalize the Trinity. Even when theological review comes into play, too often the goal is limited to avoiding obvious error or expressing a scriptural sentiment. Few composers seek to include theological contemplation of the triune God.

Rather than focusing on the Trinity, CWM is concerned to share and express affective experience in worship. To use its language, worship is expressing our hearts and ministering to the heart of God. It is this law of love, *lex amandi,* that determines the rule of praying, *lex orandi.*

This concern with affections can be seen in the available literature from and about the composers of this study's songs.[22] The composers frequently describe worship as authentically singing to God from one's heart to express true affection directly to God;[23] they often use a cluster of related terms to emphasize the affective dimension of worship. Terms like relationship, closeness, intimacy, and the immediacy of divine presence are common. Composers who write songs that express their heart and create a sense of closeness with God do not see a need for the Trinity.

---

[21] Even a cursory examination of CCLI's online database shows that there are many trinitarian songs in CWM, just not in the corpus studied here; some are by the same composers. The present study seeks to investigate the nature of the songs most used in order to indicate trends in CWM as a whole.

[22] I found background data on forty-four of the seventy-two songs. Three books were especially helpful: L. Terry, *The Sacrifice of Praise: Stories behind the Greatest Praise and Worship Songs of All Time* (Nashville, TN: Integrity Publishers, 2002); P. Christensen and S. MacDonald, *Our God Reigns: The Stories behind Your Favorite Praise and Worship Songs* (Grand Rapids, MI: Kregel, 2000); and idem, *Celebrate Jesus: The Stories Behind Your Favorite Praise and Worship Songs* (Grand Rapids, MI: Kregel, 2003). Issues of the magazine *Worship Leader* also provided background.

[23] See Christensen and MacDonald, *Our God Reigns,* 127; *Celebrate Jesus,* 46, 66; and Terry, *The Sacrifice of Praise,* 45.

The actual dynamics of composing contribute to a lack of trinitarian emphasis. For one thing, many of the songs were written spontaneously, often in one sitting, and sometimes even during a worship service itself. Of the forty-four songs for which I found background information, twenty-nine were spontaneous creations. There was no time for deeper theological revision. If a composer felt God had directly given a song, there was no need for further theological reflection.

Another important compositional dynamic is the life situation of many composers. Many of these songs were written at a low point in the composer's life, expressing an encounter with God at that point. The economy of salvation in these songs is a personal story of salvation. In such personal expressions of the composer's experience and affections there would be little desire for theological reflection.

A final compositional dynamic that marginalizes trinitarian content is, ironically, the source of many of the songs: Scripture, particularly the Psalms. Many of the composers mention deriving their songs from Scripture, either by directly singing a biblical text, or by scriptural allusion or short phrases. The Psalms are the scriptural material most mentioned in the accounts of composition and most suggested for future compositions.[24] While the use of Psalms is commendable and historical, it contributes to the lack of trinitarian content in this study's songs since the triune God is not obvious there. Moreover, if a song is scripturally derived the biblical connection is self-validating; there seems to be no need for theological revision.

The system by which CWM is produced and marketed to churches is also responsible for the trinitarian omission. Several commercial sources make CWM available to churches.[25] This system of distribution helps to marginalize trinitarian concerns in that it reinforces the piety that creates and chooses these songs. Christians within this system seem to have the same piety as the composers and the churches using the songs. These Christians have not seen the omission because they have valued the songs on other grounds.

For those involved in this system, the sale of CWM is business as well as ministry. Business concerns provide little motivation to ad-

---

[24] For an example, see M. D. Roberts, "3 Songwriting Essentials: Theology, Poetry, & Community." *Worship Leader* 13, no. 2 (2004) 23–25.

[25] See R. Redman, *The Great Worship Awakening: Singing a New Song in the Postmodern Church* (San Francisco: Jossey-Bass, 2002) 55–67.

dress the omission of a theological dimension in these songs. Good theology does not necessarily sell songs. Robb Redman, a former vice president at Maranatha! Music, acknowledges that decisions about repertoire and presentations often have been defined "by the needs of the recording and marketing process (projected revenue and expenses, available musical talent, advertising, and so on) instead of the needs of the congregation for worship music people can sing with theological integrity."[26]

Finally, the reasons these seventy-two songs have become the most used CWM songs for the last fifteen years reside with the churches that choose them.[27] An important factor is the churches' expectations for worship music. CWM-related literature speaks of the desire for an experience of God's presence in and through the music. When the theology of the Vineyard movement has been influential, for example, worshipers express this desire in terms of intimacy. The criteria for discerning achievement of this goal are affective. Whether a song truly expresses the heart seems a higher concern than doctrinal content.

In discussing how to use CWM in "worship sets," worship leaders (the usual term for musicians) place a strong emphasis on the instrumentality of the music to create an experience of divine presence. One explanation is the Old Testament typology found in certain pentecostal and charismatic writers. In this typology the areas and thresholds of the temple or tabernacle provide the framework for the musical

[26] Ibid., 69; Redman offers a caveat that these concerns can be overstated and do not apply to all.

[27] The CCLI Web site notes more than 136,000 churches holding licenses in the United States. Each top 25 list represents a sampling of these license holders. I obtained from CCLI a denominational breakdown of the churches represented in the October 1989, October 1996, and October 2003 lists. In each sample at least 130 denominations were represented. The October 1989 list represents 8,270 churches with the following as the largest participants in the sample: Southern Baptist (1,147); Assemblies of God (712); independent Charismatic (452); and Nazarene (341). The October 1996 lists represents 6,470 churches with the following as the largest participants: Southern Baptist (1,024); United Methodist (416); Assemblies of God (340); and Lutheran–Missouri Synod (213). The October 2003 list represents 8,106 churches with the following as the largest participants: Southern Baptist (1,198); United Methodist (638); Assemblies of God (455); and Evangelical Lutheran Church in America/Canada (286).

journey to an experience of God's presence in a musically achieved "Holy of Holies."[28]

Even if other churches do not use this precise typology to explain the musical order, these churches often replicate a similar order for the set. The movement tends to go from "praise" or "high praise" to "worship" understood as intimate communion with God. There is often a shift in the tempo of the songs from fast to slow. There is also an increasing focus on the divine "You" directly addressed by the song lyric. To achieve this end of entering God's presence, musical worship leaders often learn to structure the musical set by "flow."[29] Most explanations of achieving "flow" do not address it by theological concerns but by theme, tempo, and key. Key is important to allow easy and effective transitions between songs. Tempo is a concern to allow the common movement from faster to slower. Theme is a concern for it allows songs to be gathered together on a central topic, perhaps to anticipate the main sermon idea. This theme-based approach to planning a musical set contributed to the widespread use of these seventy-two songs. Theme-based approaches tend to emphasize nouns (names for God) and adjectives (attributes for God). These songs excel in these qualities; what they lack is a corresponding emphasis on verbs, understood as the activity of God within the economy of salvation and inter-trinitarian dynamics.

This emphasis on the use of musical sets to facilitate an experience of God erodes a classic understanding of Jesus Christ as the mediator between humans and God the Father. Typical use of CWM places expectations on music to mediate worshipers' approach to God. Perhaps displacing Christ as mediator with the Father goes hand in hand with the central focus on an exalted, divine Christ in CWM. If worship's primary end is communion or intimacy with the Son, not with God the Father, the need for Christ as mediator is itself lessened. Mediation is shifted to the music. Thus prayer in CWM is not to the Father through the Son but to the Son through the music.

[28] See J. Cornwall, *Let Us Worship* (South Plainfield, NJ: Bridge Publications, 1983), 153–58, and D. K. Blomgren et al., *Restoring Praise & Worship in the Church* (Shippensburg, PA: Revival Press, 1999).

[29] See [P. Baloche], *Leading Worship: Creating Flow.* Modern Worship Series Instructional DVD (Lindale, TX: Lead Worship, 2003).

WILL CWM CHANGE?

What will future years of CCLI data indicate? If this method is applied to future most-used songs, what will the study show?

Several signs indicate a possible shift. One is the increased number of songs about the Trinity recently registered with CCLI. Another is the growing awareness by CWM composers of the power of liturgical songs to shape people's faith. Many of the new composers speak of their practice of submitting songs to those who can provide a theological review. This increased theological dialogue is reflected in the works of composers like Graham Kendrick and Matt Redman.[30] Moreover, a growing number of theologians and pastors respected within the CWM world, publishing in venues accessed by CWM users, have called for theologically enriched lyrics.[31]

While these signs indicate a potential shift in the most-used songs for the next fifteen years, widespread change will depend upon doing more than creating a more trinitarian theology among CWM composers and users. The key will be developing a more trinitarian piety. These Christians will write and choose more trinitarian songs only if love for the Trinity resides in their hearts. The dynamics of *lex amandi, lex orandi* will not go away. Consider the *lex amandi* in how the composer Brian Doerksen explains a song's goal. He says that the aim of a song is "to unlock the language of a people's hearts and for them to say, 'This is exactly what I wanted to say to God.'"[32] Since Doerksen accurately assesses the way CWM is valued, the implication is clear: to see a shift will mean planting adoration of the Trinity within people's hearts. Song composition and use will shift as these Christians learn to

---

[30] For Kendrick, see D. Di Sabatino, "Table Talk: An Interview with Graham Kendrick." *Worship Leader* 10, no. 7 (2001): 30. For Redman, see his comments in Parry, *Worshipping Trinity*, xi, and P. Baloche et al., *God Songs: How to Write and Select Songs for Worship* (Lindale, TX: Lead Worship, 2004), 215–16. For the latter's trinitarian theology of worship, see M. Redman, *Facedown* (Ventura, CA: Regal Books, 2004) 52.

[31] R. E. Webber, "Is Our Worship Adequately Triune?" *Reformation & Revival Journal* 9, no. 3 (2000) 121–32; B. McLaren, "An Open Letter to Songwriters." *Worship Leader* 10, no. 1 (2002): 44–45; B. Waggoner, "Leading Trinitarian Worship." *Inside Worship* 52 (2004): 5–6.

[32] "Songwriting." In *Songwriting for Worship: Study Tools for the DVD*. Equip Resources for Worship Series Instructional DVD. Vineyard Music Global.

love the triune God for being triune. The Trinity must become the language of this people's hearts.

The 72 Songs Appearing on Top 25 CCLI Lists from April 1989 to March 2004
(Note: Lack of data in 5-year columns means no appearance on those lists.)

Title	15 year rank	# of times on lists 15 years	Last 5 years rank	# of times on lists in last 5 years
Above All	39	4	24	4
Ah Lord God	49	5		
All Hail King Jesus	10	22	42	2
Arise and Sing	71	1		
As the Deer	4	29	5	10
Awesome God	9	25	8	10
Because He Lives	53	4		
Better Is One Day	54	4	36	4
Bind Us Together	63	1		
Bless His Holy Name	38	7		
Breathe	30	5	16	5
Celebrate Jesus Celebrate	52	5	35	4
Change My Heart O God	22	17	13	10
Come Now Is the Time to Worship	24	7	9	7
Draw Me Close	47	4	30	4
Emmanuel	29	13	36	2
Father I Adore You	63	2		
Forever	45	3	29	3
Give Thanks	2	29	7	9
Glorify Thy Name	8	24	23	5

(Continued)

Title	15 year rank	# of times on lists 15 years	Last 5 years rank	# of times on lists in last 5 years
God of Wonders	39	3	24	3
Great Is the Lord	33	18	34	5
He Has Made Me Glad	5	26	14	7
He Is Exalted	11	25	15	8
Here I Am to Worship	35	3	19	3
His Name Is Wonderful	51	6		
Holy Ground	26	20		
How Can We Name a Love	55	1		
How Majestic Is Your Name	23	19		
I Could Sing Your Love Forever	28	9	11	9
I Exalt Thee	12	25	31	5
I Give You My Heart	66	1	44	1
I Love You Lord	1	28	6	9
I Stand in Awe	66	1	44	1
I Will Call Upon the Lord	12	24	33	4
I Worship You Almighty God	56	3	43	1
In Moments Like These	61	1		
Jesus Name Above All Names	15	21	40	2
Joy to the World	66	1		
Let There Be Glory and Honor and Praises	66	1		
Lord Be Glorified	56	4		

(Continued)

Title	15 year rank	# of times on lists 15 years	Last 5 years rank	# of times on lists in last 5 years
Lord I Lift Your Name on High	6	21	1	10
Lord Reign in Me	56	2	39	2
Majesty	3	27	10	8
More Precious Than Silver	25	14	21	6
My Life Is in You Lord	44	7	28	7
Oh How He Loves You and Me	42	9		
Open Our Eyes	17	22	40	3
Open the Eyes of my Heart	19	9	3	9
Our God Reigns	27	10		
Praise the Name of Jesus	18	17		
Sanctuary	41	5	26	5
Seek Ye First	36	13		
Shine Jesus Shine	21	19	12	10
Shout to the Lord	14	13	2	10
Surely the Presence of the Lord	62	1		
The Heart of Worship	31	5	17	5
There's Something about that Name	59	1		
This Is the Day	16	22	36	4
Thou Art Worthy	34	8		
Thy Loving-kindness	60	1		
Trading My Sorrows	37	4	22	4

(Continued)

Title	15 year rank	# of times on lists 15 years	Last 5 years rank	# of times on lists in last 5 years
Turn Your Eyes upon Jesus	65	1		
We Bring the Sacrifice of Praise	7	26	20	6
We Fall Down	42	5	27	5
We Have Come into His House	47	5		
We Will Glorify	45	9		
What a Mighty God We Serve	70	2		
When I Look into Your Holiness	70	1		
You Are My All in All	20	11	4	10
You Are My King	31	5	17	5
You're Worthy of My Praise	50	4	32	4

Chapter 15

Feminist Liturgical Trinities and a Generous Orthodoxy

Kathryn Greene-McCreight
St. John's Episcopal Church, New Haven, Connecticut

> We certainly seek a trinity, not any trinity,
> but that Trinity which is God,
> and the true and supreme and only God.
>
> Augustine, *De Trinitate* 9.1.1

In an earlier work I examined feminist reconstructions of Christian doctrine, focusing particularly on hermeneutics, christology, and the doctrine of the Trinity. I asked there how and to what extent the biblical narrative's identification of God informs and shapes Christian feminist theology. Does the biblical narrative's depiction of God hold authority for feminist theologians? If so, how and to what extent?[1] The answers to these questions proved quite complicated, and of course varied from feminist theologian to feminist theologian, but the overall conclusion was that the biblical narrative begins to lose shape slowly and subtly, and then quite markedly, in many feminist reconstructions of Christian doctrine. Of course this is no terribly earth-shattering conclusion, as in many cases feminists do want to break the stranglehold that the biblical narrative traditionally claims over doctrine. Even somebody as traditional as Margaret Farley, whose classic statement still holds sway, has said that

> . . . included in feminist consciousness are some fundamental convictions so basic and so important that contradictory assertions cannot be accepted by feminists without violence being done to their understand-

[1] Kathryn Greene-McCreight, *Feminist Reconstructions of Christian Doctrine: Narrative Analysis and Appraisal* (New York: Oxford University Press, 2000) 3.

360

ings and valuations. These convictions serve as a kind of negative test for any revelation in knowledge. They can serve, too, as a positive key to the fullness of revelation regarding the reality and destiny of human persons. These convictions must, then, function in a feminist interpretation of Scripture—discerning the meaning of the biblical witness as a whole and in its parts and thus (though not only thus) whether it is to be believed.[2]

Around the time my *Feminist Reconstructions of Christian Doctrine* was published there arose significant offerings in feminist liturgy that I did not deal with in my book. I think in particular of *Praising God: The Trinity in Christian Worship*[3] and *Gleanings: Essays on Expansive Language with Prayers for Various Occasions*.[4] All of the revisions of liturgies boil down to the following assumption: "Using many masculine images and no feminine images for God sends the message that women are not made in the image of God and thus are less valuable than men." The correlate assumption is that such liturgical language can be damaging societally: the claim is made that such language and the implicit teachings that women are worth less than men yield "credence to values that condone the violation of females by males—from rape to battering to sexual abuse to economic discrimination."[5] The task, then, of inclusive and expansive language in feminist liturgies is to provide alternative images along with familiar images, literally to "expand" the repertoire of images by which we name and know God.[6]

As I noted in *Feminist Reconstructions* (29 ff.), many feminist theologians base their work on (usually implicit) assumptions grounded in the claims of Friedrich Schleiermacher (1768–1834). This is not surprising, since Schleiermacher has been called the "father" [sic] of modern Protestant theology. It was Schleiermacher who affirmed the role of

---

[2] "Feminist Consciousness and the Interpretation of Scripture," in *Feminist Interpretation of the Bible*, ed. Letty Russell (Philadelphia: Westminster, 1985) 44.

[3] By Ruth C. Duck and Patricia Wilson-Kastner (Louisville, KY: Westminster John Knox, 1999).

[4] Edited by Ruth A. Meyers and Phoebe Pettingell (New York: Church Publishing, 2001); to these may be added the two volumes of *Enriching our Worship* from the Standing Liturgical Commission of the Church Pension Fund (New York: Church Publishing, 1998).

[5] Duck and Wilson-Kastner, 6.

[6] See Meyers and Pettingell.

experience in theology. Faith in God, for Schleiermacher, is the experience of "absolute dependence." Feminists have taken Schleiermacher's ball and run with it, declaring that the governing theme of theology is personal and/or communal experience. Of course they leave aside the absolute dependence, which is a specifically non- or even antifeminist theme. Instead, most feminist theologians, Duck and Wilson-Kastner included, choose implicitly to advance the theme of the religious life as experience-driven.

Another theologian in the background of feminist work is Immanuel Kant (1724–1804). From him derive the triumph of the ethical over the dogmatic, a trust in contemporary experience combined with a distrust of tradition, and a vision of theological study's goal as rescuing the tradition from error and irrelevance.

Probably one of the most important theological underpinnings to the feminist quest for a rarefied Christian doctrine, however, is represented by the thought of Ludwig Feuerbach (1804–1872), who thought that religion is "too important to leave to the theologians."[7] For Feuerbach and most feminist theologians religion involves the subconscious projection of individual or communal values or norms onto the grand screen of religious belief. Feuerbach did not discern the danger here that feminist theologians now see: if theology is left to men, it is a male projection of God that Christians will worship. This of course will only reinscribe patriarchy and the subjugation of women. Indeed, it is on the basis of Feuerbach's thought that Mary Daly can later claim: "If God is male, then Male is God."[8]

There are, of course, many miles between the feminist theologians with whom I will deal in this paper and Mary Daly, who has explicitly and openly left the church. Still, her statement above is programmatic for expansive, balanced, and inclusive language. In some respects, then: as Karl Barth observed of Feuerbach,[9] I would observe of many feminist theologians such as Mary Daly, that they are at times "more theological than many of the theologians" for they pose questions that are vitally important for theology and liturgy.

---

[7] V. A. Harvey, *Feuerbach and the Interpretation of Religion* (New York: Cambridge University Press, 1995) 6.

[8] See *Gyn/Ecology: The Metaethics of Radical Feminism* (Boston: Beacon Press, 1978).

[9] *Theology and Church*, trans. L. P. Smith (New York: Harper and Row, 1928) 217.

It is a sign, then, that feminist theology is beginning to come of age that these books were written at all. The fact that Patricia Wilson-Kastner and Ruth Duck want to return to a "traditional" doctrine while holding on implicitly to the nonclassical modern claims of a Feuerbach, etc., is part of the impressive growth of feminist theology. Specifically, this coming of age brings with it a certain patience and forbearance with the traditional doctrines that have not marked much of previous feminist reconstructions.

PRAISING GOD

As regards the doctrine of the Trinity and trinitarian language in liturgy, Ruth Duck and Patricia Wilson-Kastner believe, unlike some feminist liturgists and theologians, that "the Trinity is central to Christian faith and worship." This in itself is a step forward from many feminists, such as Daphne Hampson, who have broken with Christian tradition.[10] Here Duck and Wilson-Kastner follow in the footsteps of Elizabeth Johnson[11] and most especially Catherine La Cugna,[12] both trinitarian feminist scholars who remain Christians.

Duck and Wilson-Kastner also believe that, secondly, language used in worship to speak about the Trinity should be gender-inclusive.[13] They seek a renewed sense of the reality of the Trinity rather than a "white-out theology"[14] that rids liturgy of the doctrine of the Trinity and other specific doctrines. It attempts to do this in ways that "reflect the just and egalitarian nature of the gospel."[15] In any case, the authors note that their view of the importance of the doctrine of the Trinity sets them off from other liberal liturgists who see that doctrine as relatively unimportant and necessary to delete because of its "sexist" nature. Instead Duck and Wilson-Kastner align themselves

---

[10] *After Christianity* (London: SCM Press, 1996).

[11] *She Who Is: The Mystery of God in Feminist Theological Discourse* (New York: Crossroads, 1992).

[12] *God for Us: The Trinity and the Christian Life* (San Francisco: HarperSan-Francisco, 1991).

[13] Duck and Wilson-Kastner, 2.

[14] J. Campbell, "The Feminine as Omitted, Optional, or Alternative Story: A Review of the Episcopal Eucharistic Lectionary," in *How Shall We Pray?*, ed. Ruth A. Meyers, 57–68. Liturgical Studies 2 (New York: Church Hymnal Corporation, 1994).

[15] Duck and Wilson-Kastner, 2.

with much of the theological work on the doctrine of the Trinity over approximately the last generation that underscores the centrality of the Trinity for Christian faith.[16] They do not, however, want to affirm uniquely and solely the classical trinitarian language of Father, Son, and Holy Spirit, because they claim that it does not in fact uphold trinitarian faith at all. They claim that the use of the language of Father, Son, and Holy Spirit to the exclusion of other metaphors "is too limited and stereotyped to encourage trinitarian faith."[17]

In order to respond to theologians both traditional and feminist,[18] Wilson-Kastner and Duck want to focus on the theological and liturgical importance of the trinitarian formula and the doctrine of the Trinity while changing the language with which to express the inner life of the Trinity. It interests me greatly here that they want to express not the doctrine of the Trinity but implicitly the inner reality of the life of the triune God. In other words, they do not engage in doctrinal reconstruction, using second order language, but in the first order language of worship. Notice the extremely important, indeed indispensable, assumption that trinitarian language refers metaphorically rather than directly to the Godhead.

Here Patricia Wilson-Kastner asks "are we addressing a divine reality . . . or talking to ourselves . . . ?"[19] Much to her credit she wants to hold on to the classical notion that the Divine Being is a reality apart from the consciousness and experience of the human subject. This is indeed a change from the modern paradigm and from earlier feminist theologies. She then takes up the distinction of God-language-as-literal versus God-language-as-metaphor-and-analogy and concludes that the latter is to be preferred because "our language cannot be a projection about a deity that is the same reality as we are . . . [and yet] . . . we do not believe the deity to be totally removed

[16] See L. Boff, *Trinity and Society* (New York: Orbis Press, 1988); T. Peters, *God as Trinity: Relationality and Temporality in Divine Life* (Louisville: Westminster John Knox, 1993); and C. La Cugna, *God for Us.*

[17] Duck and Wilson-Kastner, 2.

[18] G. Wainwright, "Trinitarian Worship," in *Speaking the Christian God*, ed. Alvin F. Kimel (Grand Rapids: Eerdmans, 1992) 209–21, and G. Ramshaw, *God Beyond Gender: Feminist Christian God-Language* (Minneapolis: Fortress, 1995) 76.

[19] Duck and Wilson-Kastner, 10.

from us and unlike us."[20] A metaphor compares two realities, one of which is accessible to understanding and the other not. Its use does not assume a necessary relationship between the realities compared. According to Wilson-Kastner, an analogy is a comparison of two realities on the basis of such a relationship; she gives as an analogy the use of the parental image of father or mother to refer to God. She declares that the only way to speak of God is by analogy, imagery, and metaphor. This is the case because literal language is "non-sensical," so she claims.[21]

Instead of laying out the entire doctrine of the Trinity, or even part of it, Wilson-Kastner notes the aspects of the doctrine that are important to feminist theology and liturgics: the claim that the nature of the Trinity (again, not the doctrine, but the Trinity itself) is communal and relational, a highly important claim over the past generation of trinitarian scholarship.[22] In addition, according to Wilson-Kastner the language for expressing this God's relation to us in trinitarian terms must be metaphorical and anagogical. Here she cites the work of Catherine La Cugna (1952–1997), who engaged these theses until her early death at age forty-four. According to La Cugna, while trinitarian language is important in expressing this nature of God, masculine terms are not only outdated but inadequate and unacceptable. For Wilson-Kastner, then, only an expanded language about God can include the experience of women and empower their liberation. This last jump in her argument, of course, is just that: a jump. Where did empowering the liberation of women come from, and why is it distinct from the empowering and liberation of men? Of course, to a feminist liturgist the answer to this question will seem obvious: it is women who need to be empowered more than men in our society, and indeed in most societies.

---

[20] Ibid., 17.

[21] Ibid., 19.

[22] See J. Moltmann, *The Trinity and the Kingdom: The Doctrine of God* (New York: Harper and Row, 1981); La Cugna, *God for Us*; ibid., ed., *Freeing Theology* (San Francisco: HarperSanFrancisco, 1993); Boff, *Trinity and Society*; R. C. Duck, *Gender and the Name of God: The Trinitarian Baptismal Formula* (New York: Pilgrim Press, 1991); D. Cunningham, *These Three Are One: The Practice of Trinitarian Theology* (Malden: Blackwell, 1998); and J. A. Bracken and M. H. Suchocki, eds., *Trinity in Process: A Relational Theology of God* (New York: Continuum, 1997).

Wilson-Kastner offers some formulas which she understands to be alternatives to the traditional "Father, Son, and Holy Spirit," declaring that the formulae are "liturgically usable, theologically responsible, and faithful to the tradition."[23] Barely recognizable as trinitarian, they are instead triadic in nature:

> Honor and glory to the holy and undivided Trinity
> God who creates, redeems and inspires:
> One in Three and Three in One,
> For ever and ever. Amen.

> Glory to you, Source of all being,
> Eternal Word and Holy Spirit:
> As it was in the beginning, is now,
> And shall be forever. Amen.

> Glory to God the Creator
> And to the Christ,
> And to the Holy Spirit:
> As it was in the beginning, is now, and will be forever. Amen.[24]

She borrows these from *Supplemental Liturgy 30*, the Carmelites, and the UCC for a reason: she knows how vital liturgy is to shaping and forming Christian identity. If liturgical language is charged with sexism, such patriarchal God-language reinforces our society's identification of the male as superior (indeed, in the Christian community, identifying the male as more in the image of God than the female).

A great complaint has arisen among those who do not value the change. A large part of the laity does not want to be formed in these new ways. The language of Scripture is understood to be uniquely revelatory, and therefore the revisions of God-language are seen at best as made-up or concocted according to whim, and at worst as heretical.[25]

Ruth Duck, like Patricia Wilson-Kastner, values the classical understanding and grammar of the doctrine of the Trinity. Our talk of the

---

[23] Duck and Wilson-Kastner, 22.

[24] Ibid., 21.

[25] See A. F. Kimel Jr., *Speaking the Christian God* (Grand Rapids: Eerdmans, 1992) 188–208; F. Martin, *The Feminist Question: Feminist Theology in the Light of Christian Tradition* (Grand Rapids: Eerdmans, 1994).

Trinity, she says, must (1) reflect coequality among the three persons rather than the subordination of one person to another; (2) reflect the unity of the persons of the trinitarian godhead; and (3) acknowledge the distinctiveness of each person of the Trinity. This is a major step forward for feminist scholars of the doctrine of the Trinity. Indeed, the more radical scholars may see this as a step backward since they themselves attempt to unchain Christian theology from many of its traditional moorings.

Duck renames the traditional persons of the Trinity. Instead of Father, the first person of the Trinity, one can easily use the metaphors of Mother, Source, Creator, Holy One, Eternal Living God, and Mystery "for the unoriginate source who begets Jesus Christ, breathes forth the Holy Spirit and creates everything else in the universe."[26]

The second person of the Trinity according to Duck, the incarnate Word of God in Jesus, can be spoken of, in addition to Son, with the metaphors of Word, Christ, Sophia, Redeemer, risen One, incarnate One, and, following Julian of Norwich, Mother.

The third person of the Trinity according to Duck is the eternal presence of God in life. The Spirit leads into all truth and calls to mind the words and deeds of Jesus. It is active in baptism, it sanctifies and brings us into the image of God in Christ. The metaphors that Duck offers for the Spirit are Wind and Breath, translations of the Hebrew *ru'ach*, Spirit, as well as Giver of Life, Sanctifier, Comforter, and Sustainer.

The doctrine of the Trinity, however, is not a problem to be solved but rather a solution to a problem. It is the reasoning out of the problem of the relationships between Jesus of Nazareth, his Father God, and the Holy Spirit. The doctrine of the Trinity does not unnecessarily set up obscure questions just to trip up feminists who want to transfer talk of God into nonsexist terms. It presents a solution to the doctrine of God, christology, and pneumatology, not an obfuscation. To Duck's credit, she does assert that speaking of God as "three persons or three partners is not to speak of three Gods." However, it seems that the ultimate reason that Duck is interested in the life of the Trinity is not, as with Augustine, to love God all the more. Instead, Duck apparently sees it as useful for feminist purposes: "a trinitarian ethic promotes a lifestyle of love, justice and concern for all persons."[27] There is of

[26] Duck and Wilson-Kastner, 28–29.
[27] Ibid., 29.

course nothing wrong with promoting these things. Indeed it seems eminently righteous—but perhaps more for Duck's own purposes than for the purpose of glorifying and enjoying God, in the words of the first question of the Westminster Catechism. I say this with full respect for her concern for a feminist credo.

Now to explore some other suggestions for language on the Trinity. One that I find particularly beautiful is "God who is Source of Life, Word of Truth, and Spirit of Love."[28] Whether or not this formula is trinitarian is debatable, but it is certainly triadic, and especially in personal prayer has the potential for profoundly connecting the soul to the Godhead, even though it does not name the Godhead directly. We can welcome this as an alternative as long as it is not intended to erase entirely the trinitarian name.

Many prayers are included at the back of the book. They are rich and creative, but how trinitarian they actually are is another question. The sung doxologies[29] by Ruth Duck offer a locus for seeing how the theory intersects with the reality of liturgical reconstructions. An Advent doxology, sung to the tune of *Veni Emmanuel*, is beautiful to the ears and soul:

> Praise Spirit-God who comes with fire.
> Praise Jesus Christ, our heart's desire.
> Praise Love who comes to seek us all,
> One God on whom our Spirits call.
> God comes! God comes!
> Lift heart and voice.
> The Savior comes; let earth rejoice.

This is beautiful, and especially useful as a change of pace from the usual doxology a congregation might sing during Advent. However, Spirit-God, Jesus Christ, Love, One God do not replace functionally, or even allude to, Father, Son, and Holy Spirit, except by the phrase "One God." While it is triadic it is not trinitarian.

A doxology for Christmastide, sung to *Antioch*, is as follows:

> Praise the eternal Holy One, and tell the Spirit's worth.

---

[28] Ibid., 138.

[29] Ibid., 140–42. First and second excerpts below from p. 140, third, fourth and fifth from p. 141, and final doxology from pp. 141–42.

To Christ sing praise, God-with-us all our days.
O sing the Savior's birth, O sing the Savior's birth,
O sing, O sing the Savior's birth.

Here again we have a nice doxology to use as an alternative. There is nothing theologically amiss about calling God Holy One, and Spirit, God-with-us, Savior, but this is not even triadic much less trinitarian.

For Epiphany, the following is suggested, to the tune of the *Old Hundredth*:

Praise Love who made all time and space,
Praise Love who came in truth and grace.
Praise Love on humankind outpoured,
That all may love forevermore.

This is a bit more successful than either of the above. Of course there is no attempt here to "inclusivize" the name of the Godhead but instead to illustrate each of the persons' activities. The repetition of the word "love" fits the repetitious melody of the *Old Hundredth*. The problem here is that it illustrates only the activities of the persons of the Trinity, while it has been held for centuries that the Trinity is more than the sum of its actions. Surprisingly, this Trinity does not indicate relationality among the persons, and relationality is a key ingredient, so it is claimed, of feminist reconstructions of the doctrine and name of the Trinity.

For Lent, the following is suggested, sung to the tune of *Redhead*.

Praise the Source who gives us life.
Praise to Christ, who shares our strife.
Praise the Spirit who sustains,
bearing us through grief and pain.
To the Holy Trinity glory praise and honor be.

Source, Christ, Spirit, Holy Trinity. But the Father is more than Source. Actually Source sounds more like Near Eastern goddess religions where the goddess bears of herself to create. Maybe this is intended to include women's voices, but there is no hint of the Hebrew faith. Judaism and Christianity have traditionally held that God the Father is creator not out of the substance of himself but out of nothing, so that the world is complete grace and not part of the Father. "Christ" speaks of the second person of the Trinity, but posits no relationality between the first and second persons. "Spirit" therefore seems "out there," disconnected from the first two persons. Attempting to fix these problems by concluding the Doxology with "To the Holy Trinity . . ." does not work. Here the Holy Trinity bears no relation to the triadic formula suggested, and sounds like a fourth divinity.

For Eastertide, sung to the tune of *Lasst Uns Erfreuen*, we have the following:

> Praise Jesus Christ who rose from death!
> Praise to the Source of life and breath!
> Alleluia! Alleluia!
> Praise to the Spirit, holy dove,
> Giver of life, of peace, of love.
> Alleluia! Christ is risen!
> Alleluia! Christ is risen! Alleluia!

Again, we have not even a trace of the trinitarian formula, except insofar as there is threefold imagery: Spirit, dove; Giver of life; Christ . . . Those who are not familiar with the doctrine of the Trinity might think that "dove" is not in apposition to "Spirit" but stands alone as another divinity. And why a dove? Some feminists have complained that a dove descending from overhead trivializes the Spirit.

For Pentecost, sung to the tune of *Lobe den Herren*, the authors suggest the following:

> Praise to the One who has destined us all to salvation.
> Praise to Christ Jesus, who sends us in love to all nations.
> Worship afresh One who is poured on all flesh,
> Spirit of love and vocation!

Here we have a trinitarian formula that is as follows: One, Christ Jesus, One . . . Spirit of love and vocation. How does "One" speak of the Father? Certainly Christ Jesus speaks of the Son, and the Spirit of love and vocation is reminiscent of the Holy Spirit. But does this formula indicate how to relate theologically this One with Christ and with the Spirit? One might refer to the whole Godhead, but then the person of the Father is left out of this formula.

For Trinity Sunday, sung to *Old One Hundredth*, the following is suggested:

> Praise God the Father and the Son

and Holy Spirit always one,
the God whose holy name we call,
one God and Mother of us all.

Here we have a greater stress on the unity of the Godhead ("always one"). This uses the traditional formula, Father, Son, and Holy Spirit, adding the Riverside appendix "One God and Mother of us all."[30] As I pointed out in my previously cited article, adding "Mother of us all" is not biblical, nor does it add to the trinitarian formula anything that would help the worshiper singing this doxology to understand better the doctrine of the Trinity. Mother language, as I noted above, is derived from Julian of Norwich, who sometimes called the Godhead and the second person of the Trinity "Mother."

In a suggested baptismal rite the formula used would be one of these four:[31]

> [Name], you are baptized in the name of the Father and of the Son and of the Holy Spirit, one God, Mother of us all.

> [Name], you are baptized in the name of God the Source, Word and Spirit.

> [Name], I baptize you in the name of God, Source of love, in the name of Jesus Christ, love incarnate, and in the name of the Holy Spirit, love's power.

> [Name], I baptize you in the name of God the Father and Mother, and of Jesus Christ, God Incarnate, and of the Spirit, God ever-present.

These are by far the most creative and expansive baptismal formulae I have ever encountered. Of course, the Riverside formula, the first above, is a long-standing option. Adding Mother to the end of the traditional formula gives the impression that while the persons of the Trinity are Father, Son, and Holy Spirit, Mother is the name of the Godhead. This is useful liturgically for it attempts to include maternal imagery, but brings in the foreign idea that the Godhead is female. This it shares with ancient Near Eastern religions that praise female gods, but it is absolutely forbidden in the Old Testament.

---

[30] See Duck, *Gender and the Name of God*; K. Greene-McCreight, "What's in a Name? On the Ecumenical Baptismal Formula." *Pro Ecclesia* 6 (1997) 289–308.
[31] Duck and Wilson-Kastner, 152.

The second option, God the Source, Word, and Spirit, is also misleading. If Source replaces Father, there is no indication of a relationship (and, I repeat, what feminist theologians want to stress is relationality) between the Father and the Son and therefore also with the Spirit. If God the Father is Source, what does this mean? That the Son (here, Word) is not active in creation? That the world emanates from God the Father as though from a gnostic deity?

The third option is from the United Church of Canada. This is the wordiest of all of the options suggested. Focusing on the concept of love, God the Father is Source of love, God the Son becomes Jesus Christ, love incarnate, and the Holy Spirit is love's power. This is evocative, even beautiful. However, we have no explicit relationship among the persons other than love. Is God the Father the only Source of love? Is not God the Son a source as well, and the Spirit too? These three do not seem one. This gives the impression shared by many non-Christians that our God is three Gods. How do these three actually relate to one another in their expression of love? The traditional formula is shorthand for much theological reflection, including the relations and distinctions between the persons of the Trinity. If we sweep the traditional formula aside we have much work to do theologically, which is not accomplished by this (albeit attractive) attempt.

The fourth option founders on similar shoals. Aesthetically it is not as pleasing as is the focus on love of the previous offering. What is a "Father and Mother" if not a plural? How does this represent the singularity of God the Father? "Jesus Christ, God incarnate" and "Spirit, God ever-present" do indeed describe the actions and essences of the second and third persons of the Trinity, and yet again do not deal with the relationality. This kind of "Trinity" is not triadic but quadratic.

GLEANINGS

This work, subtitled *Essays on Expansive Language with Prayers for Various Occasions*, is in some respects a most interesting piece of feminist scholarship, as it tries to avoid "white-out" inclusive theology and replace it with what the authors, Ruth Meyers and Phoebe Pettingell, call "expansive" language.[32] Expansive language attempts to push be-

[32] "The development of 'expansive language' liturgies came about as many Episcopalians realised that the voice of women had been largely excluded from the language of contemporary liturgical prayer. . . . One of the initia-

yond the bounds of so-called exclusive language, not in negative but in positive ways. The first half of the book is a series of essays on expansive language, and the second half is a collection of prayers that use expansive language arranged according to the liturgical year, the calendar of the saints, and various pastoral occasions.

The first essay, by Jennifer M. Phillips, suggests some key criteria by which liturgy can be judged. The first is that good liturgy must be "virtuous," that is, that it must mature reason, memory, will, desire, and intuition, and motivate and train the congregation to do the good. This element of liturgy focuses on the moral dimension. Phillips then offers nine principles of virtuous worship. Good liturgy is "evocative, thick, layered with allusion, imagery." Here she refers to "the universal experience of the womb," evoked in a liturgical text, the prayer "For Rest" (proposed to General Convention 2000, and then included in *Enriching Our Worship* 2), "O God my refuge and strength: in this place of unrelenting light and noise, enfold me in your holy darkness and silence, that I may rest secure under the shadow of your wings,"[33] and points out how this draws in allusions to the psalms, the versicle for Compline from the fourth century, and even Dylan Thomas's "close and holy darkness."

Another necessity is vigor. Thus liturgy will foster fortitude, strengthen the soul to overcome fear. "The language of prayer needs juiciness and passion." In addition, good liturgical imagery should fall between the extremes of being too fresh and daring and too trite and quaint. Effective liturgy is also just, "truthful when it seeks commonweal,"[34] and hospitable. It should make all worshipers feel welcome and included. Therefore, liturgy must also express "fitting" theology."[35] What this means is not clear to me. "Fitting theology" for one person may be teeth-grinding for another. How do we determine what is fitting and what is not? One way is that the major part of liturgical imagery should be biblical. Liturgical texts, according to Phillips, should be elegant, touching the hearts and minds of diverse

---

tives of expansive language has been to bring prayers and canticles by these women and some of their sisters in religion [e.g.,Teresa of Avila, Thérèse of Lisieux, Hildegard of Bingen, Julian of Norwich] into the liturgy . . ." Meyers and Pettingell, 14–15.

[33] In Meyers and Pettingell, 6.

[34] Meyers and Pettingell, 8.

[35] Ibid., 9.

worshipers across time. They should be able to spring to the hearts and lips in times of stress and happiness. One thing I note is the absence of praise of God. Maybe that seemed too obvious a trait of good liturgy.

Having established how liturgical texts function ideally according to the feminist paradigm, we turn to an essay by Phoebe Pettingell on expansive language. This is the heart and soul of the book, for it speaks of a new approach to inclusive language. Instead of deleting references to the male God of Israel, expansive language builds a new conceptuality. Why is it needed? Because Episcopalians (in particular here) are coming to realize that the voices of women have largely been excluded from liturgies. By the 1980s, says Pettingell, the laity was reading the works of female mystics such as Teresa of Avila, Thérèse of Lisieux, Hildegard of Bingen, and Julian of Norwich. She suggests that through reading these women she and her feminist colleagues began to realize that the characteristics of women's prayer are different from men's prayer. Pettingell claims that whether or not these differences stem from nature or nurture does not matter: they exist. What are some of the characteristics of this kind of womens' prayer? Pettingell specifies here:

> And this voice—often ecstatic, frequently lamenting, by turns gentle or angry—was absent from our corporate liturgies, and rarely present even in Anglican anthologies of prayers for private devotion. One of the initiatives of expansive language has been to bring prayers and canticles by these women and some of their sisters in religion into the liturgy.[36]

Many factors have led to the development of expansive language. Certainly the feminist movement is one. Rosemary Radford Ruether, Elizabeth Schüssler Fiorenza, Mary Daly, and others have paved the way for a feminist critique of religion and therefore the development of expansive language in liturgy. But, interestingly enough, Pettingell also credits the self-help movement, which she suggests was rooted partly in Jung's vision of a divine nurturing force. She compares this view with Freud's vision of an inner self fraught with competitive and self-destructive urges. She claims that the new expansive prayers invoke a loving God, the God of the self-help Jungian movement, a loving mother nurturing the infant.

[36] Ibid., 15.

This camp of feminists holds that the tradition of Anglican prayer is not to be abandoned but rather reshaped and expanded. Notice how different this is from the more radical inclusivists who would seek to abandon traditions and key liturgical elements for the sake of a feminist liturgy. According to Pettingell we should make it "more and more ours" rather than making liturgy shocking to ears and soul. Following Leonel Mitchell[37] she understands that

> we do Cranmer and his work no honor by gilding it and putting it on display. We best follow the lead of the first Book of Common Prayer by making liturgy life in our own day, for our own people. It is not an heirloom of our cultural heritage to be displayed in a showcase for our children to admire, it is a working tool to be used by us and them. And so today we give thanks for the gift of the English liturgy, and we ask that we may pray with our spirit and understanding, to make that liturgy alive today.[38]

Expansive language is unlike inclusive language insofar as it does not represent the struggle of an oppressed group over against a dominant group. Rather, it represents the struggle to develop an authentic language for liturgy, common to males and females, Americans and foreigners, and all ethnicities.[39] Expansive language bears truth, insofar as it offers a full range of language to express our relationship to the Sacred. "More recently, the term 'expansive language' has been used to emphasize the need for a wide range of language and imagery in order to speak of the inexhaustible mystery of God . . . the revisers have sought to offer a fuller vision of God by expanding the imagery used in liturgical texts."[40]

In the essay by Ruth A. Meyers, we find that while "Father" has become a central metaphor in Christian liturgical language, "careful study of Scripture shows that it is not the only or even the primary term used to speak about and to God. The Old Testament includes only a handful of references to God as Father. In the new Testament, 'Father' is one of numerous metaphors Jesus uses to address God and teach about God."[41] She says that the most obvious complement to "father"

---

[37] L. Mitchell, "The First Book of Common Prayer." *Open* (Fall 1999) 7.
[38] Meyers and Pettingell, 21.
[39] Ibid., 22.
[40] Ibid., 29.
[41] Ibid., 30.

is "mother," and she points to the maternal imagery found throughout the Old Testament, apparently in order to justify its use in liturgical texts. Here she indicates that the Hebrew word for compassion (*rahamim*) is etymologically related to the noun for womb (*rehem*). She suggests an analogy between divine compassion and the intimacy and nurture of the mother's womb. Certainly she is correct about the etymological relation between "compassion" and "womb," but sometimes etymology does not equal meaning. The places in the Old Testament in which God is imaged as a mother do not always employ positive female imagery. One text that Meyers points to as showing a nurturing motherly God is Isaiah 42:14 where birth imagery is violent, and God is said to lay waste mountains and hills and dry up all plants.

Meyers insists that "Father" is a metaphor for "God."[42] Clearly this is not the case for the biblical writers. Jesus is almost unique in addressing God as Father. An address is semantically a name; it can be a nasty one, in which case we say that people "call us names," but never a metaphor. Certainly Jesus never addresses God as Mother. Father is the name that Jesus uses to refer to God, and to refer to his relationship to God. It is a relationship of a Son to a Father. Not only this, God is Father. When we come to the baptismal formula in Matthew 28:19, Jesus tells us to baptize in the name (singular) of the Father, and of the Son, and of the Holy Spirit. This means that Jesus discloses to us the very name of God—not a metaphor, not an image, but the name. Whereas in Jewish worship that name is the unpronounceable *yhwh*, for Christians that name is threefold: Father, Son, and Holy Spirit. "Some claim," says Meyers, "that 'Father, Son and Holy Spirit' is the revealed name of God and must be used in order to maintain the historic identity of Christian worship. . . . Trinitarian doctrine asserts that relationship is central to the being of God, that God is in relationship with Godself and the world. Within God there is both unity and diversity."[43]

How can someone not claim that "Father, Son, and Holy Spirit" is the revealed name of God unless that person is unwilling to admit the category of revelation to begin with? In other words, talk of metaphor and analogy permits the invention and multiplication of further metaphor and analogy, since the concept of revelation is set aside.

[42] Ibid.
[43] Ibid., 33.

Along with the notion of the Divine Name as metaphor, Meyers claims that God is both unity and diversity. Surely Meyers is correct: classically we say that in the Godhead we have one God in three persons, but to say there is diversity is a completely different concept. What could it mean that there is diversity in the Godhead? That we can map ourselves in our diversities onto the Godhead? Would Augustine, for example, have agreed with this?

Interestingly enough, Meyers does not object to the term "Lord" insofar as historically it meant that Jesus is sovereign and is not Caesar. The name of God in the Old Testament (Lord) is to be applied to Jesus: Jesus is God. While sometimes Christ or Savior is used instead, usually the title Lord remains, as Pettingell says especially of the Sursum Corda and the Sanctus of the eucharistic prayers. But to whom do we lift our hearts in the Sursum Corda, God or Jesus? Who is the Lord? Such revisions as are suggested here obscure these questions and domesticate Christian claims about Jesus as the Lord to whom we lift up our hearts.

CONCLUSIONS

Many liturgical revisions are eloquent and beautiful, but as we have seen they may not express the doctrine of the Trinity. The substance of God, and the reality to which the trinitarian name points, should not be compromised in our attempts to expand and inclusivize our language. We must still be able to speak of that "Trinity which is God, and the true and supreme and only God."[44] The effort to make language more contemporary has constantly challenged translators of the Bible from the early church to the modern/postmodern periods. Inclusivizing is therefore in some sense no new project. The question is this: how can we hold on to that reality of which Augustine and Paul and indeed Jesus speak? Theology must not simply be a rearranging of surface signs and symbols, but must express in our own faulty language the substance of our faith, the trinitarian God. Are we teaching of a three-fold god? Are we praising one God in a triad? Different names and different ways of address may be sought. They may supplement the divine name, but they can never, for the orthodox, replace the divine name, either in baptism or in general worship.

[44] Augustine, *De Trinitate* 9.1.1.

Here are my suggestions for inclusive language: we need to make two key distinctions, one between personal and public prayer, and one between God-language and humanity-language. First, inclusive language and/or expansive language may be harder to introduce in public prayer than in personal, private prayer. Calling God "Mother" may shock the faithful, distracting them rather than producing a worshipful mood. Is such language being introduced in order to shock? In private prayer this way of broadening one's way of addressing God may be easier.

On a different level, the other distinction I would make is a more crucial one: there is a world of difference theologically between God-language and humanity-language. This is not because of our language, but because of the God whom we invoke, address, and adore. Unlike Feuerbach, the Christian holding to the classical confession cannot say that God is humanity shouted in a loud voice. In addition, this Christian cannot say that God-language is metaphor rather than name, for name is the mode of biblical address, Jesus to the Father, the Father to the Son.

If we are to agree on something, orthodox and revisionist can both agree that humanity-language must be made inclusive: "brethren" becoming sisters and brothers; "man" becoming mortal or some such option; masculine pronouns referring to humans in general being avoided. For the orthodox, even the generous orthodox, the second distinction remains a sine qua non. Failure to make this distinction is linked hermeneutically to the theological errors made above in the feminist trinitarian liturgical revisions.